Exploring the Relationship between Child Abuse and Delinquency

Exploring the Relationship between Child Abuse and Delinquency

edited by ROBERT J. HUNNER
and YVONNE ELDER WALKER

ALLANHELD, OSMUN Montclair

ALLANHELD, OSMUN & CO. PUBLISHERS, INC.

Published in the United States of America in 1981
by Allanheld, Osmun & Co. Publishers, Inc.
6 South Fullerton Avenue, Montclair, New Jersey 07042

Library of Congress Cataloging in Publication Data

Main entry under title:

Exploring the relationship between child abuse and delinquency.

Includes index.
1. Child abuse—Addresses, essays, lectures.
2. Juvenile delinquency—Addresses, essays, lectures.
I. Hunner, Robert J.
HV713.E9 362.7'044 79-5178
ISBN 0-916672-31-X

Printed in the United States of America

Contents

Foreword

More years ago than I care to remember, when I was working with street gangs at the New York City Youth Board, the relationship between child abuse and juvenile delinquency was an issue that never came up. I can't recall ever questioning whether any of the kids who were part of the gangs I worked with had been victims of child abuse. Nor do I remember any of my colleagues ever raising the question.

Thinking about it today, I recognize that the question would have been an important one to ask. On reflection, there's little doubt that many of those youths were victims of neglect, if not physical and sexual abuse as well.

So for me, this book provides an opportunity to come full circle from my first professional job, working in the area of delinquency, to my present involvement with the Children's Bureau in issues of child abuse and neglect. It is with great pleasure that I participate in a major effort to examine the relationship between two of the most serious and disturbing social problems affecting children today.

On the surface, the relationship between child abuse and neglect and juvenile delinquency appears to be one of simple causality—the victim of early childhood battering, growing up to vent that violence on society. This may be a sufficient explanation of the dynamics which produce delinquent behavior in some adolescents. However, it is not true in all cases. If the relationship could be characterized so easily, we could then assume that our efforts to prevent or reduce child abuse and neglect would result in similar reductions in the incidence of juvenile delinquency. But my experience tells me that this is not the case. Child abuse, child neglect and juvenile delinquency are complex and interrelated problems, and as such, defy singular, cursory solutions.

Certainly there is enough research and clinical experience to support the notion that a linkage exists between those phenomena. But to explain this linkage as exclusively causal is to miss the complexity of social relationships and social problems. As important as our attempts are to establish cause and effect for particular social problems, it is equally necessary to understand the symptomatic nature of the kinds of social problems which are the focus of this conference .

The relationship that exists between child abuse and delinquency is probably not that different from the relationship between child abuse and drug abuse; or child abuse and emotional disturbances; or child abuse and alcoholism; or child abuse and wife abuse.

All of these can be viewed as one kind of aberrant behavior possibly triggering the other; and certainly linked in the person or persons involved. The task you have before you is a difficult and challenging one. It is not enough to explain the relationship between child abuse and neglect and juvenile delinquency as primarily causal; to do so is to risk oversimplification. But to dismiss it as merely symptomatic is to avoid addressing those larger, underlying issues which must be confronted if we are to deal effectively with these problems.

Every effort to increase our knowledge about the relationships between the various forms of social deviance represents a step toward effective solutions and reduction of human suffering. But the scientific establishment of a relationship between different symptoms is only the first step in addressing problems as pervasive as these.

I think all of us can agree that problems are rarely resolved by treating symptoms. The challenge that confronts us today is to look beneath the web of immediate and visible social problems to the underlying position of the social structure which governs human relationships. By focusing our efforts on the relationships between individual behavior and social context, we are gradually moving away from earlier, more exclusive emphasis on individual pathology and individual blame.

Over a hundred years ago, Elbridge Gerry, a founder of the New York SPCC, noted that "most of the juvenile culprits are the children of heartless and cruel parents . . . forced into the streets to pick up a living as they can." Today we recognize that this is a limited one-dimensional perspective. We have come to realize that the 'cruelty and heartlessness' once attributed solely to parents are more characteristic of the circumstances in which many families live than they are of the individuals involved.

The nature of the circumstances under which a family lives cannot help but affect the quality of parental care and childhood experience within a family. Both child abuse and juvenile delinquency have been viewed historically as criminal violations and as separate issues requiring individual' punitive responses. As we recognize the interrelatedness of these and other social problems, the need for both individual treatment and comprehensive social policy becomes clearer. Any attempts to find solutions or design treatment strategies must ultimately focus on those factors which most threaten the fundamental structure of society—the family unit.

It is true, as Bronfenbrenner has pointed out, that unprecedented changes have rocked the structure of families in this country over the last 25 years. Among those changes—aside from a dramatic increase in the divorce rate—is the fact that the extended family is rapidly disappearing. The number of grandparents, uncles and aunts, or unmarried older siblings in the home has been reduced by half since the early 1950's. The number of children under 18 living in single-parent homes (now one out of six) has almost doubled in the past 25 years. Perhaps more importantly, there are fewer stable neighborhoods, real communities where individual family isolation is unusual and interdependence is the norm.

Today, parental responsibility has been intensified because many parents have fewer trusted family members or close friends and neighbors on whom they can rely for affirmation and support as individuals and as parents. At the same time that parental responsibility has become intensified, parental time with children has been cut drastically. There are many economic, social and cultural reasons for these changes. In 1975, for the first time in history, a majority of American mothers of school-age children held jobs outside the home. One out of every three mothers with children under six is in paid employment.

It is dangerous to draw conclusions about the quality of the time that parents spend with their children on the basis of the number of hours they spend together. But it does seem clear that the parent-child relationship, like so much of the rest of modern life, is being increasingly compartmentalized and time-limited.

Bronfenbrenner reports that one study of middle-class fathers of year-old infants found that they spent an average of only twenty minutes a day with their children. Meanwhile, older children were averaging 50 hours a week with television.

Other recent research has found that at every age level, today's children show a greater dependency on their peers than they did ten years ago. There are increasing numbers of 'latch-key children': those who come home from school to an empty house and a community, a neighborhood, which no longer exists. It is these 'latch-key children' who contribute in disproportionate numbers to the ranks of the runaways, the groups of youngsters with school problems and drug problems, and, of course, to the rising toll of juvenile delinquency.

For many families, the general caregiving role has, of necessity, become a shared function—with babysitters, day care centers, schools and peer groups. It seems pointless to try to place blame for this development or to try to totally reverse it. It is these factors, as well as the other social and economic stresses with which today's parents must contend. Together, they are creating the circumstances which allow for intolerable family tensions, family disintegration, abused and neglected children and teenagers whose lack of supervision and discipline are expressed in antisocial behavior of various kinds. Thus, we must turn our attention to measures which will counter these effects and enhance the quality of family life.

Social problems, such as the ones which bring us together today, do not allow the luxury of taking a single approach or a single strategy. It is not enough for us to focus our attention on the neglectful behavior of parents. We need also to recognize that the effects of the societal neglect of family needs play an equally destructive role in the process of family breakdown.

This is highlighted in the following excerpt from the 1970 White House conference on children and youth which I quote to you by way of emphasis:

> "A host of factors conspire to isolate children from the rest of society," said the report. It then went on to note that the fragmentation of the extended family, the separation of residential and business areas, the disappearance of neighborhoods, zoning ordinances, occupational mobility, child labor laws, the abolishment of the apprentice system, consolidated schools, separate patterns of social life for different age groups, the working mother, the delegation of child care to specialists—all of these manifestations of progress operate to decrease opportunity and incentive for meaningful contact between children and persons older or younger than themselves.

In 1975, James Coleman in his study, "Youth: Transition to Adulthood," documented the same things, and so have many others.

In our discussions about the effects of social change on families it is important to be clear about whom we are speaking. When I say families and children, I mean ALL families and children. It is simply not instructive or fruitful to continue focusing exclusive attention on low income families. The symptoms, including abuse and juvenile delinquency, are emerging within all social and economic groups. All families are being plagued today by the same kinds of problems in the broad social areas.

This was recently brought home to me very forcefully in a report I read about a conference on the social costs of the maltreatment of children, sponsored by the Protective Services Resource Institute of New Jersey.

In a follow-up report on the conference, Institute Director Frank Schneiger noted that the participants expressed profound concern over some of the social trends in America. He noted that there were expressions of deep-seated disillusionment with the performance of human services institutions and systems which are supposedly designed to meet the needs of children and families.

In describing the mood of the conference, Schneiger said there was a feeling that the problems are structural and systemic and that tinkering at the peripheries was pointless and served primarily to mask the ongoing erosion.

The conference issued a strong call for the involvement of all segments of society—especially local communities—in developing new efforts for serving the needs of families and children.

Having said all this, perhaps my contribution to this book comes from my own efforts to explore the various relationships as I have seen and experienced them. In doing so, I raise more questions than answers.

To reiterate, I think that the relationship between child abuse and neglect and juvenile delinquency is not a singular one. It is no more useful to talk in simple terms of cause and effect than it is to look to the larger social context for all the answers. Similarly, our recognition of the symptomatic nature of these and other indicators of social and family dysfunction represents only a first step in combatting them. There are still many issues which demand our attention before we can even begin to develop solutions.

Why is it, for example, that some children who have been subjected to childhood abuse and neglect never become involved in juvenile delinquency or other forms of social deviance, while some children who do, have come from what most of us would call exemplary homes?

Perhaps we need to ask, too, what are the most promising answers of research and the areas for program demonstration that can lead to more effective prevention of the kinds of family dissolution which express themselves in child abuse and neglect and juvenile delinquency?

Or, what can be done about the institutional abuse and neglect of the children who have been co-mingled with juvenile offenders and branded as juvenile delinquents and placed in inadequately staffed reform or training schools and detention homes?

Finally, perhaps it is most productive to see the relationship between child abuse and neglect and juvenile delinquency as one which is primarily indicative of an unhealthy social ecology. In the case of child abuse and neglect, the effects are manifested in the parent and result in his or her destructive behavior. In the case of juvenile delinquency, the effects are manifested in older children and result in their destructive behavior toward society. In both cases, both the individual and society are the victims.

Frank Ferro
Associate Chief, Children's Bureau
Office of Child Development
Department of Health, Education & Welfare

Exploring the Relationship between Child Abuse and Delinquency

Introduction

PETER FORSYTHE

Vice-President
Edna McConnell Clark Foundation
New York, New York 10017

These are exciting times. They are times that involve all of the kinds of children that we are talking about in this book, a broad spectrum of children and not just two separate pieces. We aren't limited to just the little child who is abused, and the abuser who perpetrates the act, or just the delinquent who emerges in teenage years to ravage a community or do something less, often much less, such as we saw in parts of New York during the blackout. In between these extremes are all of the other manifestations of troubled children, of disorganized families and families under stress that aren't disorganized in the usual sense of the term. All acting out children whether it be school rejection, inappropriate peer pressure on each other, or warped attitudes about childhood, adult life and blocked visions of the future are on the spectrum. All of this ought to come within the challenge we've laid before ourselves in exploring the relationship between child abuse and delinquency.

I'd like to take the liberty of expanding on two pieces of my history since I have a somewhat different perspective than that which will be the basis for many of the chapters. When I was asked to participate in this volume I welcomed the opportunity but questioned my appropriateness—not because I haven't been involved in these issues, but because I've been involved in them in a way other than research.

On the delinquency side, it was mentioned that I am a lawyer. I'm a former prosecutor and a city attorney who worked in law enforcement for six years. I spent three years responsible for the Michigan delinquency program at the state level, not only training schools and institutions, but group homes and other community based programs, as well as parole. Since that time I have been involved in statute drafting and other system reform efforts, some with the Clark Foundation and some before I went there. I have participated in many of the standard-setting efforts around questions of delinquency, status offenders and other kinds of troubled children.

With regard to child abuse and, I would add in capital letters, NEGLECT, I began as an advisor to a pilot child protection project in Michigan in 1964, and the termination of that responsibility was an eye-opener in terms of the way we deal with social problems. In the early 60's, child protection, child protective services, ways to be more imaginative and constructive in intervening in the lives of older children who are the victims of disorganization and anger in parents, substandard conditions, family stress, and so on, were new topics. They were not terribly popular ones, and in many ways seemed, and sometimes still seem, to be threatening to standard methods of delivery of service. A group of citizens , chosen by the local department of social services which had been designated as a pilot county to develop a child protection service, met repeatedly and looked at the pattern of service and non-service in our community. After thoughtful, and I think hard-headed and creative service, we made a significant, strong, hard hitting proposal on behalf of the county to the State Department of Social Services. The chairperson, who obviously was better-connected with the establishment than I, thanked me as the chairman of that subcommittee for the recommendations that were made and, I think with a comma (not even with a period or a new paragraph), dissolved the citizen advocacy group.

I don't think it had anything to do with the quality of what we had recommended, because nobody knew what that was going to be when the dissolution action was decided. I do think that it was a misguided effort to silence a community concern that was headed in the direction of trying to make basic changes in the ways such families were helped.

That is where I cut my teeth in the area of child abuse and child protection. Since then I've served the state in a variety of advisory ways, and then ran the child neglect and abuse programs for the state of Michigan for about three years, and have spent about 15 years with an interest in foster care and adoption.

I believe deeply in a coordinated system. I believe, as a lawyer, that much of what we do in segmenting our thinking is the result of a forced process of labeling for jurisdictional, funding and service provision reasons, many of which are indefensible. The first step in overcoming the negative impact of such practice is to recognize it for the limited and limiting kind of phenomenon it is. I believe in a coordinated system and fought hard for it and, in fact, administered one in Michigan in which delinquency and neglect, dependency and abuse were all part of the same agency. This was on a very deeply held philosophy that these were heavily over-lapping categories, particularly in the middle years of childhood. Many of these children were at one time both the victims of neglect and perpetrators of other anti-social behavior. Segregating them for program purposes was counter-productive, reinforcing of labels and perpetuating the inability of service to be responsive to an individual child, or group of children and their families' needs.

Unfortunately, when DHEW had an opportunity to have a similar broad spectrum, and it was not convinced that there were important relationships between these two kinds of children, it passively abandoned delinquency and prevention programs to LEAA. I have no objections to LEAA. I've served on the crime commission in Michigan and worked with LEAA funds and ideas, task forces, and so on, for many years. It does seem to me, however, a shame to segregate delinquent kids to one federal department and neglected and abused kids into another federal department when in legislative or congressional wisdom they were once together. We let them come apart. Many are hopeful that in a more appropriate environment they may be returned to a common administration in the future. I sincerely hope that with some vigorous advocacy this will be possible.

In any event, I have a background in delinquency, a background in abuse and neglect, but it is all in the role of advocate and as an administrator and as someone who tries to carry out the best of what we already know. I am not a researcher—not a speck of research in that background—and I say that only for perspective. My real question is why we don't use what we already know. I deplore the fact that so much of that which we already know goes by the wayside and is ignored in policy and practice. It goes by the wayside unnecessarily and unwisely. I think the implications of not making use of such knowledge are profound for what we do in research and further exploration of significant relationships in days like these.

I'm most interested in knowing more about what information will really be helpful to the kids themselves. Somehow, the way in which we organize that which we explore in research has, I believe, a heavy influence on the use that will be made of it. I'm delighted that some of the chapters directly address questions of implications for policy. And I hope that they take very, very seriously the realistic limitations in the formulation of policy so that we can explore ways to effectively implement that which we learn, rather than to simply decry its lack of implementation.

DEFINING THE ISSUES—ABUSE

I take the process of exploring seriously. Exploring, to me, means an examination of all sides, the nooks and crannies, the shadows and the bright spots of some phenomenon. I found the chapters fascinating; and yet, if real exploring suggests looking at all sides, I'm not sure that breadth of self-examination is present in what I read. I hope I'm wrong. Where are those who doubt that there is any meaningful relationship or specific one-to-one relationship between abuse and delinquency?

One of the things we can't do is explore adequately without some cleanness of definition. This may be my lawyer training poking its head through, but I think one of the things we must ask ourselves at every turn is whether we are being precise enough to be useful, or fuzzy out of laziness. I feel very strongly that we ought to seriously examine, as some of the chapters do, the boundaries of what has been in the title classified as 'abuse.' Just as it seems to me that there is indeed some relationship between abuse and delinquency, each of those is part of a spectrum of neglect on the one hand and antisocial behavior on the other that is difficult to define with precision. Yet such an effort is needed to make any dicussion of this topic productive.

I've had an awful time with the current public enthusiasm for the labeling of child abuse, or what sometimes is described as child abuse and neglect (it used to be neglect and dependency). When one looks at the figures, those experts that I've heard suggest that physical abuse of children is probably not 5% of the behavior that occurs in the area of neglect and dependency that we take seriously as a society, or those areas covered by the statutes that govern us.

Yet, it's obviously the 5% that has fascinated us for the last half-decade ; I suggest that it has fascinated us out of all proportion to its actual impact on families. Not that it isn't serious—it is extremely serious. Not that we gave adequate attention to physical abuse before—we did not. Not that we now know all we need to know—we do not. But it's terribly important that we be reasonably precise in what we mean by 'child abuse.' Is it, as some of the chapters explore, or should it be limited, in terms of implications for delinquency, to those circumstances where there is a separation between parent and child which follows? At least we need to be clear that the impact of abuse + separation is vastly different, or one would at least expect it to be different, from the impact of abuse where there is no separation. And what about the repetitiveness of the abuse; and what about the extensiveness of it?

I am puzzled, as I watch our society evolve new standards of how parents ought to treat children, that we so often lose the historical perspective. If one believes that physical abuse ought to lead in close correlation to delinquency, and if one looks back at the way children were treated, historically, in many societies, including western ones, the peaks of delinquency ought to be seen in previous years, rather than in the present.

So I think that it's a complex phenomenon that requires us to look carefully at what we mean. Do we believe that adjudicated abuse will allow a useful correlation in spite of all the differences in statutes, all the imprecision in court procedures, all the variations in intake and diversion? Do we mean those that have been prosecuted? Historically we have looked at child abuse as a criminal offense by adults—not one that we've punished unless it became very, very severe—and only recently have we struggled with our ambivalence of wishing to lash out at those who attack innocent children and hurt them permanently and the serious family disintegration that can result, not just from the abuse, but also from the lashing out itself.

Are we talking about only reported abuse, and, if so, reported by whom? That which is reported in our official statistics varies widely. If you put up billboards in Florida, or construct networks and have hot-lines, you get many more reports than if you don't. The level of reporting varies and we've seen proven ways to greatly escalate the community consciousness about child abuse.

We also know something about the timeliness of reports with regard to veracity. So, when we're talking about reported child abuse, we must ask not only about differences between the reporter's definition and ours, as well as his or her perception of what we would like to be told, but also the timeliness of those reports and the context in which they were made.

In talking about the correlation between child abuse and delinquency, we must look not only at the abused, but at the abuser as well. I suggest that we should look at how often the delinquent becomes the adult criminal and then abuser all over again. We've explored the link between intergenerational repetition of abuse and strongly believe that it exists. I'm not sure that we've established that delinquent or antisocial behavior which comes to the attention of the authorities is a typical intervening pattern between the years of being victimized and, in turn, being a parent with inappropriate abusive reactions and relationships with one's own children.

What is the severity of the child abuse we're talking about? You may think that all of this is nonsense, but I've spent enough time listening, for instance, to some of the key experts in this field describe to judges the ways in which we as a society ought to respond to abuse to know that we're talking about widely divergent levels of activity. We have to clarify what part of the spectrum will be our focus. Are we talking about all levels of corporal punishment? There are those who suggest, as I'm sure you are aware, that corporal punishment *per se* is inappropriate. Children just plain shouldn't be spanked; and spankings, if they're harder than some other non-parent authority determines they should be, are child abuse. I'll have to confess that in raising five children, two of them adults at this point, spanking, or some sort of corporal punishment always seemed essential with young children.

Dr. Ten Bensel from Minnesota, in a very interesting recent dialogue with some juvenile court judges, was able to pinpoint what he thought were the thresholds between appropriate kinds of corporal punishment and abuse—defined by the age of the child, the place on the child where the punishment was inflicted, the amount of force used, the damage which might or might not have been predictable from the force used, etc. He suggested that some behavior generally accepted as being non-abusive, such as shaking a child, actually has severe, long-range, permanent physical effect. We should consider the possibility that it isn't just an abuse event, report or adjudication that is the issue but, indeed, the nature of that interrelationship (the extensiveness of the abuse and the context in which it occurs) that provides the correlation with delinquency, more than the label itself.

We know that abuse is defined differently by statutes in different states. It's defined differently by the mores, customs and lifestyles of ethnic groups, religious groups, and so forth. How can we compare one place with another? What about the historical context? I've touched on that, yet less than careful inquiry bothers me when we insist on defining the proper role of a parent in relation to a child so differently today than we ever have done before.

DEFINING THE ISSUES—DELINQUENCY

When we turn to the delinquency side, are we talking only about those acts which would be criminal if committed by adults? That's what most of us would now use as a proper definition of 'delinquency.' Yet the majority of states define it more broadly. Are we talking only about those violent acts that one might think are influenced by violence of others, including abuse by parents; or about a correlation between property crimes, petty misbehavior or other kinds of nuisance 'delinquency' and being abused as a child? If we're talking about reported delinquency, then by whom, and with whose standards? Is it by the child's definition of misbehavior or delinquency, or by something more precise?

Are we talking about those kids who are adjudicated; those who are diverted; only those who are caught? This is especially important in view of Martin Gold's work that suggests that delinquency is a virtually universal phenomenon. The question is: Who gets caught and **not** who is engaged in it. And, indeed, if delinquency is universal, one might be able to make a simple correlation that all abused children will engage in delinquent behavior. Is there some disproportionate propensity to getting caught if one comes out of a family where the kind of interaction which we call abuse has happened?

FAMILY IMPACT ASSESSMENT

Another issue that is important to discuss is whether or not the title of this book leads us astray by suggesting a gross correlation between two extremely complex phenomena. If it does, merely the recognition of the oversimplification may be sufficient solution to the problem. But I think we ought also to ask ourselves if our mutually shared assumption that there is a relationship between abuse and delinquency may reduce the integrity of the exploration of all of the possible relationships, and also the possibility of the absence of any relationships at all. In our exploration are we going to discriminate sufficiently between correlation and causation, between the complexity of the causation among some subfactors and the overall gross label itself? Is the reported difference in perception of treatment by parents between delinquents and non-delinquents an absolute difference, or is it one in which the perception tells us a great deal more about the impact of the behavior on the child rather than about what actually occurred?

All of this—all of our frustration about abuse, delinquency, and everything in between—comes down to a simply stated, but very complex, question of family dynamics. How much mystery those two words cover. I sit on a National Commission on Family Policy that is trying to examine some of these phenomena. We are looking at what is happening to our almost romantically alleged traditional 'family strengths' in this nation. We are, I think, at a very exciting time because what has been a loose, non-specific and meaningless, yet harsh, rhetoric about family values disintegration is now coming to the fore. We are being asked, and hopefully will ask ourselves, to examine it in hard detail—not lamenting that everything isn't all it once was, not wishing for that typical ticky-tacky 'everything is fine' family that never did exist (and never will)—but looking in hard ways at the very tough, conflicting choices we have.

I do not accept the proposition that there is nothing we can do about family structure or family life. We have made conscious decisions in this country over the last decade and a half, and we continue to make them, without carefully examining their impact on family life, In fact, I suggest, these decisions are a reflection of issues on which we place much higher value than family life itself. We shouldn't be surprised that the recognition of those other values is sometimes destructive of the very things that we on alternate Wednesdays lament as having passed. It should not be surprising—it's the obvious, should have been expected result of what we have consciously done. However, it has happened without consciously exploring the reasons behind, or the impact of, what we've done, in the name of higher values.

I'm excited to see a national administration with a family orientation, with an interest in talking about the family. But also it's sad to see how often there is a 'duck and run' response when the detailed hard work, or the funds, or the reorganization needed to implement sensitivity to family issues dynamics are called for. Partly, I think, this results from our not knowing all that we ought to know or all that we ought to do with regard to family policy.

There is an effort going on in Washington, D.C., to develop a family impact statement similar to that which we have adopted for environmental issues. It's an exciting process, but if you talk with those involved in it, you find that it has been extremely frustrating because of the complexities of trying to be specific within an idea that seems too simple and so easy at first blush. This effort shows that we must look, scrupulously and with careful detail, at what it is we do and what our trade-offs and underlying values may be when we're talking about family policy. Clearly, 'family' is the best buzz word around, and everybody is getting on the bandwagon. In this regard, we must be concerned with family interaction at all levels—adult, child, and then the child becoming an adult with a new child, children and peers. I suspect, if one looks at abuse, there has to be heavy attention to interaction among adults and peers, and among adults and the extended family, and its absence in understanding, if one is to make any real, significant headway.

I believe we have created many of the changes in the environment which affect families and we've created them consciously— not necessarily aware of the results, but consciously taking the steps and promoting the values that have caused many of the basic changes. I think we would agree that the family still has to fulfill functions of socialization and social control, but in these two areas family dysfunction is too often causing inappropriate socialization and lack of social control.

All one has to do in order to get into a horrible snarl when talking about family function or dysfunction is to ask what cultural, ethnic or lifestyle group we are talking about. This raises questions about whose values are going to be established as across-the-board standards, trying to search out the variations in those standards, and whether we mean that anything is acceptable if any group espouses it.

I suspect that I may already be in trouble with some researchers, and maybe others for other reasons, but if not I'll probably really get in trouble now. I suggest that much of what we have done or failed to do in terms of family policy proves not only that we are not a family-oriented society, but that we are an anti-family society. We are anti-family in some ways that touch us right in the very center of some of the most basic values and current movements that affect us all. We are anti-family because we have put an emphasis on individualization in the last 20 years that has never been done before. We are concerned about individual programs for people, individual entitlements, individual circumstances to a degree never before shown in any other society. People can quality on their own, and not as members of groups, for most of the benefits that government and the private sector make available within our communities. If one looks at this anti-interdependence attitude, I'm not surc that we are willing to reverse it, but we clearly creatd it by a number of conscious social decisions.

The whole question of children's rights is of major importance. I believe in children's rights and have been fighting for children's rights to have families, not to be inappropriately treated or abused, to have services which will meet their needs and not exploit them at the hands of service providers, to have rights before courts, rights to representation, etc. The very idea that children have rights outside of their relationship within the family is a revolutionary one. As most of you know, a hundred years ago in western societies a parent, basically the father, had virtually unlimited control over children up to and including the taking of their lives. As a society, we simply did not respond to that kind of intrafamilial behavior. As we have moved first to recognize the independent rights of older children, then children's rights to be protected within the family setting, and I'm not saying that we shouldn't have done that, we have undercut the basic context of forced dependence within the family, which may be the basic thread that traditionally held families together, or created them in the first place.

If that isn't controversial enough for you, let me talk for a moment about the women's movement and about women's rights. The other day as I listened to a discussion of equal wages—and I believe as an individual in the justice of equal wages—it occurred to me that one of the obvious impacts of our move to equal wages and the recognition of female heads of households and female employment as being absolutely as worthy of recompense at the same level as for men (and who can quarrel with that), has been to undo one of the oldest social mechanisms for interdependence. Now, I'm not saying that we should not do that, but if we do not recognize that this makes a revolutionary change in whether or not families are forced to be held together, then we are not really looking at the impact of that which we have consciously promoted and significantly, although not totally, succeeded in changing. It may well be, talk about hard choices, one of the circumstances most destructive of the family, as we have known it, that one could describe.

I'm sure that many will say, "Who wants a family that's based on those kinds of forced ties, the absence of options and choices?" Well, maybe nobody does, but I think we have to take a look at the fact that maybe the way families are formed and have survived as possibly the most basic association in our society does not necessarily stem from the need to come together to procreate. Large numbers of single parents illustrate that the 'traditional family' is not necessarily the only mode of childrearing; and other kinds of dependencies may be the glue which stabilized and perpetuated family relationships.

As we seek to carry out the commitment to individualization, to individual rights, to justice, to freedom, to choices, to opportunities for individual people, by very definition we are undercutting their interdependence. We may not be prepared to go back to trying to force interdependence. One option is to see them as individuals interrelating on an individual basis, occasionally by choice, but not on a permanent basis, and increasingly interacting with others outside of what we have called the family structure. This includes looking to the government or others to make up the deficits which, in the past, interdependence might have covered. Everything from pensions and social security—which freed many of us from dependence on our children as we got older—children's rights, women's rights, mobility in society, change in employment patterns, forced retirement, the whole range has had tremendous impact on families. Rarely in the past have we asked questions about causation and correlation at this level. Although we have a small beginning, I suggest that even at this point we aren't serious enough about it on a national level.

It's only recently that people have asked, "What's the impact on the family unit? Now it's easy to look for a scapegoat and it's easy to say, "Isn't it a shame that religious values are breaking down?" or "Somebody else is to blame." or "It's just a sign of the times and it's not reversible." It's easy to say, "Wouldn't it be great if we went back to a strong family structure?" Historians and sociologists and others tell us that this is an illusion. Families didn't exist the way we think they did. Going backward is no solution when we are going forward in terms of perpetuating and strengthening those very things which are tearing any remnants of the old family model apart.

We can change some of this direction if we have the will. I seriously question whether we have the will. I am also in doubt as to whether it would be appropriate for us to do so. But for heaven's sake, we've got to begin to recognize much more clearly that family change is largely the result of conscious decisions in other areas that we don't want to question or examine. For example, in the area of child care, is it better for children to be raised with less contact with the biological parents or the nurturing family unit? Well, many of us are not willing to ask that question from a child-centered or family-oriented perspective because it treads so heavily on the individual rights of women and others who have had few options within the family structure. But we have to ask these questions. It seems to me that they have to be faced if we are at all serious about putting some flesh on the bones of this emerging concern—skeletal concern, if you will—for family structure and our lament for its disintegration.

SO WHAT?

The last of my random thoughts is the most important of all. It is: So what? So there's a correlation, a relationship. So we explore it and figure out that this sample correlates with that sample, or determine the statistical relevance of this, that, or the other thing; and then so what? I hope that there is a 'so what,' and I'd like to take a look at it for a moment.

The 'so what' for me is what difference this book will make. Yes, it may refine some thinking and reflection; but what difference will it make for children or parents or judges? Are there ways in which our learning will change the way we intervene in child abuse situations or in delinquency? I'm a little skeptical about that, having run large bureaucratic organizations, struggled with advocates, sat by the hour with judges and explored the limits of their knowledge and their attitudes, fallibility, and frustrations. I think one has to seriously ask the question because in asking it and responding to the limits of the answer, maybe what we do will be a little different.

One of the 'so whats' will be that a book will emerge capturing the wisdom that is distilled in this process. It is vital to publish and make available to others some of the important research and thinking that is contained in the papers we will hear. But going back to the initial reason why I'm involved in this business at all, the 'so what' for me is what difference it will make. Yes, it may spawn some additional research. Yes, it may refine some thinking and reflection; but what difference will it make for children or parents or judges? Are there ways in which our learning will change the way we intervene in child abuse situations or in delinquency? I'm a little skeptical about that, having run large bureaucratic organizations, struggled with advocates, sat by the hour with judges and explored the limits of their knowledge and their attitudes, fallibility, and frustrations. I think one has to seriously ask the question because in asking it and responding to the limits of the answer, maybe what we do will be a little different.

One of the things we may do, because of the tremendous fear in this society about delinquency and the anti-social behavior and the growing phenomenon of children out of control, is to raise the resource credibility for both research and programs in this area. One of the things the Clark Foundation has funded, outside of our usual program interest, is a study of incarcerated adults to see what correlations there are between their dysfunctional family backgrounds, their placement in foster care, their living in institutions, their perceptions of the disintegrated family relationship and their appearance in penal custody as adults. Indeed, there is some disproportionate relationship, although the final results are not yet available.

We undertook the financing of this study not because, with all due respect, the correlation would somehow be terribly important for how we treated neglected and dependent children. We did it because it was important to tackle some of those things which trigger the money, the people, the credibility and the priorities in human services. If we can convince people that there is a correlation between what happens in terms of child abuse, or neglect, or separation, or years in foster care, or institutionalization, or repeated attachments and separations, or failure to have any plans made for such children, or failure to mobilize services in a constructive, goal-oriented way, or the inadequacy of treatment that doesn't provide any help for children in treatment settings, and the secondary consequences to society of increased disorganization, frustration, violence, crime and delinquency, then we may have increased the level of acceptability of work in what is regarded by many as this less significant area of neglect and child protection.

Neglect of children is seen by some as a marginal issue. Child welfare is obviously important, but we shouldn't be bothered too much by it. Senators have asked with apparent seriousness whether we shouldn't just abolish the whole child welfare program, toss it in with everything else. After all, it's just one more area of concern with no special reason for separate attention. One can take that position only if one does not really believe that there are enormous secondary costs to this society of doing badly in its job of rearing and protecting children. I believe the costs there are enormous and may be one important answer to my 'so what.'

But what about other uses of this knowledge? It's important to consider that the failure to use some of our knowledge, or the belief that some of it is not usable, has contributed to our continuing problem of lack of research funds. When I first went to the Clark Foundation, I had the opportunity to participate in a seminar at a place called Johnnycake Child Study Center in Arkansas. I remember two things about it: the conference result, and the fact that it's located in a virtually inaccessible place.

That we have failed to use the research that we already have has been an unarticulated concern of mine from my days as a social services administrator. It's been a more articulated concern of mine since then because after talking for two days with researchers, program administrators, and policy makers who were talking past each other hour after hour after hour it became apparent that we were participating in a live demonstration of the real problem of the utilization of research: we were missing each other by a mile. Each group was unwilling to recognize the rules of the others' game. That's an oversimplification: it isn't that none were willing to try, but all were shocked at the breadth of the gap.

Part of the answer to 'so what' seems to me to be to address the basic question of who is going to use research, and for what. This is essential in the design, the deployment, the writing up and the marketing of research. Did we so tightly control the research that we were in an unrealistic environment that made it inapplicable to anything other than a laboratory? I don't want to get into an argument about the value of knowledge for knowledge's sake, of course there is such value. But as we're talking about a restriction in resources, as we're talking about limitations on what we can do, and as we're talking about a tremendous social need to do better in service provision, adjudication, policy making, and legislating, I believe it is urgent for us to make as valuable, as transferable and as effective as possible, the capacity to learn from good research and to put those lessons to some kind of useful application.

What is the research going to do for the policy maker? Some of these chapters will address that question. What difference will it make to the probation officer who sits in a hot, stuffy cubicle, maybe with one other probation officer and no privacy, trying to deal with a huge caseload? Don't tell me the answer is just to make the caseload smaller. The research shows that is an oversimplification that alone doesn't solve the problem; and the people aren't going to fund it anyhow. What difference does it make to the judges—the judge who has 2.5 minutes per case, or spends only one day a week as a juvenile judge, or the judge who doesn't want to be a juvenile judge at all but got the short straw in the drawing and has to be one for six months?

What does it do for the therapist? Is it going to help in terms of those who seek to do therapy whether or not they're properly trained and retrained? What does it do for the policeman on the beat who has to deal with the frustration of a community mixed with the anger of the acting out of its own children and the untouchable circumstances which cause them to rebel? What is it going to do for the public anger that is turning us backward at an alarming rate toward a repressive and punishment-oriented response to children? Is it going to make any real difference in our understanding?

What is it going to do for legislators, most recently those Senators who are attempting to change the way our child welfare, social service and family oriented service provision laws in this country are shaped? There are some terribly important decisions being made right now in Washington, D.C., which are significantly affecting the long run future of programs for children in this country.

People get permanently hurt by these problems every day, every hour, in families all across the country and in every community from which we come. I sincerely hope that this work will lead to reducing some of that hurt.

1

Policy and Program Implications in the Child Delinquency Correlation

ADRIENNE A. HAEUSER, JANET STENLUND
& LAURA DANIEL

Midwest Parent-Child Welfare Resource Center
Center for Advanced Studies in Human Services
Milwaukee, Wisconsin 53201

Widespread evidence of family dysfunction in our society is apparent in many areas, particularly in child abuse/neglect and in juvenile delinquency. The correlation between child abuse/neglect and juvenile delinquency is documented in the literature by examples including the following:

> The New York State Assembly Select Committee has found that the abuse of children, whether by parents or institutions, turns the abused child inward toward aggression, violence and criminalization. It views the mistreatment of children as a major contributing factor to increasing violence and rising crime rates. One study has shown that seven out of thirty-nine abused children were in court as juvenile delinquents after being reported abused. Although he may say it too often Dr. Vincent Fontana is right when he points out that abuse is a dynamic phenomenon reflected in all our statistics on crime (Chase, 1975, p. 117).

Another study indicates an even higher correlation, namely 42% of children reported to protective services were subsequently identified as delinquent or ungovernable (*Proceedings of the First National Conference on Child Abuse and Neglect,* 1976, p. 118).

Based on this correlation, the authors of this paper will focus on: first, analyzing current child abuse/neglect policies and programs which promote juvenile delinquency, and, secondly, changing current policies and program practices toward preventing both child abuse/neglect and juvenile delinquency.

We undertake our discussion from the perspective that our nation's attitude toward children is ambivalent; indulgent and claiming to be child-centered, but also hostile and expecting discipline and controlled child behavior. We therefore have policies and programs with ambivalent and contradictory goals. Historically, the nineteenth century house-of-refuge movement and the later crusades by the Society for the Prevention of Cruelty to Children evolved "not to save children from cruel or abusive parents but to save society from future delinquents (Pfohl, 1977, p. 311)." Society's concern for order, regularity and obedience in children's behavior persists, e.g. the recent Supreme Court ruling allowing corporal punishment in the schools, and we must be aware of these values as we examine child abuse/neglect policies and programs.

Even before the battered child syndrome was identified, professional journals were presenting articles on the etiology of delinquency in parent-child relationships (Jenkins, 1943; Easson and Steinkilber, 1961; Curtis, 1963). With the advent of child abuse/neglect reporting laws and more recently with the Child Abuse Prevention and Treatment Act, child abuse/neglect has been viewed as a discreet, and unique problem rather than one of family dysfunction leading to a multiplicity of other problems, including juvenile delinquency. In our haste to enact legislation and provide programs to identify child abuse/neglect, we have provided a service delivery mechanism which is stigmatizing and therefore used largely for crisis intervention. At the same time, we have poured billions into equally discreet juvenile crime programs. We knew long ago that violence breeds violence, but we have built fragmented services for symptoms rather than treating the root of the problem in the home.

CHILD REARING PRACTICES BREEDING VIOLENCE

Although the main topic of this paper focuses on policy and needed policy changes, it is within the family that the effects of policy or lack of policy exert the most direct impact. Experiences within the family, such as child rearing practices, are linked to the norms and values outside the family system. Lystad (1975) writes:

> . . . it is within the family that societal stress affects each individual most immediately. It is here that the child's capacity to grow and develop is nurtured. And it is here that the child learns future adult roles of a violent or non-violent character (p. 340).

Thus, in establishing a knowledge base for policy, a brief overview of the research on child rearing practices, particularly discipline, should be informative.

As noted previously, society expects parents and other caretakers to keep children under control. Physical punishment, most universally known as "spanking," is often used to obtain this control. While the effects of physical punishment are complex, being dependent on both the intensity of the punishment and the manner in which it is administered, spanking provides an aggressive behavior model.

If the goal of discipline is to bring about self-control rather than control by others, attention must be given to the research that reports a correlation between parent responses that are warm, accepting and affectionate, and socialization of the child. Sears, Maccaby and Levin found that the withholding of parental affection until compliance occurred was especially effective in developing self-control in children (Bandura and Walters, 1963). Wesley C. Becker (1964) concurs in a summary statement in "Consequences of Different Kinds of Parental Discipline:"

> The importance of warmth and permissiveness in facilitating the growth of sociable, independent children has found repeated support. The debilitating effects of parental hostility in its many forms is certainly apparent (p. 203).

Rutter (1972) found that both "family discord and lack of affection were associated with the development of antisocial disorder but the combination of the two was particularly harmful . . . (p. 108)." Lystad (1975) found parents of delinquents to be more punitive , more sanctioning of antisocial behavior and of aggression than parents of non-delinquents.

Clearly, research indicates that family discord and punitiveness are associated with antisocial behavior of children. We also know that environmental or psychological stress affects a family's ability to provide nurturance and supervision. Thus, it would seem that policies must recognize that stress on families can lead to aggressive behavior by parents wherein violence breeds violence.

THE INVIOLABLE BOUNDARY BETWEEN FAMILY AND GOVERNMENT

Parents and individual caretakers can abuse and neglect children because in this country there has been an inviolable boundary between the family and the forces of government. Nowhere except with respect to the church is the barrier between public and private more rigid. Interestingly, at least one social and cultural historian points out that such was not always the case:

> The boundaries between private and public sectors of American life were defined far differently during pre-Revolutionary days when the community's power of intervention (often expressed through both family and church) was, at least in theory, virtually limitless.
>
> Families in the 17th century, for example, were taken as models of the large society, little commonwealths in which the vital lessons of obedience, deference, and mutual respect would be absorbed by children along with their food, shelter, and daily care. Parents shouldered burdens that in later years would be borne by schoolmasters and politicians: stringent laws protected their authority and held them responsible for juvenile misdeeds.
>
> Those who lived outside of normal family relations were suspect. Dependent and orphaned children were placed not in public institutions but in other families. Young bachelors were often required to receive public permission to

live separately. Widows and widowers swiftly remarried after bereavement, and divorce was practically unknown (Harris, April 4, 1976, p. 9).

Curiously, in the period between Revolutionary days and the present, the power of intervention diminished at the same time that the family as a value worthy of intervention diminished. Values shifted to the individual: to Horatio Alger, not his family; to self-actualization; to tax laws which penalize the married. Even the linchpin of the National Association of Social Workers *Code of Ethics* (1960, 1967) states, "I regard as my primary obligation the welfare of the individual or group served."

Our value of the individual rather than the family and our concern for family privacy has had devastating effects on our nation's children. We have enacted legislation which focuses on identifying and 'catching' abusive parents rather than mandating treatment for family dysfunction. Further, our laws don't prohibit using physical force on children in the interest of positive nurturing and deterring later violence; they just say "don't use too much and don't get caught." Because the poor are more visible, they are more likely to be reported and the service system is oriented to a social class whom we identify as dependent and unable to provide for themselves. Thus, we have structured an elaborate system of child welfare services to serve as parent substitutes for the poor in the naive belief that the state makes a good parent. Having structured these programs, it has been our inclination to overuse and protect them. In short, the authors believe that much of the 'solution' to child abuse and neglect is part of the juvenile delinquency problem.

CHILD ABUSE AND NEGLECT LEGISLATION

As a result of the congressional Subcommittee on Children and Youth hearings during 1973, the federal Child Abuse Prevention and Treatment Act (PL 93-247) was passed into law in January, 1974, Subsequently, through the National Center on Child Abuse and Neglect created by the Act, grants have been awarded for demonstration and research; information gathering and dissemination, training and technical assistance and assistance to states. Among the major objectives of PL 93-247 is the improvement of state child abuse and neglect reporting laws. Since its inception, thirty-three states have revised their laws to meet federal regulations established under this Act and are thereby receiving grants to implement new legislative provisions.

In actuality, however, while newly-revised state reporting laws mandate improved identification and reporting procedures, implementation of effective community based treatment and prevention programs is still severely lacking. The continuing widespread use of foster care and institutionalization of children, as well as the policies and practices within many of these programs, provides strong evidence of the ineffectiveness of these laws in resolving the problem of family dysfunction.

In view of staff shortages and lack of training, child protective service workers understandably recommend placement when in doubt. It has been estimated that 89% of all child welfare expenditures are for foster care (Comptroller General Report to the Congress, April 9, 1976, p. 35). The community team approach to child abuse and neglect with shared decision-making and accountability probably reduces the use of placement, but it has yet to be implemented on any significant scale. Furthermore, we must remember that child protective service units have been mandated only to investigate, and treatment, when it occurs for the parent, the child or the family, remains a privilege, not a right. When state laws are rewritten, the revisions inevitably relate to reporting rather than treatment. This emphasis on reporting distracts from treatment, as the following two-minute response to a television editorial suggests:

> The recent Channel 6 editorial, "Toughen Child Abuse Laws," may mislead the public into thinking that reporting child child all that is necessary to solve the problem.
>
> Certainly, as Channel 6 suggested, it is imperative to strengthen the law to require reporting by more professionals. However, identifying abusive or neglectful parents is no guarantee that they or their children will be helped. Furthermore, by emphasizing reporting, we tend to focus on "catching and punishing the parent" rather than helping the parent and preventing further abuse.
>
> Most abusive parents were themselves abused as children, and they are in fact victims, not criminals. Ninety per cent of them can be helped so the children do not have to be removed from the home.
>
> Children belong in families, not in the care of the government, so let's demand long-term treatment and followup as well as the reporting of child abuse. Reporting is not enough (Haeuser, May 13 and 16, 1977).

OVERUSE OF PLACEMENT

We turn now to what happens when parental abuse or neglect results in placement. Unfortunately, placement in itself is too often misconstrued as treatment. Yet we know that extricating children from the child welfare system is much more difficult than the initial placement. Specifically, New York City's Child Welfare Information Service reported for 1975 that "discharge plans provided for only one child in five to be returned to his home" and "no discharge plan at all had been drawn up for 30% of the children *(Child Protection Report,* December 4, 1975. A child, shifted from one foster home to another, exacerbated by the shrinking number of foster homes in the age of the Women's Movement, becomes emotionally distressed by this instability over and above the trauma of separation from his or her own family. Residential treatment is recommended, often far from the child's home community, and ultimately the child, perhaps now a youth, turns on others as a delinquent or on self as a mental patient and is at high risk for suicide, given the staggering adolescent suicide rate. Consider the lack of placement resources and, more importantly, the total disregard for a child's natural family and community in the following case:

> *The F case:* This case involved a 16 year old girl who was picked up by police for shoplifting and placed in a detention home in one state (State A) after having run away from a foster home in another state (State B). The State B welfare agency had legal custody of the girl and was notified of the situation by the State A welfare agency. The letter to the State B welfare agency indicated that suitable placement of the girl within its jurisdiction was unlikely.
>
> The State B welfare agency replied that it believed the girl should not be returned because the place from which she ran away represented all the bad experiences she had undergone throughout her life and that a fresh start would

probably help her. It offered to pay for all placement costs incurred in behalf of the girl.

The State A welfare agency could not find a foster home for her so she was placed in a receiving home. The girl ran away and was again picked up by the police in State A and placed in a detention home. The girl was subsequently returned to the county in State B from which she had run away initially. The caseworker involved in State A told us that a lack of resources for adolescent girls was the major problem in this case (Comptroller General Report to the Congress, April 9, 1976, p. 35).

At present, the state is the parent for 350,000 foster care children displaced from their homes (*Child Protection Report,* September 9, 1976, p. 1). We must ask ourselves how many got more consideration or skilled assistance than F and how many, for whom initial removal was to be only temporary, will end up in the foster care/institutional cycle.

Robert Mnookin, an expert in foster care, reported recently to the Family Impact Seminar that although foster care is primarily a state and local concern, federal financial incentives are all weighted toward institutional care, and "current practices, regulations, and policies of welfare agencies and institutions (e.g. with respect to the rights of parents, visiting privileges, and services) add up to a decidedly anti-family bias (*Summary Report: Second Meeting of the Family Impact Seminar,* January 25-26, 1977, p. 2)." The authors of this paper submit that the state makes a notoriously poor parent and that the rising juvenile crime rate and failure of state training schools clearly demonstrates that governmental policy and programs providing substitutes for dysfunctioning families are not very effective. The stigma of protective services and our 'hands off' policy with respect to the family means intervention is crisis oriented and not amenable to supportive services. If parental abuse begets placement and placement begets institutional abuse, is not our very own 'helping' system contributing to the problem of juvenile delinquency? Dr. Alan A. Stone, Professor of Law and Psychiatry at Harvard, makes the following observation:

> The use of courts to deal with noncriminal social problems (the abused, the abandoned, and the PINS), is part of America's monomania for legalistic solutions. The juvenile courts demonstrate the total inadequacy of that legal approach. The court's only function in many instances is to funnel children from unsuitable homes to unsuitable placements (Stone, 1975, pp. 156-157).

It is quite clear that both in terms of the scale of social welfare expenditures and the type of services developed, social services which support the family have received lower priority than those intended to replace the family (Moroney, 1976, p. 118).

INSTITUTIONAL ABUSE

While child abuse/neglect laws are primarily intended to protect children from maltreatment and to preserve family life whenever possible, we have seen that these laws have had, more often than not, counter-effects on both individual children and their families. First, child abuse/neglect registry data indicates that these laws have been applied almost exclusively to the identification and reporting of child abuse and neglect by parents and caretakers in the home. Whereas outside of the home, that is, in schools, in 'child-saving' institutions and in foster homes, abuse and neglect of children is socially and legally condoned by our society in the name of discipline. As a result, although "there are far more American children mistreated in institutions than suffer injury or neglect at home . . . our value system, as well as our politics, makes it easier to finger the parents than to blame society (Chase, 1976, p. 151)." This is well exemplified on the federal level. In contradiction to the federal Child Abuse Prevention and Treatment Act aimed at protecting children from parental as well as institutional abuse, federal level policymakers are in practice allowing institutional abuse to flourish. Recent congressional hearings on extension of this federal Act:

> . . . avoided any mention of the even more sensitive matter of institutional child abuse—the maltreatment of youngsters in institutions supported directly or indirectly by HEW funds. Despite many exposes of flagrant abuse in foster homes, reform schools, and hospitals, NCCAN has declined to take any initiatives—and Congress, in effect, is saying it is okay to ignore these out-of-sight unfortunates (*Child Protection Report,* May 12, 1977, p. 3).

Secondly, our ineffectiveness in preserving family life is demonstrated when we consider the numbers of children separated from and abandoned by their communities. In addition to the 350,000 children in foster care, the National Research Council cites over 450,000 children currently placed in public and private institutions, including 95,000 in residential hospitals and schools for mentally retarded persons; 78,000 in residential treatment centers for emotionally disturbed; 150,000 in detention and training schools for delinquents; 37,000 in institutional programs for the physically and sensorially handicapped; and 98,000 in residential programs for dependent and neglected children. It should be noted that these data represent only "estimates" for the number of children in institutional care. "No agency has a complete picture of institutions and institutionalized children in the U.S. Responsibility is scattered in Washington and fragmented and idiosyncratic in the states (National Research Council, 1976, pp. 85-89)." Consequently, we do not even know where our children are.

Moreover, since availability of space is often the determining factor in deciding where to place a child, the child's individual problems and needs are not necessarily matched with the type of placement utilized. In terms of problems, these children are referred by agencies, courts, schools and parents as being emotionally disturbed, truant, school dropouts, retarded, runaways, delinquent, 'dangerous' to self and others, dependent, abused, neglected, uncontrollable, ungovernable and persons in need of supervision (PINS).

Examples of the most blatant placement policies which promote institutional abuse and neglect and, therefore, also juvenile delinquency, have been cited by Wooden (1976) and others:

Forty-six states approve of placing children in county jails; thirty-four of these states do not require even a court order to do so. Consequently, 8,000 children are in jails on any given day, and over a one-year period, 100,000 children have spent one or more days in jails (Wooden, 1976, p. 27).

Seventy-five per cent of the children in jails are locked up with adults (Wooden, 1976, p. 28).

In all but three states, it is 'common' practice to place neglected children in facilities for juvenile offenders (Wooden, 1976, p. 24).

Thirty to fifty per cent of the population of detention centers, jails and training schools are status offenders, i.e., truants, runaways, and PINS (Wooden, 1976, p. 37).

When children from economically, socially and educationally advantaged families are neglected by their parents and communities, they may be sent off to 'first-class' boarding schools and military academies. Poor and minority children are the ones most often relegated to institutions in which the practices and care are worse than the homes from which these children are removed. Yet, in our world of double standards:

> . . . the preoccupation with personal hygiene and individual morality rather than institutional values and standards allows us to remove a child from parents whose living quarters are dirty and roach-infested, but to fund with public monies a school for retarded children where toilets are overflowing, garbage is uncollected, and children are permitted to lie in their own soiled clothes (Chase, 1975, p. 152).

These children are not only misplaced from their homes and communities but they are also 'sentenced' and 'warehoused' for indeterminate periods to inappropriate institutional settings in which the physical and emotional conditions are often severely abusive and neglectful. Abhorrent conditions and practices have been cited as "common," particularly in juvenile detention centers, training schools and 'for profit' foster homes by Chase (1975), Wooden (1976), Stone (1976) and the National Research Council (1976), and include: overcrowding; lack of sufficient numbers and types of staff; little or no provision for education; inadequate facilities; brutal and sadistic corporal punishment; lack of medical care; sexual abuse by staff and children; overuse of solitary confinement and drug abuse in place of treatment; lack of recreational facilities; and regulations serving the institution rather than the child and his family.

While "we know that most correctional institutions reinforce delinquency in children, that most institutions for the mentally retarded require low levels of intellectual functioning, and that most hospitals for mental illness perpetuate sickness (National Research Council, 1976, p. 85)," we continue to let the availability of these institutions influence decisions which are not in the best interests of children and their families or society.

With the emphasis on identification and increased reporting, communities and professionals continue to believe that the problem of child abuse and neglect is being taken care of. However, without community commitment to preserving family life and to implementing a comprehensive community-based system for the prevention and treatment of child abuse and neglect, separation and abandonment of children and families will prevail. The frequency of court referrals and subsequent court-ordered placements of children in institutions reflect parental as well as community sanctioned abandonment of children in a misguided search for legal solutions. As Milton Luger, former president of the New York State Juvenile Delinquency Programs stated:

> With the exception of relatively few youths, it would be better for all concerned if young delinquents were not detected, apprehended, and institutionalized. Too many of them get worse in our care. The public is terribly shortsighted. They just want them out of the way (Chase, 1975, p. 154).

Our shortsightedness is indeed costly in terms of human lives and tax dollars. Charles Manson is only one example. "(He) and countless thousands of children locked away from society during the late '40's and '50's became part of the bitter harvest this country reaped in the late '60's and early '70's (Wooden, 1976, p. 56).

CORPORAL PUNISHMENT IN THE SCHOOLS

One of the most flagrant examples of legally-sanctioned child abuse is the recent Supreme Court decision on *Ingraham et al vs. Wright et al* decided on April 9, 1977. For the second time in less than two years, the Supreme Court upheld corporal punishment in the schools. More specifically, the Court ruled that:

> . . . the cruel and unusual punishment clause of the Eighth Amendment did not apply to disciplinary corporal punishment in public schools and the due process clause did not require notice and hearing prior to the imposition of corporal punishment in the public schools, as that practice was authorized and limited by . . . common law (97 *Supreme Court Reporter* 1401).

In terms of constitutional rights, the Supreme Court more explicitly stated that "school children have no need for the Eighth Amendment" because "schools are open institutions subject to constant public scrutiny" and that these children have "adequate remedies under state law (97 *Supreme Court Reporter* 1421-1422)." However, currently there are only four states, Maine, New Jersey, Maryland and Massachusetts, which outlaw corporal punishment in schools, and one state, Hawaii, has temporarily suspended permission for its use. The majority, thirty-three states, permit corporal punishment, and the remaining twelve remain 'silent' in their statutes, i.e., allow local school districts to decide.

From an international perspective, the United States is one of the few countries of the world which still allows corporal punishment of children. Most other countries prohibit it, including the Scandinavian countries, Russia and France, since 1887 (National Education Association, 1972, p. 26).

Moreover, "there is a present lack of a specific statute authorizing the United States, through the Attorney General, to bring suits to remedy severe and widespread deprivations of the federal constitutional rights of handicapped persons and children (Office of Special Litigation, 1977, p. 1) ." Our society's contradiction in values and attitudes about disciplining children is apparent by our federal and state child protection legislation, on the one hand, and at the same time, the Supreme Court's approval of corporal punishment in the schools. While most of us would agree that consistency is an essential ingredient in disciplining children, it seems ridiculous that our social policies forbid parents to abuse their children and yet allow teachers the option of doing so. A recent letter from a county welfare department supervisor illustrates the confusion about this issue. Namely, foster parents have been questioning, "Since the schools are allowed to paddle...children, why aren't we?" (Letter to Midwest Parent-Child Welfare Resource Center, May 3, 1977)

With the responsibility of educating children, schools are in a position of modeling behavior for children. If schools use corporal punishment with children, indeed, violent behavior becomes the model for children. Moreover, as the aforementioned letter illustrates, parents, too, view the schools as a model for disciplining children.

FAMILY SUPPORT, NOT SUBSTITUTION, NEEDED

Even if we exclude the foster care-institutionalization-delinquency syndrome and institutional abuse, we are confronted with Gelles' research indicating that basic training for violence and the teaching of violent behavior and pro-violent norms occurs primarily through parent-child interaction and day-to-day family life (Gelles, 1972, p. 172). If our policies are targeted to substitutes for the family, how can we expect to change the violent ways of the large majority of families who are not seen by protective or other social services?

Clearly, it appears that governmental policy and program priorities with respect to families should be reversed, with priority given to support for families and less emphasis on substitution for families. As far back as 1909, the White House Conference on Dependent Children pointed out that parents care for children better and cheaper than anyone else (Schorr, 1974, p. xiii). Moreover, support for families is not synonymous with invasion of families, so family privacy is not an issue. While some authors conceive of family support policies and programs as a partnership between parents and the state wherein responsibility is shared, the authors prefer a conceptualization wherein the state provides resources, and outreach for their utilization, which facilitates parenting and family life. In short, parents are given resources to do their job. In totalitarian countries such as Russia and China, the child belongs to the state and intrusions into family life for the sake of the state are the norm. In socialist countries such as Sweden, the child belongs to the parent but the state recognizes that it is in its best interest to help the parent through a variety of social benefits and programs. Some authors, such as David Gil, believe that capitalism is incompatible with a nonviolent society and that the USA cannot adopt a family support posture without a significant movement toward socialism (Gil, 1977, pp. 5-6). The authors agree with Dr. Gil that total nonviolence is impossible in a capitalistic, economically violent society. However, we also believe that capitalism will stay for the foreseeable future and that by reversing our priorities and focusing universally on families rather than on deviant individuals, much can be done to reduce family and societal violence within our present system.

We see the emergence of family policy discussions in many areas as a hopeful sign. President Carter's focus on the family is, of course, invaluable, but there is also the Family Impact Seminar, the forthcoming National Conference on Social Welfare Commission on the Family, the recent American Orthopsychiatric Association resolution proposing national policy aimed at strengthening the family and the National Academy of Sciences 1976 report identifying the primary problem facing America's children as poverty.

At the same time, we are pessimistic because child welfare, with foster care and institutionalization as primary functions, is a very entrenched establishment, and entrenched establishments tend to perpetuate themselves. What Titmuss observed with respect to hospitals can probably be applied to child welfare programs:

Boards of Governors and Management Committees devote more of their time to conditions of work, questions of rewards, difficulties of status and dissatisfaction among the staff than they do to meet the needs of the patients. Of course, all of these questions are vital to the efficient and harmonious running of a hospital; there must be a system of settling these often difficult issues...One of the new problems is the danger that the hospital may tend increasingly to be run in the interests of those working in and for the hospital rather than in the interests of the patients. The fundamental purpose of the hospital must not be dimmed by excessive preoccupation with the means (Schorr, 1974, pp. 122-123).

Furthermore, we social workers and social scientists seem to be enchanted with needs assessments relating supply and demand. This, of course, has the serious limitation of promulgating programs as ends rather than means to achieve an objective. "They generate their own dynamism and can reduce efforts to initiate change through more flexible experimentation in as much as the emphasis tends to shift to organizational survival (Moroney, 1976, p. 104)."

With reluctance and concern for many dedicated child welfare workers, the authors have concluded that only a platform which obliterates child welfare will curb the violence in families and institutions which breeds juvenile delinquency and other problems. Parents, not children, are this country's greatest resource. Let's help them do their job by providing services to families and children in their own homes and benefits which will enable every family to enjoy a decent standard of living.

INCOME BEFORE POLICIES AND PROGRAMS

The importance of income as a deterrent to child abuse and juvenile delinquency as well as other problems cannot be overemphasized. HEW Secretary Califano underscored this by reporting to President Carter that "the most severe threat to family life stems from unemployment and lack of adequate income...Give American parents the job opportunities they seek so that they can provide for their families (Califano, September 17, 1976, p. l)." Mary Keyserling, a member of the National Academy of Sciences research committee, also recently noted that "serious economic difficulties have impact on other things. Child abuse comes out of this, poor academic performance, juvenile crime—they're all income related (Merry, December 25, 1976, p. 1)." While our American society may not welcome socialistic policies and programs to combat family dysfunction, we must accept the fact that some form of guaranteed employment or income redistribution is essential to alleviate both child abuse and neglect and juvenile delinquency.

To support our conclusion that child welfare which substitutes for the family must be obliterated and replaced with policies and programs which support the family, we cite a recent *Milwaukee Journal* newspaper article which appeared under the heading, "End of Line Arrives at Age 16." After describing a typical juvenile criminal's foster home/institution experience, the article continues:

The boy first came to the court's attention in 1963, when he was just 3 years old. The Sheriff's Department had filed a complaint at Children's Court that the boy and his siblings were neglected children. The complaint apparently stemmed from an action of their parents, who took the toddlers to the Children's Home and said they were uncontrollable (*Milwaukee Journal*, January 9, 1977).

Parents who describe their children as uncontrollable are probably parents for whom life is uncontrollable; families without adequate income, housing, etc., or knowledge of child care, and few links to resources such as family or social services. It is clear that we must provide both resources and links to assist families in controlling their destinies.

SUMMARY

While the causes of child abuse/neglect and juvenile delinquency are rooted in family dysfunction, we have elaborated separate service systems which blind us to their common origin and deter us from focusing on programs which support families and children in their own homes. We have done this in the misguided belief that we must respect family privacy until private family problems become public.

In evolving child abuse/neglect reporting legislation, we have focused on identification rather than treatment, and too often we have misconstrued placement as treatment. By not providing treatment and by permitting the foster care-institutionalization-delinquency cycle to flourish, we must admit that child abuse/neglect policies and programs are indeed promoting juvenile delinquency.

More directly, abused and neglected children who are placed in institutions often fare worse than if left in the most inadequate home. Yet we sanction institutional placements just as the Supreme Court sanctions corporal punishment in the schools. In effect we are saying we sanction abuse.

The authors believe these policies and programs for child abuse/neglect contribute to the juvenile delinquency problem. Only as we reverse our priorities and provide universal programming and benefits, particularly income, for families and children will we intervene in family dysfunction without making the solution to the child abuse/neglect problem a part of the cause of juvenile delinquency.

> When society seeks to redress deprivation, programs are designed to meet the needs of the deprived. In most instances "deprived" is synonymous with "poor." Services tend to be designed for special groups, rather than for all children. Thus the field of child welfare is oriented toward pathology and deprivation, an orientation that in overt and subtle ways affects program development and planning. There is substantial evidence that programs for the poor are often poor programs. So a system such as child welfare, designed as part of the solution, can instead become part of the problem (Schorr, 1974, p. 4).

And, as long as we have child welfare placement services available, they will be used and reversing priorities will be difficult. It may be necessary to adopt an anti-child welfare posture.

REFERENCES

Bandura , W. & Walters, R. H. *Social learning and personality development.* New York: Holt, Rinehart & Winston, 1963.

Becker, W. C. Consequences of different kinds of parental discipline. In M. L. Hoffman & L. Hoffman (Eds.), *Review of child development research.* Vol. 1. New York: Russell Sage Foundation, 1964.

Califano, J. A., Jr. *American families: Trends, pressures and recommendations.* Preliminary Report to Governor Jimmy Carter, September 17, 1976.

Chase, N. F. *A child is being beaten: Violence against children, an American tragedy.* New York: McGraw-Hill, 1975.

Child protection report. December 4, 1975, 3; September 9, 1976, 1; & May 12, 1977, 3.

Curtis, G. C. Violence breeds violence—perhaps . *American Journal of Psychiatry,* October, 1963, 386-387.

Easson, W. & Steinkilber, R. Murderous aggression by children and adolescents. *Archives of General Psychiatry,* June, 1961, 1-9.

End of line arrives at age 16. *Milwaukee Journal,* January 9.

Gelles, R. J. *The violent home.* Beverly Hills: Sage Publications, 1972.

Gil, D. G. Primary prevention of child abuse: A philosophical and political issue. *Caring,* Spring, 1977, 5-6.

Haeuser, A. Reply to editorial 5245, 'Toughen child abuse laws.' WITI-TV, Milwaukee, Wisconsin, May 13 & 16, 1977.

Harris, N. Family, church are U.S. 'boundary lines.' American Issues Forum, *Milwaukee Journal,* April 4, 1976, 9.

Jenkins, R. L. Child-parent relationships and delinquency and crime. In W. C. Reckless (Ed.), *Etiology of delinquent and criminal behavior.* New York: Social Science Research Council, 1943.

Letter to Midwest Parent-Child Welfare Resource Center, May 3, 1977.

Lystad, M. H. Violence at home: A review of the literature. *American Journal of Orthopsychiatry,* April, 1975, 328-345.

Merry, R. W. A federal policy for kids. *National Observor,* December 25, 1976.

Marony, R. M. *The family and the state.* New York: Longman, 1976.

National Association of Social Workers. *Code of ethics.* Adopted by the Delegate Assembly October 13, 1960, amended April 11, 1967.

National Education Association. *Report of the task force on corporal punishment.* New York: National Education Association, 1972.

National Research Council. *Toward a national policy for children and families.* Washington, D. C.: National Academy of Sciences, 1976.

Pfohl, S. J. The 'discovery' of child abuse. *Social Problems,* February, 1977, 310-323.

Rutter, M. *The qualities of mothering: Maternal deprivation reassessed.* New York: Jason Aronson, 1972.

Schorr, A. L. *Mental health and law: A system in transition.* In *HEW Crime and delinquency issues: A monography series.* Rockville, Maryland: National Insitute of Mental Health, 1975.

Summary report: Second meeting of the family impact seminar. January 25-26, 1977.

97 *Supreme Court Reporter* 1401.

97 *Supreme Court Reporter* 1421-1422.

U. S. Comptroller General. *More can be learned and done about the well-being of children.* Report to the Congress. Washington, D.C.: U.S. Department of Health, Education, and Welfare, April 9, 1976.

U. S. Department of Health, Education, and Welfare. *Proceedings of the first national conference on child abuse and neglect.* Washington, D.C., 1976.

U. S. Department of Justice, Office of Special Litigation. *Child protection program description.* May 12, 1977.

Wooden, K. *Weeping in the playtime of others.* New York: McGraw-Hill, 1976.

NOTE

This paper was made possible by Grant No. 90-C-600 from the National Center on Child Abuse and Neglect, Children's Bureau, Office of Child Development, Office of Human Development, U. S. DEPARTMENT OF HEALTH, EDUCATION AND WELFARE. Its contents should not be construed as official policy of the National Center on Child Abuse and Neglect or any agency of the Federal Government.

2

National Policies on Child Abuse and Delinquency: Convergence or Divergence?

VINCENT FAHERTY

Assistant Professor,
School of Social Work
University of Missouri—Columbia
Columbia, Missouri 65201

Charles Dickens has been heralded as one of the most enlightened and assertive social reformers in 19th Century England. He was, to put it mildly, an outraged humanitarian. The England which was the object of Dickens' satirical pen was an England which "...had practically forgotten childhood, or at least had ceased to think of it as something precious and beautiful...(Crotch , 1913, p. 42)." It seems appropriate to refer to Charles Dickens during this symposium since he was the first, some say the unequaled, writer to open to society's eyes the infection of child abuse and, indeed, of people abuse.

It was the child thief, the boy criminal, the juvenile robber that Dickens so skillfully portrayed in 'The Artful Dodger' and his band of gruffy pickpockets. But it is also, and more critically, the abused, neglected, destitute child that shone through the transparent veil of anti-social behavior, at times charming and comical, in Dickens' novels.

We possess no statistical data nor scientific research studies to link abuse and crime in 19th Century England, we have only Dickens' memorable scene of man's inhumanity to child:

> The evening had arrived: The boys took their places; the master in his cook's uniform, stationed himself at the copper; his pauper assistants ranged themselves behind him; the gruel was served out and a long grace was served out over the short commons. The gruel disappeared, and the boys whispered to each other and winked at Oliver, while his next neighbors nudged him. Child as he was, he was desperate with hunger, and reckless with misery. He rose from the table, and advancing, basin and spoon in hand, to the master said, somewhat alarmed at his own temerity—
>
> "Please, Sir, I want some more."
>
> The master was a fat, healthy man, but he turned very pale, He gazed in stupefied astonishment on the small rebel for some seconds, and then clung for support to the copper. The assistants were paralyzed with wonder, and the boys with fear.
>
> "What?" said the master at length, in a faint voice.
>
> "Please Sir," replied Oliver, "I want some more."
>
> The master aimed a blow at Oliver's head with the ladle, pinioned him in his arms, and shrieked aloud for the beadle (assistant) (Dickens, 1841, p. 18).

The rest of the story you know. Despite the fantasy world of Broadway and Hollywood stage productions, *Oliver Twist* is a denouncement of the brutality fostered on children and a record of the effects of that physical and emotional degradation.

During the same period, mid-19th Century, America was not faring much better. The Children's Aid Society, under the leadership of Charles Loring Brace, instituted a daring and controversial program for the homeless, vagrant and delinquent children of New York City. Starting in 1854, the first wave of 46 boys and girls were sent to a small town in Michigan from the decaying inner-city of New York. The purpose was to "drain the city,"—the exact phrase used by the Children's Aid Society, of these children, provide the children with a stable home and, in the process, provide the community to which they were sent a veritable army of unpaid farm and industry laborers. More than 50,000 were sent all over the expanding West before the program ended 25 years later.

In his *History of Social Welfare in America,* Walter Trattner notes:

> It is not surprising that such a system, or lack of one, should have met firm opposition. With the absence of any care and supervision in placement and the lack of any follow-up , all the abuses of the apprenticeship system reappeared. Families commonly overworked the children, failed to educate them, poorly fed and clothed them, and in general, mistreated them...many of the—close to 60 percent according to a study conducted by the Secretary of Minnesota's State Board of Charities—became sources of trouble and public expenditures. Mistreated and overworked in their new homes, many of the youngsters ran away and became public charges (Trattner, 1974, p. 104).

The issue that haunts current researchers and professionals revolves around the long-term effects of early child abuse and neglect. Physical effects of child abuse have been documented as encompassing slowed intellectual growth and mental retardation (Martin, 1973; Morse, et al, 1970), brain damage (Caffey, 1972), and less than average weight and height (Glaser, et al, 1968). Long-term psychological effects are more difficult to understand and therefore elude simple tracking and research. Vincent Fontana (1971) and others (Lascari, 1972) report the presence of prior abuse in the personal histories of abusing parents. Fontana concludes that the abused child has a high potential of becoming not only an abusing parent, but also a social deviant in the broader sense of the term.

Alan Button, in his post-factum study of male juvenile delinquents, did find a specific correlation between child abuse and delinquency (Button, 1973). Other studies of long-term effects of abuse and neglect universally note that children exhibit serious learning and behavior problems, both at home and during their early school years. Any professional who has worked with the adolescent offender will acknowledge that learning and behavior problems in elementary school are recurring variables, though admittedly untested, in subsequent adolescent anti-social behavior.

When one talks about the lack of research into casuality and effects of child abuse and neglect, the situation on the international level is even more disheartening. Columbia University School of Social Work initiated a cross-national child abuse research study of the United States, Canada, France, West Germany, Israel, Poland, the United Kingdom and Yugoslavia. One of the project directors, Sheila Kammerman, notes that "...formal research and evaluation studies among the seven other countries studied are even more limited than in the United States and, as we know, research is in its incipient stages here (Kammerman, 1975, p. 36)."

My discussion up to this point is designed to establish that, even though rigorous research data on the correlation between child abuse and delinquency do not exist as yet, sufficient indications—signs if you will—of this connection are present to warrant the refocusing of national priorities and allocations of resources. Indeed, the experiences of human service professionals in schools, child care agencies, adolescent treatment programs and the criminal justice system subjectively document that many clients who travel within the network of social service agencies were once the victim of child abuse or neglect.

SOCIAL POLICY ANALYSIS

The focus of this paper from this point on will be to critically analyze two pieces of national social legislation: The Child Abuse Prevention and Treatment Act (PL 93-247) passed in 1973, and the Juvenile Justice and Delinquency Prevention Act (PL 93-415) passed in 1974.

Before initiating a discussion of these two national policies, it would be well to digress for a moment and relate why it is important—actually critical—to engage in a systematic analysis of an existing policy or policies. A national policy is a societal response to an identified problem, in our case the problems child abuse and delinquency. Once a policy is drafted, whether by legislative, judicial or administrative means, it generates a program or a service. The point I will reiterate today is that if we are serious about effecting change or proposing new programs, then we must make the quantum leap and intercede at the policy, not the program, level.

To change we must understand, and to understand we must analyze. Social policy analysis is quite simply a study of social choices and social values. As Neil Gilbert and Harry Specht (1974) so bluntly and aptly put it:

...the professionals who give insufficient attention to social choices and social values in order to devote exclusive attention to development of their practice skills will be like musicians playing background music to a melody that seems to come from nowhere. Like musical themes, the directions and goals which are reflected in social welfare policy are neither accidental nor aimless—they develop because men make choices (p. 13).

The analysis which follows will be an attempt to clarify those choices, identify the values which underlie them and propose alternate courses of action. The specific components of this analytical framework are: the issues involved, the policy objectives, the value premises and the intended and unintended effects of the policies.

Issues:

David Gil in his book, *Unravelling Social Policy* (1973) makes a compelling point in suggesting that the first step in policy analysis is to identify the issues, and not simply the *problem* addressed by a specific policy. This is more than an exercise in tautology or semantics. An issue is some matter that is brought to a societal level of concern involving collective decision making and strong differences of opinion. A problem is more specific. It connotes something negative or assumes there is present some difficulty or some deviancy from an established norm. To discuss an issue rather than a problem is to elevate what or who is defined as a problem to a conceptual level free of negative assumptions or deviant labeling. Thus, instead of talking about the problem of racism, one should dialogue the issue of an individual's right in American society to liberty, freedom and equal treatment regardless of race, color or ethnic origin.

Specifically, for our situation, it would be more effective to cease using the terms 'problem of child abuse' and 'problem of juvenile delinquency,' and, instead, relate to the issue of the emotional and physical health of children and adolescents. To state the issue another way: How can we preserve and protect the health, and how can we nurture the positive development, of every child and adolescent in our society?

I repeat that this is not simply a semantic exercise. For what becomes apparent is that the two national policies—The Child Abuse Prevention and Treatment Act and The Juvenile Justice and Delinquency Prevention Act—are dealing with the same issue: the emotional and physical health of children. It appears that the policy makers were blinded to this fact because they focused solely on the problem of child abuse and the problem of delinquency. This problem-focused approach to social policy development has created, unwittingly, the present fragmented, uncoordinated and, at times, conflicting network of human service programs.

Broad definition of issues allows the analyst to judge the effectiveness of policies as they impact on the total human being in the human environmental system, and not simply whether the policies are effective for the delinquent, or the alcoholic. Thus, to take an extreme example, a policy developed to 'deal with' the problem of delinquent crime might do so effectively by institutionalizing and punishing every adolescent caught and convicted of an anti-social act. What would be overlooked, tragically, by that policy would be the existential person with distinct psychological and emotional needs and the community responsibility for treating the adolescent delinquent.

Broad definitions of issues rather than specific denotations of problems also facilitate the development of alternative policies and the acceptance of complexities or correlations between, for example, child abuse and delinquency. It facilitates that overview which is imperative in any discussion of human problems which by their very nature are never simple or uncomplicated.

To sum up this section, then, is to point out that the issues dealt with by these two policies are the same. To accept that premise and act on it would be one way to avoid fractionalization of resources, programs and personnel.

Policy Objectives:

David Gil, also in his book referred to earlier, cautions the social policy analyst to differentiate between stated objectives in a policy and stated means to achieve an objective. To quote Gil (1973):

> Thus, for instance, "constructing houses" may come to be viewed as a policy objective, replacing the socially more appropriate objective of "housing people." Constructing houses is, no doubt, an important means toward the objective of housing people. However, when this means is elevated to the level of an objective in its own right, its pursuit may, under certain conditions, produce adverse consequences for the policy objective of "housing people (p. 38)."

In the two national policies under consideration here, there are no clearly stated objectives, but many clearly stated means of achieving some goal. Thus, for example, the Child Abuse Law establishes a National Center on Child Abuse and Neglect to 'do' certain things:

compile an annual summary
serve as a national clearinghouse
publish training materials
provide technical assistance
conduct research
determine national incidence of child abuse and neglect
provide grants for demonstration projects

The Juvenile Delinquency Act similarly created a Coordinating Council on Juvenile Justice and Delinquency Prevention, headed by the Attorney General, to coordinate federal juvenile delinquency programs. The Act also established a 21-member Advisory Committee and authorized the Law Enforcement Assistance Administration to make grants available for education training and research in juvenile delinquency.

One could go on and on, but I trust the point is clear: neither of these policies clearly state their objectives. Both of them digress quickly into means, techniques, processes by which some vague, unstated objectives, hopefully, should be reached.

It is the hypothesis of this author that if the policy makers who drafted this legislation were compelled to state clearly and unequivocally their objectives, and not the technical *modus operandi,* our society would have a clearer understanding and acceptance of the multi-faceted human problems we daily confront. Legislators and public officials would then, perhaps, be able to sense the relationship between the phenomena of child abuse, dysfunctioning in school, acting-out behavior, substance abuse, flight from home and generalized depression.

Value Premises:

The single, overriding value premise that emerges from an analysis of these two policies is this: abused children should be served by the medical-social systems and the delinquent should be processed through and punished by the criminal justice system. Herein lies the crux of the present controversy and the source of future dilemmas. National policy as stated in official law assumes the abused child to be perpetrator. The consequences are equally dichotomized. The emphasis in the child abuse law is on protection, identification and treatment under the Department of Health, Education, and Welfare; while the emphasis in the Juvenile Delinquency Act is on control and retribution within The Law Enforcement Assistance Administration.

Several Senators fought vainly to maintain HEW as the responsible authority for juveniles, notably Bayh (Ind.), Hart (Mich.), Kennedy (Mass.), Tunney (Calif.) and Mathias (Md.). Thus, LEAA within the Justice Department was assigned the leadership status to prevent, treat and research into the problem of delinquency. It was undoubtedly a value mind set which directed the development of that policy, a judgment, a philosophy of life which legislated two classes of children: Those who need society's protection and those from whom society should be protected.

This aspect of policy analysis dictates that we as a society can never achieve any meaningful successes in the war on delinquency until we view the problem in its entire continuum. There is a continuum which initiates with brutality, confusion and withdrawal of love and finalizes in a person—either adolescent or adult—who is repressed, hostile and perhaps even violent. I would call for a reappraisal of the value system which is blended by an act, a delinquent act, and forgets that the act was committed by a person. And, after all, a person is nothing but a composite of feelings, experiences and needs.

Intended and Unintended Effects:

To be able to critically evaluate the effects of these two policies on the target populations they were designed to help would, at this point in time, be presumptuous. More time is needed for the programs to become fully operationalized, and for evaluative data to be collected, analyzed and disseminated. Based on our analysis of issues, objectives and value premises, however, and based on subjective reactions of professionals involved in programs of child abuse and delinquency, we can, I believe, offer some worthwhile projections.

First, the existence of two distinct policies which are problem-focused will continue to rupture the network of human service delivery systems. It appears totally inconsistent with the current federal emphasis on integration of services to have existing in the same political environment an approach to policy development which fails to see possible correlations and relationships between human-experienced problems.

Second, we as a society will continue to 'muddle through' our attempts to impact effectively upon human problems. This 'muddling through' is due to the fact that we have yet to assign any one component of the federal bureaucracy to a leadership role in the planning, delivery and monitoring of human services.

Third, the issue of boundary maintenance will exacerbate the problems. As we view the varied systems that interact, just for example on the two problems of child abuse and delinquency, several boundary issues emerge: eligibility rules, administrative procedures, overlapping funding sources and distinct professional roles. Institutions, agencies and professions will continue to isolate themselves and maintain their own territoriality.

Fourth, the most tragic effect of a problem-focused, rather than an issue-focused policy is that the consumer, the client, will be served neither efficiently nor effectively. It is absolutely true that specific programs will be needed for the delinquent, for the abused and neglected child, for the runaway, for the person exhibiting a particular problem at a point in his or her life. But no program can be truly effective or operationally efficient unless it is guided by a directing national social policy which addresses the issue of human growth and development for every citizen.

There exists no convergence of national social policies dealing with human need around a single theme or purpose. Divergence away from a central core and conflicted interrelationships of agencies, institutions and professions seems to be the present disastrous pattern.

ALTERNATIVE POLICY

This analysis ends with the projection of an alternative policy in terms as specific as possible. The approach proposed here will address not only the correlation between child abuse and delinquency, but also address other components of other human problems. I propose quite simply, perhaps too simply, to establish and institutionalize a national policy on personal social services.

Alfred Kahn (1976), in a paper delivered at The American Public Welfare Association's National Conference in 1976, developed and discussed this issue of personal social services. Kahn identified that, to date, American society has accepted and institutionalized five social service systems: education, income security, health, employment manpower and housing. Within this network, or perhaps more appropriately stated, spanning several of these network components, we know there exist subsystems such as child welfare, community services and a host of others. In Britain, these subsystems are not considered unrelated or peripheral. They are formalized into a system of their own—personal social services. They are viewed "...as needed as part of the total societal response to modern living (Kahn, p. 27)."

Several results could accrue if a national policy on personal social services were accepted and formalized. One result would be the existence of a system to disseminate information on the availability of services and information about access to these services across the entire spectrum of the six social service systems. Another result would be the potential for meaningful integration of services. The personal social service system could, and should, become the focus of coordination and planning to insure competent and efficient service delivery.

The development of this sixth social service system would, more importantly than anything else, assist the creation of social policies that are issue-focused rather than problem-focused. Thus, national policies could concentrate on the issue of housing people decently and safely and not focus on what to do about the problem of inferior housing in the inner city. Broad based definition of issues allows for flexibility so that alternative policies can be proposed if appropriate. There are several ways to house people decently and safely: build new houses, renovate old ones, purchase trailers, provide cash grants, supplement rent payments, etc. To operate from the concept of a 'problem' of inferior housing, however, tends to lock policy makers into one means of confronting the problem. It also tends to blind them to the complexity of the problem or to the acceptance of the many extraneous realities that are *causing* that inferior housing.

CONCLUSION

The theme of this symposium is the relationship between child abuse and juvenile delinquency, two phenomena that are disparate and yet related. It is urgent for these kinds of symposia to continue to meet and to search for other relationships among other human problems. Perhaps what will emerge is a tapestry of the human condition more closely woven than we have ever suspected.

To generate the immense amount of research, experimentation and creativity that is needed to accomplish this level of understanding will require a reordering of some national priorities and policies. This is no simple task. The 1976 report from The Brookings Institution entitled, *Setting National Priorities: The Next Ten Years,* is, in my view, a depressing document. My depression stems not from what is said, but rather, what is not said. The following domestic problems were singled out in the report as demanding high priority status in terms of societal response and public concern: economic stabilization; the size of federal, state and local budgets; energy and the environment; governmental regulations of health and safety for workers and consumers; and income security. There is no question that these are urgent priorities that require immediate attention. What is missing, in my estimation, is a national priority that clamors for true integration of all human services and programs, and a convergence of knowledge, resources and talents to affect positively the quality of life of our most vulnerable citizens.

REFERENCES

Button, A. Some antecedents of felonious and delinquent behavior. *Journal of Clinical Child Psychology,* 1973, *2*(3) 35-37.

Caffey, J. On the theory and practice of shaking infants. *American Journal of Diseases of Children,* 1972, *124*(2) 161-169.

Crotch, W. *Charles Dickens, social reformer.* London: Chapman & Hall, 1913.

Dickens, C. *Oliver Twist.* Philadelphia: T. B. Peterson, 1841.

Fontana, V. Which parents abuse children? *Medical Insight,* 1971, *3*(10) 16-21.

Gil, D. *Unravelling social policy.* Cambridge: Schenkman Publishing Co., 1973.

Gilbert, N. & Specht, H. *Dimensions of social welfare policy.* Englewood Cliffs, New Jersey: Prentice-Hall , 1974.

Glaser, H., et al. Physical and psychological development of children with early failure to thrive. *Journal of Pediatrics,* 1968, *73,* 690-698.

Kahn, A. New directions in social services. *Public Welfare,* 1976, *34*(2) , 23-32.

Kammerman, S. Eight countries: Cross-national perspectives on child abuse and neglect. *Children Today,* 1975, *4*(3) , 34-37.

Lascari, A. The abused child. *Journal of the Iowa Medical Society,* 1972, *62,* 229-232.

Martin, H. Follow-up studies in the development of abused children. JFK Child Development Center, National Center for the Prevention and Treatment of Child Abuse and Neglect. Unpublished manuscript, 1973.

Morse, C., et al. A three-year follow-up study of abused and neglected children. *American Journal of Diseases of Children,* 1970, *120,* 436-446.

Owen, H. & Schulte, C. (Eds.) *Setting national priorities: The next ten years.* Washington, D.C.: The Brookings Institution, 1976.

Trattner, W. *From poor law to welfare state: A history of social welfare in America.* New York: The Free Press, 1974.

3

Some Etiological Factors and Treatment Considerations in Child Abuse

JOHN A. BROWN

School of Social Work
San Jose State University
San Jose, California 95192

An effective attack on child abuse must be based on two primary considerations: l) the etiological factors which culminate in child abuse; and 2) identification of the most effective means of dealing with this problem. Perhaps no recent social problem has received the attention which has been focused on this subject. A recent item in *The Detroit News,* January 17, 1977, reports on an "Advertising Blitz Aimed at Child Abuse." This item reports that a $10,000,000 national advertising campaign on child abuse is underway in the Detroit area; and that one million children are abused or neglected by parents annually. This news article, as well as a number of others, present the conclusion that "in just about every case one or both parents were also abused as children." Most recently this position has been stated by Ackley (1977) who writes, "Thus, it is not surprising that one of the most common findings of abusive parents is that they were abused children (p. 21)." Button (1973) also reached the conclusion that child abuse was quite common in the group of delinquents studied. This view of the etiology of child abuse has become known as the 'generational hypothesis,' which holds that the victim of child abuse will become an abusive parent and, consequently, a cycle is born which is repeated from generation to generation.

Some question this view. Kadushin (1974) states, "There is little valid evidence to support the theory that abusive parents were themselves abused as children.'' This cautionary remark is necessary so that one does not, on the basis of limited evidence, accept such views as being totally valid.

Here I would like to suggest the danger present in accepting such views and attempting to develop them into some kind of predictive theory, such as 'the child who is abused will become an abusive parent or a future delinquent.' If this is done, we blind ourselves to the other variables which may be equally influential in bringing child abuse into existence. I remembered while working in adoptions it was a frequently stated observation that if a couple without children adopted, the wife would become pregnant. This was true in some cases, but was not true in a greater number of cases. I think the same applies to child abuse and delinquency. Linear interpretations must be questioned. Too many exceptions appear to permit broad generalizations about the outcome or future behavior of children who are abused.

In 1965, Stott's study, which attempted to analyze family situations of delinquents, concluded, ''Relating delinquent behavior to abnormalities of family structure has on the whole failed to establish decisive correlations (p. 15).'' However, Monahan (1966) reached the conclusion that abnormal or defective family relationships are more prevalent among families of delinquent children than among families of comparable children who do not become delinquent. A review of the literature on child abuse and etiological factors involved in this act produces contradictory findings which suggest that research has not advanced to the degree that cause and effect can be predicted with any great degree of certainty.

Contradictory findings also are located in other areas, especially that of social class. Gil (1970) reached the conclusion that physical abuse of children was found to be overly concentrated among the poor and among non-white minorities (p. 392). Others suggest that the child abusers come from all strata of society. Laskin (1973) expresses the view that child abusers are generally ''well adjusted'' and can be middle or upper class. Leinski (1976) states, ''People who beat their kids obey all the rules of society. They are usually in their late 20s, better educated high school students, have gone to college, are employed, attend church regularly, are legally married and registered to vote (p. 6).''

These contradictory findings should not be viewed as a cause for dismay. Knowledge can be extrapolated from past research, which can be of value in providing a frame of reference from which to view this problem relative to identifying etiological factors, planning treatment considerations and in formulating policy. Some of this knowledge is as follows:

1) The child abuser is peculiar to no social class.

2) The victim of child abuse is more than likely to show the adverse effects of this abuse in his later years.

3) It is necessary to make a distinction between acts of abuse and neglect, although the outcome may be the same.

4) An evaluation of the nature and cause of the abuse must be based on a differential diagnosis.

5) Child abuse may be of a chronic, episodic or acute nature.

6) Emotional immaturity plays an important role in the act of child abuse.

7) Severe stress is a frequent precipitant of child abuse.

8) The problem of child abuse must be attacked at three levels of prevention: primary, secondary and tertiary.

The purpose of this paper is to discuss etiological factors in child abuse and to suggest treatment considerations in working with abusive parents. The author subscribes to a psychodynamic framework in working with abusive parents (Brown and Daniels, 1968). This framework focuses on personality disorders as being largely responsible for the acts of child abuse. Within this framework, the social worker identifies the problem, makes a diagnosis of the social and personality forces acting on the child abuser and, based on this assessment, comes up with an intervention plan. It is necessary that the social worker approach abusive parents with some frame of reference for evaluating behavior. Wasserman (1974) suggests that without a characterology, i.e., structural concept of some sort, it is not possible to make the differential diagnosis which guides practice:

> Unless the worker is clear in his assessment of the client's total situation (external and internal), his ego strengths, intact areas, gaps and weaknesses, his model for intervention will be affected by cloudiness, groping and undifferentiated kinds of action (or inaction) (p. 57).

CHILD ABUSE AND NEGLECT: A DISTINCTION

Fontana (1975) stresses the view that little value results from categorizing physical abuse as one thing and neglect as another. In stressing this view, Fontana overlooks a positive consideration. Different acts call for different planning. The type of act, physical abuse or neglect, and the identifiable reasons for it must influence treatment considerations. The social worker not only must determine the nature of the act, abuse or neglect, but also the 'why' of it, if his planning is to be diagnostically sound. In an earlier article (Brown and Daniels, 1968), we defined neglect primarily as acts of omission, usually having some degree of chronicity attached to them, in which a parent failed to carry out his parental role in a manner consistent with societal norms. Physical abuse was defined as acts of commission, acts committed on a child which arouse concern for the child's life and physical well-being. We still view this distinction as being workable in distinguishing between acts of abuse and neglect.

ETIOLOGICAL FACTORS

It is the author's view that emotional stress plays a crucial and decisive role in the act of child abuse. Therefore, it is suggested that if individuals are helped to deal with emotional stress, the possibility of child abuse decreases. In identifying emotional stress, the social worker must take into consideration the influences of the environment and its contributions to the stress which a person faces in a chronic sense, or, at a given moment, a crisis. Accepting stress as a primary factor in the etiology of child abuse removes it from being the peculiar characteristic of a particular social class, and brings into focus the fact that everyone, regardless of his class status, is a potential child abuser if placed in a given situation in which normal coping patterns are overwhelmed. As Walkenstein (1977) states so well, we all have potential for some form of violence and under certain circumstances each of us could commit child abuse.

We once believed that we could identify characteristics of people as a means of predicting if they might become future child abusers. This ambition was quickly given up as impossible. We recognized that we could not evaluate a person's stress tolerance until he was faced with stress. In working in adoptions, we frequently came across adoptive parents who had been abused as children, but were coping very well in their present situations. These parents spoke of the desire to be good parents, not to discipline their children in a manner similar to the way they had been disciplined. They had developed reaction formations and vowed within themselves to be better parents to their children than their parents were to them. This attitude is also an outcome of situations in which children have been abused, and in some situations children were placed with them, since the previous history of abuse was not sufficient to contraindicate adoption. Similarly, in other situations no background of abuse existed, but the person turned out to be a child abuser. Case 1, Mr. G., illustrates this point, his emotional immaturity and the stress which culminated in child abuse.

Case 1: The agency was contacted by an agency in another state to inquire if Mr. G., age 24, was willing to release his 4 year old son for adoption. This son had been placed in an institution by his mother, who had deserted Mr. G. two years previously. The mother had no subsequent contacts with the child. A relative who desired to adopt the child had provided Mr. G.'s address. Mr. G. had remarried a woman several years older than he with a young daughter age 7.

In casework interviews, Mr. G. revealed himself as a person with feelings of inadequacy, especially in the area of employment. The wife and child were also interviewed relative to their feelings. The family wanted the child and he came to live with them.

The family did not desire follow-up and appeared happy. Within two months the child was in the hospital, severely brain-damaged and near death. Contacts revealed the wife had become upset over the boy's crying and his wetting his bed. Mr.G. was facing a lay-off. Her complaints led to marital tension with threats to leave Mr. G. unless the situation improved. Mr. G., in his anxiety over the threat of losing his wife and facing unemployment, inflicted severe punishment on his son as a means of forcing a change in his behavior.

Mr. G. claimed that the abuse was a way of correcting his son's behavior. However, other questions may also be asked: Was the act a consequence of his fear of losing his wife, or fear of unemployment which would highlight his inadequacies, or did it result from a reaction of rage toward his first wife who had deserted him? Mr. G., faced with stress, regressed to a primitive state in which he lost sight of alternatives, and in which aggression was viewed as providing a solution to the problem.

Leinski (1976) suggests the child abuse pattern consists of four parts: 1) potential abuser, 2) victim, 3) incident, and 4) a lack of an escape mechanism from pressure. Helfer (1973) views the child abuse pattern as consisting of *The Parent The Child + The Situation* which ends in abuse. Our view of abuse follows the stress-reactor pattern: Stress*Acts on Adult who, in turn, acts abusively on the Child.* Stress is the precipitant of the abuse.

CLASSIFICATIONS OF ABUSE

From an etiological perspective, child abuse can be divided into three classifications: 1) Chronic Abuse, 2) Episodic Abuse, and 3) Acute Abuse. These classifications are important for treatment considerations.

Chronic Abuse appears more correlated with a socialization pattern in which abuse has become a way of life. However, we seek etiological factors not in the socioeconomic status of the parents, though these may be contributing factors, but in the dynamic make-up of their personalities. Chronic abuse presents itself when this behavior has become inbred in the abuser, and thus forms a part of his personality. We view these abusive patterns as being concretized in the person. Nothing is viewed as being wrong with the behavior and no anxiety results from the behavior or its consequences. This parent is liable to remark, "He deserved it," or "He had it coming." These people are viewed as having characterological disorders, and the likelihood of their changing is nil.

Episodic Abuse usually occurs at irregular intervals, brought on by stress, anxiety, frustration, anger or feelings of helplessness. In these instances, the parents may feel some guilt. The guilt is shortlived, and, inasmuch as they do not learn different coping patterns, the act is repeated. These parents may find themselves in chronic situations, continually exposed to crises, and their children bear the brunt of their rage. When their situation is going well, they respond more favorably to their children. We think episodic abuse is more characteristic of families of low socioeconomic circumstances.

Acute Abuse occurs when the person is totally overwhelmed when faced with a threatening, anxiety provoking situation. Normal coping patterns are weakened. The ego is weakened and primitive impulses break through. The parent may not remember the act, and truly might have been in a psychotic state momentarily. Following the act, he recovers his equilibrium and must cope with what he has done. Denial may present itself in all three of these categories. In considering treatment planning, the social worker must determine in which classification the act of abuse falls.

Classifications	Treatment Considerations
Chronic Abuse	Permanent removal of the child
Episodic Abuse	Treatment, parenting skills, support, modification of environment
Acute Abuse	Treatment, supportive, insight development

In Chronic Abuse, the child should always be removed from the home. In Acute and Episodic, the child can remain in the home while the parent is in therapy.

LEVELS OF PREVENTION

We have suggested that the problem of child abuse must be attacked at three levels of prevention: primary, secondary and tertiary. To accomplish this task, child abuse must be viewed as a social, instead of an individual, problem. This view has implications for social policy formulation and the nation must develop child abuse programs which aim at prevention instead of early casefinding and reporting. Shankan (1973) has expressed a similar view. He suggests that public policy must evolve from a residual to an institutional approach. Since child abusers come from all strata of society, this view has much merit. Programs must be made available to combat this problem before it happens, since that is the true meaning of prevention. By catching it in its early stages and through early screening and diagnosing, as well as by offering some form of rehabilitation to the parents when it has occurred, a way of preventing it from happening again will be developed. In the following section, we shall discuss what we view as effective approaches to coping with this problem on three preventive levels.

Primary— A preventive program must be directed at a total population. Attention must be directed at educating people to positive parenting skills and child rearing practices before they enter marriage or the family state. The public schools provide a good setting for such programs to be introduced. Since all children are required to attend school, educational institutions are ideal for providing this kind of information. This kind of material should be introduced into the curriculum. Present programs which aim at early screening, diagnosing and casefinding, while valuable, have a secondary preventive focus. A number of writers have come to view the importance of the school in coping with this problem, but invariably they focus on the school as a mechanism for early detection of child abuse (Murdock, 1970; Gil, 1969; Martin, 1973; Broadhurst, 1975).

We view the school as a mechanism for preventing child abuse through educating students on how to be good parents. At the present time no institution fulfills this need, and many children have no information by which they can make comparisons. They learn from what they have been exposed to. The suggestion is made that educational classes on parenting and child discipline be made available in the school, as well as information on community resources. This appears a feasible way of breaking into the so-called "generational cycle of abuse."

Secondary— Programs also must be made available for parents to learn effective parenting skills, receive support and improve their self-images. Literature on abusive parents describes their loneliness, their apathy and their isolation. Programs such as Parents Anonymous, Parental Stress Services and Child Abuse Listening Mediation do provide parents with supportive help and give them a place to turn to in time of need. However, we see the need for a more comprehensive program along the lines of Head Start with a number of components present. Perhaps such a program can best be described through an illustration.

Before presenting the illustration, some information on what is required for good parenting should be provided. In identifying what parents need, Elizabeth Philbrick (1975) states that parenthood requires mature responsibility, which includes the ability to organize, the ability to delay gratification, the ability to accept responsibility, the ability to make judgments and decisions, the ability to tolerate stress and exercise patience, the ability to set limits and to discipline appropriately and consistently. The Head Start program assists the parents who use its services to gain these skills. Head Start came into existence in 1965 and was one of the programs which resulted from the War on Poverty. Through early childhood education and the provision of a number of other services, Head Start was to improve the lives of children and families from marginal circumstances. Its components were nutrition, social services, mental health, education, volunteers and parent involvement. Eligibility was determined by poverty guidelines.

Case 2: Mrs. Jackson, age 27, lived alone with her three children, ages 4, 2½ and 1 year. She came to the attention of the Head Start program through the teachers who were recruiting in the neighborhood. Initially she was reluctant, but enrolled the older child. The teachers noted the children were listless, nonverbal and unkempt. The 1 year old was confined to the playpen during the visit. One child had a severe burn. The teachers suspected child abuse and neglect, which later were confirmed through Mrs. J's social worker.

Mrs. Jackson was separated and isolated from her parents. Through encouragement she became involved in the program. She participated in program activities, served as a volunteer in the classroom and took on the project of decorating several rooms. She was elected secretary of the Parents' Committee. She developed more realistic ways of handling her children and arrived at an understanding of their needs. Whenever she had to go somewhere she could call on a parent to babysit or could leave the children at the center. Her horizons expanded greatly. She became pregnant again, but this did not place her in a state of depression or stress. She continued to be accepted by staff and parents and received much support. She spoke of entering job training following the birth of the child.

Mrs. J., when she became involved in Head Start, entered into a structured environment which provided her with a great deal of acceptance and support. In Head Start she could learn how to become a good parent and to develop a more positive image about herself. If her environment had not undergone change, more than likely her neglect and abuse of the children would have become greater as she faced greater stress, loneliness and alienation. Such programs as Head Start, with its structural components, should be made available to the population at large on a universal, rather than a selective, basis. Within such programs parents can learn effective parenting skills and gain greater confidence in themselves whereby they can more adequately cope with stress or have a place to turn for assistance. Head Start took Mrs. J. out of her isolation and provided her with a consistent round of activities on a daily basis. She gained some release from constant child rearing and focusing on her own needs. It is these kinds of supportive, educationally oriented, experiential programs which provide positive learning experiences which can be most effective in tackling child abuse at the secondary level.

Tertiary— Tertiary prevention is of a rehabilitative nature and seeks to prevent future abuse through some kind of therapeutic program such as crisis intervention, group therapy or casework counseling. Utilizing the classifications of abuse stated earlier, the rehabilitative approach in chronic abuse is to remove the child permanently, since little hope is held out for bringing about any positive change in the parents. In cases of episodic and acute abuse, therapy programs can be effective. In these situations the objective is to assist the parents in developing improved coping mechanisms and sometimes to understand why the abuse has occurred. Parents Anonymous can be viewed as offering secondary and tertiary prevention.

The literature of child abuse stresses the importance of having some kind of educational component in therapeutic programs, since an objective is to improve parenting skills. These programs should be made easily accessible to abusive parents. Crisis centers should operate 24 hours/day and have emergency placement facilities. In addition, the program must be flexible enough to meet the needs of the parent.

SUMMARY

Child abuse is an act which occurs due to a number of factors, of which emotional stress looms as a most important one. The child abuser is peculiar to no social class. Therefore any real attempt at dealing with this problem effectively must be approached from three levels of prevention: primary, secondary and tertiary. These approaches call for the formulation of a public policy on child abuse and the implementation of programs to carry out the policy objectives. A classification system of child abuse has been presented and the social worker, based on a differential diagnosis, must determine into which classification the abuse falls and plan intervention strategies on this assessment.

This Symposium seeks to shed light on the possibility of a correlation between child abuse and future delinquent behavior. It is my opinion that some children who have been abused will indeed exhibit future delinquent behavior, but too many exceptions will exist to allow for any broad generalization. Attention must be given to other variables. Single interpretations of child abuse, as well as delinquent behavior, should be avoided.

The programs of prevention cited and described in this paper offer the possibility of mounting a comprehensive approach to deal with this problem. If child abuse is ever to be eradicated or controlled, programs directed at primary, secondary and tertiary prevention must be instituted.

REFERENCES

Ackley, D. C. A brief overview of child abuse. *Social Casework,* January, 1977, *58.*

Broadhurst, D. Project Protection: A school program to detect and prevent child abuse and neglect. *Children Today,* May-June , 1975.

Brown, J. A. & Daniels, R. Some observations on abusive parents. *Child Welfare,* February, 1968.

Button, A. Some antecedents of felonious and delinquent behavior. *Journal of Clinical Child Psychology,* Fall, 1973, *2*

Gil, D. What schools can do about child abuse. *American Educator,* April, 1969.

Gil, D. *Violence against children.* Cambridge: Harvard University Press, 1970.

Helfer, R. The etiology of child abuse. *Pediatrics,* April, 1973, *51.*

Kadushin, A. *Child welfare services.* New York: MacMillan Co., 1974.

Laskin, D. M. The battered child syndrome . *Journal of Oral Surgery,* December, 1973, *31.*

Leinski, E. College graduates abuse kids. *San Jose Spartan Daily,* November 22, 1976, p. 6.

Martin, D. L. The growing horror of child abuse and the unreliable role of the school in putting an end to it. *American School Board Journal,* 1973, *160*(11).

Monahan, T. P. Family status and the delinquent child: A reappraisal and some new findings. In R. Giallombardo (Ed.), *Juvenile delinquency.* New York: John Wiley & Sons, Inc., 1966.

Murdock, G. The abused child and the school system. *American Journal of Public Health,* January, 1970, *60.*

Philbrick, E. The role of child protection services. Paper presented at the American Humane Association Conference in San Diego, California, October 29, 1975.

Polansky, N., et al. *Profile of neglect: A survey of the state of knowledge of child neglect.* Washington, D.C.: U.S. Department of Health, Education, and Welfare, 1975.

Shankan, Y. A. The abused child: A reminder of despair. *Canadian Welfare,* 1973, *49.*

Stott, D. H. Family structure conducive to behavior disturbances in delinquents. *Social Work,* April, 1965, *1.*

Walkenstein, A. The fear of committing child abuse: A discussion of eight families. *Child Welfare,* April, 1977, *56.*

Wasserman, S. L. Ego psychology. In F. Turner (Ed.), *Social work treatment.* New York: The Free Press, 1974.

A factor analysis of the 20 item Childhood Social Functioning Inventory yielded a first factor cluster of nine items with overt aggressive behavior content. The items loaded from .561 to .713 and accounted for 47% of the behavioral variance among the children's Inventory scores. The mean factor score of the abused children was 3.3 (aggressive several times daily); of the neglected children, 2.5 (aggressive several times weekly). The F value of 1.17 indicated that the finding was statistically significant at the .05 level and supported the hypothesis. Therefore, it appears that the abused children in the study have learned to cope with life in an overtly aggressive fashion.

Depressive Affect

Both groups of foster children in this study have experienced: 1) actual separation from the family, and 2) distorted parental relationships ranging from failure to perform parental duties to commission of abusive acts. The physically abused children have experienced loss of self well-being associated with hostility and physical violence. The neglected children, by contrast, have experienced loss of self well-being associated with omissions in child caring. Although we know something of the prior life experiences of the study children, we do not know how they have coped with the preplacement and placement loss experiences. For instance, are they affectively depressed?

In order to take into account age appropriate manifestations of childhood depression, the following measures of depression were included in the research design: 1) obtaining fantasy material through psychosocial diagnostic interviews and rating the material according to a depressive theme scale (interrater reliability, +.91); 2) obtaining a social worker's and foster mother's independent ratings of each child's behavior on an affective mood scale (interrater reliability, +.89); and 3) obtaining a social worker's and foster mother's independent ratings of each child's behavior on a verbal expression scale (interrater reliability, +.68) A strong direct positive correlation (R, +.94) among the three measures of depression confirmed that the subscales provided different ways of measuring the same behavior.

On the basis of the strong correlation among the three measures and the high interrater reliability, the affective mood scale was selected as representative of the measures of depression for preliminary data analysis. The range of affective mood scores (1-10 out of a possible 21) and a mean of three (1-3 indicate high depression) confirmed the research hypothesis that this sample of foster children did indeed score high on depression. There was no statistically significant difference between the groups of children.

Situational Social Functioning

So far, the overt aggressive behaviors and depressive affect of the physically abused and the neglected children in the study have been considered piecemeal. Bibring (1953) theorizes that the absence of consistent love objects and the lack of emotional response from the social environment frustrate a child and precipitate angry aggressive responses. If the frustration continues, aggressive behavior is replaced by exhaustion, helplessness and depression. Through this process, the emotional expression of a basic angry affective state changes from overt aggressive behavior to depressive reaction. Applying this theory to foster children, Littner (1956) points out that foster children believe they were rejected and abandoned for being bad. In an attempt to ward off the devastating knowledge of parental rejection, foster children assume a bad guy role. Such defensive-adaptive coping behavior creates a negative self image and concomitant negative acts. The foster child then directs the depression and the aggression toward others or toward self.

As noted earlier, the depressive nucleus described by Bibring and Littner appears to be present throughout the sample of foster children under study. The outwardly directed aggressive behavior, on the other hand, was more prevalent among the physically abused foster children than among the neglected foster children. However, does imitative learning alone account for this behavioral difference between two groups of children who have experienced family disturbance and actual separation from their families? Or, might there be certain social situations which are more likely to trigger overtly aggressive responses by physically abused foster children than by neglected foster children?

The researcher hypothesized that there would be an association among overt aggressive behavior, being a victim of physical abuse, depression, school performance and social functioning in the foster home. Multiple correlation was used to examine the system of relationships between the dependent variable (overt expression of aggression) and six independent variables. The independent variables included one measure of experienced parenting style (being a victim of abuse), three measures of depression (affective behavior, verbal expression and fantasy expression), and two measures of social functioning (foster home replacement and repeating first grade). Multiple step-wise regression analysis was computed to assess which combinations of the independent variables most influenced overt expression of aggression. Table 1 shows the component variance of overt aggressive behavior among the study children which was accounted for by each of the independent variables in the regression model.

The coefficient of multiple correlation (R, +.79) indicates a strong relationship between overt expression of aggression and the six predictor variables: 1) victim of physical abuse, 2) affective mood depressive themes, 3) foster home replacement, 4) repeating first grade, 5) fantasy depressive themes, and 6) verbal depressive themes. The square of the multiple correlation coefficient, the communality estimate, indicates that 62% of the variability in overt aggressive behavior among the children was explained by the known variance of the combined independent variable predictors in Table 1.

As predicted, being a victim of physical abuse accounted for the highest proportion (34%) of the variance in overt aggressive behavior among the foster children. In other words, the findings supported the theoretical perspective that aggressive behavior is imitative learned behavior. Depressive behavior themes measured on the Affective Mood Scale accounted for an additional 13% of the variance. This finding supports the theory that aggressive actions serve as an escape from painful feelings. When children's patterns of communication are taken into account, it is not surprising that behavioral or action measures of depressive process 13%) accounted for four times the aggressive behavior accounted for by fantasy and verbal measures (3%). That is, children tend to translate impulse and affect into action behaviors, since conceptual thinking and reality testing are inmaturely developed in early latency.

The Multiple R (.79) points to the strength of the simultaneous association among overt aggressive behaviors, depressive process and social situation. This finding ap-

TABLE I MULTIPLE STEPWISE REGRESSION MODEL OF OVERT AGGRESSION

Source of Variance	Multiple R	R^2	R^2 Change	B Values
Victim of Physical Abuse	.585	.342	.342	.585
Affective Mood Depressive Themes	.686	.471	.128	.530
Foster Home Placement	.737	.543	.073	.485
Repeating First Grade	.765	.585	.042	.443
Fantasy Depressive Themes	.781	.610	.024	.400
Verbal Depressive Themes	.787	.620	.010	.409
Totals: N=112			R=.79	
$P<.05$			R^2=.62	

pears to differ from Despert's (1952) conclusion that there is a coincidence of depression and aggression in children which manifests either singularly or alternately. The apparent difference may be a function of the research methodology and sampling procedures of the two studies. On the other hand, the difference may be real, since the current study of maladaptive coping patterns considers behavior within the context of social situation. Thus, the current study may point to a third pattern of maladaptive coping with a coincidence of aggressive impulse and depressive process in a particular kind of social situation—a pattern of simultaneous manifestation of depression and aggression.

For a physically abused child, the possibility of intense closeness to a parenting figure represents threat rather than a potential source of gratification because he has been so frequently frustrated and rejected by an abusive parent. Therefore, in social situations involving parental figures, the physically abused child in foster care is likely to resort to earlier learned patterns of releasing frustration-aggression through violent actions. In this manner the child practices and develops maladaptive skills in social functioning. Furthermore, it appears likely that the child's overtly aggressive coping strategies, associated with the simultaneous manifestation of aggressive impulse and depressive process, push away the new parental figures. Thereby, the abused child's actual behavior sets in motion a repetition compulsion pattern of rejection by parental love objects and reconfirms anxieties around both rejection and faulty self images.

As the six and seven year olds in the study grow up, therefore, it seems likely that the aggressive interpersonal response patterns will become established in a life style of externalized aggression. Assuming the continuity between minor and severe forms of aggression in interpersonal violence, it seems likely that such an aggressive stance will increasingly bring the abused child in contact with the juvenile justice system (See Erlanger, 1971; Eron, 1959). Thus, by way of the cumulative effect of social learning, of identification with the aggressor, of repetitive use of aggression to avoid painful affect and of the self image projected to society, the overt aggressive mechanisms of the six and seven year old physically abused child become the more violent aggressive mechanisms of the delinquent adolescent.

CHANGING THE AGGRESSIVE/DEPRESSIVE STANCE

The research study accepts the purpose of the federal foster care program as preparing physically abused children for reintegration into their families and communities. From this perspective, a simultaneous rehabilitative effort is considered essential for the abusive parents and for the abused children for whom separation was deemed the "least detrimental alternative (Goldstein, Solnit, and Freud, 1973). Viable methods of treating the parents and modifying violent social functioning patterns within the family have been reported elsewhere in the literature (Ebeling and Hill, 1975; *Social Casework, 58* January, 1977). The intervention focus in this paper, therefore, is the implications of the research findings for: 1) improving the child caring capabilities of the foster care system, specifically the foster parents; and 2) promoting child development through building ego capacity to the point that an abused child can use foster family relationships for social identification and continued ego development.

The data suggest changing the abused child's maladaptive aggressive/depressive stance in order to increase social effectiveness, to enhance sense of self, and to decrease violent actions. Such change for the physically abused child in foster care does not merely involve the development of new patterns of behavior and a new orientation to family life. To accomplish change, a child must first relinquish past adaptive coping styles. He must undo old learning prior to linking new learning to action behavior in social situations. Only as the physically abused child is able to build expectations of a new future without abuse from a different life base, his daily corrective experiences in foster care, can his image of the future impact on his overt aggressive behavior. That is, experienced "abused" past, experiencing "cared for" present and anticipated future are incorporated into the child's present aggressive/depressive stance.

It seems probable that the most important factor connected with the child's actual change in social functioning—i.e., success in the foster care program and reintegration into his family—will be the foster parents' image of the physically abused child's future. Will he become increasingly aggressive and destructive? Will he return home? What will he be like in a few years; as an adolescent; as an adult; as a parent? Only by making assumptions about where a child is growing and going can a foster parent deduce the kinds of human abilities, skills and growth patterns that need to be encouraged. With a future that is questionable or ignored, the present expands and minimizes both experienced past and anticipated future (Singer, 1974). In an expanded present, the externalized aggression and negative image are highlighted and operate like Merton's self-fulfilling prophecy (Merton, 1959). That is, the overt aggressive defenses of the physically abused child become the focal point for foster parent and foster child interaction. The physically abused child demonstrates his increasing competency in aggressive behavior to himself and to others. Indeed, he confirms his already established image of himself as bad and experiences further loss of self well-being . Thus, to the nurturing and protecting aspects of daily child caring, the foster parent must integrate a change function and an orientation to the future which includes: 1) valuing the physically abused child as a person with a right to a future and 2) imaging the abused child's future functioning in life situations.

Within this climate of change, the abused child, the foster parents, the teacher and the social worker focus on growth and development in the social domains of the child's life experience: foster home, school and peer groups. The following treatment principles provide an action framework for engaging the child's maturational forces and for teaching basic living skills.

Principle I: The child relives and works through in a direct manner the feelings connected with earlier violence, parental deprivation and actual separation. Unless the conflicted behavior in the aggressive/depressive stance is resolved, the child's changed behavior may revert back to externalized aggression under stress. This task, worked on directly in therapy sessions, is also worked on in complementary fashion through day to day activities.

Principle II: Life space teaching and learning promotes the stepwise development of the child's capacity to cope with current everyday losses. The focus is on the developmental opportunities available in both unstructured and programmed daily life space (Redl, 1959). Attention to the implications of daily events for coping with loss sensitizes the adult helpers to the vulnerability of the physically abused child in foster care and to the teaching-learning opportunities in small losses within the child's life space. To observe and make constructive use of the minutiae of everyday events, however, is a demanding task for social worker, foster parent and teacher. For example, adult attention to the abused child's ability to cope with ordinary losses such as ending an activity, going to bed and handling school vacations with its absence of teacher and friends encourages mastery of loss experiences. Adult attention is not only needed for loss related to ending events, but also for loss of possessions or other extensions of self and for loss of self esteem. Thus, breaking a toy and losing a game take on greater significance in the life space of a vulnerable child—both to the child and to the adult helping the child work on specific problems of adjustment.

Principle III: Daily life management does not reward the overtly aggressive life stance. Stimuli which maintain the aggressive response behavior are minimized by anticipation of the child's needs. Such clinical exploitation of foster care and school life events in order to help the physically abused child work on specific problems of coping with loss in a nonaggressive manner promotes a therapeutic alliance between the adult and that part of the child struggling toward conflict resolution and growth. The destructive aggressive behavior associated with parent figure closeness and with ordinary loss-related events reflects both the child's protest over his difficulty coping with the loss and the child's learned pattern of expressing feelings. Thus, adult attention to vulnerable times helps to keep behavior within reasonable limits by: 1) preventing excess affect build-up; 2) bringing affect and behavior to the level of ego manageability; and 3) teaching new skills in coping with loss and with the affects in general. In this manner, firm limits are set gently, with avoidance of aggressive behavior and physical punishment.

Principle IV: Daily life management includes development of new activity areas of interest and achievement skills. Ambivalent parental attitudes have not helped the abused child achieve success in academic learning or activity learning such as sports, games, arts and crafts. Nor has the child experienced the satisfaction that accompanies the development of his own knowledge and skills. The abused child, therefore, needs active involvement and realistic help in school and recreational learning. He needs praise for and satisfaction from actual achievement to enhance his self esteem. He needs an opportunity for commitment of self to an interest area within which he can demonstrate competence to himself. In sum, the physically abused child needs an opportunity to begin the psychosocial tasks of latency.

Principle V: There is an effort to provide peer presence learning, as well as peer group reinforcement of the new behavior style in school and other social settings. The abused child needs to engage in activities aimed at developing skill in interpersonal relationships, as well as skill in dealing with physical objects. The peer presence learning revolves around the child's public image in a peer group situation in order to: 1) modify transactions damaging to identity, self esteem and social functioning; and 2) modify transactions destructive to the social and physical environment.

Principle VI: There is a concern with value formation within the physically abused child during the interactional processes between the child, his peers and significant adults. The abused child is encouraged to weigh facts, to think through alternatives and to take age-appropriate responsibility for his decisions.

Within the life model treatment approach described (See Bibring, 1947; Austin, 1948), the physically abused child in foster care becomes increasingly free to cope more adequately with succeeding events. The life processes of normal child development which form the theoretical framework of the life model for child welfare practice (Erikson, 1959) have become our guiding principles in engaging the adaptive potential of the child, in mobilizing the social environment to provide supplementary developmental processes and in altering portions of the social and physical environment. Use of the life processes also points to the progressive sequence of mastery opportunities in relation to coping with loss, with change and with aggressive impulse. These opportunities may be converted into stepwise treatment principles for teaching-learning life skills.

CONCLUSION

Although not generalizable beyond the small sample of 112, the findings point to behavioral trends among physically abused children, ages 6 and 7, and suggest ideas for foster care service delivery in order to prevent escalation of externalized aggressive behavior in adolescence. The regression analysis suggests that the child is simultaneously attempting to separate from his own family and to establish ties with new parental figures. For detachment-attachment to occur, the child's new significant other adults need more than understanding of and frustration tolerance for an aggressive/depressive life stance. We also need to develop skill in using the life processes of normal development to promote social and emotional competence of the physically abused child in foster care. Then, the physically abused child in foster care can learn to cope with tomorrow as he engages with us today in the processes of learning how to learn, learning how to value, learning how to play and learning how to cope with change. Thereby, foster care will indeed become a social work resource for violence prevention through planned change of aggressive social interaction patterns. As a specialized tool in social work practice, foster caring becomes one tool among many available to support family functioning.

REFERENCES

Austin, L. Trends in differential treatment in social casework. *Journal of Social Casework,* June, 1948, *29.*

Bibring, E. The mechanisms of depression. In P. Greenacre (Ed.), *Affective disorders.* New York: International Universities Press, 1953.

Bibring, G. Psychiatry and social work. *Journal of Social Casework,* June, 1947.

Bronfenbrenner, U. The calamitous decline of the American family. *The Washington Post,* January 2, 1977.

Curtis, G. Violence breeds violence—Perhaps? *American Journal of Psychiatry,* April, 1963, *120.*

Despert, L. Suicide and depression in children. *Nervous Child,* 1952, *9.*

Ebeling, N. & Hill, D. (Eds.) *Child abuse, intervention and treatment.* New York: Publishing Science, 1975.

Erikson, E. Identity and the life cycle. *Psychological Issues, Monograph 1* (l). New York: International Universities Press, 1959.

Erlanger, H. *The anatomy of violence: An empirical examination of sociological theories of aggression.* Ann Arbor: University Microfilms, 1971.

Eron, L. Symposium: The application of role and learning theories to the study of the development of aggression in children. *Proceedings of the Rip Van Winkle Clinic,* January-February , 1959, *10.*

Goldstein, J., Solnit, A., & Freud, A. *Beyond the best interests of the child.* New York: The Free Press, 1973.

Kopernik, L. The family as a breeding ground of violence. *Corrective Psychiatry and Journal of Social Therapy,* June, 1964, *10.*

Lefkowitz, M., et al. Punishment, identification, and aggression. *Merrill Palmer Quarterly of Behavior and Development,* March, 1963, *9.*

Levitch, J. & Vlock, L. Violent street kids—Must it be jail? *Parade,* May 1, 1977.

Littner, N. *Some traumatic effects of separation and placement.* New York: Child Welfare League of America, 1956.

Merton, R. *Social theory and social structure.* Glencoe: Free Press, 1959.

Morris, M., et al. Toward prevention of child abuse. *Children,* 1964, *11.*

Ohlin, L. The prevention and control of delinquent acts. In N. Talbot (Ed.), *Raising children in modern America.* Boston: Little, Brown & Co., 1976.

Redl, R. Strategy and techniques of the life space interview. *American Journal of Orthopsychiatry,* January, 1959, *29.*

Silver, L., et al. Does violence breed violence? *American Journal of Psychiatry,* March, 1969, *126.*

Singer, B. The future focussed role image. In A. Toffler (Ed.), *Learning for tomorrow.* New York: Vintage Books, 1974.

Special issue on child abuse, *Social Casework,* January, 1977, *58.*

5

Treatment of Abusing Parents: An Alternative Method of Delinquency Control

GEORGE W. AYERS

Associate Professor
School of Social Work
University of Tennessee
Knoxville, Tennessee 37916

In the following presentation I shall address the issue of child abuse as it relates to delinquency and offer an alternative method of preventing a continuation of the relationship between the two. What I propose is a method of group treatment for parents who have been identified as either potential or actual abusers and offer an interventive strategy to break the cycle which begins with abuse and ends with delinquency.

This presentation is offered in two parts. The first will be a brief examination of relevant research relating to the relationship between abuse and delinquency and methods of treatment for these phenomena. The second will cover the mechanics of the proposed interventive strategy which utilizes the issue-oriented group method in agencies which deal with abusers.

The relationship between child abuse in all of its forms and juvenile delinquency has been noted as a clinical phenomenon for many years. However, there is a genuine dearth of material of a definitive, empirical nature in the literature which deals with this subject.

This is strange, for man has been fascinated with all types of crime and delinquency for many years. Certainly child abuse has not been one of the more 'attractive crimes' to be examined. However, there has been at least a peripheral examination of the relationship in certain classics of literature, for example *Oliver Twist.* It is amazing that man has a unique capacity to dilute any painful social issue; and, in spite of Dickens' moving social commentary which was contained in the pages of *Oliver Twist,* present day man has managed to blunt this commentary and turn Oliver into a musical.

I don't really know why I should be surprised at this, since "West Side Story," which also dealt markedly with the issue of delinquency, neglect and various other social problems, was similarly turned into a musical some ten years prior to "Oliver."

All of this simply serves to demonstrate that man is capable of dealing with a number, yes, an infinite variety, of traumatic issues in a way which blunts their trauma.

However, those of us who are clinicians are finding that practice presents phenomena which can never be stereotyped, and we can no longer accept either political or academic versions of what the real world is about. We know, for example, in spite of the dearth of research in the area, that there is a relationship between abuse and delinquency. We must, however, begin to describe it. We know, for example, that no longer are abuse or delinquency confined to the lower socioeconomic classes who have been so aptly described in many of the classic works on delinquency or childrens' social problems; but rather, that both of these major social ills span the entire spectrum of socioeconomic classes. If one searches, one may begin to locate areas in which abuse and delinquency are described and related to one another. However, almost to a citation, the literature portrays the abuse in the form of neglect, not physical or sexual abuse.

I will begin this brief discussion of the literature by referring to what I consider to be a seminal article in the area. G. Partridge, in 1928, described 50 cases of psychopathic personalities. Given the point in time that this study occurred, there was a radical departure from the constitutional theories of criminality currently in vogue. Partridge spent considerable time examining environmental influences affecting diagnosed psychopaths. Among his sample were 12 delinquents, all of whom were found to have been rejected and/or neglected as children. Unfortunately the terms psychopath, delinquency, neglect, rejection, etc. are not defined in great detail. However, they point out that some fifty years ago there was some concern about the relationship between the phenomena of abuse/neglect and delinquency. Partridge's findings have been replicated in one fashion or another since that time by Schachtel and Levi (1945), Bender (1947), Glueck and Glueck (1950), and others. These studies have continued to show a peripheral, however unexplored, relationship between the two phenomena. The Gluecks go so far as to say that there were few of their samples, delinquent or otherwise, who had parents who consistently mistreated them. They then go on to point out that there were inconsistencies, however, in discipline and that discipline was not necessarily appropriate for the situation.

In 1959 Reiner and Kaufman published one of the first definitive works which not only recognized the relationship between child abuse and delinquency but examined, in depth, a method of treatment that was comprehensive; it included suggested treatment approaches for parent and child. The major weakness of both the research and the treatment was that the approach was bound to the psychoanalytic model, and to the child guidance methodology of the day. It did not use a systems framework in examining either the families or the causes of the various types of pathology.

Further case histories which document the existence of a relationship between delinquency and abuse are contained in the works of Bell and Hall (1971) concerning child molestation; may be found graphically documented in Gerald Frank's (1966) account of the Boston strangler; and may be gleaned from Krystal's (1968) edited works concerning the survivors of German concentration camps.

It has only been in the last decade that a definitive set of literature concerning child abuse has begun to emerge within the helping professions. Certainly an individual who must be given pioneer credit in this regard is Ray Helfer (1968) who has co-authored what I consider to be the most comprehensive work in the field in terms of identification and prevention. In regard to treatment strategies, we must look to the work of Blair and Rita Justice (1976), who have only recently published a comprehensive text dealing with a group treatment of abusing families. I shall refer in forthcoming parts in this presentation to the similarities between their work and my own.

Certainly the psychoanalytic approach and its inordinate concern with child rearing practices has laid the ground work to show that any type of emotional deprivation or inappropriate physical behavior toward a child will somehow affect the ability of that child to successfully complete subsequent developmental stages. Most of the research in the area of delinquency which points to background deficiencies, constantly refers to emotional deprivation and neglect as precursors of delinquent behavior. The Reiner and Kaufman work previously cited indicated almost consistent problems of characterological disabilities in parents of defined delinquents.

All of this groundwork, at least, indicates that there must be a relationship between abuse and delinquency. Perhaps Helfer, in a recent publication completed for the National Office of Child Development (1975), has said it best. He develops what is called the WAR cycle or the World of Abnormal Rearing. He definitively indicates how abuse begets abuse and how the abused child, in the process of growing up to become an abusing parent, is involved in an almost infinite series of other aberrant or nonfunctional behaviors and relationships. In summary, a review of the literature in this area reveals there are many peripheral studies which deal with the relationship between abuse and delinquency. However, the basic proof of this relationship appears to be found primarily in clinical observations.

I think that, without having to suffer too much from the criticism of my colleagues for lack of thoroughness, I can conclude that there is a relationship between abuse and delinquency; and if one is going to make any effort to deal with abuse, that the interventive thrust must be made not only toward the child, in an effort to repair damage that has already been done, but also toward the parents in an effort to prevent further damage to this and any other children they produce.

THE ISSUE-ORIENTED GROUP

A recent publication by Brant Steel (1975) indicates that there is "an increasing use of group therapy as a mode of working with abusive parents, but as yet there is a dearth of published reports describing fully either techniques or long-term results." The following description of an issue-oriented model of group treatment for abusing parents deals with one of Steel's criticisms, that is, it attempts to alleviate the lack of descriptions of group technique. It however, admittedly, does not deal with the other criticism, in that at this point and time I cannot report long-term results.

The group process I will describe was developed for women hospitalized in a setting which had as its primary mission the treatment of acute psychiatric disorders. The group was designed for women who had marital problems as a primary symptom at the time of admission, and was oriented toward dealing with these problems on a short-term basis. The group was developed on the premise that normal group techniques did not work, given the organizational structure of the setting, because there was inadequate time to build a usable group dynamic and there was a constant turnover of patients; hence, an unstable flow of members in and out of the group. The group was based on the assumption that marital problems were a result of role dysfunction (Burr, 1972), and the therapist and co-therapist used the concept of role conflict as a basic premise for conducting the group.

What was not realized at the time and what did not really come into play until I began an analysis of the data after the group had terminated, was that in addition to having a primary symptom of marital dysfunction at the time of admission, approximately 70% of the group members were or had been child abusers. The child abuse would only become known in the group after the patient had been a member for a sufficient length of time in which to develop rapport with the therapists. They would then reveal the fact that they had great difficulty disciplining their children and had on occasion gone so far as to discipline the children to such an extent that they later became concerned for the children's or child's safety. Generally speaking, these periods of abuse were not consistent, in that they occurred constantly over a period of time. Rather, they would occur sporadically; but often enough to establish a pattern that concerned the patient and caused the patient to identify herself as an individual who had abused her child or children.

Since I was not really aware of the total significance of the child abuse as a secondary symptom, I never dealt with the issue of abuse in conducting the group any more specifically than I did with any other issue. I only became aware of its significance when I could look at the data as a whole.

However, in retrospect it seems to me that what we did do was deal with the abuse as one symptom in an entire constellation of symptoms, reflecting marital disharmony. I would also assume at this point, given data which will be covered at a later place in the paper, that the abuse was a further indication of severe role dysfunction within the patient and that an issue-oriented group composed of abusers and oriented toward dealing with role dysfunction as a precursor of abuse would produce results similar to that produced by the group I am describing.

Before dealing further with the issue of child abuse as manifested by members of this group, I should describe the group itself and the mechanics involved in establishing it. As I have mentioned, the group had as its basic premise that role conflicts were the cause of marital discord, which in turn became a major factor in the presenting symptomatology of this group of psychiatric admissions. As a portion of this distorted role conflict, there were decided problems in the area of expectations on the part of both husband and wife as to how they were to fulfill the marital role. Therefore, in an effort to provide patients with the opportunity of dealing with healthy males and females, I chose to use male and female co-therapists. This was not done in an effort to create the so called 'healthy couple' phenomenon used by some family therapists, but was employed to provide the patients with exposure to people who had successfully negotiated some of life's stressful situations and from whom the patients could learn.

This idea of using two therapists is covered in the works of other group leaders. The Justice family (1976) sees it as being essential, and Helfer (1968) has indicated that it is of value in preventing a group member from withholding anger toward one therapist or another, but not expressing it for fear of rejection. Justice additionally points out that it allows for an extra pair of eyes (for observing group interaction) during the therapy session.

I would agree with all of the above justifications for using co-therapists, however, I believe for purposes of the issue-oriented group, it is extremely important to allow the abusing parent to see healthy relationships in action and to have an opportunity to interact effectively with both a healthy member of their own sex and with the opposite sex. If we follow the premise of distorted role expectations to a logical conclusion, we might surmise that much of the anger which results in abuse stems from what are perceived to be unrealistic, unequal or unfair expectations placed on the abusing parent by another adult, or by a child.

The issue-oriented group extensively employed a concept which I developed several years ago in conducting marital therapy. That concept is "therapeutic didactics (Ayers, 1976)". I define "therapeutic didactics" as a nonthreatening provision of technical psycho-sociological information to patients in order to permit them to understand the possible sources of their dysfunctional behavior. The Justice family also indicates that much of their model is didactic and that the introduction of didactic material prevents an extensive opportunity to interpret dynamic behavior (Justice, 1976). It is the emphasis on role disharmony and the use of therapeutic didactics which have, in my opinion, led to the major successes enjoyed by the issue-oriented group. The variables surrounding use of a particular type of co-therapist, or a co-therapist with a particular type of training, do not seem to have significance in the issue-oriented group. I employed a variety of co-therapists (all of whom were females) and found that there was really no single type of individual who performed any more effectively than any other. What did seem to make a difference was the length of time I worked with the co-therapist: the longer we worked together, the more effective we became as a team. This seems a rather simple, almost ridiculous, statement to make, however, given staff turnover in many treatment facilities, it would seem a very important fact to note.

One might ask, appropriately I believe, at this point how the issue-oriented group differs from a standard group. In order to answer that question, we must concurrently examine the two processes, standard or traditional versus issue-oriented, in contrast to each other.

Kadis, Krasner, and Winick (1963) defined therapy groups as falling into two basic categories: closed groups and open groups. They indicate that closed groups have been particularly effective in treating homogeneous groups of patients. They also indicate that these types of groups have a relatively long life. They discuss the notion of open groups by indicating that they have both advantages and disadvantages; however, they indicate that the length of the group is an important topic and that both length and infusion of new patients should be controlled by the therapist, based on group needs (Kadis, 1963).

They do not approach the concept of the issue-oriented group in either the open or closed category. The closest to that subject that they come is in the discussion of homogenity of patient placement. In that case, however, the patients rather than the content are similar. Therefore, we can say that, based on this one theoretical formulation, which I have found to be relatively typical, the issue-oriented group is a somewhat reactionary idea in terms of group composition and formulation.

The role of the therapist has been much discussed in published material dealing with various types of group psychotherapy. There appears to be little consensus concerning what the role should be; rather, consensus is obtained only in looking at relatively pristine descriptions of various philosophies of group process. If there is any type of agreement, it seems to center around the fact that the therapist must be active; positive in his capacity to facilitate; and constantly aware of transference potential. I have found little that directly approaches the role of the therapist in relating to a particular type of problem, with the exception of the recent Justice work (1976).

The third area of differentiation in regard to the issue-oriented group versus traditional types of groups is in the area of flexibility. Generally speaking, the research that I have reviewed indicates that the construction of therapy groups is rather like the process of manufacturing good corn whiskey, in that there is a careful selection of ingredients, a designed set of perimeters regarding sitting or fermentation, followed by a cooking process that will ultimately distill the desired result, in the presence of a healthier, or at least somewhat stronger, individual. There is little mention made regarding flexibility *per se,* although one might infer it is not a very sound idea, and that once a group is constructed it is better left alone until the end product is ready for the 'bottle.' It is in these three areas that I found the major conceptual differences of the operationalization of the issue-oriented group that I shall now discuss.

Let us look first at the area that includes composition and length. In this case, the composition of the issue-oriented group has been quite heterogeneous in terms of psychiatric population. Of 104 patients studied, 34 had diagnosis of depressive neurosis, 6 had other types of neurosis and 25 had some variation of schizophrenia. The remaining 39 were a *potpourri* of personality disorders, alcoholism, drug addiction, psycho-physiologic reactions, paranoid states and neurological diseases. I might add at this point that the child abusers spanned all these diagnostic categories and were not found centered in any one particular type.

The ages of the group members ranged from 18 through 65 and the marital status included all variations of marriage, including common law, and formally married. As an additional factor, the group members were drawn on an unstratified basis from the general hospital population, which in turn represented a socioeconomic cross section of the state in which the hospital was located. The one area in which the group was unbalanced in regard to stratification was race. This was more a reflection of the racial composition of the overall hospital population, rather than an attempt to exclude on the basis of race. However, at the time of the group's termination only two of 104 members of the group had been nonwhite.

In regard to the issue of length, the issue-oriented group is also totally at variance with generally accepted group practices. For all practical purposes the issue-oriented group had no length. It ran continuously and had periods of broken time, due only to lack of patient referrals or to the absence of the therapists. During its three years of existence, the total period of broken time would come to approximately 4 months. I would recommend, however, that were this group model to be implemented for treating child abusers only, that, because of the probable out-patient nature of the member population, the number of sessions which the patients would attend should be limited.

I do not have firm data regarding the ideal length, however, I would suggest that it be limited to a period of two months. My general experience with the issue-oriented group was that we began duplicating topic areas about every two months, or 16 sessions, depending on the number of times per week that the group met.

This time frame, while somewhat shorter than lengths suggested by other therapists who have treated abusers, does have certain advantages. A primary advantage lies in the area of assessment. For example, abusers in treatment for the first time could be evaluated by the therapists as well as by personnel of the referring agency. The added dimension that the group process could aid in making critical case management decisions would be invaluable to an agency having child protection as a primary responsibility.

In regard to the area of therapist roles, there has been a clear delineation of expectations for the issue-oriented group. Here the therapist is expected to play a role that involves active support of patients in regard to their attempts to reach solutions to their marital and/or family problems. This has included giving information in any areas of family relations that the patient considered important enough to initiate within the context of the group. I might add that the information given has involved utilizing both the previously discussed concept of therapeutic didactics and the simple provision of straight factual material on a large number of subjects, such as sex education, reproductive anatomy, medication effects, etc.

It is in the area of information giving that perhaps the issue-oriented group, as applied to a total population of defined abusers, could make its greatest contribution. It has been my experience that, more than anything else, patients who have experienced periods of abuse have great difficulty in understanding why they did what they did. It would, therefore, be possible within the context of a group for both the therapist and for other group members to provide suppositions as to what was taking place at a particular period in an individual's life when they engaged in abusing behavior and to provide them with information that will allow them to structure their life experiences to avoid coming into contact with situations which might ultimately end in the abuse of their children.

As far as the area of flexibility is concerned, it is my impression that in the issue-oriented group we attained maximum flexibility. Patients were under no constraint to attend. A patient had only to request removal from the group if she believed that it was becoming problematic to her. However, even with this great degree of flexibility, attendance was never a problem and I would estimate that 95% of the patients attended 90% of the sessions.

As I began to develop the model for implementing this type of group exclusively for abusing parents, a question was raised as to whether or not the same degree of flexibility that was attained with inpatients could be duplicated. I would suggest, therefore, that some type of contracting arrangement be added and that once an individual had agreed to attend the group as an alternative to other types of treatment or litigation, they make a firm commitment for a set number of sessions.

The therapists were able to attain great flexibility in regard to their entrances and exits from the group. Because of the fluctuating work shifts of the original nurse co-therapists, I was never certain which—or, on some occasions, if—either of the co-therapists would be present. I also was absent myself for some periods of time. My absence, or the absence of either of the co-therapists, had no apparent major negative effect on the operation of the group and it continued to function normally, regardless of whether one or both co-therapists were present. We also varied the make-up of group sessions and on occasion (with the group's permission) the sessions were video taped. None of these variations in regard to setting or mix of individuals in the treatment room adversely affected the group process. Additionally, entrances and exits of patients caused no problems and veterans of the group were willing to brief new members on the purposes and functions of the group.

This particular feature I think is particularly important for groups of abusers, in that a group would not have to go to completion before a new group could be formed nor would a group only be limited to people who began the group at a certain time. Rather, people could be added as they were needed by the agency establishing the treatment program.

Flexibility was also attained in that the issues which were discussed in a given session were consciously solicited from members of the group and an agenda for both the current session and subsequent sessions developed. This particular element of flexibility marks an extreme departure of the issue-oriented group from normal therapeutic groups. In standard groups, previous sessions are often needed as a springboard of discussion for subsequent sessions. As an additional matter, there was an absolute attempt on the part of both therapists and patients to gain closure on those issues discussed in any given session in order to clear the deck for new material to emerge.

It is this attempt to make each session a total experience, in and of itself, that I believe gives the issue-oriented group its real strength. Group members hopefully leave each session with issues settled and are not forced to deal with a great deal of ambiguous, or at least partially covered, material between meetings.

As I have conceptualized it, the issue-oriented group differs from traditional groups in three major areas; composition and length, therapist role, and flexibility. Empirically, how do these differences affect outcome? The success of the issue-oriented group can best be measured by an uncomplicated, but what I consider to be meaningful, examination of readmission rates for group members versus non-members. Of the entire population of 104 individuals treated over a period of three years, 19.4% were readmitted to the setting in which the group was conducted. I am unable to discern whether or not there were psychiatric admissions to settings other than that in which the group was conducted. If we adjust the readmission rate for group members by removing patients who were suffering from what I generally define as chronic psychiatric problems such as schizophrenia of a chronic undifferentiated type and severe neurological problems such as Huntingtons Disease, then the readmission rate drops to 15.2%. This figure is less than half of the total readmission rate for the female population of the setting during the three years the group operated. On the basis of the lower readmission rate for group members, I can only believe that the issue-oriented group had some impact upon the alleviation of the symptoms which caused patients to be admitted to the hospital in the first place. I make this statement openly, although I am fully aware of the total absence of experimental controls within either the issue-oriented group or the non-group population. On the other hand, I must emphasize that the issue-oriented group was not developed within the context of an experiment, but rather as a method of treatment. Attempts to describe the group in a systematic way were not initiated until the group was disbanded.

I am making some rather broad assumptions concerning the success rate of this group particularly as it relates to the issue of abuse. The major assumption is that because the readmission rate was markedly lower for group members, the reoccurrences of their symptoms were also significantly lower. Since I am numbering among their symptoms abuse, I, therefore, assume that these individuals controlled their abusing tendencies. I do not argue that this assumption can be questioned. However, I am including at this point a brief case vignette to indicate why I am making the assumption.

Toward the end of the three years of the operation of the group, we were referred a group member who was admitted to the hospital with a primary symptom, at the time of admission, of abuse. This, incidentally, was the only patient admitted with abuse as a primary symptom. She was hospitalized as a stipulation of the court process dealing with the documented physical abuse of her child.

The patient remained in the hospital for approximately 12 weeks, 8 of which she was a member of the group. Several significant things occurred during the hospitalization. First of all, she began to take an in-depth look at the dynamics of her marriage and at the time of her discharge from the hospital was filing for divorce from her husband. Secondly, she was, through the group process, able to acknowledge that she was unable to control her abusing tendencies and asked that her child remain in the custody of the local Department of Public Welfare and be reared under foster care until a time she felt able to have the child returned to her. Her wishes in this regard were carried out and she continued to be followed on an outpatient basis working toward the possibility of having her child returned to her.

I can state definitively in this one case that the group process was essential in helping her reach a decision not to ask for the return of her child at the time of discharge. On the basis of this one case I would then speculate that the group had a similar impact upon other members who had abusing tendencies. I know peripherally from continuing to monitor patients who were discharged from the hospital and followed in a local outpatient clinic that abusing tendencies were alleviated. I cannot, however, report any statistical material which would quantifiably support these claims.

What I am suggesting is that the issue-oriented group has demonstrated that people can be treated for the symptom of abuse in a relatively short, but intensive, time frame, and treated successfully. The exploratory experience that I have had with the model indicates that, if nothing else, it could be implemented on an empirically controlled basis with a population of specifically identified abusers.

I do not present the concept of the issue-oriented group as a panacea. Rather, I see it, because of its several inherently unique features, as having particular value in juvenile justice and child protective settings where early intervention with both abusers and parents of delinquents is possible.

In the event that the model was funded and I were given the opportunity to test it empirically, I would make several changes. The first would be to see that the referrals to the group were made as early as possible. This would involve obtaining referrals immediately upon investigation or request for investigation by the Department of Public Welfare, or from medical settings in which there was some suspicion of abuse. The second change would involve establishing a series of the groups and training, as co-therapists, individuals who had successful experiences as parents. One of my original co-therapists was a nurse who was also a grandmother. I found that this particular co-therapist was able to provide group members with highly effective information concerning successful parenting. For some reason, her age gave her experiences a greater degree of credibility than was given the other co-therapists in regard to child rearing practices.

Implementation of this concept would involve recruiting individuals who could successfully complete a screening process to measure both current health and degree of prior success in life and training them in the theoretical basics of the issue-oriented group. These individuals, under professional supervision, could then begin retraining the problem parents. Implementation, after testing, could greatly extend the treatment potential of many types of agencies.

This process also has the additional capability of intimately involving many tax-payers (and potential advocates) with the workings of public social welfare and juvenile justice programs in a meaningful way. This extensive involvement could go a long way in building public sentiment for and increasing public understanding of the work and problems of these agencies.

I will preface my summation by stating unequivocally that much of my experience with the issue-oriented group in regard to child abuse occurred by serendipity. This fact, however, should not detract from a serious examination of its potential as a method of treating abusing parents. There is enough clinical evidence to indicate that the method has merit and should be the subject of experiments in agency settings which deal with abuse, delinquency or both.

The method has proven to be economical in terms of both training time and staff involvement in the actual treatment process. Both of these features should be of interest to child caring agencies which are experiencing problems involving large case loads and small staffs. Overall, the method lends itself to implementation in settings where both the need for and scarcity of treatment resources are the most acute.

I suppose that anyone who defines and engages in a new or refined treatment process is entitled to speculate about and advance recommendations concerning methods for implementing the approach. To that end, the following suggestions are offered:

1) The issue-oriented group method could be used by family or juvenile courts as an interventive strategy with parents of children who come to the attention of the court for alleged delinquency. Implementation of the method would be both to assist these parents in dealing more effectively with their child, and as a data gathering mechanism to explore the relationship between previous abuse and current delinquency.

2) The issue-oriented group method could be used on a voluntary basis for alleged abusers whose cases were under investigation by child protective agencies. There is no doubt that this proposed form of implementation could be a 'legal nightmare'. However, I would suggest that the possible therapeutic benefit outweighs the legal difficulties and that a major interventive thrust could be attained early in the abusive relationship.

3) The issue-oriented group method could be used in a controlled sense for defined abusers and compared with a variety of other treatment methods.

Child abuse is becoming a national epidemic. Those of us who are involved in clinical practice are quickly becoming aware of the correlation between it and many other problems, not the least of which is delinquency. It is only through innovation and experimentation that we can ever hope to deal with the problem effectively. The issue-oriented group is one such experimental innovation.

REFERENCES

Ayers, G. W. A time limited approach to marital therapy. *The Psychiatric Forum,* Winter, 1976, *5*(2).

Ayers, G. W. The structured group as a potentiator of treatment. *The Psychiatric Forum,* Winter, 1977, *6*(2).

Bell, A. P. & Hall, C. S. *The personality of a child molester.* New York: Aldine, 1971.

Bender, L. Psychopathic behavior disorders in children. In R. Linder & R. Seliger (Eds.), *Handbook of correctional psychology.* New York: Psychological Library, 1947.

Burr, W. R. Role transitions: A reformation of theory. *Journal of Marriage and the Family,* 1972, *34.*

Frank, G. *The Boston strangler.* New York: The New American Library, 1966.

Glueck, S. & Glueck, E. *Unraveling juvenile delinquency.* Cambridge: Commonwealth Fund, 1950.

Helfer, R. E. & Kempe, C. H. *The battered child.* Chicago: University of Chicago Press, 1968.

Helfer, R. E. *Child abuse and neglect: The diagnostic process and treatment programs.* Washington, D.C.: U.S. Department of Health, Education, and Welfare, 1975.

Justice, B. & Justice, R. *The abusing family.* New York: Human Sciences Press, 1976.

Kadis, A. L., Krasner, J. D. & Winick, C. *A practicum of group psychotherapy.* New York: Harper & Row, 1963.

Krystal, H. *Massive psychic trauma.* New York: International Universities Press, 1968.

Partridge, G. E. A study of 50 cases of psychopathic personality. *American Journal of Psychiatry,* 1928, *7*953-973.

Reiner, B. & Kaufman, I. *Character disorders in parents of delinquents.* New York: Family Service Association of America, 1959.

Schachtel, A. H. & Levi, M. B. Character structure of day nursery children as seen through the Rorschach. *American Journal of Orthopsychiatry,* 1945, *15.*

Steel, B. F. *Working with abusive parents from a psychiatric point of view.* Washington, D.C.: U.S. Department of Health, Education and Welfare, 1975.

6

Intergenerational Treatment Approach: An Alternative Model for Working with Abusive/Neglectful and Delinquent Prone Families

ELOISE RATHBONE-McCUAN & ROBERT PIERCE

Assistant Professors
George Warren Brown School of Social Work
Washington University
St. Louis, Missouri

The most valuable resource of this nation is its young people. A vast amount of the literature dealing with children reflects the theme that America is a child-centered nation which places a high premium on its youth. However, the report from the 1970 White House Conference on Children and Youth labeled this proposition a myth (Joint Commission on Mental Health of Children, 1969). For example, the commission pointed out that despite our advances in technology and the accumulation of knowledge about our youth, there are still in our midst millions of children who are living in (or out) of family situations where they are ill-fed, ill-housed or ill-educated and often unwanted (p. 2).

Paradoxically, in this so-called child-oriented nation, many children are victimized by insensitive political, economic and social policies that are generally unresponsive to their material, physical and emotional needs. The tragic consequence for society seems to be the loss of human resources and productivity, coupled with the long-term economic burden of dependency.

The professional clinician serving children may well be aware of these gaps between our knowledge and actions on behalf of children. But due to the structure of our social service system, most clinicians do not have the legal or professional responsibility to intervene on behalf of children until after the statistical evidence indicates that a problem does exist. This is clearly demonstrated in the responses of professionals engaged in the range of abuses to children, including the most recent problem of child pornography. Child abuse is defined here as the action (or inaction) taken by a parent or an adult caretaker that results in: 1) the utilization of a child for sexual gratification; or 2) the physical harm (including neglect) of a child (Walters, 1975, 27-29).

For example, attempts to estimate the number of maltreated children in the United States abound in the literature (Sussman & Cohen, 1975). Caffey (1946), Wooley (1963), and Kempe, et al (1962) conducted early clinical studies in an effort to determine how many children in America actually were being maltreated. Surveys of various agencies and professionals serving children have been conducted in an effort to arrive at more precise estimates of the incidence of child maltreatment. The 1970 national survey of public attitudes and opinions about physical child abuse was another attempt to estimate the scope of the problem. In this survey, Gil (1971) estimated that between 2.53 and 4.07 million cases represented the lower and upper limits of the annual incidence of child abuse. Applying a more sophisticated statistical procedure to Gil's data, Light (1973) estimated that between 200,000 and 500,000 children are abused each year, with 465,000 to 1,175,000 more being severely neglected or sexually exploited. *St. Louis Post Dispatch,* November 30, 1975, reported that the National Center on Child Abuse and Neglect had estimated that 1,000,000 children will be maltreated by a parent or parent substitute each year. The confusion surrounding attempts to estimate the incidence of abuse would become even more complex if it were possible to include in these statistics the number of maltreated and exploited children who go undetected. In part, the obvious discrepancy in these figures illustrates the strong tradition of family privacy which hides many vulnerable and defenseless children in this society.

The incidence of child maltreatment, in contrast to the incidence of delinquency, is particularly revealing. If one believes that the success of a society is measured by the way it responds to the development and needs of its children, then the following statistics on the prevalence of juvenile delinquency are important. According to Besharov, juvenile delinquency, as a legal concept, is defined as any conduct which the law declares to be illegal for those it defines as juveniles. Stripped of all legalism, delinquency is "what the law says it is." (See *Juvenile Justice Advocacy: Practice in a Unique Court,* 1974, p. 174., Bronfenbrenner (1947), one of the country's foremost authorities on American family life, recently observed that since 1963 the rate of juvenile delinquency has been increasing more rapidly than the juvenile population. Also, offenses committed by juveniles appear to be more serious. For example, the *1974 Uniform Crime Report* (pp. 1-47) identified an increase in the arrest of persons under the age of 18 in the following categories. During the period 1969-1974 persons under 18 arrested for:

1) murder increased 51%
2) aggravated assault increased 52%
3) forcible rape increased 32%
4) robbery increased 33%

Similar increases were reflected in the 1976 Senate Judiciary Sub-committee's annual report on the current status of juvenile crimes in this country (*Report by the Subcommittee to Investigate Juvenile Delinquency,* 1977, p. 3). Data gathered from this subcommittee's investigation revealed that over a fifteen-year period, 1960-1975, the overall rate of juvenile crime jumped 293% while burglary, larceny and auto theft by youths under 18 increased by 132%.

The subcommittee also investigated the level and prevalence of violence and vandalism in the public schools (*Report by the Subcommittee to Investigate Juvenile Delinquency,* Part II, 1977). The report, entitled *Our Nation's Schools—A Report Card: 'A' In School Violence and Vandalism,* represents the responses from superintendents of 757 public school districts throughout the United States. The Committee found that in a three year period, 1970-1973, the incidence of:

1) homicides increased by 18.5%
2) rapes and attempted rapes increased by 40.1%
3) robberies increased by 36.7%
4) assaults on students increased by 85.3%
5) assaults on teachers increased by 77.4%
6) burglaries of school buildings increased by 11.8%
7) drugs and alcohol offenses on school property increased by 37.5%, and
8) dropouts increased by 11.7%

The Committee concluded that these findings provide compelling evidence which suggests that the ability of our educational system to carry out its primary function is seriously threatened (p. 4).

Although the data presented above on child abuse and delinquency provide some evidence of the breadth of these problems, there are some experts who still contend that these statistics only represent the tip of the iceberg. For example, Sussman and Cohen (p. 126), from their summary of available data on the incidence of child abuse in the United States, concluded that information indicating the true incidence of this problem does not exist. Walters (1957) draws a similar conclusion, noting that no one can estimate with any degree of accuracy the frequency or extent of physical and sexual abuse of children in America.

Halleck (1972), Glaser (1958), and Short (1966) have concluded that a true measure of the incidence of delinquency does not exist. Short (p. 423) candidly states that despite the almost timeless and universal concern with the problem and the feverish activity that has been generated, it is not possible to specify with certainty either the extent or the nature of juvenile delinquency.

Experts from many disciplines are attempting to develop some rational explanation as to why parents would injure children and why some children become delinquent. The statistical data currently available on child abuse and delinquency must be handled with caution. The information may prove useful for identifying and analyzing those variables which seem to contribute significantly to either parent abusive behavior or delinquency. New data and re-examination of the available data may help to clarify the popular theoretical frameworks or lead to the formulation of new ones.

Two theoretical approaches have dominated the child abuse literature. First is the psychiatric or psychopathological approach which argues for a model of causation associated with defective personality characteristics of the parent and thus implies that the parent is mentally ill. Kempe, et al (1962), Bennie, et al (1969), and Steele and Pollock (1968) are major proponents of this approach. A more recent approach is the sociological or social-environmental approach which argues that causation can best be understood by shifting the focus from the individual to the social environment (Park and Collmer, 1975; Gelles, 1973). It stresses that mounting stress and frustration encountered through daily living serve as precursors to abuse.

The conceptual frameworks used by delinquency theorists to explain causation are similar to those applied to child abuse. Hakeem (1958) reviewed the research fitting into the psychological approach which tended to define delinquent behavior as a pathological condition within the child who was perceived as mentally ill. Short (p. 424) and Weinberg (1958) discussed delinquency from a sociological approach which defines delinquency as deviant behavior. Social factors such as peer association, ethnic group affiliation, social class and community and family influence the development and maintenance of deviant behavior. A third approach not present in the abuse literature emphasizes biological or constitutional factors. McCord (1958) introduced the concept of the "bad seed" which implies some form of transmission from one generation or family member to another. The biological approach closely follows the psychological approach and ignores the interchange between the delinquent child and the external environment. This interrelationship is the core of the sociological approach.

Theorists in both fields have tended to divide into unrelated theoretical camps reflecting either one or the other approach. Researchers desiring to generate solution-oriented data challenge the narrow perspectives of their colleagues and encourage the development of an integrated causal framework.

This paper presents a conceptual scheme that implies intergenerational transference of behavioral and attitudinal predispositions for abusive and delinquent acts. The alternate approach has potential for facilitating the incorporation of all three major approaches. It also introduces an expanded concept of family influence because it directly addresses the influences of grandparents and extended kin.

Walters (p. 37) describes a case situation in which abuse was detected across three generations. Fontana's (1964) observations are similar, noting that the past history of abusive parents was marked by parents who were unloving, cruel and brutal. Gil's national survey of child abuse revealed that about 11% of his sampled population had been victims of abuse during their own childhoods (p. 117). Ounsted, et al (1975) made similar observations pointing out that their data confirmed the hypothesis that parents who abuse their children often come from families where violence has ruled down the generations. Finally, Polansky's et al (1972) observations of neglectful families show a generation-to-generation transference of a life style of neglect that comes from the sharing and passing on of family misfortunes. According to these studies it seems likely that violence does breed violence.

The delinquency literature reflects a similar concern about the generation-to-generation transfer of deviant behavior. An early example of this kind of thinking is illustrated in Charles Braces' work *The Dangerous Classes of New York* (1880). Brace writes, "A most powerful and continued source of crime with the young is inheritance—the transmitted tendencies and qualities of their parents over several generations." Fifty years later, the same theme is discussed. Burt (1931), in his book, *The Young Delinquent,* proposed that in tracing the etiology of delinquency, one must go back to the family influences that were operative long before the child himself was born. The following study by Robins (1975) summarizes these observations, as well as providing empirical evidence to support the intergenerational theme. The study investigated arrest and delinquency in two generations. It attempted to determine the conditions under which deviancy was passed from one generation to the next and the form taken by this deviancy.

Information about deviant activity was obtained by interviewing 223, 30-36 year old black, urban males, and by examining existing police and juvenile court records for any recorded offenses. The men were also asked for the names and ages of their children and the children's mothers—145 children and 79 mothers qualified for inclusion in the study.

The results of the study revealed that while there was little change in delinquency rates over generations, parental (father and mother) arrests as juveniles and adults were extremely potent predictors (accounting for 50% of the variance) of children's being arrested. It was also determined that antisocial behavior of members of the extended paternal family had an effect on children's delinquent behavior. For example, antisocial behavior of both paternal grandparents was associated with delinquency in 83% of the cases for boys and 33% of the cases for girls. In summary, these findings provide some statistical evidence that deviancy is linked across generations, thus supporting the intergeneration theme advanced by the authors of this paper.

Elements of the psychological, sociological and biological causal models of neglect/abuse and delinquency have relevance for understanding intergenerational transmission. Literature and clinical evidence in both fields directly and indirectly substantiate that behavioral and attitudinal factors may be passed down from one generation to the next.

In this section of the paper intergenerational transmission will be considered in relation to treatment and intervention. Specific aspects of the approach will be discussed. The family is the traditional focus of intervention in child abuse cases and to a lesser extent this approach is used with delinquent children. The majority of clinicians recognize the vital role that family members play in the reduction and elimination of family dysfunction and desire to strengthen this area of practice. An intergenerational approach may serve to broaden the scope of family treatment.

Solutions for upgrading the accessibility and availability of total family-intervention approaches may require a careful examination of the structural limitations of existing service delivery systems. Also it may be necessary to institute more staff opportunities for continuing education and clinical re-education. If limited agency resources affect the availability of family therapy or if this service is provided by professionals insufficiently trained to offer the service, efforts should be taken to rectify these service gaps.

Undoubtedly, there are times when the child's circumstances and presenting problems and other factors demand that the initial and immediate intervention be taken on behalf of the child. Sometimes these steps exclude the nuclear family unit. For example, when the child's life is endangered or when the legalistic demands of law enforcement agencies and juvenile courts require immediate and specific actions related only to the child. Treatment that focuses only on the child is not the preferred approach. Services that exclude the family can be seriously questioned, as clinical findings and practice wisdom emphasize total family treatment.

Family therapy may be provided directly by agency staff or made available through referral to other agencies or private practitioners. A significant portion of client families may be unable to sustain the cost of private longer-term family therapy. However, with the advent of Title XX and expansions of health insurance policies to cover a range of mental health services, the problem of financing private family therapy may be decreasing. Some agencies could strengthen their professional capacities to provide longer-term family therapy by expanding referral linkages with mental health clinics, family counseling centers, and private practitioners capitilizing on the purchase-of-service concept. No family should be denied access to family therapy because of economic factors limiting its ability to purchase private service. Families should have access to longer-term family therapy if this method of intervention appears appropriate.

Boszormenyi-Nagy and Spark (1973) make the observation that family therapists rarely encounter physically battered, neglected children. Families with these types of problems most frequently interface with physicians in medical settings, social workers in social service settings and law enforcement or juvenile authorities in legal settings. The services provided under the aegis of these agencies may include short-term family-oriented services as part of crisis intervention, case management or service planning. Many agencies are unable, even when appropriate, to provide long-term, intense family intervention.

Treatment directed toward reducing intrafamily violence, neglect of children and delinquency-promoting behaviors may necessitate family therapy. If there is clinical indication of intergenerational transmission, intergenerational family therapy is an approach to be explored. At present a multigenerational family therapy approach is rarely utilized with these types of family problems.

Family therapy is frequently provided to members of the nuclear two-generational family unit. A spectrum of professionals from different disciplines are working as family therapists. They utilize different theoretical frameworks and techniques and practice in many different settings. The common characteristic of their practice is that they work with the nuclear family. Influences exerted by the grandparents and extended family members are typically ignored even in the face of clinical material indicating their significance for family dysfunction.

Rakoff and Lefebvre (1976) succinctly summarize the current status of family therapy:

> Although psychotherapy of the family as a whole is essentially a post World War II phenomenon, by now there are a number of relatively unquestioned axioms, assumptions, and doctrinal quarrels associated with the field there is certainly not enough (empirical evidence) to substantiate either the clinical analysis frequently advanced after initial screening interviews, nor to support the various rationales which putatively shape the details of practice technique nor does research support many assertions related to expectation, outcome, suitability for therapy, therapist behavior, and manipulation of the family ...however, in spite of the blend of occasionally grandiose theory and the bewildering variety of approaches with a comparatively new field, conjoint therapy is pragmatically useful (p. 115).

Sometimes it is difficult to pinpoint the interconnectedness between clinical research and the evolution of new treatment approaches. New treatment thrusts may emerge in the absence of clinical and/or empirical research. At other times, empirical research offers guidelines for developing new directions, clinical treatment and approaches. Occasionally there is an incongruency between type of treatment implied in the empirical literature and what approaches are actually applied as treatment for a particular condition. Research and treatment in the area of the schizophrenic process is an example of the incongruency between clinically substantiated hypotheses and the focus of intervention.

During the decade of the mid 50's thru the 60's there was considerable interest in the "three-generational hypothesis of schizophrenia." L. B. Hill originally formulated an hypothesis which involved learned behaviors of grandmothers and mothers in relationship to the schizophrenic (Hill, 1965; Zuk & Rubinstein, 1965). Bowen (1960) reformulated the hypothesis which indicated that the combined immaturities of grandparents were acquired by the child who was most attached to the mother. When this child married a spouse with an equal degree of immaturity, and when the process repeated itself in the third generation, it resulted in one child (usually designated as the patient) with a high degree of immaturity, while the other siblings were more mature. The concept as originally constructed suggested that at some point tensions generated in a pathological family system are reduced by a projection of tension onto a particular family member. There may be many consequences for the scapegoated individual including the development and maintenance of schizophrenia (Zuk & Rubinstein, p. 24).

The family system dynamics reflected in the three-genera- tional hypothesis gave support for and direction to family therapy as an appropriate form of psychotherapy. The influences exerted by grandparents, patterns of intergenerational transmission and the interrelationship between past and present pathology should have alerted clinicians to the potential value of broadening the definition of the family system to include grandparents as a focus of family psychotherapy to mitigate the schizophrenic process. Despite the rather clear indication of three-generational involvements in pathology, there was minimal application of multigenerational family therapy.

Failure to adopt a multigenerational family therapy approach on a wide scale may have been related to the narrow concept of the nuclear family, which is only representative of a proportion of family types. Also the perceptions and attitudes of therapists regarding older patients may have discouraged many from work with grandparents as part of the family therapy. The importance of grandparents may have been overlooked because they were old and perceived to be irrelevant. Geographical dispersion of multiple generations of family members may reduce the immediate accessibility of grandparents. Another factor affecting the application of multigenerational family therapy may result from the difficulty encountered by therapists in working with the larger groups involved in this approach. Perhaps this incongruent direction was symptomatic of the temporal lag between the presentation of clinical research findings and their incorporation into practice techniques.

Traditional definitions of family therapy offer a point of departure in the examination of intergenerational family therapy. Nathan Ackerman's definition of family therapy emphasizes an established psychotherapeutic orientation that encompasses multiple generations and more distant significant kin:

> The therapeutic interview with a living unit, the functional family group comprising all those who live together under a single roof, and additional relatives who fulfill a significant family role, even if they reside in a separate place Rakoff and Lefebvre, p. 120).

This widely accepted definition of a family therapy establishes a certain definitional legitimacy for the multigenerational family therapy approach. The literature contains few examples of its application with families experiencing problems of child abuse and neglect. Literature describing the application of the approach emanates from situations where the aged person is the designated patient and members of younger generations (e.g., the middle aged children) seek family therapy as a means of resolving the family problems perceived to be associated with elder members (Silverstone and Hyman, 1976). For example, the help of a family therapist is sometimes sought if a bereaved aged woman is unable to manage grief and resolve her crisis without perceived serious disruption to her children and their nuclear families. A similar crisis may arise when extended families must decide about the institutional placement of an elderly patriarch or matriarch. There is some documentation to support the effectiveness of this approach in such situations (Boszormenyi-Nagy and Spark, p. 276).

Parallels exist between the aged person and the child. A very young or very old family member may be dependent upon the adults in middle generation and this creates a dependency overload. The needs of the very young and old family members can become a source of conflicting intrafamily loyalties and create a physical, emotional, and economic burden and a perceived imbalance between what is given and what is received in return. This abuse and neglect may be a common experience of both children and the aged.

Mendell published descriptive case analyses on the communication of maladaptive behavior in three, four and five generations of family members (Mendell, Cleveland & Fisher, 1968; Mendell, Fisher, 1956; and Mendell and Fisher, 1958). From an examination of these cases it is at least possible to describe some pathological forms of communication processes across multigenerations. Bell's analysis of extended family relationships of disturbed and well families gives some clues about the patterns assumed by multigenerational extended kin. These include:

l) they may serve as stimulators of conflict;
2) they may serve as countervailing forces;
3) they may serve as competing objects of support and indulgence among family members (Bell, 1962).

An important task facing practitioners is the identification and assessment of family boundaries. It would appear that some clinicians lack fundamental understanding of this concept and its diagnostic application. The complexity of boundary analysis is greater when undertaken with a three generational family and/or an extended kin structure. Realizing the current state of the diagnostic function in family situations of abuse/neglect and delinquency, the level of skill of many workers is inadequate to conduct assessments in family units with a numerically expanded number of members and multiple households that contain nuclear family units with differential patterns of interaction over time.

Family members (e.g., members of three generations and relatives representing extended kin) are engaged in a web of social relationships which can be untangled through the assessment of boundaries within the family system. These are most easily identified and understood through observation of verbal and nonverbal behavior among all members of the family unit based on the information accumulated through observation and communication. The more important objectives of boundary assessment are to understand the complex of norms and patterns of behavior both present and past, to sort these out and then to analyze them as a means of clarifying behavior involving personal sentiment, conventional rules of outward behavior and rights and duties (Radcliffe-Brown, 1968). In so doing, the clinician becomes familiar with the different structural components of the family unit and can identify the behavior within separate subsystems functioning within the boundaries of the total family system.

The clinician's boundary assessment that includes analyzing behavior of the oldest generation and more distant relatives should have relevance for intervention planning. As Pattison states, "These kinship considerations assume clinical importance both in terms of the social network conditions that may produce symptomatic behavior and as a social system to which therapeutic efforts may be addressed (Pattison, 1976, p. 135).

In cases where there are situations of neglect, abuse and/or delinquency, there is a possibility that practitioners will encounter families where the parent generation has not been able to create an equilibrium within the nuclear family and one, if not both, parent(s) manifest, participate, promote or react to conflicts associated with older generations of family members.

If older generations of family members provide a functional countervailing force to conflict within the nuclear family, the therapist may be in a position to immediately build on the grandparental subsystem to mitigate conflicts. On the other hand, if grandparents or other extended family members contribute dysfunctionally to the dynamics of the family system, it may necessitate the practitioner involving them as direct actors in the therapeutic experience.

The intergenerational family therapy approach need not be categorized as a narrow psychotherapeutic intervention nor a treatment approach that emanates from only a psychological model of causation, although those family therapists who have pioneered with this form of family therapy have been oriented in a psychoanalytic or psychotherapeutic tradition. Boszormenyi-Nagy and Spark (1973) are credited with expanding the concept into a formalized clinical approach. Their perspective on the three-generational dimension of therapy can be summarized as follows:

> We must take into consideration the three dimensions — e.g., the yearnings behind the hurt and angry feelings that are unconsciously transferred from the parent to a spouse or to children can then be directly connected back to the original sources. In other words, the multigenerational approach provides new opportunities to modify and change those relationships which presently appear hopeless, unyielding, and ungratifying. In the family accounting system (which extends over multiple generations) the injustice of parents' having been emotionally abandoned or exploited may be corrected and rebalanced. Behind the acts of aggression on the child lie the accumulation of feelings of helpless rage over having been exploited. Retaliation and revenge is thus reenacted upon the provocative, challenging child. Guilt feelings may be modified or decreased through discharging one's emotional obligation in one's close, personal relationships (p. 280).

Their operational framework for applying intergenerational family therapy emphasizes an assessment of all significant family members. Major consideration should be given to an understanding of the victimized child, abusing-victimized parent and the perpetrating grandparent. While there is no single description that can be appropriately generalized to multigenerational problem families, the following general description can be considered representative of some families:

The child—if he/she is the victim of parental neglect/abuse, it may result from some precipitating factors present in the child or behavior perceived by the abusing parent. If the child is involved in delinquent behavior, this behavior may be assessed as a form of retaliation or revenge promoted by hostile and aggressive feelings toward the abusing parent and directed within or outside the environment of the family.

The parent—the abusing parent is also defined as a sort of 'victim' subject to some form of violation from his/her parent(s) which may or may not have taken the form of physical abuse. The behavior of the grandparent, when functioning in the role of the parent, left the abusing parent with feelings of exploitation, rejection or abandonment which have remained unresolved and are most likely unrecognized and denied. The dysfunctional and destructive response to the child and possibly to the grandparent may be indicative of the parent's failure to 'come to terms' with her/his parents resulting in a delayed venting of feelings through highly dangerous patterns of interaction with the victim child.

The grandparents—the central grandparent figure may also be a victim of similar violations rendered by his/her parents, but resolution of grandparental feelings toward great-grandparents is not likely to be the focus of therapy. The therapeutic thrust may be to resolve the lifelong emotional and behavioral dysfunction between the grandparent and the parent and, where necessary, to strengthen the relationship between the grandparent and the victimized child.

The assumption we are making is that the presence of child abuse/neglect is directly associated with family dysfunction and that the delinquent behavior of a nonabused/neglected child is a reflection of individual dysfunction that may or may not be associated with family dysfunction. The presence of a combination of victimization and delinquent behavior within the same child reflects both individual and family dysfunction. It is strongly suggested that multigenerational family therapy be carefully evaluated as a potential approach with such families. If applied, the objective of therapy is one of promoting more adequate psychosocial functioning of family members in the family of origin and the nuclear family.

The interactional phenomenon of abuse/neglect and delinquency appears most frequently within the context of the nuclear family. The delinquent child enters therapy as the designated client with a history of abuse or neglect from one parent. There may be a small proportion of cases in which the abuse/neglect has been rendered by another family member (sibling or grandparent), but these more deviant cases may also be handled through an intergenerational family therapy approach.

CLINICAL ILLUSTRATION

The dynamics of intergenerational transmission become vivid to the clinician if he or she is confronted with a case involving dysfunctional patterns that reappear from one generation to another. In this section a hypothetical case illustration is presented which gives evidence of intergenerational transmission and clarifies how positive and negative relationships between and among grandparents, parents and children may be handled in family therapy.

This case illustration (see diagram, below) is incorporated into this paper because it represents a family situation in which there is a grandson who has been a victim of abuse and referred for treatment because of his delinquent behavior. In addition, the case demonstrates the transmitted patterns of abuse between men in the nuclear family and the family of origin.

Referral Information

Three months prior to the case referral, Mark, age 13, was arrested for burglary. Subsequently he was placed on probation under the auspices of the Juvenile Probation Follow-up Program. He was characterized as a rebellious, socially isolated adolescent who was considered an under-achiever in school. His father, Mr. L., age 36, had been unresponsive to the probation social worker, indicating a strong preference for his son to have been placed in a juvenile detention center rather than receive probation. Mrs. L., age 33, was the family member who requested the probation social worker to assist her family in getting counseling. During an initial conversation with the social worker she described a great deal of tension within her family that appeared to emanate from Mr. L's violent temper and physically aggressive behavior. Mrs. L. mentioned that the week before Mark broke into the neighbor's house she had entered their garage and found Mark bent over on the floor attempting to protect himself from Mr. L's blows to the neck and back. She expressed her own fear that Mr. L. would seriously injure the boy and described her efforts to detract him, but she was not successful. The L. family includes a daughter, Patty, age 8. The couple had been married when Mr. L. was 23 and Mrs. L. was age 20.

Father's History

Mr. L. is a tall, muscularly built man who is an assistant foreman in a local auto assembly plant. His parents are both living, and he was raised by them on a farm located outside of the city. His parents continued to live on the farm, but his father had recently undergone the amputation of his right foot. Mr. L. has one sister, Jana, age 34, who has never been married and works at a local junior college.

He expressed great resentment toward his father and indifference toward his mother. He felt that his father had treated him unjustly and had forced him to labor on the farm like a 'beast of burden' without providing him the financial support he thought he deserved when it was time to go to college. He entered the Navy for four years and was never able to attend college. Mr. L. considered his childhood a period of little happiness and was not willing to spend time with his parents or with his sister.

Mother's History

Mrs. L., age 30, was an attractive, small, verbal woman. She was one of three children. Her father, Mr. G., owned and operated a TV repair shop in a small community in close proximity to the city and her mother, Mrs. G., worked as a bookkeeper for the family business. Her two male siblings, age 25 and 24, were married, with infant children. Mrs. L. openly talked about her warm feelings toward her parents and other family members and mentioned that her family had always been close and supportive, as compared to Mr. L's. She was very grateful to Mr. G., who had shown great affection to Mark throughout his life and was able to reach Mark more than most other people.

Marital Relationship

Mr. L. worked full-time and accumulated much overtime at the assembly plant. When Mark was three, Mrs. L. returned to work but had not worked since the birth of their daughter, Patty. She resented Mr. L's rigid position about refusing to let her work until Patty was old enough not to require the careful guidance of her mother. Mrs. L. had little social life and Mr. L. discouraged her from developing interests that would take them outside their home. He exerted total financial control and made all decisions about money without input from his wife. Both parents expressed much pleasure with Patty; Mr. L. indicated that Mark had been born into the wrong family. Mrs. L. related that she had found Mark hard to communicate with since early childhood, but said she tried to show him love despite his general indifference to her.

Initial Phase of Treatment

Mark was very sullen and withdrawn in the first few sessions. He appeared isolated and would only respond to questions asked of him directly by the therapists. Mr. L. was consistently critical of Mark and, as a consequence, Mark would engage in conversation with his parents only when prompted by the therapists. Moreover, Mrs. L's supposedly excessive attention to Mark and insufficient management of Patty's daily routine were extremely upsetting for Mr. L. This could partially explain why Mr. L. encouraged Patty's disruptive behavior (engaging her in side-play) during these early sessions. Mark and Mrs. L. began to form a limited verbal alliance, talking together about a few topics, primarily Mark's growing interest in CB radios.

After four sessions with the nuclear family, the therapists suggested that Mrs. L. might want to invite her parents to attend a session because they had been expressing great concern over Mark and wanted to be of financial help if she decided to send Mark to a private military school. During the session with the maternal grandparents Mr. L. and Patty were unanticipatedly absent. Their absence was not desirable, but this session proved to be an important opportunity for a sharing of information between Mark and his grandfather. Mark and his mother both directly expressed their personal anger and fear of Mr. L. Mark directed his persistent stream of words toward his grandfather while begging his forgiveness over Mark's burglary. Mr. G. inquired of Mark what had led him to do such a thing. During an emotional outburst Mark said that he had wanted to get even with his father and if he was going to be beaten it might as well be for something real instead of his father's pretend excuses. Mrs. L. questioned the therapists about how to deal with her husband's temper and outbursts throughout the session. She said that any serious actions she took to discipline Patty or to protect Mark went unheeded and led to days of silence in the family. At the end of the session the grandparents left willing to come back again if the therapists thought they could be of help.

Several sessions followed with Mr. L., Mrs. L., Mark and Patty. Mr. L. made many accusations about his wife's dissatisfaction with their home life, her failure to set a good domestic example for Patty and the interference shown by her parents when they actually attended a therapy session. He challenged the legitimacy of her affection for her father and said that she had pushed Mark into loving her father and had prevented Mark from growing up to be the kind of son Mr. L. had dreamed of having when Mrs. L. was pregnant with Mark. Mark responded to his father by saying that he wished his grandfather were his father and that Mrs. G. loved both his daughter and grandson more than Mr. L. Mrs. L., through an outburst of angry retaliation, brought out new information regarding Mr. L's relationship with his parents. She said that he didn't know how to live as part of a loving household and pronounced that Mr. L. was like his father, violent and hostile, and that Mr. L. was treating Mark as Mr. L's father had treated him. She said that she felt he would never raise his children in the manner he had been raised.

Throughout these sessions, Mr. L. had become resentful and defensive and his patterns of projection on Mark had become somewhat clear to the therapists. Mr. L. had resisted any discussion of his early family life and did not respond to his wife's charge that he was acting exactly like his father. Through therapy Mark's defiance of his father grew stronger and more open. Sometimes Mrs. L. expressed fear that another violent family episode was brewing.

Future Treatment Plan

The major efforts in the initial phase of treatment could be to help the L. family to identify and understand their dysfunctional patterns of communication and interaction. The next task might be to help the family members to express their underlying emotions more directly and openly in order to clarify subsystem boundaries within the nuclear family, as well as across generations.

The therapist could be in the process of referring the initial goals to the mutual satisfaction of the family and therapists. The therapist's concern may be with identifying the functional strengths and weaknesses of multigenerational family members that may be of use in later sessions. The future direction of the therapy could be to continue to attempt to modify and redirect the expressions of anger and aggression by helping family members to understand their areas of dysfunctional communication and its effects on their daily lives. Finally, efforts might be in progress to help them understand interactional subsystems and their contributions to the intrafamily climate of violence.

CONCLUSION

Given the uncertainty surrounding the selection of appropriate individual, family or group oriented treatment approaches, and the questionable effectiveness of these approaches as evidenced by repeated cases of abuse and neglect, it would seem worthwhile to explore new family therapy approaches. The process of developing new methods of intervention is very complex and requires a significant commitment of time and resources. If intergenerational family therapy were to become an approach incorporated into the range of interventions readily available, the following will need to occur:

A. Development of a Knowledge Base about the Approach

1. The conceptual framework will have to be expanded to incorporate a family life cycle perspective.

2. A greater number of family therapy theorists will need to assume commitment for developing the frameworks which underpin the model.

3. There will need to be more clinical research which is directed toward establishing an empirical data base and the techniques which might be appropriate.

B. Introduction of the Method to Practitioners

1. Creating opportunities to reeducate practitioners who are skilled in working with the nuclear family unit;

2. Adopting this content into curriculum provided to young practitioners about to enter the field; and

3. Making judicious use of consultants to strengthen the diagnostic and therapeutic strengths of staff.

C. Restructuring the Service Delivery System

1. Revising the range of services that may be available through medical, health, social and legal settings;

2. Obtaining mechanisms to reimburse and sustain longer term family therapy; and

3. Strengthening external service delivery system linkages.

The concept of intergenerational transmission has been around a long time. There has been a tendency either to misuse the concept to reinforce the notion of unalterable family pathology or to simply ignore those dimensions of family behavior closely associated with multigenerational dynamics. In this paper the concept has been employed to link the phenomena of abuse and delinquency. Literature in both areas supports intergenerational transmittal, but more empirical research will be required to substantiate the interrelationship among the three factors. In advance of such research, intergenerational family therapy could be introduced as a complementary approach to more traditional forms of family-based intervention if an agency has sufficient resources.

Federal, state and local policies directly influence the availability of human service resources to deal with abuse and delinquency. The situation of too few resources to serve too many clients with serious and complex problems is reinforced by an absence of a national family policy.

A national family policy would help to reduce the stigma of family-based problems, facilitate the family unit's accessibility to appropriate and effective services, expand the family-based focus into all human service delivery systems and provide families with a range of incentives to counteract societal trends promoting isolation and dysfunction. Furthermore, it would have positive implications for all generations of family members and strengthen the family unit's ability to deal with problems encountered by its youngest and oldest members.

REFERENCES

Bell, N. W. Extended family relations of disturbed and well families. *Family Process*, 1962, *1* 175-193.

Bennie, E. H. & Sclare, A. B. The battered child syndrome. *American Journal of Psychiatry*, January, 1969, *125*(7), 147-151.

Boszormenyi-Nagy, I. & Spark, G. M. *Invisible Loyalties.* New York: Har] Row, 1973.

Bowen, M. A family concept of schizophrenia. . In D. D. Jackson (Ed.), *Etiol(schizophrenia.* New York: Basic Books, 1960.

Brace, C. L. *The dangerous classes of New York.* New York: Wynkoop & Hallenbeck, 1880.

Bronfenbrenner, U. The origins of alienation. *Scientific American,* August, 1974, 53-61.

Burt, C. *The young delinquents.* London: University of London Press, 1931.

Caffey, J. Multiple fractures in the long bones of children suffering from chronic subdural hematoma. *American Journal of Roentgenology,* August, 1946, *56* (2), 163-173.

Fontana, V. *The maltreated child: The maltreatment syndrome in children.* Springfield, Ill.: Charles C. Thomas, 1964.

Gelles, R. J. Child abuse as psychopathology: A sociological critique and reformulation. *American Journal of Orthopsychiatry,* 1973, *43,* 611-621.

Gil, D. Violence against children in the family. *Journal of Marriage and Family,* November, 1971, *33,* 637-648.

Glaser, D. Dimension of the problem. In J. S. Roucek (Ed.), *Juvenile Delinquency.* Freeport, N.Y.: Books for Libraries, 1958.

Hakeem, M. A critique of the psychiatric approach. In J. S. Roucek (Ed.), *Juvenile delinquency.* Freeport, N.Y.: Books for Libraries, 1958.

Halleck, S. Delinquency. In B. J. Wolman (Ed.), *Manual of child psychopathology.* New York: McGraw-Hill, 1972.

Hill, L. B. *Psychotherapeutic intervention in schizophrenia.* Chicago: University of Chicago Press, 1955.

Joint Commission on Mental Health of Children. *Crisis in child mental health: Challenge for the 1970's.* New York: Harper & Row, 1969.

Kempe, C. H., et al. The battered child syndrome. *Journal of the American Medical Association,* July, 1962, *181,* 17-24.

Kempe, C. H., et al. The battered child syndrome, *Journal of the American Medical Association,* July-September, 1962, *181,* 105-112.

Light, R. Abused and neglected children in America: A study of alternative policies. *Harvard Educational Review,* 1973, *43,* 556-598.

McCord, W. The biological bases of juvenile delinquency. In J. S. Roucek (Ed.), *Juvenile delinquency.* Freeport, N.Y.: Books for Libraries, 1958.

Mendell, D., Cleveland, S. E. & Fisher, S. A five-generation family theme. *Family Process,* 1968, *7,* 126-132.

Mendell, D. & Fisher, S. An approach to neurotic behavior in terms of a three-generation family model. *Journal of Nervous Mental Disorders,* 1956, *123,* 171-180.

Mendell, D. & Fisher, S. A multi-generational approach to treatment of psychopathology. *Journal of Nervous Mental Disorders,* 1958, *126,* 523-529.

Ounsted, C., et al. The psychopathology and psychotherapy of the families' aspects bounding failure. In A. Franklin (Ed.), *Concerning child abuse.* Edinburgh & London: Churchill Livingston, 1975.

Parke, R. & Collmet, C. Child abuse: An interdisciplinary analysis. In M. Hetherington (Ed.), *Review of child development research.* Vol. 5. Chicago: University of Chicago Press, 1975.

Pattison, E. M. Psychosocial system therapy. In R. G. Hirschowitz & B. Levy (Eds.), *The changing mental health scene.* New York: Spectrum, 1976.

Polansky, N., et al. *Child neglect: Understanding and reaching the parents.* New York: Child Welfare League of America, 1972.

Radcliffe-Brown, A. R. Introduction to the analysis of kinship systems. In N. W. Bell & E. F. Vogel (Eds.), *The family.* New York: Free Press, 1968.

Rakoff, V. M. & Lefebvre, A. Conjoint family therapy. In R. G. Hirschowitz & B. Levy, (Eds.), *The changing mental health scene.* New York: Spectrum, 1976.

Robins, L. Arrest and delinquency in two generations: A study of black urban families and their children. In S. Chess & A. Thomas (Eds.), *Annual progress in child psychiatry and child development.* New York: Brunner/Mazzl, 1975.

Short, J. Juvenile delinquency: The sociocultural context. In L. Hoffman & M. Hoffman (Eds.), *Review of child development.* Vol. 2. New York: Russell Sage Foundation, 1966.

Silverstone, B. & Hyman, H. K. *You and your aging parent.* New York: Pantheon Books, 1976.

Steele, B. F. & Pollock, D. A psychiatric study of parents who abuse infants and small children. In R. E. Helfer & C. H. Kempe (Eds.), *The battered child.* Chicago: University of Chicago Press, 1968. *St. Louis Post-Dispatch,* November 30, 1975.

Sussman, A. & Cohen, S. *Reporting child abuse and neglect: Guidelines for legislation.* Cambridge, Mass.: Ballinger Publishing Co., 1975.

U.S. Congress, Committee on the Judiciary, United States Senate. *A report by the Subcommittee to Investigate Juvenile Delinquency.* 95th Congress, 1st Session, 1977.

U.S. Congress, Committee on the Judiciary, United States Senate. *Our nation's schools—a report card: 'A' in school violence and vandalism. A report by the Subcommittee to Investigate Juvenile Delinquency.* Part 2. 95th Congress, 1st Session, 1977. *United States Crime Report.* 1974, 1-47.

Walters, D. *Physical and sexual abuse of children: Causes and treatment.* Bloomington: Indiana University Press, 1975.

Weinberg, K. Sociological processes and factors in juvenile delinquency. In J. S. Roucek (Ed.), *Juvenile delinquency.* New York: Books for Libraries, 1958.

Wooley, P. V. The pediatrician and the young child subjected to repeated physical abuse. *Journal of Pediatrics,* April, 1963, *62,* 628-630.

Zuk, G. H. & Rubenstein, D. A review of concepts in the study and treatment of families of schizophrenics. In I. Boszormenyi-Nagy & J. L. Framo (Eds.), *Intensive family therapy.* New York: Harper & Row, 1965.

7

Deviant Behaviors of Child Victims and Bystanders in Violent Families

JANE H. PFOUTS, JANICE H. SCHOPLER
& H. CARL HENLEY, JR.

School of Social Work
University of North Carolina
Chapel Hill, North Carolina 27514

Das eben ist der Fluch
der Bosen Tat,
Das sie, fortzeugend,
"immer Boses muss gebaren.
That truly is the Curse
of Evil Deeds,
That ever they give birth
to new Evil.

Friedrich von Schiller
Die Piccolomini, 5th Act, 1st Scene 1800.

All children who live in violent families are affected whether they are victims themselves or helpless bystanders to mother or sibling abuse . The web of family violence enmeshes the entire group; when one family member is abused by another, the repercussions reverberate throughout the family system (e.g., Minuchin, 1974). As the children carry the hostile world of the family with them into the larger society, a likely outcome is social and psychological deviance (e.g., Becker, et al, 1960; Hoffman, 1960; Silver, et al, 1969; Gladston, 1971; Konopka, 1976).

This paper explores the extent to which family violence is associated with deviance in children. In our view, crucial factors in distinguishing variations in deviance are the emotional climate of family and the role of the child in the structure of violence. The linkage between parental attitudes and deviance in children is well documented in the literature (e.g., Morse, et al, 1970; Walters and Stinnett, 1971; Blumberg, 1974; Green, et al, 1974; Steele and Pollock, 1974). Although there has been voluminous research on the effect of child abuse on the victim (e.g., Young, 1964, Elmer and Gregg, 1967; Martin, 1972; Justice, 1976; Acley, 1977), only one author (Moore, 1975) has researched the effect of wife abuse on children and there is only brief discussion in the literature regarding the effect of child abuse on children who are bystanders (e..g., Johnson and Morse, 1968). We will also examine sex, race, maternal vs. paternal abuse, extent of abuse; and extent of neglect as have other researchers (e.g., Gil, 1970; Giovannoni and Billingsley, 1970; Gelles, 1974).

The following hypotheses are offered to predict variations in behavior among children in differing roles and differing family climates.

Hypothesis I: Children who are bystanders to family violence will exhibit minimal deviance if their relationship with parents has some positive features and mild deviance if the relationship is characterized by parental rejection.

Hypothesis II: Children who are victims of family violence will exhibit mild deviance if their relationship with their abusing parents has some positive features and severe deviance if the relationship is characterized by paternal rejection.

METHOD OF STUDY

The population studied was chosen from over 800 cases investigated by the Protective Service Unit of the Orange County Department of Social Services in North Carolina from 1971 to 1977. (1) Initial selection was based on information obtained from the National Clearinghouse and local forms filed by Protective Service Workers on completion of investigation of reports of child abuse and neglect. When the reports related to abuse by caretakers other than parents or parent/substitutes, sexual abuse, substantiated and unsubstantiated emotional and physical neglect and abandonement, the cases were excluded from the sample. The remaining 140 cases included eighty-five cases of child abuse, twenty-seven cases of wife abuse and twenty-eight cases of child abuse combined with wife abuse.

These 140 cases were reviewed to determine whether abuse had been substantiated and whether sufficient information was available for the study. Sixty-seven cases were eliminated from the sample. Abuse was unsubstantiated in twenty cases of child abuse. In fourteen cases of child abuse, information could not be obtained beacause the family had moved or the children were infants whose behavior had not been recorded. In sixteen cases of child abuse; eleven cases of wife abuse and six cases of child abuse combined with wife abuse; information was insufficient because the case had been closed and/or the assigned social worker was no longer employed at the agency or the case had been transferred to another agency . The final sample of seventy-three families, with a total of 141 children; included thirty-five cases of child abuse, sixteen cases of wife abuse and twenty-two cases involving both wife and child abuse. Comparison of the cases selected for the sample with those rejected because of insufficient information revealed no significant demographic differences.

Data collected were obtained from the reports of investigation and from interviews with the social workers or supervisor responsible for each case. Background information on each family was recorded as follows: 1) children were described in terms of sibling number and order, age, birth status, grade level and physical or mental disabilities; 2) parent characteristics noted were marital status, parental composition and living arrangements, education; employment and income; 3) description of the abusing parent included age, sex, relationship to child and any deviant characteristics, and 4) the abuse involved and service provided were briefly summarized. Any background information not present on the reports of investigation was obtained, when possible, during the interviews.

In the interviews, the social workers were asked to describe the family members and their interactional patterns with particular emphasis on the children's behavior and on the parent/child relationships. Specific behavioral information was not always present on all of the siblings, particularly in larger families of three or more children. Children excluded from the study for lack of information comprised both abused and non-abused siblings, but more frequently were thought to be in the non-abused bystander category. Because the social workers typically were more closely involved with children who were exhibiting problems and had more information on their behavioral characteristics, the sample contains some bias in the direction of deviance. There also may be an unkown degree of bias toward reporting of acting out behaviors since withdrawn children are sometimes of less concern to parents and oth.er adults and their behavior might not be discussed with the social worker or might be reported as within the normal range.

THE SAMPLE

Characteristics of the 73 Families

The family characteristics presented in Table 1 provide an overview of the sample of 73 families. Violence is expressed by wife abuse in about 20% of the families, child abuse in almost 50% and a combination of wife and child abuse in 30%. In almost half (45.9%) of the cases of wife abuse, the beaten wives are physically combative with their spouses; the remainder (54.1%) are passive victims. Fathers and father substitutes abuse their children in almost two-thirds of these families; the mothers are abusive toward their children in over half the families; in 47.4% of the families, the father or father substitute is the sole abuser, in 35.1% of the families the mother is the sole abuser and in 17.5% of the families both parents are abusive. Slightly more than half the referrals come from official sources (medical, school, day care, police, court, social agency personnel) and the remainder are complaints by neighbors, relatives, and anonymous callers.

These families are disproportionately poor, Black, and badly educated. In 30.4% of the families the income is from Public Assistance. Only 10% of the families have incomes of $15,000 or more. Forty-five percent of the families are Black. Twenty percent have four or more children living in the home. Over half the parents did not complete high school, although in this sample, drawn from a county with a large university population, 12.7% of the mothers and 18.3% of the fathers or father substitutes hold B.A., M.A., or Ph.D. Degrees. Because these are public agency cases, we can assume there is a bias toward the lower end of the socio-economic scale and, therefore, the sample does not speak to the characteristics of violent families in the general population.

Table 2 examines the extent to which adults in the family are handicapped by

TABLE 1 CHARACTERISTICS OF 73 VIOLENT FAMILIES

SCHEDULE ITEM	No. of Cases	% of Total
Type of Family Violence		
Wife Abuse Only.	16	21.9
Child Abuse Only	35	47.9
Both Wife Abuse and Child Abuse	22	30.2
Total	73	100.0
Dynamics of Wife Abuse		
Beaten Wife is Passive Victim. .	20	54.1
Beaten Wife is Active Combatant.	17	45.9
Total	37	100.0
Dynamics of Child Abuse		
Child Abuse by Father/Substitute	27	47.4
Child Abuse by Mother.	20	35.1
Child Abuse by Father/Sub & Mother	10	17.5
Total	57	100.0
Referral Source		
Medical (M.D., Nurse, Hospital)	19	26.0
Neighbor	13	17.8
School or Day Care Center. . . .	12	16.4
Police, Courts, Social Agencies.	8	11.0
Relatives.	7	9.6
Anonymous or Unknown	14	19.2
Total	73	100.0
Number of Children Living in Home		
One	19	26.0
Two	23	31.5
Three.	16	21.9
Four or More	15	20.6
Total	73	100.0
Race		
Black.	33	45.2
White.	39	53.4
Other.	1	1.4
Total	73	100.0

SCHEDULE ITEM	No. of Cases	% of Total
Education of Father/Substitute		
Less than 12th Grade.	21	55.3
High School Graduate.	5	13.2
Some College or Post H.S. . . .	5	13.2
College or Graduate Degree. . .	7	18.3
Unknown	35	--
Total.	73	100.0
Education of Mother		
Less than 12th Grade.	32	58.2
High School Graduate.	9	16.4
Some College or Post H.S. . . .	7	12.7
College or Graduate Degree. . .	7	12.7
Unknown	18	--
Total.	73	100.0
Family Income		
Less than $6,000.	19	41.3
Between $6,000 & $11,999. . . .	14	30.4
Between $12,000 & $14,999 . . .	8	17.4
$15,000 or Over.	5	10.9
Unknown	27	--
Total	73	100.0
Receives Public Assistance		
Yes	21	30.4
No	48	69.6
Unknown	4	--
Total.	73	100.0
Age of Principal Abuser		
Under 21.	2	3.6
21-30	24	42.9
31-40	19	33.9
40 or Over	11	19.6
Unknown	17	--
Total.	73	100.0
Parents Abused as Children		
Yes	11	15.1
Unknown	62	84.9
Total	73	100.0
Frequent Parental Separation		
Yes	18	50.0
No	18	50.0
N.A. (one Parent Family). . . .	15	--
Unknown	22	--
Total.	73	100.0

TABLE 2 SERIOUS DEVIANCE EXHIBITED BY ADULTS INVOLVED IN VIOLENT FAMILIES*

Adult Roles in Family Violence	No. of Parents in each role	% of Parents With Physical, Psychological or Social Deviance
Abused mother abuses children	14	85.7%
Non-abused mother abuses children	19	78.9
Abused mother doesn't abuse children	25	60.0
Male abuses wife and/or children**	57	59.6
Non-abused mother doesn't abuse children	11	27.3
Male abuses neither wife nor children	5	20.0

*Characteristics of 4 mothers are unknown.

**The category "male abuses wife and/or children" includes 50 males living in the home plus 7 males living outside the home.

serious physical, psychological or social pathology. Abusers are much more likely to be impaired than are their non-abusive mates and women who abuse their children are the most damaged group of all. Over 85% of these women exhibit serious pathology, while abusing men are similar to abused wives in that roughly 60% of this group have severe physical, psychological or social pathology.

Characteristics of the 141 Children

The 141 children in the sample are described in Table 3: twenty-five (17.7%) were bystanders to wife abuse, twenty-four (17.0%) were bystanders to the abuse of a sib and ninety-two (65.3%) were victims of child abuse. The children are fairly evenly distributed in the sex, age and race categories. One-third are pre-school or kindergarten children, about two-thirds are in school and only three are school drop-outs.

The majority of these children have led disadvantaged lives since birth. Twenty-two percent are illegitimate. Only 41% live with both natural parents. Over 20% suffer from serious physical and mental disabilities and there are weak to strong indications of physical neglect for 66% of the children.

TABLE 3 CHARACTERISTICS OF THE 141 CHILDREN

SCHEDULE ITEM	No. of Children	% of Total
Child's Role in Family Violence		
Bystander of Wife Abuse . . .	25	17.7
Bystander of Child Abuse. . .	24	17.0
Victim of Child Abuse	92	65.3
Total.	141	100.0
Sex of Child		
Male	76	53.8
Female	65	46.1
Total.	141	100.0
Age of Child		
2-5	31	22.0
6-8	35	24.8
9-12	38	27.0
13-18	37	26.2
Total.	141	100.0
Birth Status of Child		
Legitimate	106	77.9
Illegitimate	30	22.1
Unknown	5	--
Total.	141	100.0
Child's Living Arrangements		
Lives with Mother and Father.	58	41.1
Lives With Mother & Stepfather	35	23.4
Lives With Mother Alone . . .	33	24.8
Lives With Mother & Paramour	11	7.8
Other	4	2.9
Total.	141	100.0
Child's Disabilities		
No Disabilities	98	69.5
Mental Retardation.	11	7.8
Physical Problems	1	0.7
Mental Illness.	13	9.2
Physical & Mental Disabilities	7	5.0
Unknown	11	7.8
Total.	141	100.0

SCHEDULE ITEM	No. of Children	% of Total
Grade Level of Child		
PreSchool - No Day Care. .	22	19.8
PreSchool - Day Care . . .	8	7.2
Kindergarten	6	5.4
Grades 1,2, and 3.	27	24.3
Grades 4,5, and 6.	22	19.8
Grades 7,8, and 9.	14	12.6
Grades 10,11, and 12 . . .	9	8.2
School Drop-out	3	2.7
Unknown.	30	--
Total.	141	100.0
Race of Child		
Black	71	50.4
White.	68	48.2
Other.	2	1.4
Total.	141	100.0
Relationship to Abuser		
Natural Mother	47	33.6
Natural Father	37	26.4
Both Natural Parents . . .	8	5.7
Mother & Stepfather. . . .	15	10.7
Stepfather	18	12.9
Mother's Paramour.	15	10.7
Unknown	1	--
Total	141	100.0
DSS Neglect Finding		
No Indication	46	33.4
Weak Indication	34	24.6
Strong Indication	58	42.0
Unknown	3	--
Total	141	100.0
DSS Abuse Finding		
No Indication	42	29.8
Weak Indication	48	34.0
Strong Indication	51	36.2
Total	141	100.0

As shown in Table 4, deviant behavior was widespread among the 141 children. The deviant social behaviors most often indicated were truancy (40.0%), assault (30.3%), stealing (29.9%), vandalism (24.1%), has appeared in Juvenile Court (17.0%) and running away (14.6%). Among the deviant emotional behaviors, most striking were the frequent depression (64.4%) and anxiety (66.0%) exhibited by these children. It is also significant to note the percentage of children hospitalized (7.9%) for psychiatric treatment and receiving health treatment (34.8%). School performance (See Table 5) of the eighty-eight children enrolled reflects the intellectual deficits these children bring to the classroom. Only 28.4% are average or above average students; 71.5% are below average or failing; and an additional eleven children are in special education.

TABLE 4 CHECKLIST OF DEVIANT BEHAVIORS

Behavior Category	No. of Cases for Which Information is Available	Children Exhibiting Behavior	
		No.	%
Deviant Social Behavior			
Has appeared in Juvenile Court.	140	25	17.9%
Assault	106	32	30.2
Stealing.	87	26	29.9
Vandalism	83	20	24.1
Running Away.	103	15	14.6
Drinking.	96	8	8.3
Drug Abuse.	94	5	5.3
Sexual Acting Out . . .	95	16	16.8
Truancy	100	40	40.0
Deviant Emotional Behavior			
Receiving Mental Health Treatment . . .	132	46	34.8%
Hospitalized for Psychiatric Treatment.	137	10	7.9
Hyperactivity	111	31	27.9
Depression.	104	67	64.4
Anxiety	100	66	66.0
Other	134	83	61.9%

TABLE 5 CHILD'S SCHOOL PERFORMANCE

School Behavior Category	No. of Children	% of Total
Above Average	6	6.8%
Average	19	21.6
Below Average	45	51.1
Failing	18	20.5
Special Education	11	--
Not in School	25	--
Unknown	17	--
Total.	141	100.0%

Table 6 shows the judgements made by the researchers concerning the interpersonal style of the children with their parents, sibs, peers and teachers. (2) The greatest departure from the norm (balanced style) occurs in parental relationships with only 16.3% of the children judged as balanced in their interpersonal style; the least departure from the norm is in sib relationships. The most extreme withdrawal behavior occurs in interaction with parents, the most extreme acting out behavior with peers. Table 7 summarizes the overall judgements of interpersonal style and degree of deviancy. (3) Of the 141 children, only one-fourth are viewed as having a balanced interpersonal style; twice as many deviate in the direction of acting out as in the direction of withdrawal. In relation to the overall judgement of deviancy almost three-fourths of the children are rated as mildly or severely deviant.

TABLE 6 CHILDREN'S INTERPERSONAL STYLE WITH PARENTS, SIBS, PEERS, AND TEACHERS*

Categories of Interpersonal Style	Type of Relationship			
	With Parents	With Sibs	With Peers	With Teachers
Withdrawn	22.1% (19)	12.2% (7)	10.1% (7)	12.9% (9)
Somewhat Withdrawn	11.6% (10)	7.0% (4)	14.5% (10)	10.0% (7)
Balanced	16.3% (14)	38.6% (22)	27.6% (19)	28.6% (20)
Somewhat Acting Out	24.4% (21)	21.1% (12)	11.6% (8)	17.1% (12)
Acting Out	25.6% (22)	21.1% (12)	36.2% (25)	31.4% (22)
Total Cases Scored	100.0% (86)	100.0% (57)	100.0% (69)	100.0% (70)

TABLE 7 OVERALL JUDGEMENTS OF INTERPERSONAL STYLE AND DEGREE OF DEVIANCY FOR 141 CHILDREN

Judgement Category	No. of Children	% of Total
Overall Judgement of Interpersonal Style		
Withdrawn	15	10.6%
Somewhat Withdrawn	16	11.3
Balanced	36	25.6
Somewhat Acting Out	35	24.8
Acting Out	39	27.7
Total	141	100.0%
Overall Judgement of Degree of Deviancy		
Normal	37	26.2%
Mild	49	34.8
Severe	55	39.0
Total	141	100.0%

As a final step in analyzing the total sample of children, a judgement was made about the quality of parental relationships with each child and the resulting ambivalent or rejecting family climate experienced by the child. As shown in Table 8, in 64.5% of the cases the children live in an ambivalent family climate in which, even though abuse may be present, one or both parents provide some emotional support to the child . In 35.5% of the cases, however, the emotional climate is completely rejecting.

Table 9 demonstrates that the fathers and father substitutes are significantly more rejecting of their children than are mothers (X¼ 28.5, p .001). This is compatible with the earlier finding that fathers and father substitutes are more often involved in child abuse than are mothers. In addition, it seems likely. that the emotional support

TABLE 8 EMOTIONAL RESOURCES WITHIN THE FAMILY FOR 141 CHILDREN

SCHEDULE ITEM	No. of Children	% of Total
Child's Emotional Ties With Parents		
Mother Supportive Some of the Time - Father Rejecting	53	37.8 %
Father Supportive Some of the Time - Mother Rejecting	6	4.3
Both Parents Supportive Some of the Time	26	18.4
Both Parents Rejecting All of the Time.	33	23.4
Mother Supportive Some of the Time - No Father	6	4.3
Mother Rejecting All of the Time - No Father	17	12.1
Total	141	100.0 %
Family Climate		
Parent-Child Relationship Marked by Ambivalence. . . .	91	64.5 %
Parent-Child Relationship Marked by Rejection.	50	35.5
Total	141	100.0 %

TABLE 9 PARENTAL FEELINGS TOWARD EACH OF THE 141 CHILDREN

Emotional Climate	Mothers	Fathers and Father Sub.	Total
Ambivalent	60.3% (85)	27.1% (32)	117
Rejecting	39.7% (56)	72.9% (86)	142
Total	100.0% (141)	100.0% (118)	259

$X^2 = 28.5,\ p < .001$

of the mothers is a constant, though may be mixed with rejecting behavior, because while fathers, stepfathers and paramours come and go in these families, mothers and children remain together for better or worse.

In summary, family life for this sample is chaotic and violent; both parents and children exhibit high rates of deviance the children are underachievers in school and their interpersonal relationships are distorted. Perhaps the most crucial relationship, and the most ambivalent, is that of mother and child because this is the one stable factor for the child in a world fraught with uncertainty and terror.

FINDINGS

As a first step in the analysis of these data, we determined which of the independent variables (family climate, the child's role in family violence, indications of neglect, indications of abuse, paternal vs. maternal abuser, race of the child and sex of the child) were significantly associated with the dependent variable in our study—the overall judgment of the degree of deviancy. We accomplished this step by cross-tabulating each independent variable with the dependent variable, overall judgment of the degree of deviancy, and testing the ordinal relationship for significance by using a Z test. As a second step, we tested our two hypotheses by cross-tabulating the overall judgment of the degree of deviancy by the family climate, while controlling for the child's role in family violence, and testing the two ordinal relationships for significance by using Z tests. Finally, we tested the simultaneous effect of the independent variables on the overall judgement of the degree of deviancy by using a stepwise multiple regression procedure and F tests.

By examining the percentages in Table 10, one can see that children who are members of a family in which the family climate is rejecting toward them have a higher overall degree of deviancy than do children who are members of a family in which the family climate is ambivalent toward them. These differences are significant at the .001 level of significance.

The percentages in Table 11 show that children who are victims of child abuse have a higher overall degree of deviancy than do children who are bystanders in family violence. These differences are significant at the .001 level of significance.

TABLE 10 OVERALL JUDGEMENT OF DEGREE OF DEVIANCY BY FAMILY CLIMATE FOR THE 141 CHILDREN

Family Climate	Overall Judgement of Degree of Deviancy			
	Normal	Mild	Severe	Total
Ambivalent	39.6% (36)	39.6% (36)	20.9% (19)	100% (91)
Rejecting	2.0% (1)	26.0% (13)	72.0% (36)	100% (50)
Total	(37)	(49)	(55)	(141)

Gamma = +0.82
$Z = +7.00$, $p < .001$

TABLE 11 OVERALL JUDGEMENT OF DEGREE OF DEVIANCY BY CHILD'S ROLE IN FAMILY VIOLENCE FOR THE 141 CHILDREN

Child's Role in Family Violence	Overall Judgement of Degree of Deviancy			
	Normal	Mild	Severe	Total
Bystander	46.9% (23)	32.7% (16)	20.4% (10)	100% (49)
Victim	15.2% (14)	35.9% (33)	48.9% (45)	100% (92)
Total	(37)	(49)	(55)	(141)

Gamma = + 0.57

Z = + 3.31, $p < .001$

TABLE 12 OVERALL JUDGEMENT OF DEGREE OF DEVIANCY BY INDICATIONS OF NEGLECT FOR THE 141 CHILDREN

Indications of Neglect	Overall Judgement of Degree of Deviancy			
	Normal	Mild	Severe	Total
None	34.8% (16)	43.5% (20)	21.7% (10)	100% (46)
Weak	38.2% (13)	32.4% (11)	29.4% (10)	100% (34)
Strong	13.8% (8)	27.6% (16)	58.6% (34)	100% (58)
Total	(37)	(47)	(54)	(138)*

Gamma = + 0.42

Z = + 2.57, $p < .01$

*There were three children for whom we could not determine the indications of neglect.

As can be seen by examining the percentages in Table 12, the stronger the indications of neglect in a family, the more severe the child's overall degree of deviancy is likely to be. This association is significant at the .001 level of significance.

The percentages in Table 13 show that as the indications of abuse in a family increase, the overall degree of deviancy becomes more severe. This association is significant at the .01 level of significance.

Table 14 gives the percentage distributions of the overall degree of deviancy for those children who were abused by fathers or father substitutes only and for those children who were abused by mothers only. From the table, one can see that those children who were abused by mothers only have a higher overall degree of deviancy than do those children who were abused by fathers and father substitutes only. These differences are significant at the .05 level of significance.

As the percentages in Table 15 indicate, there is no consistent relationship between race and overall degree of deviancy. Furthermore, the relationship between these two variables is not significant.

Although the percents in Table 16 indicate that females have a slightly higher overall degree of deviancy than do males, these differences are not statistically significant.

From Tables 10-16, one can see that the following variables are significantly associated with the child's overall degree of deviancy: 1) the family climate; 2) the child's role in family violence; 3) the indications of neglect; 4) the indications of abuse, and 5) paternal vs. maternal abuser.

It was originally hypothesized that children who are bystanders to family violence will exhibit minimal deviance if relationships with parents are ambivalent and mild

TABLE 13 OVERALL JUDGEMENT OF DEGREE OF DEVIANCY BY INDICATIONS OF ABUSE FOR THE 141 CHILDREN

Indications of Abuse	Overall Judgement of Degree of Deviancy			
	Normal	Mild	Severe	Total
None	47.6% (20)	33.3% (14)	19.0% (8)	100% (42)
Weak	12.5% (6)	52.1% (25)	35.4% (17)	100% (48)
Strong	21.6% (11)	19.6% (10)	58.8% (30)	100% (51)
Total	(37)	(49)	(55)	(141)

Gamma = + 0.44

$Z = +2.79$, $p < .01$

TABLE 14 OVERALL JUDGEMENT OF DEGREE OF DEVIANCY BY PATERNAL VS. MATERNAL ABUSER FOR THE 141 CHILDREN

Abuser	Overall Judgement of Degree of Deviancy			
	Normal	Mild	Severe	Total
Father or Father Substitute Only	38.3% (18)	38.3% (18)	23.4% (11)	100% (47)
Mother Only	12.5% (5)	42.5% (17)	45.0% (18)	100% (40)
Total	(23)	(35)	(29)	(87)

Gamma = + 0.48 $Z = +2.10$, $p < .05$

TABLE 15 OVERALL JUDGEMENT OF DEGREE OF DEVIANCY BY RACE FOR THE 141 CHILDREN

Race	Overall Judgement of Degree of Deviancy			
	Normal	Mild	Severe	Total
Black	33.8% (24)	23.9% (17)	42.3% (30)	100% (71)
White	17.6% (12)	47.1% (32)	35.3% (24)	100% (68)
Total	(36)	(49)	(54)	(139)*

Gamma = + 0.07 $Z = +0.34$, NS at .05

*Two children have been omitted from this Table - one Chinese and one Arab.

TABLE 16 OVERALL JUDGEMENT OF DEGREE OF DEVIANCY BY SEX FOR THE 141 CHILDREN

Sex	Overall Judgement of Degree of Deviancy			
	Normal	Mild	Severe	Total
Male	28.9% (22)	32.9% (25)	38.2% (29)	100% (76)
Female	23.1% (15)	36.9% (24)	40.0% (26)	100% (65)
Total	(37)	(49)	(55)	(141)

TABLE 17 OVERALL JUDGEMENT OF DEGREE OF DEVIANCY BY FAMILY CLIMATE FOR THE 49 CHILDREN WHO WERE BYSTANDERS IN FAMILY VIOLENCE

Family Climate	Overall Judgement of Degree of Deviancy			
	Normal	Mild	Severe	Total
Ambivalent	53.7% (22)	31.7% (13)	14.6% (6)	100% (41)
Rejecting	12.5% (1)	37.5% (3)	50.0% (4)	100% (8)
Total	(23)	(16)	(10)	(49)

Gamma = + .70 $Z = +2.18$, $p < .05$

TABLE 18 OVERALL JUDGEMENT OF DEGREE OF DEVIANCY BY FAMILY CLIMATE FOR THE 92 CHILDREN WHO WERE VICTIMS OF FAMILY VIOLENCE

Family Climate	Overall Judgement of Degree of Deviancy			
	Normal	Mild	Severe	Total
Ambivalent	28.0% (14)	46.0% (23)	26.0% (13)	100% (50)
Rejecting	0.0% (0)	23.8% (10)	76.2% (32)	100% (42)
Total	(14)	(33)	(45)	(92)

Gamma = + .82
$Z = 5.70$, $p < .001$

deviance if relationships are rejecting. It is clear from Table 17 that the overall degree of deviancy is greater than we had anticipated in both the "ambivalent" and "rejecting" categories of bystanders (14.6% of those in the "ambivalent" category are severely deviant and exactly one-half of those in the "rejecting" category are severely deviant). However, the test of significance shows that those bystanders who are rejected by their parents have a significantly greater degree of deviancy than do those bystanders who are treated with ambivalence by their parents. Therefore, our first hypothesis is supported.

It also was originally hypothesized that children who are victims of family violence will exhibit mild deviance if relationships with parents are ambivalent and severe deviance if relationships with parents are rejecting. From Table 18 it is clear that the largest percent of those victims in the "ambivalent" category were mildly deviant and that the majority of those victims in the "rejecting" category were severely deviant. In addition, it should be noted that more than one-fourth of those victims in the "ambivalent" category, but not a single victim in the "rejecting" category, showed only a normal amount of deviance.

When the association between these two variables was tested for significance, we found that those victims who were rejected by their parents had a significantly greater degree of deviancy than did those victims who were treated with ambivalence by their parents. Thus, our second hypothesis is supported.

In order to determine which of the independent variables that were significantly associated with the overall degree of deviancy are the best predictors of overall degree of deviancy, we used them as independent variables in an ordinary least squares, stepwise, multiple regression procedure. This statistical procedure considers the simultaneous effect the independent variables have on the dependent variable; that is, the effect of each independent variable is adjusted for each of the other independent variables in the regression model.

The first multiple regression analysis considers the effect of family climate, the child's role in family violence, the indications of neglect and the indications of abuse on the overall degree of deviancy. The paternal vs. maternal abuser was not included in this particular analysis since not all children were abused either by the father or father substitute only or by the mother only.

A summary of this regression analysis is presented in Table 19, and the results indicate that once one considers the effect of family climate and the role of the child in family violence on the overall degree of deviancy, neither of the other two variables needs to be considered. The regression coefficients show that children who are rejected by their parents and who are also abused by their parents are the most deviant. Together these two variables explain more than 32% of the variation in the overall degree of deviancy, with family climate being a better predictor than the child's role in family violence.

TABLE 19 MULTIPLE REGRESSION OF OVERALL DEGREE OF DEVIANCY ON FAMILY CLIMATE AND THE CHILD'S ROLE IN FAMILY VIOLENCE

(N=138)

Variable	Regression Coefficient (B)	Standard Error of B	F
Intercept	-0.54863		
Family Climate	0.77127	0.12601	37.460***
Child's Role in Family Violence	0.38102	0.12665	9.051**

Multiple R ------------------------------ .57312***
Percentage of variance explained ------- 32.85
** Significant at the .01 level
*** Significant at the .001 level

TABLE 20 MULTIPLE REGRESSION OF OVERALL DEGREE OF DEVIANCY ON FAMILY CLIMATE, PATERNAL VS. MATERNAL ABUSER, AND INDICATION OF ABUSE FOR THE 87 CHILDREN ABUSED BY THE FATHER OR FATHER SUBSTITUTE ONLY OR THE MOTHER ONLY

Variable	Regression Coefficient (B)	Standard Error of B	F
Intercept	-1.05275		
Family Climate	0.74810	0.14452	26.795***
Paternal vs. Maternal Abuser	0.41375	0.13891	8.972**
Indications of Abuse	0.21402	0.10810	3.920*

Multiple R ---------------------- 0.61825***
Percentage of Variance Explained ----- 38.22
*Significant at the .05 level
**Significant at the .01 level
***Significant at the .001 level

Table 20 gives the results of the regression analysis for those 87 children who were abused either by their father or father substitute only or by their mother only. The results indicate that of the variables family climate, paternal vs. maternal abuser, indications of abuse and indications of neglect, only the first three of these need to be considered in predicting the overall degree of deviancy. The regression coefficients indicate that abused children who exhibit the greatest degree of deviancy are those who are rejected by their parents, who are abused by their mothers and undergo the most serious abuse. Together these three variables explain more than 38% of the variance in the overall degree of deviancy, with the family climate again being the best predictor.

DISCUSSION

In accepting our hypotheses concerning causal relationships among the rol of the child in abuse, parental attitudes toward the child and the extent to whiich the child is socially and psychologically deviant, the following linkages were established:

1. Children who are bystanders to sibling abuse or wife abuse are significantly less deviant than are children who are victims of abuse.
2. Deviance varies among abused children depending on who does the abusing and on whether or not there are some positive features in the child's relationship with at least one parent.

We shall examine dynamics underlying these two assertions.

The bystanders — An examination of characteristics of the 24 bystanders to sib abuse and the 25 bystanders to wife abuse in our sample reveals important differences between the two groups. Although 80% of the bystanders to child abuse experience a positive or ambivalent family climate, they live with the knowledge that at any time they too may be battered and rejected if they incur the wrath of a violent parent. These children appear to have solved the problem of survival in a dangerous environment by strict conformity to parental demands and by developing the ability to get out of the way when trouble is brewing. These are good children. Not one of them has ever appeared in Juvenile Court or run away, and only a very few are described by their caseworkers as involved in lying and cheating (4.2%), stealing (4.2%), truancy (4.2%), vandalism (8.3%) and fighting (12.5%). Sixty-four percent of the group were judged as having a balanced relationship with parents, with 27% somewhat withdrawn and only 9% somewhat acting out. Seventy-five percent maintain a balanced relationship with sibs and 25% withdraw from them. None of these children act out in their relationship with sibs, probably because quarreling and fighting among the children invites parental anger. With teachers, too, these children are compliant, with 70% maintaining a balanced relationship, 20% somewhat withdrawn and only 10% somewhat acting out. Not only do bystanders to sib abuse have better school deportment than all other groups in the sample, but also they make better grades. Seventy-one percent are average or above average students, while 29% are below average or failing. However, these children who have been able to escape physical assault at the hands of their parents cannot escape the psychological consequences of living in the shadow of violence. Thirty-seven percent are diagnosed by their caseworkers as depressed, 40% as anxious and over 25% have undergone therapy. One wonders whether these children, like many concentration camp inmates or hostages of terrorists, have identified with their abusers because they have been spared. Perhaps they also shun the 'bad' sibs who 'deserve' the punishment which they receive. And perhaps they will grow up believing that passive acquiescence is the only safe stance in a hostile world. We really don't know because these silent witnesses to sib abuse have been largely overlooked by both researchers and clinicians.

The 25 children in the sample who are bystanders to wife abuse present a very different picture. Eighty-eight percent enjoy a reasonably positive relationship with parents. While not highly deviant, their behavior mirrors the adult violence which they observe. Fifty-three percent act out with parents and 60% act out in their interactions with sibs. Outside the violent milieu of the family, they are less provocative and quarrelsome, with only 30% acting out with peers and 33% acting out with teachers. Not surprisingly, these children have a higher rate of social deviancy than do bystanders to sib abuse, with 16% having appeared in Juvenile Court, 20% characterized as truants and 58% rated as below average or failing at school. Like the bystanders to sib abuse, they pay a high psychological price because they are exposed to family violence. They are described by caseworkers as anxious (40.0%) and depressed (48.0%), and 35% have had therapy. It is likely that some of these children will be among the abusing husbands and abused wives of the next generation unless they are given help now.

The Victims — By classifying the victims of child abuse on the basis of the identity of the abuser, we are able to see how both maternal involvement in abuse and total parental rejection are linked to the social and psychological deviance of the victims.

The most extreme deviance in our sample is found within the group of 22 children who are abused by the mother and father (45.0%) or mother and stepfather (55.0%). Roughly three-fourths of these children (72.2%) experience a family climate of total parental rejection. The incidence of severe abuse (68.0%) and the incidence of severe neglect (77.3%) found in this group are the highest of any group in the sample, as is the percentage of children who have serious mental, emotional or physical disabilities (42.9%). It was impossible to determine whether these impairments were antecedents or consequences of abuse. Eighty-six percent of these doubly abused doubly-rejected children exhibit moderate to severe psychological and social deviance. They are the most acting out children in our sample in interaction with sibs (66.7%), peers (75.0%) and teachers (73.4%). They are somewhat less likely to act out with parents (57.1%), but the perilous relationship with the abusers is still surprisingly likely to involve provocative victim behavior. It is important to note that not one of these children was rated as exhibiting a balanced style in total relationships. In all cases school performance is below average or failing. There is a high incidence of Juvenile Court appearances (54.5%) , lying and cheating (45.0%), stealing (50.0%), truancy (45.5%) and vandalism (40.0%). Widespread psychological problems include anxiety (54.4%), depression (50.0%) and hyperactivity (31.1%), with a high proportion undergoing psychiatric hospitalization (27.3%) or therapy (50.1%). For this group the linkages among maternal abuse reinforced by paternal abuse, total parental rejection and the reactive deviance of the victims appear to be well established. These pathological linkages are likely to persist unbroken and indeed to become stronger over time unless massive help is given now.

Members of our second group, victims of abuse by mother only, are somewhat less socially deviant than the victims of abuse by both parents, although their social problems still fall in the moderate range. Of the 38 children in this group, half (51.4%) live with their mothers in one parent families and the remainder live with mother and father (29.7%), or stepfather (8.1%) or paramour (10.8%). Perhaps one reason for the lower rate of social deviance for this group is that children abused by mother only more often live in a family climate where there is some degree of parental acceptance (57.1%) than do children abused by both parents (27.3%). On the other hand, we can expect to find severe psychological deviance because the abusing mothers are the most psychologically and socially damaged of all the adults in our sample (82.3%). They are also severely neglectful (50.0%), and in over half the cases carry the entire responsibility for child rearing alone. In addition, they are the youngest group of parents in our sample, and 55.6% of the children are less than 9 years of age. Thus they are in the early childhood period when a pathological mother-child relationship can be most damaging. Indeed, it is psychological deviance which is most striking in this group. More of these children are withdrawn in interpersonal relationships (35.0%), depressed (58.3%) and anxious (66.7%) than in any other group. Thirty percent have had therapy, and 75% are rated as below average or failing in school. Rates of social deviancy, which are less dramatic numerically but still important in view of the extreme youth of a large part of the group, include juvenile court appearances (22.2%), lying and cheating (38.9%), stealing (25.0%) and fighting with sibs and peers (27.8%).

Finally, we will examine our third group of 34 victims of abuse by father or father substitute only. The abusing males in this group include natural fathers (61.8%), stepfathers (29.4)and mothers' paramours (8.8%). These fathers, in contrast to the abusing mothers discussed above, tend to abuse older children. In 70.7% of the cases, children abused by father are over 9 years of age compared to 44.4% of mother abused children. Abuse from father does not appear to demoralize children to the extent that abuse from mother does but, instead, makes them angry. In 72.2%of the cases of father abuse, as opposed to 45.8% of the cases of mother abuse, the abused children act out in the parent-child relationship. In overall relationship style, only 14.5% of the father abused children are withdrawn, compared to

35.0% of mother abused children. Overall relationship style was rated as balanced for only 10% of children abused by mother while 29.4% of father abused children had a balanced relationship style, the highest percentage of all three abuse groups. What is most interesting about this group is the extremely low rate of social deviance in the areas of appearance in Juvenile Court (5.9%), lying and cheating (11.6%), stealing (8.6%), vandalism (8.6%) and running away (8.6%). Only in school performance, where 90.3% of the children are below average or failing, and in extent of truancy (44.1%) is deviance severe.

These children are slightly less likely to be depressed (41.2%) and much less likely to be anxious (29.4%) than the members of the other two abuse groups. However, over one-third are in therapy (35.3%). One explanation for the relative well being of this group of father abused children lies in the fact that 72.7% of the children live in a family climate in which there is some positive support from parents. A second possible explanation lies in the nature of the abuse. Caseworkers described almost half of these fathers (44.1%) as "stern disciplinarians" who went too far with good intentions. Many of the fathers insisted to workers that they love their children but want to raise them "right." Certainly the aim of social conformity appears to have been achieved except in the area of school performance. However, we do not know whether the high degree of school-related deviance represents a rebellion against achievement goals held by the father or is merely reflective of the low priority of school success in these poorly educated families.

SUMMARY

In summary, we have found that deviance among children in violent families varies depending on the role of the child in abuse, the family climate and identity of the abuser. The children who exhibit the greatest number of socially deviant behaviors are those who suffer abuse from both parents (X 3.5), followed by children abused by mother only (X 1.8), children abused by father only (X 1.3), bystanders to wife abuse (X 0.8) and bystanders to child abuse (X 0.3). It is important to remember that all of the children we studied, bystanders as well as victims, were psychologically harmed to some extent by violence in the home and all need help in order to cope with the milieu in which they live.

FOOTNOTES

1. Data collection with full protection of client confidentiality was approved by the Orange County Department of Social Services. The authors particularly commend the Protective Service Unit for its untiring service to violent families and extend their appreciation to the social work supervisor, Marilyn Tyroler, and the social workers, Effie Kittrell, Roberta Kyle, Teresa Shatterly, and Donna Vail who cooperated in this study.
2. Based on behavioral data obtained from interviews with the social worker, each child was rated on interpersonal scales as being either withdrawn, somewhat withdrawn, balanced, somewhat acting out, or acting out for each type of relationship for which information was available.
3. The overall judgement of interpersonal style was based on the average score of interpersonal style with parents, sibs, peers and teachers or when it was not possi-

ble to determine the child's style in specific relationships, an overall judgement was made. The overall judgment of deviancy was based on a numerical score, degree of deviation from balanced style or, when information was not available to compute this score, the judgement was made after reviewing data on social and emotional deviant behaviors, school performance and interpersonal style. A child was judged to be severely deviant if he/she had been institutionalized for social or emotional deviance and/or had a numerical score of 1.55 or over; a child was judged to be mildly deviant if he/she had exhibited a pattern of withdrawn or acting out behaviors but had not been institutionalized and/or had a numerical score between .46 and 1.54; and children were judged to be within the normal range when they exhibited infrequent or no deviant behavior and/or had a numerical deviance score of .45 or below.

REFERENCES

Ackley, D. A brief overview of child abuse. *Social Casework,* January, 1977, *58,* 21-24.

Becker, W. C., et al. Relations of factors derived from parent interview ratings to behavior problems of five-year olds. *Child Development,* 1962, *33,* 509-535.

Blumberg, M. L. Psychopathology of the abusing parent. *American Journal of Psychotherapy,* January, 1974, *28,* 21-29.

Elmer, E. & Gregg, G. S. Developmental characteristics of abused children. *Pediatrics,* October, 1967; *40;* 596-602.

Gelles, R. G. Child abuse and psychopathology: A sociological critique and reformulation. *American Journal of Orthopsychiatry,* July, 1973, *43,* 611-621.

Gil, D. G. *Violence against children.* Cambridge: Harvard University Press, 1970.

Giovannoni, J. M. & Billingsley, A. Child neglect among the poor: A study of parental adequacy in families of three ethnic groups. *Child Welfare,* April, 1970, *49,* 196-204.

Gladston , R. Violence begins at home. *Journal of the American Academy of Child Psychiatry,* April, 1971, *10,* 336-350.

Green, A. H., Gaines, R. W., & Sandgrund, A. Child abuse: Pathological syndrome of family interaction. *American Journal of Psychiatry,* August, 1974, *131,* 882-886.

Hoffman, M. Power assertion by the parent and its impact on the child. *Child Development,* 1960, *31,* 129-143.

Johnson, B. & Morse, H. A. Injured children and their parents. *Children,* August, 1968, *15,* 147-152.

Justice, B. & Justice, R. *The abusing family.* New York: Human Sciences Press, 1976.

Konopka, G. *Young girls: A portrait of adolescence.* Englewood Cliffs, N. J.: Prentice-Hall, 1976.

Martin, H. The child and his development. In C. H. Kempe & R. E. Helfer (Eds.), *Helping the battered child and his family.* Philadelphia: J. B. Lippincott Co., 1972.

Minuchin, S. *Families and family therapy.* Cambridge: Harvard University Press, 1974.

Moore, J. C. Yo-Yo-children—Victims of matrimonial violence. *Child Welfare,* September-October, 1975, *54,* 557-566.

Morse, C. W., Sahler, O. J. Z., & Friedman, S. B. A three-year follow-up study of abused and neglected children. *American Journal of the Disabled Child,* November, 1970, *120,* 439-446.

Silver, L. B., Dublin, C. C. & Lourie, R. S. Does violence breed violence? Contributions from a study of the child abuse syndrome. *American Journal of Psychiatry,* September, 1969, *126,* 404-407.

Steele, B. F. & Pollock, C. B. A psychiatric study of parents who abuse infants and small children. In R. E. Helfer & C. H. Kempe (Eds.), *The battered child.* Chicago: University of Chicago Press; 1974, 89-133.

Walters, J. & Stinnett, W. Parent-child relationships: A decade review of research. *Journal of Marriage and the Family,* February, 1971, *33,* 70-109.

Young, L. *Wednesday's children.* New York: McGraw Hill Book Co., 1964.

8

A Framework for Family Analysis Relevant to Child Abuse, Neglect and Juvenile Delinquency

PAUL GLASSER & CHARLES GARVIN

The University of Texas and The University of Michigan
Schools of Social Work
Arlington, Texas and Ann Arbor, Michigan

Increasingly social and behavioral scientists and helping professionals realize that classification of problems into discrete and disparate categories has little utility. In addition, it has become apparent that no single theoretical orientation can be expected to explain the totality of any personal or social difficulty; and further, that effective assistance at any level requires a multiplicity of intervention modalities and techniques. For this reason, this paper attempts to develop a multi-theoretical framework for the understanding of personal and social deviance.(1) The framework focuses on the family in the context of its social environment in a way that should be helpful in understanding such dysfunctional behaviors as abuse, neglect, delinquency, crime, emotional disorder of parents and children, as well as some of the relationships among these.

But before more is promised than can be delivered, it must be stated that no single conceptual framework—even a multidisciplinary one—can alone lead to the solution of all problems. This approach gives primary attention to the contemporary social conditions of families rather than internal psychological states resulting from previous experiences. It is focused on developing the kind of analysis that will be useful to the interpersonal change practitioner; and based on the belief that the large number of individuals and families referred to social agencies necessitates the development of short-term intervention methods in the context of presently available agency resources.

The family social situations focused on in this framework are: a) the social psychological (small group) dynamics of family functioning; b) the nature of the situational crisis that precipitate behaviors unacceptable to the community; and c) the relationships between the family and informal and formal neighborhood and community helping systems. The framework will be illustrated by applying it to an understanding of abuse and delinquency and the relationship between these two types of problems. Crucial questions for study of delinquency and abuse will be developed, and implications for new approaches to the prevention and treatment of these two types of socially undesirable behavior will be drawn.

THE CONCEPTUAL FRAMEWORK

Family Functioning (2)

A useful way to conceive family functioning is by its structural components.

Task Force Structure: This refers to who does what within the family unit and how often. Most tasks are the responsibility of the parents, which is usually a full-time job for two adults. Traditional sex role specialization continues to predominate in our culture but in our essentially servantless society, it is expected that one parent will substitute if the other is incapacitated or absent. When one parent is required to perform most of the instrumental and expressive tasks (Parsons and Bales, 1954), he/she may experience a sense of frustration and/or task overload. Some tasks may be almost completely avoided, including not only giving emotional support and attention to children but also providing such basics as food, clothing and shelter, as well as household safety and cleanliness.

Communication Structure: This refers to who conveys verbal and nonverbal messages to whom about what, how often, and in what manner. Parents serve as the channels of communication with the adult world in two ways: first as transmitters of the cultural value system which has previously been internalized by the parent; and secondly, as the child's contact with and representative in the adult world. A large part of the socialization process involves the child seeing the adult world through the eyes and experiences of the parents. Further, to the extent that the child identifies with the family, he or she is likely to internalize parental images of him or her. In addition, the child implicitly understands how others see his/her family. Finally, one of the child's primary means of learning is through imitation (Bandura and Walters, 1964), including how parents communicate. Therefore, inadequate and inaccurate methods of communication between spouses, as well as among parents and children and among siblings is not only likely to be disruptive to the family unit but also to have serious consequences for the functioning of individual family members in the community.

Power Structure: This refers to who influences whom, as well as who makes decisions about what, and how often. The expression of power in the family is essential if the family is to fulfill its functions. However, the way it is expressed is a major factor in determining the nature of relationships among its members. When power is exerted through the use of reward, identification, expert knowledge or legitimate norms, relationships are likely to be positive and the decision-making process more democratic and more satisfying (French and Raven, 1960). On the other hand, if power is coercive, absolute or even tyrannical, some family members are likely to live in a constant state of fear, and some of the legitimation of parents as representatives of society is removed. Or, if power is negated and denied by those responsible for the actions of the total family unit, are inhibited in their ability to make decisions and take responsibility. A balance of power among family members, appropriate to age and tasks performed, is required to maximize family functioning and individual performances in the community.

Affectional Structure: This refers to who likes whom, prefers to spend time with whom, and why, as well as the opposite: who dislikes whom. This dimension has received more attention in the literature than the others.

Children and their parents require love and security in order to adapt and develop in a healthy manner, and unless both get a sufficient amount, all will suffer. In addition, the family must function to provide a safe outlet for negative feelings. But these basic emotions, positive and negative, must have their context, manner and occasion for expression regulated, especially in the modern nuclear family where emotional relationships are intense (Glasser and Navarre, 1964).

But emotional relationships between parents and children are not entirely reciprocal, because of age and power differences in the family. While a child's love is gratifying to the adult, it cannot be seen as supportive but rather demanding in the responsibilities it places on the parent. Support can be received only from one who is equal or greater in power and discrimination. Nor can a child be a socially acceptable outlet for negative emotions to the extent that another adult can. A child's emotional and physical dependency upon the adult makes him or her more vulnerable to possible damage in this kind of situation (Steele and Pollock, 1974). Marital conflict, separation and divorce may confound solutions to these issues because the damage to the parents' self-images may intensify their very need for support and reassurance at a time when increasingly these cannot be met within the family structure.

In small groups, one of the most important devices for regulating members' emotional needs is the presence and influence of others who deter or limit demands harmful to group members or to group cohesion. These persons prevent the intensification of influence of any one individual by balancing it with the influence of others. Parental figures play such roles in families. If one parent is absent or uninvolved, the structural balance is removed. This intensifies the influence of the remaining parent upon the children, while possibly limiting the ability of this parent to withstand demands made by the children. Family members may also transfer to one or more of the remaining members the demands formerly filled by the absent or withdrawn person. This would seem to lead to the following dangers: a) emotional demands upon the children normally met within the marital relationship may prove intolerable and damaging to them because they are unable to give the required emotional support or to absorb negative feeling, or b) the combined needs of the children may be intolerable to the emotionally unsupported parent. Since the emotional requirements of children are very likely to take the form of demands for physical attention or personal service, the remaining parent may be subject to physical as well as emotional overload and exhaustion. These dynamics may often be involved at the onset of personal and family deviance.

Family Crises

Let us turn our attention from family dynamics to the situations and events that influence family functioning, another part of this framework. This analysis draws upon the family crisis literature.

Hill (1958) has provided the following model in family crisis theory: "A (the event)—interacting with B (the family's crisis meeting resources)—interacting with C (the definition the family makes of the event)—produces X (the crisis)." Family events have been classified into at least five different types (3) and the effects of a considerable number of different events upon the family have been studied (4) (Hansen and Hill, 1958). In addition, there has been research on the effects of particular events on individuals; rather than on the family as a small group, but this is not as germane to this paper.

We extend and modify this family model in the following way: Family disorganization, which often has personal deviance as a symptom, is preceeded by three possible types of stressors. First, there are chronic situations in families which serve as continuous stressors, such as poverty or the presence of a handicapped or retarded child. Second, there may be sudden or unanticipated changes in the family's situation, such as unemployment of the chief wage-earner or hospitalization of a family member. The difference between the first and second type of stressor event is the amount of time the family has lived with the situation, and this distinction is an important one.

Some families have learned to cope with chronic stressors, but their coping methods are likely to be responsible for lower and lower levels of family and/or individual organization. On the other hand, sudden or unanticipated changes in the family situation may be evident in almost immediate changes in the family's and its members' coping abilities.

The third type of event is an immediate, behavioral occurence (such as an argument between spouses or a child's perceived bad conduct) which triggers a particular incident of deviance. These types of stressors lead to tension or anxiety for one or more family members, which then is related to both unacceptable behavior on the part of one or more adults or children in the family and disorganization of the total unit.

Burr (1973) has summarized all of the family crisis studies in a recent volume on family theory. A family's vulnerability to the stressor event is dependent upon the family's definition of the seriousness of the change, externalization or blame for the change, the amount of time available to anticipate the change, the positional and personal relationships among the family members, the degree of family integration and the family's adaptability. The family's regenerative power or ability to recover from the disorganization produced by the stressor event is dependent upon the length of time the family experiences disruption; the degree to which families share sentiments, feelings and values; the relative equality of power between spouses; the wife's adjustment to activities outside the home; the couple's marital adjustment; the amount of help available from the extended family; and the amount of help available from other sources. There is considerable overlap among these factors. Two seem of special importance.

All the studies of family crisis to date have found family integration to be central to the family's vulnerability to stress and its ability to recover from it. Family integration very much involves the small group variables described above. For example, the degree of involvement of family members in this small group (Hansen and Hill, 1964), the clarity of role expectations among family members (Cottrell, 1942; Glasser and Glasser, 1966), the presence or absence of role conflict and role incompatibility (Cottrell, 1942; Goode, 1960), and the amount of facilitative interdependence and cooperation among family members (Thomas, 1954), are all relevant.

Similarly, the adaptability component has been found to be central to all of the previous studies. This factor is closely related to such other terms as role flexibility, creativity and creative problem-solving. Since it was first recognized in the marital adjustment studies by Burgess and Wallen (1953), adaptability has grown in prominence in investigations of the family as a small group. It generally refers to the ease with which family members can change roles, or the ways they behave in interaction with each other under changing circumstances. Such role flexibility is highly dependent upon not only anticipatory socialization into roles but also on the nature of the family's structural organization. Family integration and adaptability are also closely related to member consensus concerning this group's goals and values and the means by which they can be achieved.

Families in which members demonstrate deviant behavior may undergo both more stressor events and qualitatively different types of situations than other such groups. By understanding these factors, as well as how a particular type of family organization is both prone to and affected by stressor events, a number of useful clues concerning the prediction of deviance can be provided. Increasingly, it may be possible to determine the variety of ways families can be better organized to deal with such crises and how a therapeutic agent might both prevent them from occurring , as well as facilitate family reorganization when they do take place.

Social Networks (5)

The ability of a family to respond effectively to stressors is dependent not only upon the nature of the event and the organization of the family unit but also the social resources it has available to call upon for aid. This involves the social network, a topic which has been of major interest to social and behavioral scientists only in the last ten years' and which helping professionals have hardly addressed at all. (6) The term refers to a "complex set of interrelationships in a social system (Mitchell, 1969, p. 1);" kith and kin and the agencies and institutions used by a family in a community (Sussman and Burchinal, 1964; Adams, 1970). Analytically, a social network is a specific set of linkages among a defined set of persons (Mitchell, 1969, p. 2; Harary, Norman and Cartwright, 1965). The network is seen as having a **protective** element, directed toward the larger society and away from the nuclear unit, and a **regulatory** element, directed toward the nuclear unit and away from the larger society. Both elements serve as mechanisms of social control, insulating and shielding behavior within the nuclear family from control, scrutiny and stress emanating from the larger society; and intervening when the family or one of its members acts in ways the larger society defines as deviant.

Five major dimensions of the social network have been differentiated:

1. Structure: This refers to the range (number of people and institutions in the network), as well as the connectedness (density) among them (Bott, 1971). The research clearly reveals that the larger the range and the greater the connectedness of the social network of a family, the more likely the family will receive appropriate assistance when needed. It comes as no surprise then that clinical impressions reveal that abuse families and families of delinquents tend to be socially isolated (Giovannoni and Billingsley, 1970; Child Abuse and Neglect: A Report on the Status of Research., 1974).

2. Interactional Characteristics: These are used to describe the quality of the relationships among the members of a social network, and this affects how and when the network may be used by a particular family. It includes a) the similarity of persons within the network to each other (homogeneity) (Newcomb, 1961; Freedman, Carlsmith and Sears, 1970); b) the length of time persons within the network know each other; c) the frequency of contact among persons in the network (Homans, 1950); d) the geographic proximity (relative availability) of persons within the network (Festinger, Schacter and Back, 1950; Newcomb, 1961; Whyte, 1956; Dailey and Bersheid, 1967; Mirels and Mills, 1964); e) the stability of relationships among those in the network, which is closely related to geographic mobility (Adams, 1964; Litwak, 1960; Sussman and Burchinal, 1964); f) the perceived equity (nature of reciprocity) among individuals in the network; g) the degree of obligation people feel for each other in the network (Mauss, 1954); and h) the degree of balance or actual equity among members of the network (Heider, 1958; Cartwright and Harary, 1965; Newcomb, 1961; Harary, 1959). These factors are relevant for determining whether a family's social network hinders or helps in its adaptation to its environment, whether it can be called upon for aid in times of crisis and how it may be used to assist a family during a crisis.

3. Institutional Embeddedness: This dimension refers to institutions in which the family's social network is anchored, such as kinship, neighborhood, friendship, occupation, voluntary organization or professional. Numerous studies reveal that the extended family continues to be the most important social network for the majority of nuclear units in this country (Adams, 1968; Sussman and Burchinal, 1964; Dotson, 1951; Axelrod, 1956; Croog, Lipson and Levines, 1972; Dow, 1965; Hayes and Mindel, 1973; McAllister, Butler and Lee, 1973; Gibson, 1972; Warren and Clifford, 1975). Among the services performed by the extended family are child care, health care, financial aid and living accommodation during trips. However, studies indicate that different types of problems lead to less extensive use of some parts of the social network and more extensive use of other parts.

4. Shared Values: The more values are shared among the participants in a network, the more likely it is to be helpful to each. Two particular values are of special importance for our purposes: Privacy vs. involvement and protectiveness vs. independence. These affect the ways networks influence the social control of the family. For example, a network high on involvement and protection will supply both regulatory and protective functions to the family. A network low on these will offer little regulation and protection.

5. Utilization: This refers to the specific ways particular segments of the network are used by a family. This knowledge is essential for the practitioner who wishes to make use of the network in the helping process. It distinguishes those who may be helpful with financial concerns, employment and occupational issues, health, legal and political areas, child rearing and child care, etc., and how this aid may be put to use for the family in trouble.

Summary

These sets of variables, and the relationships among them, are portrayed in Figure 1. As can be seen in that illustration of our model, stressor events are presumed to act on the family's functioning in ways mediated by the family structure and network. The service system in turn, can have an effect upon the events, the mediating variables or the family's functioning itself.

UNDERSTANDING ABUSE, NEGLECT AND DELINQUENCY

Definitional Problems

One of the first difficulties to be faced is the ambiguity in meaning for each of these terms. How do we distinguish between the commitment of an offense, apprehension, prosecution and a finding which leads to some form of community intervention for the individual and/or the family, especially since we know the last three factors but not necessarily the first (Rodman and Grams, 1967; Toby, 1967). In addition, we are dealing with two very different systems, which process clients differently because they have relatively different aims. In abuse and neglect the primary purpose of the community agency is protection of the child and rehabilitation of the family, so that less than 15% of all cases go to court nationally and there are very few criminal prosecutions (Helfer and Kempe, 1974). In delinquency the primary goal is protection of the community and secondarily rehabilitation of the child, and a very high number of apprehended children are prosecuted (Task Force on Juvenile Delinquency, 1967). Further, it is known that more than 90% of all children receive physical punishment at some time during the child's growth and more than half of all children receive injuries as a result (Straus, Gelles and Steinmetz, 1973). Similarly, almost all children violate the law at some time before they are eighteen. For this reason this discussion will focus on individuals who are apprehended for either abuse or neglect or delinquency.

In general child abuse refers to "nonaccidental physical or mental injury, sexual abuse, or maltreatment;" child neglect is defined as "negligent treatment including failure to provide adequate food, clothing, shelter or medical care by a person responsible for the child's health or welfare." (7) These definitions are quite vague, and in practice apprehension varies considerably from one place to another based on community standards.

Delinquency usually refers to a violation of the law by someone under the age of eighteen. This definition also is problematic since some laws apply only to minors—status offenses—and would not result in a criminal charge if committed by an adult. Typical examples are "truancy," "promiscuity," "curfew violation," "running away," "using profanity," "growing up in idleness" and "incorrigibili ty" (Sarri, 1975, p. 3). These examples make clear that status offenses refer both to specific behaviors and to general character or personality characteristics. Many are catchalls for a youth's alleged pattern of stubbornness or rebelliousness against authority. The state often believes it necessary to intervene in order to constrain such adolescent development. Other types of delinquent acts will be referred to as criminal acts, that is, those for which adults also would be prosecuted.

FIGURE 1 GENERAL MODEL

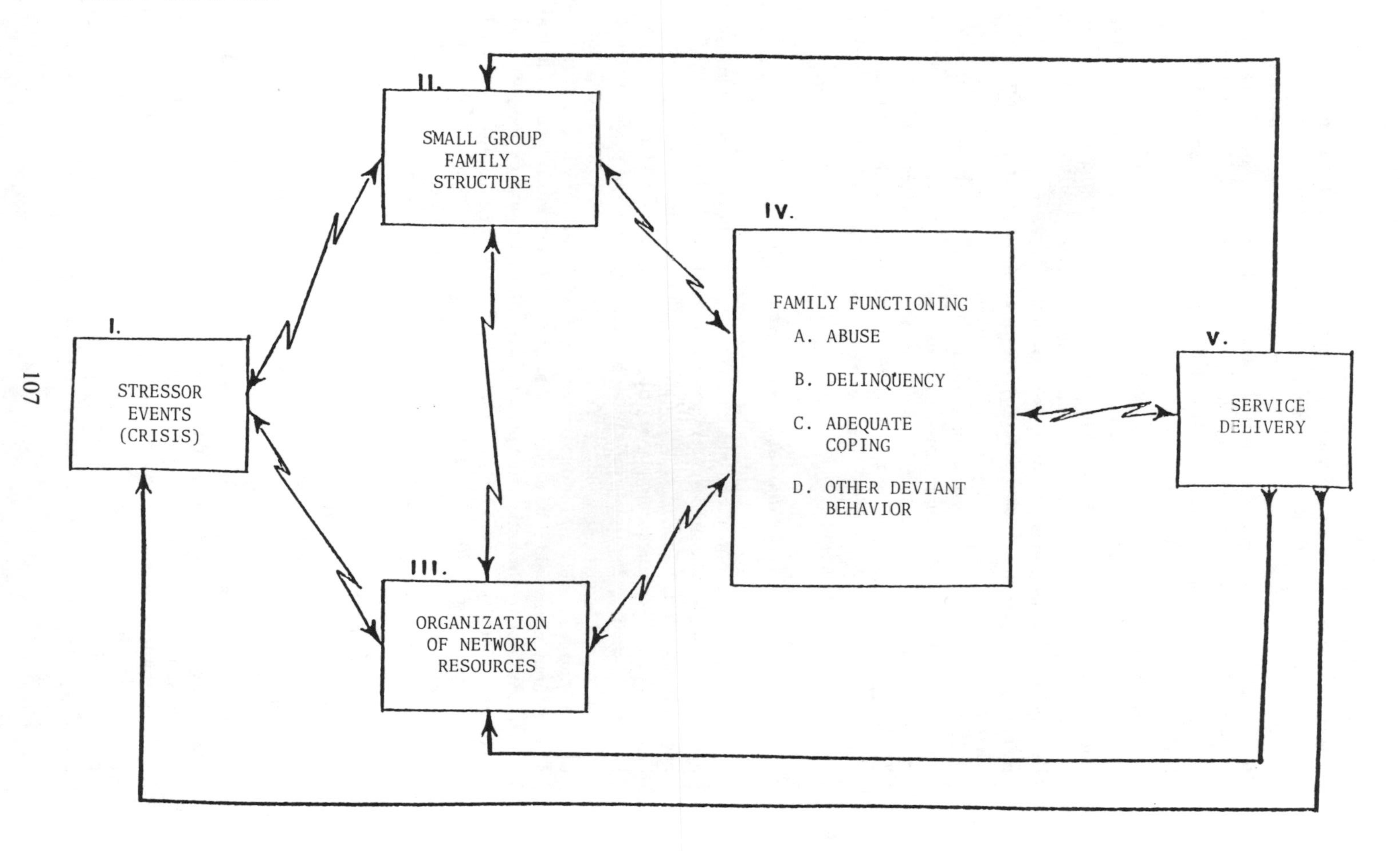

It is fairly apparent that child abuse and neglect and delinquency are likely to be closely connected and inter-dependent. Some delinquency offenses, such as truancy, are likely to relate to violations of abuse and neglect laws as well. In addition, in some localities, it is much easier to adjudicate a case for delinquency than abuse or neglect, and therefore, with the rationale of protecting the child, he/she is made a ward of the court for a status offense instead of challenging the parents. But, most importantly, most status offenses, like running away or incorrigibility, are responses to the abuse of children (physical and emotional) by parents, and therefore involve serious family problems (Sarri, 1975; Barton, Isenstadt and Selo, 1976). Therefore, status offenses and child abuse are seen as interrelated in the discussion that follows.

Criminal offenses of children and child neglect also seem somewhat related, although this connection is not found as often in the literature. However, from the point of view of the conceptual framework presented in this paper it is proposed that a link exists.

Before turning to the analysis of these relationships in the next section it must be pointed out that the literature related to abuse, neglect and delinquency and the family is quite speculative and too often based on clinical judgments rather than well controlled studies (Jayartne, 1977; Hirschi, 1969, Rodman and Grams, 1967). Under these circumstances the framework is useful primarily for generating hypotheses rather than explicating findings.

Abuse and Status Offenses (8)

The dynamics of family life in which these two types of inter-connected problems are present is likely to be similar. Members are probably highly involved in the family group with strong bonds of affection among some of them. However, there may be a considerable conflict among sub-groups and/or some of the relationships may be dysfunctional or disturbed, preventing adequate growth and personal freedom for a parent and some or all children. Yet, there is likely to be high interdependence of tasks, and task overload for one or two members. Power may not be distributed appropriately nor would it be expected that there will be democratic decision making. Instead one might anticipate absolute or tyrannical power on the part of one member, although this need not be pressed overtly or necessarily under the control of the child abuser. Communication among some family members, particularly among individuals in some subgroups; will be considerable, but poor between subgroups, and often distorted. Thus, integration will be high for sub-units but low between subgroups. Adaptability to change is likely to be low, particularly family and individual developmental changes. Thus, we see a family in which there is high involvement but also high levels of individual frustration by some members who are unable to meet new and developing needs. The result is abuse of some members out of frustration, or behavior defined as status offense in rebellion against inappropriate demands by an authority with whom it is difficult to deal.

These families may often be viewed by the community as functioning adequately. Their network range is probably typical of other families, but the density is low. Further, some of their relationships in the network may be dysfunctional; for example, a symbiotic affinity between a married daughter and her mother which is disruptive of the husband-wife bond. Further, the network may often place a high value on privacy and independence. For all these reasons it cannot effectively intervene when a crisis occurs, and the family's lack of adaptability and flexibility make it more prone to stressor events than other families. Then when these situations occur, the organizational problems of the family unit may come to the surface—what was covert becomes overt and abuse or behavior indicative of status offenses are brought to the attention of the community. This is particularly so if the family has a history of violence, which often is covered up and kept secret.

Neglect and Criminal Acts

The dynamics of these families are hypothesized to be relatively different. Affectional bonds are likely to be relatively weak, and there is little attempt to meet the physical or emotional needs of its members. Not all tasks are carried out or performed responsibly, and therefore there is little interdependence among members, although one or more members may be assigned tasks which are an overload. Power tends to be abdicated rather than authoritarian, and little formal or rational decision making takes place. Communication among members of the unit is low and probably ineffective. Integration is low, as is adaptability, since the unit has few organizational resources to deal with change.

Both the range and density of the social network of such families can be expected to be low. The exception is the adolescent peer group, which in many ways is used by the teenager as a means for meeting needs not satisfied in the family itself. These families may be seen by the community as strange over a long period of time. Some may have been the object of services by formal health and welfare agencies for many years, which the family may view as a punishing response from the network, and leads them to try to avoid outside interference. Many of these families may have had to deal with chronic stressor events over a long period, coping with them at a barely adequate level. They may be brought to the attention of the authorities either because their coping abilities have become less and less or a new situation takes them over the brink. These tend to be isolated families in which children must seek personal satisfactions outside, and in communities in which criminal behavior is relatively normative, the teenager is prone to gang delinquency and/or alcohol and drug addiction. In middle class localities the adolescent gang may be motivated by the search for excitement since he or she is unable to find satisfaction in the home. The result may be criminal behavior. These two sections are summarized in the table that follows.

Time Sequence

What has been described are ideal family types, with the assumption that 'normal' families are well organized and well integrated internally, as well as with a wide and dense network. Further, the more typical family is adaptable to both developmental and outside stressor events. Finally, such families undergo fewer stressor situations, and these are qualitatively different from the two types described above.

There is a difference in developmental stages between families in which there is child abuse and those in which there is apprehension for a status offense by an adolescent. A similar time difference is found between the family apprehended for neglect and charges of a criminal act against a minor. The family accused of abuse and neglect will tend to be at an earlier stage of development than the family which has a teenager charged with delinquency. Thus, there is the hypothesis that abuse

TABLE 1 A COMPARISON OF ABUSE, NEGLECT AND DELINQUENCY PRONE FAMILIES

Patterns of Family Functioning	Abuse and Status Offenses	Neglect and Criminal Acts
Most Important Type of Stress	Acute	Chronic
Personal Involvement In Family Group	High	Low
Conflict Among Sub-groups	High	Low
Task Interdependence	High	Low
Task Overload	Varied - for some	Varied - for some
Democratic Decision Making	Absent	Absent
Power Distribution	Absolute and/or Tyranical By One or Two Members	Abdicated By Most or All Members
Communication	High Within Sub-Groups But Low Across Sub-Groups	Low Among All Members
Adaptability to Change	Low	Low
Network Range	Normative or Typical	Low Except for Delinquent Subculture
Network Density	Low	Low Except for Delinquent Subculture
Network Relationships	Dysfunctional	Isolated

may be a source of the development of status offense violations while neglect may be closely associated with the initiation of criminal behavior by minors.

INTERVENTION

Many authors have pointed to the need for social policies that reduce stress in the family (Gil, 1970; Rodman and Grams, 1967). Full employment, better services to families with children who are physically and mentally handicapped and other such programs will be effective in reducing all of the problems discussed in this paper.

But beyond that, how might this analysis be helpful to the interpersonal practitioner required to work with families identified with one of the four categories of problems? Families suspected of child abuse or in which a child is apprehended for a status offense have members committed and involved in the unit, albeit some of the relationships may be disturbed and distorted. With this in mind, some form of intensive family therapy which makes use of the social network may be the preferable treatment approach. On the other hand, families suspected of neglect or in which there is criminal behavior by a minor are not likely to have high member involvement or commitment to the unit or any extensive social network. In many ways they may be more difficult to deal with. The formal agencies in the community may have to expend considerable effort in reaching out to these families with the provision of a variety of services to demonstrate that they care. The use of paraprofessionals such as homemakers, parent aides and big brothers may be particularly helpful in such situations. (9)

Space does not permit more specific suggestions. However, analysis of specific families through the use of each of the sub-categories under each of the major variables will provide more specific interpersonal intervention possibilities.

CONCLUSION

The purpose of this paper has been to provide a multi-disciplinary conceptual framework for the analysis of child abuse, child neglect and delinquency. This was followed by the application of the concepts to an understanding of these personal and social problems, in which comparisons were made between family functioning and social networks of child abusers and status offenders versus child neglecters and minor criminal offenders. The paper ended with some implications for interpersonal practice.

FOOTNOTES

1. This framework was developed as part of a doctoral seminar on child abuse and neglect in the Ph.D. Program in Social Work and Social Science at the University of Michigan School of Social Work, and became part of a research proposal submitted and approved by the National Institutes of Mental Health. The authors are indebted to all of the students and faculty who participated in this effort.
2. The authors wish to thank Kathleen Faller who did much of the literature review for this section.
3. These are (a) external, such as a flood, a tornado, or unemployment; (b) dismemberment only, such as death of a spouse or child, or separation due to hospitalization or military service; (c) accession only, such as an unwanted pregnancy, a new step-parent in the home, adding a grandparent to the home, adoption; (d) demoralization only, such as incidents of infidelity, alcoholism, drug addiction, or delinquency; and (e) combined events, such as illegitimacy, desertion, divorce, imprisonment of a spouse, suicide or homicide. In terms of our model any of these events can be either chronic or unanticipated stressors.
4. These have included the effects of unemployment during the depression (Angell, 1936; Cavan and Ranck, 1938), war, separation and reunion (Hill, 1949), death (Eliot, 1960), the birth of a retarded child (Farber, 1960), the birth of a premature child (Kaplan, 1964), divorce (Goode, 1956) and mental illness (Glasser, 1963; and Glasser and Glasser, 1966).

5. The authors wish to thank Bennett Wolper who did much of the literature review for this section.
6. The first major study in recent times which served to stimulate much that has come along since then was by Bott, 1971. This is a review of all of her previous work.
7. This definition is taken from Enrolled House Bill No. 4214, State of Michigan, Seventy-Eighth Legislature, Regular Session of 1975. It is very similar to that found in the legislation in other states and in much of the literature.
8. The next two sections can be considered a series of hypotheses based upon a review of the literature relevant to the framework, child abuse and neglect and delinquency.
9. The treatment literature relevant to this discussion is enormous, and therefore a bibliography cannot be provided. A number of summaries are available however, such as Olson, 1976.

REFERENCES

Adams, B. Isolation, function and beyond: American kinship in the 1960's. In Broderick (ed.), *A decade of family research and action.* Minneapolis: National Council on Family Relations, 1970.

Adams, B. *Kinship in urban settings.* Chicago: Markham, 1968.

Adams, B. Structural factors affecting paramental aid to married children. *Journal of Marriage and the Family,* 1964; *26,* 327-331.

Angell, R. C. *The family encounters the depression.* New York: Scribner, 1936.

Axelrod, M. Urban structure and social participation. *American Sociological Review,* 1956, *21,* 13-18.

Bakke, E. W. *The unemployed worker.* New York: Yale University Press, 1940.

Bandura, A. & Walters, R. H. *Social learning and personality development.* New York: Holt, Rinehart & Winston, 1964.

Barton, W., Isenstadt, P. & Selo, E. *Analysis of data on status offenders in correctional programs.* U.S. DHEW Project 100-76-0081 Report, Ann Arbor, Michigan, 1976, mimeographed.

Bott, E. *Family and social network: Roles, norms, and external relationships in ordinary urban families.* (2nd ed.) New York: The Free Press, 1971.

Cartwright, D. & Harary, F. Structural balance: A generalization of Heider's theory. *Psychological Review,* 1956, *63,* 227-293.

Cavan, R, S. & Ranck., K. H. *The family and the depression.* Chicago: University of Chicago Press, 1938.

Cottrell, L. S., Jr. The adjustment of the individual to his age and sex roles. *American Sociological Review,* 1942, *7,* 617-620.

Croog, S. L. & Levines, A. Help patterns in severe illness. *Journal of Marriage and the Family,* 1972, *34,* 687-693.

Dailey, J. M. & Bersheid, E. Increased liking caused by the anticipation of personal contact. *Human Relations,* 1967, *20,* 29-40.

Dotson, F. Patterns of voluntary association among urban working class families. *American Sociological Review,* 1951, *16,* 687-693.

Dow, T. Families' reaction to crisis. *Journal of Marriage and the Family,* 1965, *27,* 363-370.

Eliot, T. D. Adjusting to the death of a loved one. In R. Cavan (ed.), *Marriage and family in the modern world.* New York: Crowell, 1960.

Farber, B. Family organization and crisis. *Monograph of Social Research and Child Development,* 1960, *25,* No. 75.

Festinger, J., Schacter, S. & Back, K. *Social pressure in informal groups: A study of human factors in housing.* New York: Harper & Row, 1950.

Freedman, J., Carlsmith, M. J. & Sears, P. O. *Social psychology.* Englewood Cliffs, N. J.: Prentice-Hall, 1970.

French, J. R. P., Jr. & Raven, B. The bases of social power. In Cartwright & Zander (eds), *Group dynamics, research and theory.* Evanston, Illinois: Row, Peterson & Co., 1960.

Gibson, Kin family network. *Journal of Marriage and the Family,* 1972, *34,* 12-23.

Gil, D. G. *Violence against children.* Cambridge: Harvard University Press, 1970.

Giovannoni, J. & Billingsley, A. Child neglect among the poor: A study of parental adequacy in families of three ethnic groups. *Child Welfare,* April, 1970, 196-204.

Glasser, P. H. Changes in family equilibrium during psychotherapy. *Family Process,* 1963, *2,* 245-264.

Glasser, P. H. & Navarre, E. Structural problems of the one-parent family. *Journal of Social Issues,* 1964, *21,* 98-109.

Glasser, P. H. Glasser, L. N. Adequate family functioning. In I. M. Cohen (ed.), *Family structure, dynamics and therapy, psychiatric research report #20. Washington, D. C.: American Psychiatric Association, 1966.*

Goode, W. After divorce. Glencoe, Illinois: Free Press, 1956.

Goode, W. J. A theory of role strain. *American Sociological Review,* 1960, *25,* 488-496.

Hansen, D. & Hill, R. Families under stress. In Christensen (ed.), *Handbook of marriage and the family.* Chicago: Rand-McNally & Co., 1964.

Harary, F. On the measurement of structural balance. *Behavioral Science,* 1959, *4,* 316-323.

Harary, F., Norman, R. Z. & Cartwright, D. *Structural models and introduction to the theory of directed groups.* New York: Wiley, 1965.

Hayes, W. & Mindel, C. Extended kinship relations in white and black families. *Journal of Marriage and the Family,* 1973, *35,* 51-57.

Heider, F. *The psychology of interpersonal relations.* New York: Wiley, 1958.

Helfer, R. E. & Kempe, C. H. *The battered child.* (2nd ed.) Chicago: University of Chicago Press, 1974.

Hill, R. *Families under stress.* New York: Harper, 1949.

Hill, R. Generic features of families under stress. *Social Casework,* 1957, *39,* 139-150.

Hirschi, T. *Causes of delinquency.* Berkeley: University of California Press, 1969.

Homans, G. C. *The human group.* New York: Harcourt, Brace & World, 1950.

Jayartne S. Child abusers as parents and children: A review. *Social Work,* 1977, *22* (1), 5-9.

Kaplan, D. M. Problem conception and planned intervention, In *Health and disability concepts in social work education.* Minneapolis: U.S. DHEW, 1964, 5-15.

Komarovsky, M. *The unemployed man and his family.* New York: Dryden Press, 1940.

Litwak, E. Geographic mobility and extended family cohesion. *American Sociological Review,* 1960, *25,* 385-394.

Mauss, M. *The gift.* London: Cohen & West, 1954.

McAllister, R. J., Butler, E. W. & Lee, T. Patterns of social interaction among families of behaviorally retarded children. *Journal of Marriage and the Family,* 1973, *35,* 93-100.

Mirels, H. & Mills, J. Perception of the pleasantness and competence of a partner. *Journal of Abnormal and Social Psychology,* 1964, *68,* 456-460.

Mitchell, J. C. The concept and use of social networks. In J. C. Mitchell (Ed.), *Social networks in urban situations: Analysis of personal relationships in central African towns.* Manchester: Manchester University Press, 1969.

Newcomb, T. *The acquaintance process.* New York: Holt, 1961.

Olson, D. H. L. *Treating relationships.* Lake Mills, Iowa: Graphic Publishing Co., Inc., 1976.

Parsons, T. & Bales, R. F. *Family socialization and interaction processes.* Glencoe, Illinois: The Free Press, 1954.

Rodman, H. & Grams, P. Juvenile delinquency and the family: A review and discussion. In *Juvenile delinquency and youth crime: Report on juvenile justice and consultant papers.* Washington, D.C.: U.S. Government Printing Office, 1967.

Sarri, R. Adolescent 'status offenders'—A national problem. Paper prepared for the Child Welfare League of America and the Children's Bureau of the U.S. Department of Health, Education, and Welfare, Ann Arbor, Michigan, 1975, mimeographed.

Steele, B. F. & Pollack, C. B. A psychiatric study of parents who abuse infants and small children. In R. Helfer & C. H. Kempe (eds.), *The battered child.* Chicago: University of Chicago Press, 1974.

Straus, M. A., Gelles, R. J. & Steinmetz , S. K. *Theories, methods and controversies in the study of violence between family members.* University of New Hampshire, June, 1973, mimeographed.

Sussman, M. & Burchinal , L. Kin family network, unheralded studies in current conceptualizations of family functioning. *Journal of Marriage and the Family,* 1964, *24,* 231-240.

Task Force on Juvenile Delinquency. The administration of juvenile justice—The juvenile court and related methods of delinquency control. In *Juvenile delinquency and youth crime: Report on juvenile justice and consultant papers.* Washington, D.C.: U.S. Government Printing Office, 1967.

Thomas, E. Effects of facilitative role interdependence on group functioning. *Human Relations,* 1957, *10,* 347-366.

Toby, J. Affluence and adolescent crime. In *Juvenile delinquency and youth crime: Report on juvenile justice and consultant papers.* Washington, D.C.: U.S. Government Printing Office, 1967.

U.S. Department of Health, Education, and Welfare, Office of Human Development, Office of Child Development. *Child abuse and neglect: A report on the status of the research.* DHEW Publications No. (OHD) 74-20, 1974.

Whyte, W. H., Jr. *The organization man.* New York.: Simon & Schuster, 1956.

9

Child Abuse and Juvenile Delinquency: The Developmental Impact of Social Isolation

JAMES GARBARINO

Fellow, Research Division
Center for the Study of Youth Development
Boys Town
Omaha, Nebraska 68144

As part of a series of articles titled "Radical Perspectives on Social Problems" Steven Pfohl (1977) spoke of "The 'Discovery' of Child Abuse." Pfohl's analysis highlights the role of social and cultural forces in defining phenomena as "problems." This process operates in at least two distinct forms. In the first, a change in the conditions of social life or in the behavior of individuals is defined as self-evidently a "problem." In the minds of much of the professional and public communities, for example, recent alterations in the composition and structure of families indisputably constitute a social problem. As a colleague is fond of pointing out, however, there has been a marked change in the proportion of children growing up without a horse in their backyard, and there is little public or professional outcry about the 'problem' of 'horse absent' families. Clearly, change is not itself *prima facie* evidence of a social problem. It is the process of labeling by the public and by professionals that creates problems.

Pfohl, however, addresses the second form of problem definition in which an historical condition is 'discovered' to be a social problem. Child abuse is such a problem. As Radbill (1975) and others have made clear, abuse and neglect have been dominant themes in the history of children—particularly in Western societies. Child abuse as a social problem is a relatively recent 'discovery' by the public and professional communities. It is still being conceptually and empirically defined. The purpose of this paper is to aid in that process of definition, and, in so doing, shed some light on the quality of life for children and youth in American society.

CHILD ABUSE AND JUVENILE DELINQUENCY

Many within the field of social science are familiar with Thomas Kuhn's classic essay on "The Nature of Scientific Revolutions" (1962). In that essay Kuhn proposed that the focal point for scientific activity is the creation, maintenance and revision of "paradigms." These paradigms are the way scientists understand and study reality. They are thus the dominant rules for evaluating the legitimacy of both scientists and scientific ideas. While it is not entirely clear that social science actually employs paradigms in the sense that Kuhn uses the term, the concept has great appeal (and at least metaphorical validity) in understanding the study and students of human behavior.

Richard Gelles (1973) wrote an essay, entitled "Child Abuse as Psychopathology: A Sociological Critique and Reformulation," in which he challenged the dominant paradigm in the study of child abuse that stressed parental psychopathology as the overarching cause. He offered a sociologically-oriented model in its place. In the course of that essay Gelles observed that the study of child abuse seemed to be following the route taken by students of juvenile delinquency, an initial formulation stressing moral deficiency, followed by a 'medical' model stressing personality deficit and/or psychopathology. Such medical models have been challenged in many of the fields where they have been applied, e.g., penology (MacNamara, 1977), education (Ginsburg, 1972) and psychiatry (Szasz, 1960). It is instructive for the present purpose to expand upon Gelles' observation and note several similarities between child abuse and juvenile delinquency, both as concepts and as phenomena.

Both child abuse and juvenile delinquency are subject to a variety of definitions and interpretations which bring into play key issues in the sociology of knowledge and the organization of society. How do we respond to behavior which disturbs us, as do both child abuse and juvenile delinquency? While sociologists have elaborated complex theories of 'deviance' to describe, categorize and explain such behavior, their answers are not genuinely convincing to most Americans. Much more in tune with our individualistic ideology are explanations stressing individual moral defect, deficient personality and psychopathology. Our individualistic culture makes us think as psychologists rather than as sociologists.

In addition to this intellectual problem there are several other parallels. Both abuse and delinquency are symptomatic of inadequate personal and social control and cultural deviance (at least when compared with dominant, public norms). Both are also extreme forms of behavior found among the 'normal' population, however. Surveys reveal that many adults can relate personally to child abuse. Gil's (1970) national survey found that 16% of the respondents admitted coming very close to injuring a child in their care and that more than 22% thought they "could at some time injure a child." A recent survey by Gelles, Strauss and Steinmetz (1976) confirms and expands these findings by documenting the widespread prevalence of domestic violence in America. On the other hand, Gold (1963) and others report that many people admit to delinquent acts in their background. Both child abuse and juvenile delinquency are culturally determined labels used to formally identify persons who for a variety of reasons cannot or will not behave within the 'normal' range of physical force against children or youthful anti-social behavior. One of the critical tasks facing students of child abuse and juvenile delinquency is to specify the conditions that place some people outside the normal range of behavior.

There can be little doubt that child abuse and juvenile delinquency are similar in that they are both extreme forms of behavior that occur among the 'normal' population, and involve complex difficulties for research (given their ill defined status, their illegality and their secretive nature). These phenomena cannot be understood without an appreciation for the interaction of the individual and the environmental systems that surround him. This 'ecological' perspective will be elaborated at a subsequent point in the discussion. These parallels are not the whole story by any means, however. There is a second, more substantive, sense in which child abuse and juvenile delinquency are related.

Several direct and indirect linkages exist between abuse and delinquency. Abuse and delinquency can be direct causes of each other. The youth adjudged as a juvenile may be sentenced to an institution in which abuse is present. This is not rare. The theme of the 'crime of punishment' is very real when it comes to juvenile institutions (Wooden, 1976). The juvenile delinquent may likewise be the direct product of child abuse. Many abused children and youth attempt to avoid or escape their parents. In so doing they are likely to become involved in a variety of delinquent behaviors related to their status (unsupervised, uncared for minors), as well as their personal history (inadequate learning of social skills.) They also become highly vulnerable to victimization from all quarters. A second consequence of child abuse (particularly severe physical abuse) is removal of the child from the home. Recent surveys have found from 25% to 50% of the children in foster care are there because of removal for abuse and/or neglect (Fanshel, 1976). Where do such children go? What becomes of them? If institutionalized they are subject to child abuse from 'caretakers' and other inmates. If placed in foster care they are vulnerable to abuse by the foster family (Mnookin, 1973).

In addition to these incidental links, there are two others. We can presume that many delinquents were (and are) abused in their homes. Many studies have documented an association between child abuse and juvenile delinquency (Steele, 1976). As is usual in the study of child abuse, the relationships are often very strong (particularly when retrospective methods are used in institutionally identified samples). Steele (1976) reports a study by Weston in which 82% of the youth within a sample of juvenile offenders were found to have a history of neglect and abuse and 43% had a recollection of being knocked unconscious by one or the other parent. The phrase 'violence breeds violence' rings true.

While abuse may play a substantial role in directly causing delinquency, it is not the focal point of this discussion. Nor is the goal to illuminate the way delinquency can stimulate abuse, e.g., by eliciting harsh punishment for wrongdoing. Rather, the goal here is to explore the *shared* epidemiology of child abuse and juvenile delinquency with an eye to identifying common etiology. As will be shown, this interest has important implications for science, policy and practice as they address the difficult issues of prevention and treatment.

THE NECESSARY AND SUFFICIENT CONDITIONS FOR CHILD ABUSE AND JUVENILE DELINQUENCY

Since the relationship between child abuse and juvenile delinquency is only beginning to receive the serious and systematic attention of scholars, it seems appropriate to go out on a conceptual limb, at least for the sake of stimulating discussion. Such discussion needs the discipline of a presumptuous analysis, particularly in the early stages of investigation, to aid in identifying and defining the important questions in need of answers. For this reason it seems simultaneously presumptuous and obligatory to define the commonalities of child abuse and juvenile delinquency in terms of their shared necessary conditions because specification of necessary conditions is the most radical (in the sense of 'getting to the roots') of intellectual enterprises.

The distinction between necessary and sufficient conditions is of fundamental importance to scientific inquiry and social policy. However, it is elusive and rarely taken seriously outside textbooks and classes in 'the logic and methods of science.' The distinction boils down to this: For any particular sufficient condition to be considered the cause of a specific 'effect' all relevant necessary conditions must be met (Bronfenbrenner and Mahoney, 1975). The absence of required necessary conditions effectively 'disarms' the sufficient conditions.

> ...Within a given set of boundary conditions, x is a sufficient condition, if a change in x produces a change in y ... Necessary means that the effect cannot occur except under the specified condition (Bronfenbrenner and Mahoney, 1975, pp. 6-7).

There are multiple and diverse sufficient conditions for both child abuse and juvenile delinquency. The research literature is full of them. At the risk of oversimplification, however, all can be classified as 'psychopathology' (the small minority of cases), cultural deviance, or ''situationally defined role incompetence.'' Most persons involved in child abuse or juvenile delinquency do so as part of a general pattern of ineffective life management (Garbarino, 1977). They experience the stress of disrupted roles, poor timing and sequencing of important social and personal events, and inadequate socialization to adulthood (Garbarino, in press).

Responsibility is the key to adulthood. This is clear in a recent government advisory panel's discussion of youth as a period of ''transition to adulthood'':

> ...the opportunities for responsible action, situations in which (the person) came to have authority over matters that affected other persons, occasions in which he experienced the consequences of his own actions, and was strengthened by facing them—in short, all that is implied by 'becoming adult' in matters other than gaining cognitive skills (Coleman, et al., 1974).

Adulthood may be usefully defined not primarily as a state of mind or set of personality characteristics, but as a set of interlocking roles that define and assign the responsibilities upon which social habitability depends.

Brim (1958), and Brim and Wheeler (1966) offer a model of socialization that stresses the performance of social roles and is thus useful in the present discussion. His analysis focuses on developing knowledge of role demands, in addition to the motivation and ability to perform those roles. Socialization thus becomes goal directed and context specific (Inkcles, 1966). For our purposes we may adapt this sociologically-oriented approach to yield a kind of operational definition of adulthood in terms of three roles: worker, citizen and procreator (by which we mean both parent and sexual being). The social habitability of the environment of families is dependent upon the responsible performance of these roles. Families are economic and reproductive entities that are at the same time the focal point of the individual's relationship with public institutions. Thus families are built on the roles of worker, procreator and citizen. Such responsible role performance is, in effect, the operational definition of competent adulthood in American society. Moreover, it cannot take place in isolation from potent pro-social support systems.

Responsibilities, obligations and authority do not exist in a free floating contextless state. They are real as they are embodied in patterns of social interaction, in enduring relationships, in short, in social roles. In sociological terms, a role is . . . "a pattern of behavior associated with a distinctive social position ... The ideal role prescribes the rights and duties belonging to a social position (Broom and Selznick, 1968)." Adulthood is thus ideally defined in terms of the ideological description of what the worker, citizen and procreator are. It is operationally defined by the actual social performance of that set of interlocking roles. The gap between the prescriptive (ideal) role and the empirical (actual) roles is a matter of great concern in any assessment of the quality of life in a society. Our specific focus, of course, is on the conditions that produce breakdown in socialization to adulthood as it is expressed in child abuse and juvenile delinquency. Provision for the smooth learning and performance of the roles of adulthood is certainly a prime ingredient in social habitability. Abuse and delinquency are indications of a socially inadequate environment, one which does not provide adequate controls and resources. The individual 'causes' of abuse and delinquency are found in those factors which produce inadequate performance of adult roles (Friedman, 1976; Garbarino, 1977; Parke and Collmer, 1975). They are expressed in poor timing of key developmental events, poor coping skills, deviant attitudes, and the other components of 'ineffective life management skills.' When one examines family biographies characterized by child abuse and juvenile delinquency, one finds the stresses of lives out of control—unwanted pregnancies, incompetent handling of social, emotional and material resources, inadequate empathy, values that doom the individual to interpersonal conflict and a generally 'unwise' pattern of life-course development of which abuse and delinquency are but parts.

With the foregoing discussion of sufficient conditions as a backdrop, identifying necessary conditions is possible. This process begins with the following proposition: **child abuse and juvenile delinquency are fundamentally cultural problems.** They are an outgrowth of our individualistic ethos. Moreover, our science, policy and practice concerning abuse and delinquency also reflect that ideology. The implications of this statement cannot be adequately understood without first briefly outlining an emerging 'ecological model of human development.'

The ecological study of human development begins with several assumptions (Bronfenbrenner, 1977; Garbarino and Bronfenbrenner, 1977) This model is based on four propositions:

1. There is no validity to the concept of 'context-free' or 'pure' human development. Issues of social policy and practice are intrinsic, not tangential, to the study of human development.

2. An adequate understanding of child abuse and juvenile delinquency requires that these phenomena be seen as part of a larger issue, the 'maltreatment of children,' which in turn must be understood in the context of a concern for the 'social habitability' of the environment. Abuse and delinquency are 'indicators' of the quality of life for families and youth.

3. Like all significant human phenomena, child abuse and juvenile delinquency are developmental outcomes resulting from many sources. These outcomes derive from the mutual accommodation and adaptations of organism and environment. This process is the action of multiple systems operating at and between multiple levels. Many of the most important factors are those that operate outside dyads to influence, even control, behavior.

4. A sound model for studying and understanding child abuse and juvenile delinquency must contain a life-span developmental perspective that considers issues of event timing and social change. Programs aimed at prevention and treatment must take into account their ability to 'fix' the enduring relationships of an individual if specific behavioral and/or attitudinal changes are to have lasting impact. Because individual and environment are mutually adaptive there must be social support sufficient to interact positively with individual changes. The congruence of organism and environmental systems over time cannot be discounted, in either direction. Change in one can produce change in the other if it is sufficiently powerful.

With this outline in mind, we need to ask, what is the proper focal point for investigating and dealing with the relationship between child abuse and delinquency? That point is to be found in the operation of support systems in the day-to-day life of youth, for it is here that the conditions necessary for child abuse and juvenile delinquency operate. It is here that science, policy and practice must be addressed to the integrated tasks of comprehension and intervention. The hypothesis emerging from such an analysis is this: **the major necessary condition for child abuse and juvenile delinquency is isolation from potent pro-social support systems.**

The concept of support system has been developed and elaborated by several investigators, among them Gerald Caplan (1975, 1976). In his terms, a support system performs several critical social functions that are relevant to the dynamics of child abuse and juvenile delinquency acting as

> ...continuing social aggregates that provide individuals with opportunities for feedback about themselves and for validations for their expectations about others, which may offset deficiencies in these communications within the large community context...
>
> People have a variety of specific needs that demand satisfaction through enduring interpersonal relationships, such as for love and affection, for intimacy that provides the freedom to express feelings easily and unselfconsciously, for validation of personal identity and worth, for satisfaction of nurturance and dependency, for help with tasks, and for *support in handling emotion and controlling impulses* (emphasis added) (Caplan, 1975, pp. 4-5).

They tell him (the individual) what is expected of him and guide him in what to do. They watch what he does and they judge his performance (Caplan, 1975, pp. 5-6).

The importance of such support systems increases, of course, as a function of the stressfulness of the family's external environment, the individual's values and attitudes, and the sources of stress emanating from within the family itself. These factors have been linked to the maltreatment of children whenever research has been designed to identify them. The 'specialness' of the child (e.g., prematurity, mental retardation, etc.), difficulties in the marital relationship, unemployment, unwanted pregnancy, crowded housing conditions and a myriad of other indicators of stress have been found to be correlates of abuse (Parke and Collmer, 1975), as well as of delinquency (Bronfenbrenner, 1975). The rapidity of changes requiring social adjustment has been seen to be related to the onset of abusive behavior (Justice and Duncan, 1976). This more precise rendering of the social stress hypothesis highlights the interactive nature of the relationship between stress and maltreatment. It is the unmanageability of the stresses that is the most important factor, and that unmanageability is a product of a mismatch between the level of stress and the availability and potency of support systems.

The principal vehicles through which support system functions are accomplished are social networks (Bott, 1951; Cochran, 1977; Mitchell, 1967; Stack, 1974). While the concept of social network has been developed and utilized by sociologists and anthropologists to describe complex communication webs, it has not been applied to the study of developmental issues. Recently, ecologically-oriented students of development have begun to adapt the concept for assessing the support systems for families (e.g., Brassard, 1976; Bronfenbrenner and Cochran, 1976; Cochran, 1977; Collins and Pancoast, 1976; Garbarino, et al., 1977; Tietjen, 1977). These studies are concerned with social networks as both an independent and dependent variable in development.

Cochran (1977) defines the properties of social networks relevant to development as size and diversity of membership, interconnectedness among members, content of activities engaged in, and directionality of contacts (more or less reciprocal). He has begun elaborating their role in the dynamics through which the micro-system of the family is interactively related to the meso-systems of neighborhood, social services, politics, and economy. Studying the social networks of families promises to systematically operationalize the concepts of social isolation and social integration. This is an important advance because it may address the ideological and social isolation which gives rise to abuse and delinquency.

The key is the absence of effective performance of the functions outlined by Caplan. It would be misleading to assume that the 'fault' for social isolation is entirely external to the individual. It becomes necessary to distinguish between lack of social supports and failure to use available supports. While the net result (social isolation) is the same, the implications for policy and practice are quite different. For example, several studies have suggested that the failure to use social supports is common among abusive and neglectful families. Elmer (1967) found such parents particularly anomic—distrusting of and retreating from society. Lenoski (1974) reported that 81% of the abusive families in his sample preferred to resolve crises alone. Young (1964) found abusive parents attempted to prevent their children from forming relationships outside the home.

This is crucial to understanding the connection between abuse and delinquency. What happens when a child is denied adequate involvement in 'normal' social relationships in childhood? One consequence is often a hypersensitivity to anti-social peer pressure in adolescence (Garbarino and Bronfenbrenner, 1976). The key to adequate moral development is "social pluralism"—a balanced web of relationships each competing for the individual's loyalty within a common set of rules governing behavior on fundamental moral issues. Social isolation has the effect of depriving the child of involvement in progressively more complex pro-social support systems. Without these support systems the individual becomes easy prey to both pathogenic stresses and antisocial influences. The social dynamics of abuse and delinquency testify to the importance of social diversity as a bulwark against anti-social deviance. Abuse and delinquency among the affluent are testimony to the fact that while there is some positive correlation between social and material resources, the relationship is far from perfect. Many among the affluent are affected by 'social poverty.'

Alfaro (1976) reports that when the records of abused and neglected children (1952-53) were checked, some twelve or more years later, 30% were found to be delinquent or in need of supervision. If siblings of the index cases were added, the figure reached 62%. The social isolation of families has multiple consequences that may extend across generations. The often repeated statement that "abusing parents were themselves abused as children" may rest upon the intergenerational transmission of social isolation as much as, if not more than, the transmission of defective childrearing practices. Social isolation, like virtually all important human phenomena, is determined by an interaction between the individual and the environment. The "World of Abnormal Rearing" (Helfer and Kempe, 1976) is a social concept as much as it is a psychological one. Indeed, it may be its social implications that control its importance as a factor in human development.

Child abuse and juvenile delinquency can occur only when feedback and support are not being adequately addressed to persons in the role of caregiver either through an absence of structure (i.e., social networks) or through cultural or psychological deviance (e.g., norms of parent-child relations that tolerate or even approve of abuse or antisocial behavior). For the sufficient conditions noted previously to 'cause' abuse or delinquency they must occur in a context that 'permits' the perpetrator-victim dyad to develop and be sustained. Abuse and delinquency feed on privacy (Garbarino, 1976.) Affluent families may appear to be involved in adequate pro-social support systems but in actuality only be protected by their privacy, by an illusion of social involvement that hides a lack of adequate feedback. Where research has been designed to document the role of isolation from support systems in child maltreatment, it has consistently done so (Friedman, 1976).

COMPREHENSION AND INTERVENTION: IMPLICATIONS FOR SCIENCE, POLICY AND PRACTICE CONCERNING CHILD ABUSE AND JUVENILE DELINQUENCY

"I hate the son-of-a-bitch, but I don't beat him up anymore."

—comment by a member of Parents Anonymous

"I'm no goody-goody but I ain't been in trouble since I quit hanging out and joined this group."

—comment by an anonymous youth participating in a church-sponsored group

While the connections between child abuse and juvenile delinquency are many and diverse, it is their shared necessary condition that promises to advance the cause of science, policy and practice. The conceptual beauty of necessary conditions for the purpose of policy and practice is that, by dealing with them, one can effectively disarm the sufficient conditions. It is possible to experience aggressive psychopathology or incompetence in key roles without producing child abuse or juvenile delinquency if there is an enduring and intensive pro-social support system to observe and reinforce behavior (both positively and negatively). That is the point of the statements by a 'reformed' abuser and delinquent, cited above. Neither has changed his 'personality' (as it is understood by conventional psychodynamic thinking), but in both cases their behavior has been controlled through involvement in a potent, pro-social support system.

Social isolation is the villain in this piece, aided and abetted by the individualistic ethos that legitimized unbridled privacy in law and custom and that attributes both failure and success preeminently to the solitary individual (Garbarino, 1977b). Our overarching goal should be to reduce social isolation. This is the agenda for science, policy and practice. What does this mean programmatically?

When put this way, the answers are easily seen, although they are complex and difficult to implement. These answers pertain to several levels of analysis.

1. At the neighborhood level, we would focus our attention and resources on the identification and encouragement of 'natural neighbors' who can identify isolated families and intervene to create support system relationships (Collins and Pancoast, 1976). Such people do exist already. The role they fill should be developed and elaborated to provide an important component of the social infrastructure necessary for potent, pro-social support systems to operate.

2. At the level of formal human service delivery systems, we should focus our treatment programs on the creation of enduring pro-social personal support systems. Examples include Parents Anonymous groups for parents (Helfer and Kempe, 1976) and involvement in pro-social peer groups for adolescents (Feldman, 1974). These programs provide a lifeline and a social web to support and control individuals experiencing the sufficient conditions for abuse and delinquency. Our preoccupation with the individual blinds us to the wide range of behavioral outcomes possible for any given configuration of personality and attitudes. The location of an individual's behavior within the range of possibilities depends upon the surrounding social structure. Treatment programs can build a web of relationships that suppress abuse and delinquency without necessarily 'reforming' the individual. This social 'first aid' can be supplemented by activities that teach new skills designed to improve life management and the performance of adult roles. The Teaching-Family Model exemplifies this approach (Phillips, et al., 1971).

3. We can focus educational efforts on socialization to adulthood by emphasizing effective life management as it pertains to the key roles of citizen, worker and procreator (Garbarino, 1977a). The schools are one of three key settings in this regard. Schools can do much to train youth for parenthood and citizenship and thus reduce

the joint problems of child abuse and juvenile delinquency. Two other settings that can help are the neighborhood and the health care system.

4. We should develop bureaucratic systems to identify the objective correlates of social isolation, e.g., mobility, disrupted formal relationships, nonparticipation in civic affairs, etc. At present, we institutionally tolerate social isolation, and in some cases even encourage it. This reveals our ambivalence about the relationship of individuals to the collectivity. Our system currently operates on the assumption that a substantial minority of the population are superfluous and that, as long as these marginal people do not cause trouble, their status is not a legitimate public issue. We need a more active, positive institutional commitment to account for all persons. Such an accounting system is intrusive and does 'threaten' the autonomy of individuals. However, it seems a wise alternative to the tyranny of circumstances which damage children and youth through abuse and delinquency. The key is to make this observation as personal as possible (Wynne, 1975). To accomplish this goal we must strive to establish preventive relationships between families and institutions. This requires greater attention to neighborhood level organization, programming and policy. There are many illustrations of this orientation that can be adopted and adapted as needed (Collins and Pancoast, 1976). Enduring interpersonal relationships are the only contexts in which 'personal' observation can be expected to occur. 'Small' settings are the most reliable way to allow such relationships to develop and persist (Garbarino, in press).

5. We need to create public awareness campaigns to promote social integration and combat isolation. This means facing the issue of privacy squarely (Garbarino, 1977b). As Campbell (1976) has demonstrated, psychology and other social sciences have articulated the essentially ideological position that liberation from social constraint is a positive goal. This proposition needs to be countered. A knowledge base documenting the developmental value of social identity is needed. Privacy is the handmaiden of isolation and thus aids and abets child abuse and delinquency.

6. We should use the opportunity afforded by key developmental transitions to assess the family social networks' and routinely insert pro-social relationships where needed. Thus, at birth, entrance to school, change of school (e.g., elementary to secondary) and initiation or change of employment, we should add interested adults to the lives of children, youth and families, particularly in cases where existing forces push toward isolation. A recent study of Henry Kempe and his colleagues (Gray, Cutler, Dean and Kempe , 1977) illustrates the value of this approach. Even isolated families at risk for abuse proved receptive to the insertion of a health visitor into their life at the birth of a child. The start of school is another time when families are ripe for intervention. The key is to define the situation in such a way that the new relationship seems a natural accompaniment to the situational or role transition.

To defuse the multiple sufficient conditions for child abuse and juvenile delinquency, it seems imperative to systematically prevent social isolation. This strategy can be expected to produce a variety of beneficial outcomes, only one of which is controlling the immediate 'causes' of abuse and delinquency. We can all benefit from the sense of identity which derives from social integration. Child abuse and juvenile delinquency are products of personal crisis born of social deprivation. As Campbell (1976) has noted, it is not the material conditions of life which produce a sense of value and personal meaningfulness, but the richness of social relations and personal networks.

The author extends his gratitude to colleagues who read and commented on an earlier draft of this paper: Ann Crouter, Susan Collins, Mary Davis, Deborah Sherman and Anne Garbarino.

REFERENCES

Alfaro, J. Report of the New York State Assembly Select Committee on Child Abuse. *Child Protection Report,* 1976, *2*(l).

Bott, E. *Family and social network.* New York: The Free Press, 1971.

Brassard, J. *The nature and utilization of social networks in families confronting different life circumstances.* Thesis, Cornell University, lthaca, New York, 1976.

Brim, O. *Education for child rearing.* New York: Russell Sage Foundation, 1959.

Brim, O. G., Jr. & Wheeler, S. *Socialization after childhood: Two essays.* New York: John Wiley & Sons, 1966.

Bronfenbrenner, U. The origins of alienation. In U. Bronfenbrenner & M. Mahoney (Eds.), *Influences on human development.* Hinsdale, Illinois: Dryden Press, 1972.

Bronfenbrenner, U. & Mahoney, M. The structure and verification of hypotheses. In U. Bronfenbrenner & M. Mahoney (Eds.), *Influences on human development* Hinsdale, Illinois: Dryden Press, 1972.

Bronfenbrenner, U. & Cochran, M. Thc comparative ecology of human development: A research proposal. Cornell University, Ithaca, New York, 1976, mimeograph.

Bronfenbrenner, U. Toward an experimental ecology of human development. *American Psychologist,* 1977, *32,* 513-531.

Broom, L. & Selznick, P. *Sociology.* New York: Harpr & Row, 1968.

Caplan, G. *Support systems and community mental health.* New York: Behavioral Publications, 1974.

Caplan, G. & Killiea, M. *Support systems and mutual help.* New York: Grune & Stratton, 1976.

Cochran, M. Social networks and social development in childhood. Paper presented at the biennial meeting of the Society for Research in Child Development, New Orleans, March 17-20, 1977.

Coleman, J. S., et al. *Youth: Transition to adulthood.* Chicago: University of Chicago Press, 1974.

Collins, A. & Pancoast, D. *Natural helping networks.* Washington, D.C.: National Association of Social Workers, 1976.

Elmer, E. *Children in jeopardy.* Pittsburg: University of Pittsburg Press, 1967.

Fanshel, D. Computerized information systems and foster care. *Children Today,* 1976, *5*(6), 14-18.

Feldman, R. A. *The St. Louis experiment: Group integration and behavioral change.* NIMH Center for Studies of Crime and Delinquency Research Report Series. Washington, D.C.: U.S. Government Printing Office, 1974.

Friedman, R. Child Abuse: A review of the psychosocial research. In Herner & Company (Eds.), *Four perspectives on the status of child abuse and neglect research.* Washington, D.C.: National Center on Child Abuse and Neglect, 1976.

Garbarino, J. & Bronfenbrenner, U. The socialization of moral judgment and behavior in cross-cultural perspective. In T. Lickona (Ed.), *Moral development and behavior.* New York: Holt, Rinehart & Winston, 1976.

Garbarino, J. & Bronfenbrenner, U. Research on parent-child relations and social policy: Who needs whom? Paper presented at the symposium on Parent-Child Relations: Theoretical, Methodological and Practical Implications, University of Trier, Trier, West Germany, May, 1976.

Garbarino, J. The human ecology of child maltreatment: A conceptual model for research. *Journal of Marriage and the Family.* 1977, *39,* 731-736. (a)

Garbarino, J. The price of privacy: An analysis of the social dynamics of child abuse. *Child Welfare,* 1977, *56,* 565-575. (b)

Garbarino, J. The role of schools in socialization to adulthood. *The Educational Forum,* in press.

Gelles, R. J. Child abuse as psychopathology: A sociological critique and reformulation. *American Journal of Orthopsychiatry,* 1973, *43,* 611-621.

Gil, D. G. *Violence against children: Physical child abuse in the United States.* Cambridge, Mass.: Harvard University Press, 1970 and 1973.

Ginsburg, H. *The myth of the deprived child.* Englewood Cliffs, New Jersey: Prentice-Hall, 1972.

Gold, M. *Status forces in delinquent boys.* Ann Arbor: University of Michigan Press, 1963.

Gray, J., et al. Perinatal assessment of mother-baby interaction. In R. Helger & C. H. Kempe (Eds.), *Child abuse and neglect: The family and the community.* Cambridge, Mass.: Ballinger, 1976.

Inkeles, A. Social structure and the socialization of competence. *Harvard Educational Review,* 1966, *36,* 280-289.

Justice, B. & Duncan, D. F. Life crises as a precursor to child abuse. *Public Health Reports,* 1976, *91,* 110-115.

Kempe, C. H. A practical approach to the protection of the abused child and rehabilitation of the abusing parent. *Pediatrics,* 1973, *51,* 804-812.

Kuhn, T. *The structure of scientific revolutions.* Chicago: University of Chicago Press, 1962.

Lenoski, E. F. Translating injury data into preventive and health-care-services-physical child abuse. Unpublished manuscript, University of Southern California School of Medicine, Los Angeles, 1974.

MacNamara, D. The medical model in correction. *Criminology,* 1977, *14,* 439-448.

Mitchell, J. *Social networks in urban situations.* Atlantic Highland, New Jersey: Humanities Press, 1969.

Mnookin, R. H. Foster care: In whose best interest? *Harvard Educational Review,* 1973, *43,* 599-638.

Parke, R. & Collmer, C. W. Child abuse: An interdisciplinary analysis. In E. M. Hetherington (Ed.), *Review of child development research.* Vol. 5 Chicago: University of Chicago Press, 1975.

Pfohl, S. The 'discovery' of child abuse. *Social Problems,* 1971, *24,* 310-323.

Phillips, E. L., et al. *The teaching family handbook.* Lawrence, Kansas: The University of Kansas Press, 1972.

Radbill, S. A history of child abuse and infanticide. In R. Helfer & C. H. Kempe (Eds.), *The battered child.* Chicago: University of Chicago Press, 1974.

Stack, C. *All our kin.* New York: Harper & Row, 1974.

Steele, B. Violence in the family. In R. Helfer & C. H. Kempe (Eds.), *Child abuse and neglect: The family and the community.* Cambridge, Mass.: Ballinger, 1976.

Szasz, T. The myth of mental illness. *American Psychologist,* 1960, *15,* 113-118.

Tietjen, A. M. *Formal and informal support systems: Services and social networks in Swedish planned communities.* Thesis, Cornell University, Ithaca, New York, 1977.

Wooden, K. *Weeping in the playtime of others: The plight of incarcerated children.* New York: McGraw-Hill, 1976.

Wynne, W. Adolescent alienation and social policy. *Teachers College Record,* 1976, *78,* 33-39.

Wynne, E. Privacy and socialization to adulthood. Paper presented at the annual meeting of the American Educational Research Association, Washington, D.C., March 31, 1975.

Young, L. *Wednesday's children.* New York: McGraw-Hill, 1964.

10

Child Abuse, Cross-Cultural Childrearing Practices and Juvenile Delinquency: A Synthesis

ROBERT J. BENTLEY

The National Testing Service
Durham, North Carolina 27707

Juvenile delinquency, culturally-related childrearing practices and child abuse are topics of perennial interest and concern. Juvenile delinquency, in particular, is of concern as a sub-focus of society's ongoing 'war on crime and delinquency' and general preoccupation with the subject.

'Juvenile delinquency' refers to juvenile crime, violent and property, and 'juvenile status offenses' refers to ungovernability, truancy and running away (*Juvenile Delinquency Annual Report,* 1975-1976). Status offenses require further clarification:

> the distinguishing characteristic of these offenses is that if they were committed by an adult there would be no legal consequence. While the effect of the offenses on society is not as obvious as criminal offenses, the child often suffers permanently damaging legal and emotional consequences (*Juvenile Delinquency Annual Report,* 1975-1976, p. 4).

Childrearing practices and their relation to cultural variables have been of interest to social scientists since the initial cross-cultural studies carried out by anthropologists (Bartlett, F. C., 1970; Bartlett, F. C., 1932; Boas, F., 1965; Levy-Bruhl , L., 1966). Other studies, Schaeffer (1959), Bell (1968) and Davis and Havighurst (1946) have documented reliable intercultural differences. Childrearing practices are all of those behaviors engaged in by caretakers in the socialization of children and youth, e.g., punishment, discipline, reward systems and nurturance. Culture refers to those ethnic, socioeconomic and racial factors that differentiate social groups along a continuum.

Child abuse, comparatively new as a national concern, has been in the limelight since the late sixties (Kempe & Helfer, 1968). The realization that Americans, a child-centered society at the ideational level, actually batter and physically harm their own children is a shocking reality. National concern was evidenced through the 1974 enactment of the federal Child Abuse Prevention and Treatment Act (P.L. No. 93-247) and comparable legislation at the state level (Alvy, 1975).

Physical abuse will be the focus of this paper because of the many confounding variables present in the analysis of child neglect (Giovannoni & Billingsley, 1970). In addition, psychoemotional abuse and neglect are difficult, if not impossible, to define or agree on. Gil (1971, p. 639) defined physical abuse of children as:

> intentional, non-accidental use of physical force, or intentional, non-accidental acts of omission, on the part of a parent or other caretaker in interaction with a child in his care, aimed at hurting, injuring or destroying that child. Apart from the difficulty of ascertaining the presence or absence of elements of intentionality, which by definition, constitute a *sine qua non* of child abuse, the definition reduces ambiquity by including all use of physical force and all acts of omission aimed at hurting, injuring or destroying a child, irrespective of the act, the omission and/or the outcome. Thus the relativity of personal and community standards and judgments is avoided.

Child abuse is currently a relatively widespread and elusive phenomenon. It has been estimated that between one-half and one million children are abused annually (Gelles, 1975).

This paper will focus on a review of selected juvenile delinquency, cross-cultural childrearing and child abuse literature, with emphasis on coassociations and antecedents. In addition, some implications for social research and policy formulation will be discussed.

REVIEW OF THE LITERATURE

A. Juvenile Delinquency

Juvenile delinquency literature is characterized by outdated, impressionistic data and is more useful for hypothesis formulation than for determining emperically sound research directions. Large families, criminality in the family, church attendance, incompetency on the job, low socioeconomic status (SES), employment of the mother outside the home, low school achievement, truancy and broken homes have all been associated with delinquency (Hirschi & Selvin, 1967). The focus here, however, will be on: 1) physical or corporal punishment; 2) family disruption; 3) SES; and 4) child abuse as they relate to delinquency.

1. Parental punitiveness — Parental punitiveness has been associated with juvenile delinquency (Maurer, 1974; Bandura & Walters, 1959; Welsh, 1976; McCord, et al, 1961, and Winder & Rau, 1962). Higher rates of physical punishment in the home have been found when comparing delinquent and non-delinquent fifteen and sixteen year olds (Bandura & Walters, 1959). A recent review of the literature on corporal punishment concluded that a high correlation existed between severity of punishment experienced by a child from ages 2-12 and antisocial, aggressive behavior exhibited during adolescence (Maurer, 1974).

Non-delinquent aggression in males has been analyzed in order to determine whether an association existed between verbal and physical abuse in the home and aggressive behavior (McCord, et al, 1961). Respondents were categorized according to the following classifications: overly aggressive, 25; non-aggressive, 52; and normal, 97. Aggression was defined as "behavior intended to hurt or injure someone; we sought to limit the term aggression to those acts which, objectively, hurt or injured (McCord, et al, 1961, p. 80)." It was concluded that male, non-delinquent aggression was associated with rejection, punitiveness and parental threat. In addition, literature was cited in which overt juvenile aggression in low and middle SES subjects was associated with punitive discipline practices within the family.

The relationship between parental attitudes and 'social deviance' in pre-adolescent (4th, 5th and 6th grades) boys also has been examined (Winder & Rau, 1962). In this study, extreme deviance was defined as "extreme scores on the Peer Nominations Inventory (PNI), an instrument which utilized classmates' ratings (p. 424)." The PNI was administered to the pre-adolescent boys and the Stanford Parent Attitude Questionnaire was given to the parents—alternate forms were provided for husbands and wives. PNI deviancy measures correlated highly with parental ambivalence, restrictiveness and punitiveness.

A series of investigations into the relationship between "severe parental punishment (SPP)" and delinquency have been carried out (Welsh, 1976). In the first survey by Welsh, there were 48 juvenile delinquents from the courts—19 female and 29 male. All of the males had experienced severe parental punishment (SPP); only 12 of the girls indicated having experienced SPP. A second survey involved 132 laundromat patrons who were interviewed about their willingness to use a strap on a hypothetical misbehaving eight-year old. The percentages willing to use the strap by respondent sample were: minority non-college, 54%; minority with some college, 33%; white-ethnic non-college, 15%; and white-ethnic with some college, 11%.

Relative to the laundromat samples, it was found that:

> apparently our uneducated Black and Puerto Rican subjects were three times more willing to use a belt on their children than were uneducated white subjects, and the same ratio (3 to 1) held for our educated subjects. This data, showing a higher use of SPP by educated minority than uneducated whites, strikingly parallels the puzzling delinquency statistics reported earlier by Wolfgang who found higher crime rates among higher SES non-whites than among lower SES whites (Welsh, 1976, p. 18).

Subjects were asked if they had used the strap in childrearing. Forty-two percent of the respondents reported that they had, 58% had not. In addition, more of those who reported having used the strap also indicated having an aggressive child in the family.

A fourth study by Welsh surveyed 14 students in an adolescent psychology class about whether they had used the belt on their own children. Those respondents who admitted having used the belt also were more likely to report having more aggressive children than their cohorts. Eleven "inner-city service club students" were interviewed, in a fifth study, to determine which had been "raised on a belt." Three subjects who had been suspended from school had been raised with the belt; none of the five who were never exposed to the belt had ever been suspended or arrested.

The sixth, and final survey correlated SPP with 77 juvenile court referrals. White-ethnic, Black and Puerto Rican subjects were studied to determine the relationship between the aggression level among the subjects and the severity of parental punishment. Using judges to determine the SPP, a significant relationship was found for males only. It was noted that the high correlation between SPP and childhood and youth aggression is a reasonable basis for predicting juvenile delinquency from abused children.

2. Broken Homes — A reliable relationship between broken homes and juvenile delinquency is commonly assumed. It has been found that children adjudged delinquent are more frequently from broken homes than their non-delinquent peers (Glueck & Glueck, 1950; Monahan, 1957).

Juvenile delinquent cases in juvenile and county courts in Florida during 1969 were examined to relate juvenile delinquency and family disruption (Chilton & Markle, 1972). Fifty-eight percent were white-ethnic and 66 percent were Black. In comparison with normal youth, the court cases indicated that delinquents lived in disrupted homes more frequently; serious delinquents are more often from disrupted homes than less serious offenders; and family and race explain the link between delinquency and family disruption to a greater extent than age, sex or urban-rural residence. It was concluded that delinquents were more frequently from disrupted families than their non-delinquent cohorts. The relationship was more marked for the Blacks than for the white-ethnics.

3. Socioeconomic Status — Juvenile delinquency and SES are generally assumed to be related; the nature of the relationship, however, remains equivocal. Both Porterfield (1946) and Murphy (1946) found SES unrelated to juvenile delinquency. The former noted, in a survey of undergraduates, that middle class juveniles admitted having committed as many crimes of comparable seriousness as their low SES cohorts, but were not subjected to equal punishment or justice for the acts.

To examine the validity of several assumptions presented by Moynihan (Glazer & Moynihan, 1963; Office of Policy Planning and Research, 1965) which relate to juvenile delinquency, family disruption and SES, a multi-stage probability sampling of the 14 to 18 year old population of Illinois was conducted (Berger & Simon, 1974, p. 146). Moynihan stated that:

> The history of Blacks in the United States has been such that slavery has produced a matrifocal family pattern, especially in the lower class.
>
> The matrifocal family, caused by low rates of employment and high rates of illegitimacy, leads to unstable family life—again, mainly in the lower class.
>
> This unstable lower-class Black family is productive of a variety of socially undesirable behaviors summarized as the tangle of pathology, which is unique to the lower-class Black population.

Adolescents were interviewed for approximately 45 minutes using a self-administered questionnaire. It was concluded that

> just as our research has shown that the broken family is not, in general, the crucial causative factor in juvenile delinquency that it is often taken to be, so too social science will apparently have to seek another 'cause' for the problems of the Black community though we doubt that any single factor will provide an adequate explanation (Berger & Simon, 1974, pp. 160-161).

The relationship between SES and delinquency also has been explored through an analysis of data on suburban runaways (Shellow, et al, 1967). Several prior studies were cited linking runaways to the "lower end of the socioeconomic scale." Data sources are summarized below:

> To summarize, there were several separate sources of data. The police missing persons report (a) served chiefly as a preliminary to the interview with the parents (b), our primary source of data. Intensive interviews with children (c) were used principally as a means of interpreting findings generally. Other supplementary sources were agency records from schools (d), police department (e), and juvenile court (f). And finally, the student questionnaire (g) served as the source of comparative data (Shellow, et al, 1967).

It was concluded that suburban runaways were comparable to their non-runaway peers. The methodology used in this study, especially the collaboration with community agencies, has much to recommend itself for future research use in third world communities.

Nye, et al (1958), in order to determine whether or not delinquent behavior occurs differentially by SES, administered an anonymous delinquency checklist to 9th-12th graders from 3 areas of residence: urban, rural and suburban. SES was equated with fathers' occupations. It was concluded that delinquent behavior was unrelated to SES or place of residence. The authors also cited previous studies which indicated no over-representation of the poor among juvenile delinquents. They also pointed out the importance of differentiating between "official delinquency" and actual delinquent behavior.

A 10-year longitudinal study of 3rd graders conducted by Eron, et al (1974), beginning in 1960 with a total of 875 subjects, was conducted to determine the learn-

TABLE 1 SOURCES AND QUALITY OF DATA

Sources of Information	N Attempted	N Completed
Police missing persons report	1,026	993
Report of follow-up interview	993	951
Intensive interview	243	96
School records	731	562
Police records	834	834
Court records	834	834
Student questionnaires	1,350	1,327

ing conditions of aggression. Approximately one-half of the original respondents were reinterviewed. Peer ratings, MMPI and self-ratings were the measures.

> Measures of the learning conditions were taken from parent interviews conducted individually in face to face situations. The interviews, completely objective and precoded, yielded measures on four general types of variables presumed to be antecedent to aggression in children—instigators, reinforcers, identification and social class (p. 413).

Modal age at the time of the re-interview was 19, with a mean of 12.6 years of school completed. Aggression was defined as "an act which injures or irritates another person (p. 412)." Positive relationships were found between the four antecedent conditions and observed in school aggression. Two antecedent variables, identification and social class, predicted from age 8, aggression at age 19.

4. Child Abuse — A link between child abuse and juvenile delinquency has been hypothesized. A relationship has been theorized between child beating and delinquency (Curtis & Lukianowicz, 1971).

Adolescent homicide has also been related to parental brutality and abuse (Duncan & Duncan, 1971). In this study, five cases of adolescent homicide were examined and it was concluded that a pattern of parental brutality had existed in all five families. King (1975) looked at nine homicidal youths and concluded that in each case childhood environments were characterized by violence and brutality.

Three generations of abused children and their families were studied (Silver, 1969) and it was concluded that children experiencing violence are more likely to exhibit and commit violence in later life. Finally, Button (1973) reviewed juvenile delinquency case histories and concluded that child abuse had been commonplace.

Juvenile Delinquency Summary — Several variables seem to be related to juvenile delinquency: severe parental punishment (Bandura & Walters, 1959; Maurer, 1974; Welsh, 1976) and parental attitudes of rejection, punitiveness and ambivalence (McCord, et al, 1961; Winder & Rau, 1962). Severe parental punishment seems to be a relatively reliable antecedent variable. The direction of the relationship between parental attitudes is less clear, but clearly suggested by the data.

Family disruption characterized most cases of juvenile delinquency (Chilton & Markle, 1972; Glueck & Glueck, 1950).

Socioeconomic status did not differentiate juvenile delinquents; case materials (Shellow, et al, 1967), multistage probability sampling (Berger & Simon, 1974) and self-admitted delinquent behavior (Nye et al, 1958; Porterfield, 1946) all failed to associate SES and juvenile delinquency. In only one study cited is such a link found (Eron, et al, 1974). Parental brutality or child abuse was linked to both adolescent homicide (Duncan & Duncan, 1971; King, 1975) and violence (Button, 1973; Silver, 1969).

B. Cross-cultural Childrearing

The relationship between cultural identity and childrearing practices is reliable, if not totally understood by social scientists and the professions. Observations of childrearing environments in different cultures (social classes and/or ethnic groups) have attested to consistent intro-cultural invariation (Anders, 1968). The poor, as an example, have been observed to exhibit reliable molar and molecular differences from upper class Americans relative to what they do with their children and why.

Two major variables, 1) SES and 2) ethnicity, are discussed below in relation to childrearing practices.

1. Socioeconomic Status — While focusing primarily on early socialization among working class families, McDonald (1969, p. 12) noted that deviations from middle class norms were found in several areas: 1) childrearing techniques; 2) attitudes; 3) educational and vocational aspirations; 4) use of language; and 5) leisure activities.

Reliable ethnic and SES differences have been found to exist in: 1) feeding and weaning; 2) toilet training; 3) father-child relations; 4) educational expectations; 5) age for assuming responsibilities; and 6) strictness of regime (Davis & Havighurst, 1946).

In this study, it was concluded that "there are considerable social class differences in childrearing practices and these differences are greater than the differences between Negroes and whites of the same social class (p. 717)." It was also noted that the central "meaning of social class to students of human development is that it defines and systematizes different learning environments for children of different classes (p. 699)." The culture of the United States was viewed as consisting of the following elements: the general American system of cultural behaviors, the social class cultures, and the ethnic group cultures.

Erlanger (1974) set out, through a review of the literature and analysis of the data, to question the hypothesis that punitive childrearing practices are linked to the higher incidence of working class homicide when compared to the middle class. The following hypotheses were tested:

> Physical punishment leads to working class authoritarianism; childhood punishment experiences explain the greater probability that working class adults, as opposed to middle class adults, will commit homicide; the general use of corporal punishment is a precursor to child abuse; and that the use of corporal punishment is part of a subcultural positive evaluation of violence (p. 68).

A major purpose of the reanalysis was to examine Bronfenbrenner's (1958) earlier thesis that working class parents predominantly use physical punishment, while those in the middle class use psychological techniques. It was noted that only six studies formed the basis of Bronfenbrenner's generalization. Erlanger (1974, p. 69) noted that "although various studies have found a statistically significant relationship, the relationship between social class and the use of spanking is relatively weak." This observation held when reanalyses were conducted separately for Blacks and whites. In concluding, it was noted that:

> some previous commentary has made the mistake of assuming or implying that class or ethnic groups can be characterized by their methods of punishment. To avoid this tendency to over-generalize, future research should be sensitive to absolute percentages and the strength of correlations, rather than primarily to establish statistical significance (p. 84).

The relationship between childrearing goals, practices and SES were examined by Kamii & Radin (1967). Two groups of mothers drawn from lower-lower class (LLC) and middle class (MC) populations, respectively, were interviewed and observed in their homes. The following hypotheses were to be tested:

1. LLC childrearing goals did not differ from MC goals;

2. LLC were lower than MC in responsiveness to explicit socioemotional needs children express;

3. LLC were lower than MC relative to initiating interactions, meeting children's implicit companionship and affective needs;

4. LLC were greater than MC relative to unilaterial techniques and LLC were lower than MC relative to bilaterial techniques; and

5. LLC were lower than MC relative to rewards for desirable child behavior and LLC were higher than MC relative to punishment for undesirable child behavior. Among these, the authors concluded that hypotheses 1, 2, 4, and the first part of 5 were confirmed; hypothesis 3 was not confirmed.

2. Ethnicity —In addition to SES, ethnic identity as a cultural factor is a reliable determinant of childrearing practices. Peterson and Migliorino (1967) used the Sears, Maccoby and Levin (1957) questionnaire to survey American and Sicilian families. It was concluded that American and Sicilian families differed relative to control of sex and aggression; the former were significantly more permissive.

Sollenberg (1968) hypothesized that:

> the relative absence of aggressive behavior in general, and delinquent behavior in particular, among the young Chinese-Americans is a result of the differences in the cultural values, in the familial structure, and in the childrearing of the Chinese, as compared to other ethnic groups (p. 14).

Mothers with children approximately 5 years of age were surveyed using the Sears, Maccoby and Levin (1957) interview and personal observations. Generally, it was concluded that low juvenile delinquency rates come from childrearing practices, cultural values and familial structure. More specifically, the following factors were deemed significant: 1) a pattern of family indulgence and integration during the child's first 6 years; 2) discouragement of physical aggression and competition; 3) provision of appropriate behavior models for children; and 4) the total acceptance by parents of responsibility for the child's social behavior. The families were also found to be significantly more nurturant and higher on controlling than the Cambridge norms.

The sociocultural and multiethnic nature of childrearing practices were the focus of an investigation by Kriger and Kroes (1972). The Parental Attitude Research Instrument (PARI) was administered to Jewish, Chinese and Protestant mothers. The control and rejection scales were of particular interest. Parents were selected according to the following criteria: 1) self-identification with the culture; 2) having between 12 and 16 years of education; 3) being middle SES; 4) being between 35 and 45 years of age; and 5) having a minimum of 2 children with at least one 10 years old or older. It was hypothesized that Chinese mothers would be different from Protestant mothers. The study concluded that the Chinese were highest on the control scale; Jews and Protestants did not differ. No interethnic differences were found on the PARI rejections scale.

Three groups of low SES maternity cases were interviewed to determine modal socialization values for their children (Green, 1971). Social breadth, autonomy and expressionism were the three indices used. Ethnically, the groups were selected from

West Africans (Gambian), Trinidadians and East Indians (both resided in Trinidad). These prospective mothers were asked about their goals and preferences for training their children. The following predictions were made: 1) the answers from the three samples would differ significantly; 2) the West African sample would rank highest; 3) the East Indian sample would be lowest in relation to *social breadth, autonomy and expressionism*.

It was concluded that:

> Two predictions for differences between the West African and Negro women were not upheld: First, the West African and Negro samples did not differ significantly on Autonomy, and the Negro sample ranked higher than the West African sample on Social Breadth (p. 312).

Childrearing practices of Black parents relative to their teaching behaviors with their fifth grade sons was the subject of an investigation by Busse and Busse (1972). The fact that the father largely has been ignored in childrearing research was given as the reason for their inclusion in the observations. Forty-eight Black, male fifth--graders were observed with both parents. The mean age for the boys was 11.3, with a range of 10.5 to 13.3 years. It was concluded that:

> mothers' education was significantly linked to their autonomy-fostering behavior, their sufficiency of orientation, and their number of words. Fathers' education was positively associated with their smiling behavior. Fathers' occupation was positively related to the mothers' autonomy-fostering behavior (p. 293).

Cross-cultural Childrearing Summary — The relationship between SES, as a cultural variable, and childrearing was unclear. Differences were found in some studies (Davis & Havighurst, 1946; Kamii & Radin, 1967); no differences were found in others (Erlanger, 1974); and a statistically significant, but weak, relationship in another (McDonald, 1969).

Ethnicity, both as race and as national origin, has been linked to reliable differences in childrearing practices. West Africans have been differentiated from native Islanders (Green, 1971); Chinese-Americans differed from the Cambridge norms (Sollenberger, 1968); and Chinese-Americans and Jewish-Americans were different from a comparison group (Kriger & Kroes, 1972). In many instances, however, differences were not found across ethnic and national cultural groups. Chinese, Jews and Protestants did not differ (Kriger & Kroes, 1972); immigrant Chinese Hawaiians were comparable to their local peers; and Sicilian families did not differ from their American comparison groups (Peterson & Migliorino, 1967).

C. Child Abuse

Child abuse is an enigma. The mere existence of adults who abuse children in a child advocacy-oriented society is problematic. What are some causes and associated conditions? How does the child figure in the configuration of physical abuse? What are salient preconditions? This discussion will focus on: 1) child characteristics; 2) abuser characteristics; and 3) ecological correlatives.

1. Child characteristics — Social and psychological attributes of abused children, themselves, have been theorized to be a factor in abusive incidents (Johnson & Morse, 1968; Strauss, et al, 1976). This line of reasoning indicates that the abused child, not unlike the abused adult, can play a role in creating the situation in which physical abuse occurs. As in many other facets of abuse research and theory, the available evidence in this area is not systematic.

Certain handicapping conditions are thought to predispose children to, and be associated with, child abuse (Fontana, et al, 1963). Intellectual deficits have been found to characterize more abused children than their non-handicapped peers (Herner, 1976). Herner also indicated that developmental deviations in children and child abuse were related, although the exact nature of the relationship was not clear. For example, premature and/or low birth weight children were found to be over-represented among physical abuse cases.

Age and sex of the abused child have been associated with abuse (Herner, 1976). Sex *per se* did not reliably differentiate abused from non-abused but a sex-by-age interaction did seem to exist. For ages 12 and under, boys outnumbered girls; the opposite was found for older, teenaged victims (Herner, 1976; Gil, 1971).

A consistent age-related finding has been the predominance of more serious injuries among younger children (Herner, 1976). The age of the abused child may be a function of sampling procedures, however. For example, Herner found that hospital data indicated high percentages of young children, 60% of the abused children were under 3 years of age; agency referrals, on the other hand, showed a preponderance of older children, only 36%, or less, were under the age of three.

2. Abuser characteristics — The range of abuser characteristics hypothesized to be associated with child abuse is quite broad. Selected variables, however, have withstood empirical testing. Age and sex have been the subjects of several analyses (Paulsen & Blake, 1969; Herner, 1976). Herner found mothers and mother substitutes to outnumber fathers and father substitutes in reported cases of abuse. In addition, an age-by-sex-of-the-abuser interaction was reported. Mothers outnumbered fathers in abusing younger children; fathers were more likely to be abusers of older children.

Family-related characteristics and family history have been related to child abuse. The most widely held belief is that most parents of abused children were, themselves, abused during their childhoods (Gil, 1971; Van Stolk, 1974; Spinetta & Rigler, 1972). This cycle of violence across generations has been variously explained using psychodynamic and/or learning principles. This notion should be taken with some caution, however, because "the amount of data that has been presented dealing directly with this question at this point is minimal (Herner, 1976, p. 31)."

In both white and Black-ethnic abusive homes, the single-parent family predominated (Giovannoni & Billingsley, 1970; Herner, 1976). Another family-related characteristic was family size: abusing families were larger (Herner, 1976). A higher incidence of marital discord and the mother's first child being born when she was relatively young were also characteristic of the abuse cases.

Several social psychological variables have been associated with abusive parents. Intrapsychic disorders have been attributed to abusers (Giovannoni, 1971; Melnick & Hurley, 1969; Young, 1964; Spinetta & Rigler, 1972). Abusing parents have been found to share gross misunderstandings about the nature of childrearing and often have looked to the abused child to satisfy adult ego needs (Spinetta & Rigler, 1972). Giovannoni, in comparing adequate, neglectful and abusive mothers, concluded that "indices of interpersonal difficulty in intra-psychic disorder did differentiate the neglectful and abusive families as well as both groups from the more adequate ones (p. 650)." Abusing mothers, it could be reasoned, exhibit more psychopathology than either neglectfuls or normals (Griswold & Billingsley, 1967). It should be cautioned that the issue is not settled and a relatively small proportion of abusers are actually estimated to be psychotic (Kempe, 1973; Delsordo, 1963; Melnick & Hurley, 1969; Schmitt & Kempe, 1975). Data have indicated that abusers were generally social isolates (Giovannoni, 1971).

Ethnicity of the abuser also has been associated with child abuse (Gil, 1971; Herner, 1976). Comparing white and non-white ethnics, "non-white children were over-represented in the study cohorts. Nationwide reporting rates per 100,000 were 6.7 for white children and 21.0 for non-white children (Gil, 1971, p. 640)." This , "over-representation" is widely cited and subscribed to. In contrast, a more recent, comprehensive survey of the research indicated no ethnic over-representation (Herner, 1976).

Socioeconomic status has frequently been associated with abuser identity (Goode, 1971; Gil, 1971; Spinetta & Rigler, 1972; Strauss, et al, 1976). Abusers, according to one group of studies, are predominantly from the lower SES populations (Goode, 1971; Gil, 1971). The stress of poverty, a cultural adaptation to violence and similar reasons are offered as supporting evidence. Another group of studies have not found a link between SES and the child abusing parent (Spinetta & Rigler, 1972; Strauss et al, 1976; Zalba, 1967). These investigations concluded that child abuse, as well as related intrafamily violence, occurred with equal frequency in all classes. Differences in reporting practices and accessibility were thought to account for SES over-representation, when it occurred.

3. The human ecology — In addition to child- and abuser-related correlates, ecological factors also have been related to child abuse (Bronfenbrenner, 1975 & 1977; Garbarino, 1976 & 1977). This relatively recent interpretive framework requires some preliminary statements:

> With reference to human growth, an ecological perspective focuses attention on development as a function of interaction between the developing organism and the enduring environments or contexts in which it lives out its life (Bronfenbrenner, 1975, p. 439).

This ecological focus on child abuse and neglect involves the analysis of "the complex interplay between individual, social, and institutional levels operating in the community (Garbarino, 1977, p. 6)."

One major study looked at child abuse in relation to the human ecology's effect on the mother (Garbarino, 1976). Human ecology was operationalized by listing institutional, parent support systems impinging on the lives of mothers. Data covering the period September, 1973 through January, 1974, from approximately five New York counties were analyzed. The major hypothesis was that:

> the socioeconomic support system for the family in each county is directly associated with the rate of child abuse/maltreatment for that county; where support systems are better, where the family has more human resources, the rate of child abuse/maltreatment will be lower, and vice versa (Garbarino, 1976, p. 180).

In essence, "the mediation of the immediate family settings by socioeconomic forces is hypothesized to be related to the degree to which children experience abuse/maltreatment (Garbarino, 1976, p. 179)."

Transience, economic development, educational development, rural vs. urban location and socioeconomic situation of the mothers were the free variables entered into the analysis; 12 indicators were examined depicting these variables. They were deemed important components of human ecology and to that extent representative of the 'quality of life' or 'standard of living.' It was noted that:

> child abuse occurs as a function of the degree to which the human ecology enhances or undermines parenting. Where the total human ecology provides adequate support, child abuse is minimized; where support is inadequate and stress great, the personality and cultural factors cited by Gil are manifested in child abuse (Garbarino, 1976, pp. 178-179).

The following correlates were, in descending order, statistically significant: 1) the percent of women in the labor force who have children under eighteen years of age; 2) the median income of families with female heads; and 3) the median income of all families. It was concluded that these three major correlates of abuse suggest that the impact of institutional systems on children is 'channeled' through the mother because of her preeminent importance as a parent.

The ecological approach also has been applied to data drawn from reported cases of child abuse and neglect (Garbarino, 1977). The major problems with the pertinence of these data to child abuse were the systematic socioeconomic and related biases inherent in using reported cases to infer actual incidence. Basically, the approach consists of the following:

> the demographic and socioeconomic correlates of reports, the relation of abuse to neglect cases, differentiations of reports by source, and the geographical pattern of reporting within a given jurisdiction, an agency can develop a community profile which will more accurately portray the 'human ecology of child abuse and neglect' and thus enhance intervention through informing policy and directing research (Garbarino, 1977, p. 1).

Child Abuse Summary — Several 'at risk' conditions have been reliably associated with child abuse. Low birth weight and intellectual deficits (Herner, 1976) are examples of these. Various other handicapping conditions of the child also have been linked to the occurrence of child abuse (Fontana, 1963).

The sex and age of the abused child were noted to be subject to an interaction effect: younger children were more seriously injured (Herner, 1976); and boys were over-represented among children 12 and younger, while girls were over-represented among the children 12 and older (Gil, 1971).

Considerable agreement exists in the literature concerning the following abuser-related attributes (Herner, 1976): 1) more marital discord than normals; 2) mothers were younger when their first child was born; 3) larger families; 4) more females; 5) more mothers abusing younger children; 6) more fathers abusing older children; and 7) a preponderance of single parent families.

Much less agreement characterized the relationship of other variables to abuser characteristics. It is unclear if an abusive childhood is an antecedent (Gil, 1971). Socioeconomic status, ethnicity and intrapsychic disorders have not reliably linked abuser characteristics and child abuse (Strauss, et al, 1976; Gil, 1971; Herner, 1976; Melnick & Hurley, 1969; Giovannoni, 1971; Young, 1964).

Certain characteristics of the human ecology have been linked to child abuse (Bronfenbrenner, 1958; Garbarino, 1976 & 1977). The percentage of women in the labor force with minor children, the median income of female-headed households and median income of all families have been associated with child abuse (Garbarino, 1976).

DISCUSSION AND IMPLICATIONS FOR RESEARCH

The three areas, juvenile delinquency, cross-cultural childrearing and child abuse, can best be related through an explication of salient associations. The following illustration provides a variable-by-subject area outline. These 14 factors are generally agreed upon as relating to the areas of interest.

Area	Associated Variable
Juvenile Delinquency	1. Severe parental discipline
	2. Family disruption
	3. Child abuse
Cross-cultural Childrearing	4. Strictness of regime
	5. Psychological shaping techniques
	6. Spanking
	7. Controlling aggression
	8. Exertion of control
Child Abuse	9. At risk birth conditions
	10. Handicapping conditions
	11. Marital discord
	12. Younger mothers
	13. Large families
	14. Single parent household

Child abuse and juvenile delinquency, on initial inspection, have several associated variables in common. Taken together, variables 1, 3 and 11 could be combined under the label 'high aggression level'; variables 2, 12, 13 and 14 could be combined under atypical family structure'. So, it would seem, high aggression level and atypical family structure are common to both child abuse and juvenile delinquency.

Variables 4 through 8 have been found to differentiate cultural groups relative to childrearing practices. It would seem that these are areas in which critical incidents arise relative to childrearing practices when viewed from the perspective of an unacculturated person. In other words, because of the cultural loading of these variables, it would seem difficult for an outside observer to adequately and validly assess extreme variation from that culture's norms or standards. In essence, it would seem that the factors common to both child abuse and juvenile delinquency are subject to cultural variation and this variation ought to be taken into account more frequently.

Several implications exist for social science research. The initial implication concerns the social trend toward creating additional categories of criminal behavior. Research into the effect on the criminal justice system and the newly criminalized population is needed. The latter is pertinent to the survival of urban populations, since they rely on police and social services for support. Labeling, itself, is related to this issue. Both areas, child abuse and juvenile delinquency, can profit from research focused on the following questions raised by Gelles (1975, p. 368):

1) To what degree does educational and occupational status insulate a person from being labelled an abuser?
2) What are the labeler's conceptions of the 'routine grounds' of child abuse?
3) Upon what are these routine conceptualizations based?

A contextual study of the Black adolescent is needed. Ecological methodology can be used in order to address a variety of questions with pertinence to this 'at risk' population. For example, the relationship between juvenile delinquency and intellectual giftedness among Black youths should be explored.

Child abuse and delinquency research from a culturally pertinent perspective should focus on the bi-directionality of socialization effects (Bell, 1968). It was suggested that:

> to predict interaction in particular parent-child pairs it is necessary to know the behavior characteristics of the child, the cultural demands on the parent, and the parents' own individual assimilation of these demands into a set of expectations for the child (Bell, 1968, p. 88).

With juveniles and children, both the 'child-to-parent effect' and the more traditional 'parent-to-child effect' would yield needed data on the effects of socialization.

The final suggested research direction is the need to focus on the whole family as the basic unit of analysis. Research on children serves as a faulty basis for social policy formulation relative to family intervention. This also applies to investigations focusing on one-parent families.

REFERENCES

Alvy, K. T. Preventing child abuse. *American Psychologist*, 1975, *30*, 921-928.

Anders, S. F. New dimensions in ethnicity and childrearing attitudes. *American Journal of Mental Deficiency*, 1968, *73*, (3), 505-508.

Bandura, A. & Walters, R. *Adolescent aggression.* New York: Ronald, 1959.

Bartlett, F. C. *Psychology and primitive culture.* Westport, Conn.: Grunwood Press, 1970.

Bartlett, F. C. *Remembering.* London: Cambridge University Press, 1932.

Bell, J. A reinterpretation of the direction of effects in studies of socialization. *Psychological Review*, 1968, *75*, 81-95.

Berger, A. S. & Simon, W. Black families and the Moynihan Report: A research evaluation. *Social Problems*, 1974, (2), 145-161.

Bronfenbrenner, U. Socialization and social class through time and space. In E. E. Macoby, T. M. Newcomb, & E. L. Hartley (Eds.), *Readings in social psychology.* New York: Holt, 1958.

Bronfenbrenner, U. Reality and research in the ecology of human development. *Proceedings of the American Philosophical Society,* 1975, *119,* 439-469.

Busse, T. V. & Busse, P. Negro parental behavior and social class variables. *Journal of Genetic Psychology,* 1972, *120,* (2), 287-294.

Button, A. D. Some antecedents of felonious and delinquent behavior. *Journal of Clinical Child Psychology,* 1973, *2,* 35-37.

Chilton, R. & Markle, G. E. Family disruption, delinquent conduct and the effect of subclassification. *American Sociological Review,* 1972, *34,* 93-99.

Davis, A. & Havighurst, R. J. Social class and color differences in childrearing. *American Sociological Review,* December, 1946, *11,* 698-710.

Delsordo, J. D. Protective casework for abused children. *Children,* 1963, *10,* 213-218.

Erlanger, H. S. Social class and corporal punishment in childrearing: A reassessment. *American Sociological Review,* 1974, *39,* 68-85.

Eron, L. D. et al. How learning conditions in early childhood—including mass media—relate to aggression in late adolescence. *American Journal of Orthospychiatry,* April, 1974, *44,* (3), 412-423.

Fontana, V. J., Donovan, D., & Wong, R. J. The maltreatment syndrome in children. *New England Journal of Medicine,* 1963, *269,* 1389-1394.

Garbarino, J. A preliminary study of some ecological correlates of child abuse: The impact of socioeconomic stress on mothers. *Child Development,* 1976, *47,* 178-185.

Garbarino, J., Crouter, A., & Sherman, D. Using report data in defining the community context of child abuse and neglect. Paper presented at the Second National Conference on Child Abuse and Neglect, Houston, Texas, April 17-20, 1977.

Gelles, R. J. The social construction of child abuse. *American Journal of Orthopsychiatry,* 1975, *44,* 363-371.

Gil, D. G. Violence against children. *Journal of Marriage and the Family,* 1971, *33,* 637-648.

Giovannoni, J. M. Parental mistreatment: Perpetrators and victims. *Journal of Marriage and the Family,* 1971, *33,* (4), 649-657.

Giovannoni, J. M. & Billingsley, A. Child neglect among the poor: A study of parental adequacy in families of three ethnic groups. *Child Welfare,* 1970, *49,* (4), 196-204.

Glazer, N. & Moynihan, D. *Beyond the melting pot.* Cambridge: MIT Press, 1963.

Glueck, S. & Glueck, E. *Unraveling juvenile delinquency.* Cambridge: Harvard University Press, 1950.

Goode, W. J. Force and violence in the family. *Journal of Marriage and the Family,* 1971, *33,* (4), 624-636.

Green, H. B. Socialization values in West African Negro and East Indian cultures: A cross-cultural comparison. *Journal of Cross-Cultural Psychology,* September 2, 1971, (3), 309-312.

Griswold, B. & Billingsley, A. Psychological functioning of parents who mistreat their children and those who do not. Unpublished manuscript, Berkeley, California, 1967.

Herner & Company. *Four perspectives on the status of child abuse and neglect research,* 1976.

Hirschi, T. & Selvin, H. C. *Delinquency research: An appraisal of analytic methods.* New York: Free Press, 1967.

Johnson, B. & Morse, H. *The battered child: A study of children with inflicted injuries.* Denver: Colorado Welfare Department, 1968.

Kamii, C. K. & Radin, N. L. Class differences in the socialization practices of Negro mothers. *Journal of Marriage and the Family,* 1967, *29,* (2), 302-310.

Kempe, C. H. A practical approach to the protection of the abused child and the rehabilitation of the abusing parent. *Pediatrics,* 1973, *51,* 804-812.

Kempe, C. H. & Helfer, R. *The battered child.* Chicago: The University of Chicago Press, 1968.

King, C. H. The ego and the integration of violence in homicidal youth. *Journal of Orthopsychiatry,* January, 1975, *45,* (1), 134-135.

Kriger, S. F. & Kroes, W. H. Childrearing attitudes of Chinese, Jewish, and Protestant mothers. *Journal of Social Psychology,* 1972, *86,* (2), 205-210.

Levy-Bruhl, L. *Primitive mentality.* Boston: Beacon Press, 1966.

McCord, W., McCord, J. & Howard, A. Familial correlates of aggression in nondelinquent male children. *Journal of Abnormal and Social Psychology,* 1962, *62,* 79-93.

McDonald, L. *Social class and delinquency.* Hamden, Conn.: Archon Books, 1969.

Maurer, A. Corporal punishment. *American Psychologist,* 1974, *29,* (8), 614-626.

Melnick, B. & Hurley, R. J. Distinctive personality attributes of child-abusing mothers. *Journal of Consulting and Clinical Psychology,* 1969, *33,* 746-749.

Monahan, T. P. Family status and the delinquent child; A reappraisal and some new findings. *Social Forces,* 1957, *35,* 250-258.

Murphy, F. J., Shirley, M., & Witner, H. L. The incidence of hidden delinquency. *American Journal of Orthopsychiatry,* 1946, *16,* 686-696.

Nye, F. I., Short, J. G., & Olson, V. J. Socioeconomic status and delinquent behavior. *American Journal of Sociology,* 1958; *63,* 381-389.

Paulsen, M G. & Blakc, P. R. The physically abused child. A focus on prevention. *Child Welfare,* 1969, *48,* 86-95.

Peterson, D. R. & Migliorino, G. Pancultural factors of parental behavior in Sicily and the United States. *Child Development,* 1967, *38,* (4), 967-991.

Porterfield, A. L. *Youth in trouble.* Fort Worth: Leo Potishman Foundation, 1946.

Schaeffer, E. A circumplex model for maternal behavior. *Journal of Abnormal and Social Psychology,* 1959, *59,* 226-235.

Schmitt, B. D. & Kempe, C. H. The pediatrician's role in child abuse and neglect. *Current Problems in Pediatrics,* 1975, *5,* 3-47.

Sears, R. R., Maccoby, B., & Levin, N. *Patterns of child rearing.* New York: Harper, 1957.

Shellow, R., Schamp, J. R., Liebow, E., & Unger, E. Suburban runaways of the 1960's. *Monographs of the Society for Research in Child Development,* 1967, *32,* (3), Serial No. 111.

Silver, L. B. Does violence breed violence? Contributions from a study of the child abuse syndrome. *American Journal of Psychiatry,* 1969, *126,* (3), 152-155.

Sollenberger, R. T. Chinese American childrearing practices and juvenile delinquency. *Journal of Social Psychology,* 1968, *74;* (1), 13-23.

Spinetta, J. J. & Rigler, D. The child abusing parent: A psychological review. *Psychological Bulletin,* 1972, *77,* 296''304.

Strauss, M. A., Gelles, R. J., & Steinmetz; S. K. *Violence in the family: An assessment of knowledge and research needs.* Paper presented at the American Association for the Advancement of Science, Boston, February 23, 1976.

U.S. Department of Labor, Office of Policy Planning and Research. *The Negro family: The case for national action.* Washington, D.C.: U. S. Government Printing Office, 1965. (This volume is more commonly known as the Moynihan Report.)

Van Stolk, M. *The battered child in Canada.* Toronto: McClelland and Stewart, Ltd., 1974.

Welsh, R. S. Severe parental punishment and delinquency: A developmental theory. *Journal of Clinical Child Psychology,* 1976, 17-21.

Winder, C. L. & Rau, L. Parental attitudes associated with social deviance in preadolescent boys. *Journal of Abnormal and Social Psychology,* 1962, *64,* 418-424.

Young, L. *Wednesday's children.* New York: McGraw-Hill, 1964.

Zalba, S. R. Battered children. *Trans-Action,* 1971, *8,* 58-61.

Zalba, S. R. The abused child. II. A typology for classification and treatment. *Social Work,* 1967, *12,* (1), 70-79.

11

Perspectives on the Juvenile Sex Offender

GARY A. WENET, TONI R. CLARK
& ROBERT J. HUNNER

Adolescent Clinic
Division of Adolescent Medicine
University of Washington
Seattle, Washington 98195

In recent years a great deal of public attention has been focused on sex crimes in the United States. Concerned citizens, media personnel, governmental jurisdictions and social service agencies have been bringing to light one of the more hidden and forbidden topics in our culture: sex crimes against children and adults. Most of the attention has been directed toward programs and services to alleviate the suffering and self-devaluation of the victims and toward the more sensational adult offenders; scant attention is being directed toward youthful sexual offenders.

Yet, according to recent FBI figures, 20% of the individuals arrested for committing rape in the United States during the past year were juveniles. Non-violent moral offenses, such as indecent liberties, indecent exposure and peeping, are committed by juveniles at rates greater than for the adult population. The exact numbers of such youthful offenders are virtually impossible to obtain, since few jurisdictions in the country maintain the necessary statistical information on juvenile offenders, as shown in the literature available. Knowledgeable authorities estimate that the number of unreported and/or uninvestigated cases of juvenile sexual offenses committed would equal or surpass the number of reported cases, if such information were available. It is, therefore, possible to state that the actual number of sexual offenses committed by juveniles is in excess of the number which are eventually reported in the limited statistics available.

The Adolescent Program at the University of Washington has been involved in studying juvenile sexual offenders in Washington state since 1975. This interest followed a report by the State Bureau of Juvenile Rehabilitation which documented that within the juvenile justice system in the state there was no systematic way to identify youngsters who had committed sexual offenses. The study demonstrated that juvenile courts were reluctant to identify teenagers as sexual offenders, and that institutions were similarly concerned with labeling youngsters prematurely. The consequences of this reluctance were: 1) ignorance of the number of youngsters in state institutions with serious sexual problems; and 2) a lack of treatment resources for youngsters who did have sexual offense histories.

In June, 1975, the Adolescent Program, in conjunction with the Bureau of Juvenile Rehabilitation, held a conference to discuss these issues. Conference participants came from every area of the state and included institutional staff, probation and parole officers, police, juvenile rehabilitation administrators, juvenile court judges and faculty and staff from the University of Washington. At the conference, a commitment was made to study the problems posed by the juvenile sex offender population. Funds were sought and the Adolescent Program contracted to conduct evaluations of 60 juvenile sexual offenders. Data from these evaluations indicate that there does exist a sizable population of juvenile sexual offenders in Washington state.

THE JUVENILE SEX OFFENDER POPULATION

The following characteristics were noted in the demographic data from these evaluations. The population we saw came from juvenile courts and institutions throughout the state; from both the eastern and western regions, in a distribution that reflects the urban and rural populations of the state. The ages of the offenders in the study ranged from 12 to 18. The study group reflected the racial breakdown of the statewide population. Youngsters in the group came from every socioeconomic status. We found that their school performance typically fell below their ability. They often, but not always, had a history of behavior problems prior to their sexual offenses.

We found that juvenile sex offenders committed every kind of sexual offense that adults commit. We saw youngsters whose offenses included rape, indecent liberties, voyeurism and exhibitionism. The sexual behavior patterns of these offender groups differed. By far the largest category of offenders were those who committed indecent liberties with children. Rape appeared less frequently in this group of juvenile offenders than it does in the adult sex offender population. There were many assaults by juveniles on peers or older women, however, which appeared to be unsuccessful attempts at rape. It is possible that, were these youngsters more sophisticated, the assaults might have been rapes. About one-fourth of the offenses committed by our population were considered violent. We defined as violent any offense involving coercion, either by threat or by physical violence. The offenses we called non-violent typically involved seduction of a younger child into a sexual act.

Youngsters who committed sexual offenses tended to repeat the same kind of offense. The number of youngsters committing offenses in more than one offense category was extremely low, 9%. Among our population, about 45% of the child molesters had a record of being abused, either physically or sexually, as children. This was interesting, when contrasted with the rapists and those brought in for indecent liberties with peers or adults, where only 16% had a history of physical or sexual abuse.

There was a significant indication that sex offenders lack sexual information. About one-fourth of the offenders were rated by our interviewers as sexually naive, as compared to 61% of the nonoffending control group. The rapists tended to discuss sex more openly and with bravado. It was more likely that the child molesters would be reluctant to talk about sexual behavior, or be misinformed.

Youngsters and adults who commit sexual offenses have been observed to deny their offenses, but it is important to make a distinction about the *kind* of denial. It appeared that the greatest amount of denial that the offense had actually occurred was found in the indecent liberties group. There was no actual denial among rapists, but there was a tendency for this group to minimize the significance of their offense.

About 50% of the offenders we saw sought help for their problem. However, we have not followed enough of these youngsters at this time to know whether this desire for help would continue through actual participation in treatment. Youngsters from all offense categories tended to rate mother as the most important parent. In the control group, the youngsters had a greater tendency to check either the mother or the father, or to say that both parents were equally important. No youngsters in the group were labeled as psychotic by the interviewers.

Our evaluation of the young sexual offender presents a complex profile. He is between the ages of 12 and 18. While he may be of average intelligence, he typically has problems performing to his ability in the school situation. If he has molested children, he has a 50-50 chance of having been molested or physically abused, himself. If he has molested children, his social skills are less developed than those of most youngsters. He tends to have few close friends and no group of companions with which to spend his time. If he is a rapist, however, he may have many friends, but hold them all at a distance. He has no intimate friends. The young sex offender tends to repeat the offense for which he was originally caught. About one-half of the rapists and child molesters were repeaters; exposers are the most consistent group to repeat their offenses, and we saw this group later in their offense history.

The fact that juveniles are committing sexual offenses has been documented for some time. However, the lack of research in the area has made it difficult to determine the extent of this problem in our communities, as well as to develop any understanding of such behavior. We feel that our studies have established that there is a significant number of juvenile sexual offenders in our communities. More focused studies need to be conducted in order to outline those critical variables which lead to the development of such behavior, and to establish effective treatment models.

DEVELOPMENT OF SEXUAL BEHAVIOR

In our work with the juvenile sexual offender, we are highly interested in development. Within a developmental framework, it becomes possible to apply a variety of theoretical models, all of which can contribute to better understanding of the behavior with which we are asked to deal. The psychoanalytic, Adlerian, interpersonal, cognitive, behaviorist and developmental perspectives have each helped us clarify the diagnostic and treatment issues with the sexual offender. In the assessment phase of our work, we evaluate the significance of the individual's behavior in relation to his chronological age, level of physical maturation, early parent/child relationships, current family dynamics and his relationship with peers. In addition, we are interested in the perceived intent or goal of the sexual behavior, as well as any learning history, both from a conditioning perspective and in terms of the social/sexual models which were available to the individual.

At this point, it seems that a review of some of the basic factors involved in the development of sexual behavior would be helpful for understanding our target population. The literature on sexual behavior suggests that deviant sexual behavior is far more common among males than it is among females. In fact, there is generally a 6-to-1 ratio of males to females for various kinds of sexually deviant behavior, including such groups as transsexuals, transvestites, homosexuals and gender identity disorders in children. This suggests that developmental factors predispose males to some forms of deviant sexual development.

Looking at development, the first opportunity for error would come in the actual anatomical development of the sexual organs. In simplified terms, development follows this process: two months following conception, the fetus, which until that time has been sexually undifferentiated, assumes male or female characteristics in normal development. During the two months prior to this, the fetus is actually anatomically female. It is only with the addition of the androgens in the male that the female structures recede and the male structures develop. Once the male or female structures are developed, at age two or three months, the structures themselves begin to take over the job of producing hormones for the fetus. At this point in the development of the male, it is important that the male testes produce an adequate amount of androgen. Without the correct mix of hormones at this stage, it is possible that the fetus will develop ambiguous genitalia. At its extreme, the resulting condition is known as hermaphrodism.

The literature, however, has produced little evidence to suggest that such hormonal imbalances can be held responsible for the majority of deviant sexual behavior. In fact, in their classic study of hermaphroditic children, Money, Hampson and Hampson (1955) found that if children were assigned, in a consistent fashion, to a particular gender at an early age, they would develop normally with respect to both gender identity and appropriate sex-role behavior. Money hypothesizes that this crystallization of gender identity may coincide with the development of language. This would tend to highlight the importance of the socialization process in the development of sexual behavior and sexual identity, in general.

In the normal developmental process, the gender identity and sex-role behavior are consistent with the rearing of the child. Green and Stoller (1974), in their studies of gender identity disorders of children, suggest that early imprinting of certain cross-gender behavior patterns in children seems to lead to behavior patterns consistent with transsexualism in adults. (Transsexualism is defined as having a gender identity inconsistent with the biological sex assignment.) The studies suggest that this behavior is well established prior to age 6 and, in fact, may occur at the time language develops, that is, as early as two years.

The importance of the socialization process is again highlighted in Maccoby and Jacklin's recent book (1974) on the psychology of sex differences. One of the most salient differences between male and female children outlined in their book involves the considerably more rigid sex-role stereotyping which occurs for boys, and not for girls, prior to adolescence. Specifically, boys are far more likely to be punished for aberrant sex-role behavior prior to adolescence than are girls. This process becomes more equal during adolescence, when the reins are pulled in on girls and sex-role expectations become far more rigid than they were in childhood. The significant point to consider about boys is that the rigid sex-role defining takes place during what may be a critical period for gender identity and sexual development, that is, during the first six years of life.

Freud (1963), in his early theoretical work, also emphasized the importance of socialization processes in the development of sexual identity. The necessity for the male child to fully resolve his Oedipal impulses through identification with the same sex parent was seen as important. If, in fact, that resolution did not occur, the chances of some deviant sexual behavior occurring were seen as increased. Also, the impending doom associated with castration anxiety, according to Freud, would introduce yet another pressure or anxiety for the male child, which was not seen to have a counterpart in female children.

Although Freud (1963) suggested that the lack of identification with an appropriate male model would lead to the development of sexual maladjustment in adolescence and adulthood, his theory proved to be less than adequate in explaining why, or how, particular types of sexual offense behavior develops in juveniles. For instance, we find the theories do not explain the development of different sexual behavior patterns, such as the development of child molestation behavior rather than exhibitionistic behavior. Even with the apparent limitations of psychoanalytic theory, it remains important to evaluate the young person's current psychological adjustment in light of early parent-child relationships and family dynamics. Doing so has often surfaced a long history of emotional deprivation and lack of appropriate identification.

THE LEARNING THEORY PERSPECTIVE

Our work has repeatedly pointed to the value of considering the learning history which may have contributed to the development of sexual offense behavior. Basically, we can consider two kinds of learning models, a conditioning model and a vicarious learning model. Early conditioning can be illustrated by the case of a 16 year old boy referred for three counts of sexual assault on boys aged 8 to 10. This youngster's first sexual experience involved an invitation to have oral and anal sex with a 9 year old neighbor boy. Soon, the offender began using a similar fantasy to accompany daily masturbation. Eventually, he sought out other child victims with whom to share sexual experiences. Even when incarcerated for his offense, the boy maintained doubts that this behavior could actually have hurt the boys involved. He felt that although they expressed some anger or disturbance about the act, they may have actually enjoyed it, as he had with his first partner.

Another boy whom we saw recently, aged 14, had been having sex with younger boys since he was age 9, all of the relationships having been mutually consenting and pleasurable, apparently, to both parties. After being referred to us for sexually molesting two male cousins on a number of occasions, his response was, "Well, I really don't see why this is such a big deal. No one ever complained about it before." His sexual behavior patterns seemed to be already solidly entrenched. So, the conditioning process and the importance of early sexual experiences certainly seem to be related to the development of sexual offense behavior for some of our youngsters.

In other youngsters, we have seen evidence of modeling. One youngster reported seeing an article in *Penthouse* magazine about a woman who exposed herself in public places and was described as deriving much pleasure and, of course, attention, from that behavior. He then began masturbating to the fantasy of exhibiting himself to attractive young women. Following a period of regular masturbation to that fantasy, he acted out that fantasy and was arrested for exhibitionism. During evaluation, he reported that he hoped that the women he had exposed himself to might invite him to have sexual intercourse.

Still another youngster, having read an article in *Playboy* magazine about a man who fantasized having sex with his teacher, began to masturbate to the fantasy of having sex with a particular teacher at school. This eventually led to his attempting to sexually assault that teacher. More recently, we have had a referral of a youngster who watched the program "Roots" on television, including the episode in which a master raped his slave. The next day he was arrested for assaulting an elderly woman. She reported that during the assault he said to her, "Didn't you see 'Roots' last night? If you did, you'd know why I'm here."

SEXUAL ABUSE AND SEXUAL OFFENSES

This symposium has committed the participants to examine the possible relationship between a child's experience with either physical or sexual abuse and the subsequent development of delinquent behavior. The main finding in our study of juvenile sex offenders which speaks directly to this issue pertains to a trend which suggests that child molesters were physically or sexually abused as children. This is consistent with the data on adult child abusers, who, as a group, tend to have been child victims themselves. This trend for child molesters in our sample did not surface for any other offense category evaluated.

The findings point to the need for longitudinal research on the psychosocial development of child victims of sex offenses. It will take this type of research to adequately speak to the issues addressed by this symposium.

In the meantime, we might offer some hypotheses. Recently, Nathaniel Wagner and Mavis Tsai studied adult women who had been sexually molested as children (personal communication, 1977). They have suggested that there may be a relationship between whether a child experiences positive or negative coercion and her subsequent sexual adjustment as an adult. Wagner and Tsai's findings may provide some interesting leads to understanding the development of sexual offense behavior.

Most of the offenders in our study who reported having been sexually molested as children stated that they were willing participants, rather than victims of force. It is possible that the pleasurable nature of these early sexual experiences predisposed them to molesting younger children once they were sexually mature. They may have learned that such experiences are pleasurable to the younger child, and thus view them as acceptable. An alternate explanation could be that, because of considerable unresolved guilt related to the early sexual experience, these youngsters are more likely to seek out child victims, themselves.

The other victim type, the child who was forced, generally is considered to be of more concern to both parents and professionals. These victims are more often provided with immediate medical and/or psychological intervention; and parents worry about the long-range effects of such a sexual experience. Although this victim group may well experience sexual adjustment difficulties in adolescence, they may, as a group, be less likely to seek out child victims. The long-range effects of sexual abuse on a child are still undetermined. Such a determination will require longitudinal research of child victims, from childhood through adolescence, in order to measure the extent of psychosocial adjustment problems which they face. Specifically, it would provide information about the sexual behavior patterns adopted, particularly as they relate to sexual offense behavior.

At the present time, researchers are studying the relationship, for females, between early experiences of sexual abuse and later sexual adjustment. There is attention being paid, also, to the relationship between teenage runaways and their experience with being sexually abused. The subjects in our previous studies have been almost exclusively male. While females may manifest these early sexual abuse experiences by running away or becoming sexually active during early adolescence, males may be more likely to commit sexual offenses. Such possible gender differences must be documented more fully before a final determination can be made.

REFERENCES

Freud, S. *The sexual enlightenment of children.* New York: Crowell-Collier Publishing Co., 1963.

Green, R. *Sexual identity conflict in children and adults.* New York: Basic Books, Inc., 1974.

Maccoby, E. E. & Jacklin, C. N. *The psychology of sex differences.* Stanford, California: Stanford University Press, 1974.

Money, J., Hampson, J. G. & Hampson, J. L. An examination of some basic sexual concepts: Evidence of human hermaphroditism. *Bulletin of the Johns Hopkins Hospital,* 1955, *97,* 301-319.

Stoller, R. J. *Sex and gender: The development of masculinity and femininity.* New York: Science House, 1968.

12

Child Abuse and the Etiology of Violent Delinquent Behavior

ARTHUR H. GREEN, M.D.

Director, Brooklyn Family Center and
Clinical Associate Professor,
Division of Child and Adolescent Psychiatry,
Downstate Medical Center,
Brooklyn, New York 11203

While recent studies have suggested correlations between child abuse and subsequent delinquent and violent behavior and appear to justify the adage "violence breeds violence," the mechanisms by which the physical abuse of an infant or young child transforms him into an acting out delinquent adolescent or an impulsive child-battering adult are as yet unknown.

The purpose of this paper is to examine this relationship between child abuse and subsequent delinquency by in-depth psychological explorations of abused children who have exhibited extreme violent and/or delinquent behavior by the time they reached preadolescence or adolescence. These data are derived from psychoanalytic psychotherapy of abused preadolescents and adolescents who are out-patients at the Comprehensive Treatment Center for Abused Children and Their Families at the Downstate Medical Center.

Simultaneous therapeutic intervention with the parents of these children has provided additional information about the family interaction which produced child abuse.

Child abuse may be regarded as a complex experience consisting of several interrelated components, rather than as a single variable. Repeated injury of the child occurs within the context of a pathological parent/child and family relationship. The traumatic physical assault is accompanied by harsh and punitive childrearing, conveying parental hostility and rejection and leading to scapegoating. In our inner city population, a general background of family disorganization with interruption of maternal care was common. Neurological impairment was often present in the abused children.

Each of these components of the child abuse syndrome contributes to the formation of specific pathological personality characteristics and to the development of violent behavior in the following manner.

PHYSICAL ASSAULT RESULTING IN TRAUMATIC CONDITION

It is hard to imagine anything more terrifying to an infant or young child than physical assault at the hands of a screaming, uncontrolled parental figure. How does a child cope with being beaten, punched, burned, kicked or hurled across a room without warning by a person from whom nurturance and protection are usually expected? One might expect that his physical or psychological integrity would be severely threatened with the appearance of massive anxiety or its equivalent. This type of massive noxious stimulation obviously cannot be adequately processed or controlled by the young victim's defensive organization.

Freud's concept of the "stimulus barrier" is useful in the conceptualization of child abuse as a traumatic event. Freud (1920) regarded the infant's high threshhold for the perception of stimuli as a protective shield, or stimulus barrier. He described as "traumatic" any excitation powerful enough to break through this protective shield. He described the "traumatic situation" as the helplessness on the part of the ego in the fact of accumulation of excitation, whether of external or internal origin (Freud, 1926). Boyer (1964) stressed the mother's role as a supplementary stimulus barrier to compensate for the loss of efficiency in the original protective shield.

In the case of child abuse, the physical assault, bearing the threat of annihilation and/or abandonment, is perceived as an overwhelming trauma by the child. When the stimulus barrier is breached, the ego is rendered helpless, and a 'traumatic situation' ensues and a painful affect is experienced. The mother's failure to exercise her protective function adds to the child's discomfort. The infant may respond to the battering with undifferentiated negative affect, consisting of diffuse motor discharge, crying states, distress at being handled and disturbances in feeding and sleeping, indicating a disruption of his sensory-motor, physiological and affective equilibrium.

The older child, who is overwhelmed by the traumatic stimulation, will resort to primitive defenses, such as denial, avoidance or raising of sensory threshholds. Repeated abuse might interfere with the reception, processing and integration of sensory stimuli, resulting in sensory overload, panic and flight.

These defensive efforts are usually not successful in dealing with the anxiety and helplessness generated by the repeated episodes of physical assault, which results in a fixation to the trauma, as described by Freud in his last article on the subject (1937).

As a consequence, the original traumatic impression derived from parental assault and violence permeates the dreams, fantasies, play and object relationships of the abused children. They reenact the trauma by actively repeating the physical assault in which they attack and injure others in play and fantasy. The patterns of diffuse motor discharge exhibited by traumatized infants might be the prototype for this type of impulsive and repetitive acting out. Trauma inflicted on the child before and during the rapid acquisition of speech and language might foster the use of action instead of verbal communication with an incapacity for delay (Greenacre, 1950).

This fixation to the trauma in abused children seems to have some adaptive value. It permits active mastery of a passively experienced danger. In identifying with the aggressor, feelings of power and omnipotence replace feelings of helplessness. The timing of the trauma is controlled so that the child can prepare himself for it.

HARSH AND PUNITIVE MATERNAL ATTITUDE, CONVEYING ANGER AND HOSTILITY

Early exposure of an infant to a harsh and punitive parental figure may have numerous adverse sequelae. This promotes a primary identification with the aggressive parent, which facilitates the subsequent development of 'identification with the aggressor' as a major defense mechanism. Observations of abusing parent/abused child interaction have revealed a marked tendency of the children to imitate the parent's aggressive and impulsive characteristics. In his irritable, impulsive and destructive manipulation of toys and objects, one can envision the small abused child as a miniature edition of the 'angry' parent. In the subsequent development of these children, aggressive and assaultive behavior often becomes the primary vehicle for establishing object ties.

SCAPEGOATING

The abused child is usually blamed for the shortcomings and inadequacy of the parents. Most commonly, abuse is limited to one child in a family, and the scapegoat is the child most closely identified with the abusing parent. The scapegoated child reminds the parent of his own unacceptable traits and impulses. These parental deficiencies are projected onto the child, who, being unaware of the illogical nature of the scapegoating process, assumes that he is to blame and is deserving of the punishment. This increases his self-hatred and low self-esteem, which become the nucleus for subsequent self-destructive behavior.

Actual physical defects or psychological deviancy in the child will enhance the scapegoating process. The child accepts the role of the scapegoat because it is the easiest way of maintaining his identity in a pathological family environment in which the alternatives of neglect or abandonment might be more frightening. The parents reinforce the scapegoating process by ignoring the child when he is not disruptive.

The scapegoating process is finally stabilized when the 'badness' of the parent is transferred to the scapegoated child. The child thus complies with the unconscious wishes of the parents, completing the self-fulfilling prophecy.

The ultimate fate of this negative self-image is subject to fluctuation. In some cases, the child will retain the identity of the scapegoat, which becomes internalized and forms the prototype for subsequent object relationships. When these children become adolescents and adults, they often retain the masochistic ties to their families, or become involved with cruel and sadistic love objects. Other former scapegoats are unable to tolerate the accompanying guilt and anxiety, and narcissistic injury. They reject this negatively perceived self-image by means of projection and externalization onto others. Ultimately their own children become the most convenient targets for this displacement, as the cycle of scapegoating and abuse repeats itself in each generation. At this juncture, the former scapegoat assumes an identification with his own abusing parent ('identification with the aggressor').

MATERNAL DEPRIVATION AND FAMILY DISORGANIZATION

Child abuse, especially in the inner cities, is often associated with other signs of parental dysfunction such as neglect and a failure to provide the child with average expectable psychological and physical nurturance. Defects in parenting are often compounded by a highly stressful environment which includes poverty, poor housing, family disorganization and lack of support systems. Parental deprivation and neglect act as cumulative trauma (Khan, 1963), interfering with ego development. The children have been frequently exposed to separations from primary objects during their early years. This has often resulted from the migration of parents from rural areas to urban areas to seek employment. Thus, the detrimental effects of deprivation, which have been documented by numerous investigators (apathy, withdrawal, intellectual impairment, affect hunger with superficiality of object relations, poor superego development, low frustration tolerance, lack of basic trust and impaired object constancy) will be added to the sequelae of abuse.

The more pervasive elements of neglect experienced by the abused child might then add to the more circumscribed pathological impact of the abuse, increasing the cumulative damage to developing ego functions.

Abused children suffering from pronounced maternal deprivation and neglect often display severe separation anxiety based upon their inability to achieve object constancy. Their cognitive impairment and/or the lack of a dependable primary object, interfere with the construction and internalization of the mental representation of the absent object. They become vulnerable to object loss. Their difficulty in tolerating separation was frequently observed in the treatment situation in response to the therapist's vacations or departure from the hospital. Their feelings of physical and emotional impoverishment are translated into coercive and exploitative behavior. Stealing, mugging and robbery are the ultimate responses to feelings of deprivation and rejection.

CENTRAL NERVOUS SYSTEM IMPAIRMENT

Neurological abnormalities have been frequently discovered in abused children (Martin, 1975; Bacon, et al, 1970). Neurological damage may result from injury to the child's brain, as a consequence of direct trauma to the head (skull fracture, cerebral hemorrhage) or indirect trauma, such as the "shaking injury" described by Caffey (1972).

Martin also attributed some of the neurological impairment in abused children without brain injury to malnutrition and maternal deprivation. Sandgrund, Gaines, and Green (1974), described a high incidence of mental retardation in our population of abused children who had no evidence of head trauma. We concluded that in many of these children, the prior brain damage and retardation was regarded as a cause of, rather than a consequence of, abuse.

Regardless of etiology, a child with neurological impairment will be at greater risk for aggressive and violent behavior. The CNS impairment in itself will further undermine the cognitive, adaptive and defensive functions of the ego during their response to trauma, and interfere with controls over impulses and motility."

To summarize, an abused child reared under conditions of parental assault, punishment, deprivation, rejection and scapegoating learns to regard his environment with fear and distrust. He anticipates pain and frustration from parental encounters, rather than comfort and gratification. He gradually generalizes from these negative experiences with primary caretakers and soon regards the outside world as an extension of the sadomasochistic pattern of family life. The 'angry parent /bad child' interaction becomes the prototype for subsequent dyadic relationships. The absence of memories of paternal love, care and tenderness robs him of the capacity for optimism, affection and empathy. His relationships with others are characterized by expressions of uninhibited aggression, often accentuated by the presence of brain damage.

The violent behavior of the abused children occurs in the following manner: threats to the child's fragile self-esteem such as beatings, rejection, abandonment, etc., constitute a narcissistic injury giving rise to feelings of anxiety, helplessness and depressive effect which evoke memories of the earlier physical assaults. This results in the mobilization of 'identification with the aggressor' as a primary defense. This defense enables the child to reenact and repeat the earlier traumatic situations and allows him to actively assume the role of the aggressor rather than that of the passive victim. The current threatening object is unconsciously linked to the 'abusing parent' and the child's pent up rage toward his original tormentor is mobilized and displaced onto this new object.

'Identification with the aggressor' has additional adaptive value for the abused adolescent. It is used as a device for relieving tension, and as a pathological form of self-esteem regulation in which depression and helplessness are replaced by aggressive and destructive activities associated with omnipotent fantasies. To the abused adolescent, all human relationships consist of encounters between aggressors and victims. He is distrustful and uncomfortable in the presence of benign, caring individuals and usually seeks to restore the familiar sadomasochistic interaction by engaging in provocative behavior. This protects him against possible betrayal and rationalizes his continued defensive use of aggression.

IMPACT OF ADOLESCENCE ON THE ETIOLOGY OF VIOLENT BEHAVIOR

It is during the adolescent period that the aggressive, impulsive abused child may turn into a violent delinquent. This transformation is catalyzed by the following biological, psychological and social events during adolescence.

The rapid increase in physical growth and musculature provides the child with increased strength to execute violent antisocial activities. The incessant pressure of sexual and aggressive drives further upsets the unstable equilibrium between ego controls and impulses, resulting in a surplus of aggression which permeates object relationships. The characteristic 'acting out' behavior during the adolescent period further enhances the overt expression of aggressive thoughts and fantasies which is used as a defense against passivity.

The usual restructuring of superego, ego ideal and ego identification from childhood fails to occur in these adolescents after disengagement from their parents. In the normal adolescent, changes in these structures are effected through contact with new peers and adults who provide models for identification quite different from the parents. In the case of child abuse, fixation to the sadomasochistic identifications from childhood limits the freedom of the abused adolescents to experiment with new object identifications. Their compulsions to repeat the original trauma propel them toward violent and aggressive peers and adults who are extensions of the sadistic 'bad' parents. Thus the adolescent process perpetuates the earliest pathological identifications of these children, rather than modifying them.

Lower class membership and a subculture characterized by social disorganization, poverty and crime create a plentiful supply of violent antisocial individuals as models for identification.

CASE HISTORIES

Case histories of three abused children will illustrate the relationship between the early exposure to abuse and pathological childrearing and the subsequent development of violent, aggressive behavior. Each child represents a different age group to demonstrate the evolution of early childhood aggression into adolescent violence and delinquency.

Case History 1: Earl, a 6 year old black youngster, had been beaten and burned with an iron by his mother and her boyfriend. When he was hospitalized, untreated fractures of both cheek bones were discovered and his entire body was covered with marks and scars. He was placed in a foster home following discharge from the hospital. He exhibited severe behavior problems following his enrollment in kindergarten. He was found to be distractable and unmanageable in the classroom. He hit other children with toys and ignored instructions and reprimands from the teacher. When he became aggressive and destructive with his foster parents he was returned to the agency for replacement and placed in psychotherapy in our program. His new foster parents were simultaneously involved in counseling. In the initial stage of treatment, Earl symbolically reenacted his original traumatic experiences in the playroom in his play with dolls. He identified with a 'spider man' doll who was being beaten by a black 'mother' doll. Spider man then 'beat up' the female doll. Earl also carried on imaginary phone calls with his maternal grandmother, threatening to "beat her butt." He reacted to the placement with his new foster parents by bedwetting and soiling, and became provocative with his therapist, who refused to give him money and office supplies, which he demanded. At this point, Earl expected his therapist to hit him.

Earl's impulsive behavior soon began to interfere with his precarious adjustment in his new foster home. He exhibited an intense jealousy of the 4 year old boy who was his foster sibling at home. Earl would destroy this child's toys and physically attack him, when his inordinate demands for attention could not be provided by the foster parents. Earl began to steal and finally destroyed some furniture. The foster parents returned Earl to the agency for replacement after he set fire to his foster brother's bed.

Case History 2: Louis, a small, waif-like ll year old Puerto Rican boy, was recently referred for psychiatric treatment after he persuaded his 3 year old half-brother to drink some lye. This child required a resection of his esophagus and managed to survive after being hospitalized for over a year. Louis returned to his mother and her boyfriend when he was 9, after living with his abusive father and stepmother in Puerto Rico since the age of 2. He had been subjected to chronic physical abuse during this 7 year period which included beating on the head with a hammer and burns on his body inflicted with a hot iron. Since rejoining his mother, Louis had been extremely rough and aggressive with his two younger half-brothers. He also displayed hyperactive, aggressive behavior in school, frequently hitting and kicking his classmates' Louis conveys his violent feelings quite dramatically. "Sometimes I hate people because they bother or hit me. Once I hit a teacher in Puerto Rico because she punished me. I hit a kid in school who stole my pencil. I knocked him down the stairs. I hit my little brother when he makes too much noise. When I get nervous I punch the wall and hit my head against the radiator."

During his initial months of psychotherapy, Louis was extremely hyperactive and could not remain in the playroom for more than 20 minutes. When frustrated he would bang his fists or head against the wall. One of Louis' favorite activities at home consisted of catching mice and smashing their heads with a hammer. He would then flush them down the toilet. When asked to explain the reasons for this behavior, Louis pointed to the scars and ridges on his scalp, exclaiming, "This is what my father did to me." Louis could also be charming and ingratiating. He usually related to adults as need-satisfying objects. When frustrated, however, he would become impulsive and violent. Whenever he felt challenged or humiliated, he would try to engage his 'adversary' in physical combat. Louis' extreme sibling rivalry was expressed in therapeutic relationships. He became irate whenever he saw other children entering or leaving his therapist's office and expressed the desire to fight with them.

Case History 3: Charles T., a tall, well-built 16 year old black youngster, was reunited with his mother in New York at the age of 15, after spending the majority of his childhood with his maternal aunt and grandfather in the South. Charles was returned to his mother by his aunt after he was placed on probation for shooting his junior high school teacher with a pellet gun. This incident occurred after he was reprimanded by the teacher in front of the class for picking on a classmate. After this teacher hit him with a ruler, Charles announced that he would return with a gun and take revenge. He carried out the threat and proceeded to shoot the teacher in the leg.

Since his return to New York, Charles continued to exhibit difficulties in school. He has been abusive to a younger brother and has been involved in stealing. Another violent incident occurred when Charles shot a gun into a crowd of hostile white youths who were taunting him and several of his friends because they had entered the white neighborhood after a rock concert. Luckily no one was hit and Charles was arrested on the spot. Charles obtained the gun by stealing it from his friend's father. He carried the weapon with him in anticipation of attack. He had recently been mugged at knife point. As he ran away, he vowed never to allow himself to be victimized again. Charles seemed unperturbed when confronted with the possibility that his use of firearms might have resulted in someone's death or severe injury. He blandly responded, "If someone was killed, he deserved it."

Charles' current social adjustment is poor. He associates with children younger than himself because he has trouble competing with his peers. His principal interest and hobby is training dogs. He is fascinated with bull terriers because "they can be trained to kill men." In a recurrent fantasy, his bull terrier carries out his command to kill a menacing German shepherd."

Charles had experienced a traumatic early childhood. He was born when his mother, Miss T., was 13. Miss T. had been living with a female cousin and her husband when Charles was conceived. Miss T. had been repeatedly physically and sexually abused by the cousin and her husband. She was sent to live with them at the age of 4, after her mother died. Miss T.'s mother had also beaten her. When Charles was born, Miss T. lived alone in the room and did not have enough money to adequately feed and clothe him. She regarded the baby as "unreal, like a doll." When Charles cried out of hunger, she beat him "so he would go to sleep. I beat him so long, he'd be crazy," Miss T. confessed, "I hit with a belt, extension cord and a clothes hanger." Miss T. had two more children at ages 15 and 16. She continued to abuse Charles and also mistreated the two younger boys. Charles was sent to live with his maternal aunt at the age of 4, but he rejoined his mother at age 6 and remained with her until he was 10, when he returned to the South to live with his aunt.

Miss T. is fully aware of Charles' violent potential as an adult. She's afraid he will become a child abuser or murderer. She explains, "If someone hits him or threatens him, he gets crazy." Although Charles recalls having been beaten by his aunt and some teachers, he has no conscious recollection of the physical abuse experienced at the hands of his mother during the first 4 years of life.

DISCUSSION

The behavior of these children is typical of the abused boys of their age, with whom they share several features in common. (Abused girls may display similar aggressive patterns prior to puberty; but during adolescence their delinquent activity is more frequently complicated by sexual promiscuity, running away and masochistic behavior.) These boys were exposed to physical and psychological abuse, neglect and separation from parents since early childhood, which resulted in substantial psychological and cognitive impairment with poor impulse control and damaged self-esteem. Their identification with violent, aggressive parents were not modified by positive attachments to loving parental figures. Identification with the aggressor was used as a primary defense in situations of anxiety provoked by fears of attack, humiliation and abandonment, which were linked unconsciously to memories of traumatic victimization in early childhood. Their aggressive behavior was an adaptive maneuver designed to master the original trauma by active repetition. Their action orientation was accompanied by difficulties in language and symbolization. These children manifested little or no guilt during their violent behavior, and lacked a capacity to empathize or identify with their victims.

IMPLICATIONS FOR TREATMENT

Safeguarding an abused child from further maltreatment by therapeutic intervention with his parents or placement outside of the family will not be sufficient to alleviate his suffering and inner turmoil. Damage to the abused child's ego functions, cognitive capacity and self-esteem requires vigorous psychotherapeutic and psychoeducational intervention. The abused child will perpetuate the original sadomasochistic interaction with his parents in all subsequent relationships unless changes can be effected in his pathological inner world. Modification of pathological internalized self and object representations can be effected through play therapy and psychotherapy, but it is essential that treatment begin during childhood. It is more difficult, and at times impossible, to reverse the emotional impairment in an abused teenager who has already experienced the chaotic biological and psychological upheaval of adolescence and is committed to a violent, delinquent life style.

REFERENCES

Bacon, M., Bejar, R., & Scheaff, P. Neurological manifestations of the battered child syndrome. *Pediatrics,* 1970, *45,* 1003-1007.

Boyer, L. On maternal overstimulation and ego deficits. In *The psychoanalytic study of the child.* Vol. 2. New York: International Universities Press, 1964.

Caffey, J. On the theory and practice of shaking infants: Its potential residual affects of permanent brain damage and mental retardation. *American Journal of Diseases of Children,* 1972, *124,* 161-169.

Freud, S. *Beyond the pleasure principle (1920).* Standard Edition, 1955, Vol. 18, 7-64.

Freud, S. *Inhibitions, symptoms and anxiety (1926).* Standard Edition, 1959, Vol. 20, 77-175.

Freud, S. *Moses and monotheism, three essays (1937).* Standard Edition, 1964, Vol. 23, 7-56.

Greenacre, P. General problems of acting out. *Psychoanalytic Quarterly,* 1950, *19,* 455-467.

Khan, M. The concept of cumulative trauma. In *The psychoanalytic study of the child.* Vol. 18. New York: International Universities Press, 1963.

Martin, H. The development of abused children. *Advances in Pediatrics,* 1974, *21,* 25-73.

Sandgrund, A., Gaines, R., & Green, A. Child abuse and mental retardation: A problem of causes and effect. *American Journal of Mental Deficiency* , 1974, *79,* 327-330.

13

Theoretical Linkages Between Child Abuse and Juvenile Delinquency

ROBERT W. WEINBACH, DON E. ADAMS,
H. ARNOLD ISHIZUKA & KAREN L. ISHIZUKA

College of Social Work
University of South Carolina
Columbia, South Carolina

Nothing seems quite so logical as a relationship between the child abuse syndrome and delinquency. It simply makes sense that a person who has been abused as a child should want to strike out at someone. Society is there, yet impersonal, and not in a position to retaliate in a one-to-one manner. Delinquent behavior against society or its representatives would seem to offer good opportunity for completing a cycle of violence which began as unwarranted aggressive behavior toward a confused and terrified child.

But, is the relationship one of simple cause and effect? Very few relationships outside of the laboratory and in the complex world of human interaction are all that simple. It would not be too difficult, for example to build a case for a cause-effect relationship in the opposite direction—a certain indicator of the complexity of the relationship. Imagine a parent of an eleven year old boy who has just returned from a mandatory juvenile court appearance. The son's delinquent behavior has just resulted in a half day of lost work time, suggestions about inadequacy in his or her role as parent, the loss of a vacation fund which must now be spent for restitution and general mortification in front of neighbors and professionals. The most rational, sophisticated, understanding parent might see the need for warmth and understanding in building a better rapport with the boy; the more common (and, perhaps, honest) reaction would be to want to beat the hell out of him!

The point is this: we would be both naive and grandiose if we were to assert that we can document a relationship of cause and effect when we attempt to associate delinquency and child abuse. No pure *ex post facto* experimental home situation exists for its verification. Furthermore, as some of our recent research suggests, we cannot assume that all child abuse, as defined by rigid and, perhaps, culturally biased definitions, is motivated by sadism, frustration or ignorance of human development. There exists a thin, highly mobile line between willful abuse and well-intentioned, culturally sanctioned punishment viewed by the perpetrator (and sometimes the victim as well) as 'parenting.'

The purpose of this examination of the literature is to attempt to document that there exists a theoretical linkage between the two behaviors, and nothing more. If such a theoretical underpinning can be shown to exist, perhaps both phenomena can be understood more fully and more relevant preventive and treatment approaches can be developed.

In recent research (Adams, Ishizuka, Ishizuka, 1977) the authors were able to locate a great deal of theoretical justification for the hypothesis that a high percentage of delinquents had been abused as children. The support was chiefly contextual, i.e., the descriptive knowledge which had been compiled about conditions related to delinquency bore a startling resemblence to those which had been found to exist when the child abuse syndrome was present. It is the most dramatic of these contextual similarities, culled from the scholarly books and journals, which we present as evidence for a 'logical' (and the term is used with trepidation) association between the two social phenomena.

1. *Definitions and Management.* Both delinquency and child abuse definitions are characterized by the same variations. They express the limits of behavior which can be tolerated by a society. The statement that "delinquency is a legal term for a social problem" (Thurston, 1942) is also reflective of a number of similar conclusions regarding child abuse (e.g., Mauss, 1975). While legal definitions are available for prosecution and management of both phenomena, they tend to vary from community to community and from subgroup to subgroup. The family is seen as the most desirable vehicle for change in both. The courts and social agencies are rarely involved before behavior has become so repetitive and offensive to community members that it can no longer be tolerated. Even then, agency and court professionals can choose to proceed no further in alleged delinquency and abuse cases, either because of professional judgments, insufficient evidence or even the realities of existing case overloads. The result is a 'tip of the iceberg' statistic which is far from reflective of true rates of incidence (Lobsenz, 1975; Curlee, 1976).

2. *Patterns of Incidence.* Among reported incidence of delinquency and abuse there exists a similar pattern suggesting that both phenomena are cross-cultural, cross-racial and tend to appear in all socioeconomic classes (U.S. Department of Health, Education and Welfare, *Child Abuse and Neglect: An Overview of the Problem,* 1975.) Deprivation and/or affluence cannot be linked to either problem in any consistent way. Patterns exist, however, in the way socioeconomic groups employ the courts in management of both delinquency and abuse. With both problems, a relatively high percentage of lower socioeconomic group cases reach the judicial system; the greater resources of the upper classes seem to result in a frequent

'cover-up' of both delinquent behavior and child abuse (Weaver and Wilson, 1973; Helfer and Kempe, 1968; Nye, 1958).

3. *Intergenerational Characteristics of the Problem.* While not all parents of delinquents and abused children experienced similar problems when young, there is considerable evidence in the literature to suggest that both problems are intergenerational. Parents of delinquents have consistently been described as having characteristics of emotional disturbances and delinquent behavior (Glueck and Glueck, 1968).

Abusive parents are likely to have been victims of abuse (Helfer and Kempe, 1968). They are characterized by the inability to develop a genuine relationship with another person, feelings of being unloved as a child, excessive dependency, inability to delay gratification, yearning for care, consideration and satisfaction and a disproportionately high incidence of abuse as a child (Wasserman, 1967; U.S. Department of Health, Education, and Welfare, *The Problem and Its Management,* 1975; Zalba, 1966). Are delinquency (as reflected in adult manifestations of delinquent behavior and attitudes) and child abuse learned as a part of role identification? It appears likely that with both phenomena some early identification with the interactional 'style' of significant adult figures may relate to later behavioral problems.

4. *Parental Approaches to Discipline.* The literature suggests that, with both delinquency and abuse, a dichotomy may take place in relation to effects of discipline practices. The nebulous term 'excessive' on either end of the discipline continuum seems to result in characteristic forms of delinquency and abuse. The absence of or inadequate discipline may provoke aggressive acts of delinquency which are less overt and which may be aimed at attention getting or peer acceptance and sanction. Excessively severe, physical security threatening and physically violent discipline have been associated with aggressive, destructive acts of delinquency (Deykin, 1972; Shore, 1971; Haskell and Yablonsky, 1974). While lack of discipline may suggest lack of concern and, thereby, hinder the development of a child's inner controls, violent or excessive discipline may provide a violent role model which may be reflected in more overtly violent forms of delinquency.

Similarly, too little or too severe discipline are believed to result in different forms of abuse. Insufficient discipline, not surprisingly, is characteristic of a parenting style of irresponsibility which is also associated with abandonment or neglect, i.e., a lack of discipline is found in cases where children are abandoned or uncared for but not overtly abused. The overtly abused child more commonly lives in a home where discipline is violent, severe and brutal. The disciplinary measures themselves, of course, may constitute all or only part of abusive behavior. The violent type of discipline observed by the child may serve as an example (role model) of how he should act when he becomes angry with someone (Gold, 1963).

5. *Stability of the Family.* Homes which seem to be associated with delinquent behavior may be characterized by instability. One study concluded that psychologically broken homes that were quarrelsome and negligent tended to be more associated with delinquency than did broken homes (Zax and Stricker, 1968). Dysfunctional families of this type are believed to produce tension and strain within the child. A sense of apprehension and uncertainty is thought to lead to delinquency (Commins, 1971).

Both delinquents and abused children are likely to have experienced foster placement (Glueck and Glueck, 1968). Interestingly, foster homes and institutional settings may bring together these two not so discrete groups for the first time. While abuse and early delinquent behavior likely occurred in the home of origin, the similarity of subsequent life experience which abused children and delinquents experience may suggest yet another linkage between the two social problems.

6. *Role in the Family.* Both the delinquent and the abused child apparently possess a non-vital role in the family. The delinquent's role may tend to enforce a feeling of not belonging. He has been found to be the least preferred child and has become the family scapegoat (Commins, 1971). Perfectly adequate relationships may exist among parents and other siblings, but the delinquent child may be excluded from gratifying relationships and may be made to feel an outsider (Bremner, 1970).

Severe social stress within the family is also seen in families where child abuse occurs. Problems such as marital difficulties, financial mismanagement and faulty community relationships (social isolation) are relatively common (Zalba, 1966; Holter and Freedman, 1968). The frustrations of racial suppression and economic failure may be alleviated in part by projecting responsibility for disappointments onto a child. The scapegoating may be limited to a single child who is perceived (either validly or out of ignorance) to be a slow learner, unduly defiant, hyperactive or withdrawn. As with delinquency, other children may be admitted into gratifying relationships. Scapegoating may also be applied to all the children who through a process of rationalization can be believed to represent the major obstacles to a life of prosperity and success (Zalba, 1966; Hetherington, 1975).

7. *Characteristics of the Child.* Both biologically and psychologically, the delinquent child may possess characteristics which relate to his behavior. Mental defectiveness has long been thought to increase vulnerability to delinquent behavior because such a child may be easily manipulated due to instability or suggestibility to peer pressures (Bovet, 1951). Studies in Great Britain have identified a relatively high percentage of adult criminals and delinquents who were mentally retarded or of borderline intelligence (Kolb, 1973).

The lack of psychological nurturance is viewed as contributory to delinquent behavior. The child who has been inadequately loved or who has never developed a sense of trust may become delinquent (Commins, 1971). The child is viewed as having a common human need to perceive himself as a person of worth. Unfortunately, the psychological dynamics of becoming somebody may be the same as those involved in becoming delinquent (Zietz, 1959). Peer acceptance, to an adolescent, may assume equal or greater priority than adult acceptance; the delinquent may find a needed identity among an anti-social reference group. Unmet needs are met by a process of reacting to and reaching out which may also serve as a "redress for the misfortunes of childhood" (Gold, 1963, p. 13) and as an "indirect expression of aggression against parents" (Gold, 1963, p. 360). Is it unreasonable to assume that a childhood of abuse will tend to increase the likelihood of such a reaction?

In describing the abused child it is difficult to say with certainty whether many of the physical and psychologically unique characteristics of the child preceded or resulted from abusive behavior. They are often different from other children in a subtle way that goes beyond physical bruises or inappropriate dress designed to obscure scars or malnutrition. Parents' perceptions of 'differentness' may be substantiated by (or they may indirectly precipitate) unexplainable learning difficulties, tendencies to cry often or not at all, fearlessness or excessive fearfulness of adult authority, aggressiveness or passiveness *(Child Abuse and Neglect: An Overview,* 1975).

The same emotional deprivation and lack of a sense of worth which is seen in the delinquent can be seen among abused children. Even the abuse itself elicits little sympathy or acceptance, and then of only brief duration. The parent may be critical of the child for being injured and expect him to assume the adult role and to calm the parent. His inability to do so may result in further denigration of worth, both by parents and by himself *(Proceedings from Project Protection,* 1974).

SUMMARY

There are, quite simply, many more contextual similarities to delinquency and child abuse than there are differences. We have described only a few of the more obvious examples of 'common denominators' which were uncovered in the scientific literature. Other similarities in such diverse areas as family cohesion, parental fixations, patterns of child supervision and legal responses to the problems could be described in depth. Perhaps the most important similarity of all is the high level of concern presently reflected in our society's commitment to intervene in family functioning and to act on behalf of the child whether he is abused, delinquent or both.

Researchers and scholars have generally been reticent to state that child abuse results in delinquency or vice versa. A notable exception is Simmons (1970) who states that "a brutal parent tends to produce a criminal child" (p. 48). Simmons suggests that hostility toward the parents who have brutally treated a child is transfered to the world in general and he becomes delinquent.

Haskell and Yablonsky (1974) concluded that juvenile institutions are populated by persons who are victims of abusive treatment and family pathology. In our own study of 653 delinquents, 43% were shown to have been abused, neglected or abandoned at some point in their lives (Adams, Ishizuka and Ishizuka, 1977).

The circumstantial evidence for association continues to build. Whether the relationship is ultimately found to be a complicated chain of cause and effect or two parallel, interrelated phenomena linked to one or more other social variables is, perhaps, less important than the demonstration of some interrelationship which will preclude a myopic prevention or treatment approach to either phenomena. Having concluded that the two are inseparable, it is time to address them with broad, comprehensive solutions.

REFERENCES

Adams, D. E., Ishizuka, H.A., & Ishizuka, K. S. *The child abuse delinquent: An exploratory/descriptive study.* Unpublished MSW thesis, University of South Carolina, Columbia, 1977.

Bovet, L. *Psychiatric aspects of juvenile delinquency.* Geneva: World Health Organization, 1951.

Bremner, R. H. (Ed.) *Children and youth in America.* Cambridge: Harvard University Press, 1970.

Commins, N. *The essence of delinquency.* Cambridge: Cambridge Aids to Learning, Ltd., 1971.

Curlee, M. Interview, Columbia, South Carolina, November 17, 1976.

Deykin, E. Y. Life functioning in families of delinquent boys: An assessment model, *Social Service Review*, 1971, *46*(1), 90-91.

Glueck, S. & Glueck, E. *Delinquents and non-delinquents in perspective.* Cambridge: Harvard University Press, 1968.

Gold, M. *Status forces in delinquent boys.* Ann Arbor: The University of Michigan Press, 1963.

Haskell, M. R. & Yablonsky, L. *Crime and delinquency.* (2nd ed.) Chicago: Rand-McNally College Publishing Co., 1974.

Helfer, R. E. & Kempe, C. H. (Eds.) *The battered child.* Chicago: The University of Chicago Press, 1968.

Hetherington, E. M. (Ed.) *Review of child development research.* Vol. 5. Chicago: The University of Chicago Press, 1975.

Holter, J. C. & Freedman, S. B. Principles of management in child abuse cases. *American Journal of Orthopsychiatry,* January, 1968, *28,* 130-132.

Kolb, L. C. *Modern clinical psychiatry.* Philadelphia: W. B. Saunders Co. 1973.

Lobsenz, N. One woman's war against child abuse. *Good Housekeeping,* July, 1975, 82-83, 118-120.

Mauss, A. L. *Social problems as social movements.* Philadelphia: J. B. Lippincott Co., 1975.

Nye, I. F. *Family relationships and delinquent behavior.* New York: John Wiley & Sons, Inc., 1958.

Proceedings from Project Protection, Montgomery County Public Schools, Child Abuse and Neglect Conference Workshop, Rockville, Maryland, 1974.

Simmons, H. E. *Protective Services for children.* (2nd ed.) Sacramento: The Citadel Press, 1970.

Shore, M. F. Psychological theories of the causes of antisocial behavior, *Crime and delinquency,* 1971, *17*(4), 456-468.

Thurston, H. W. *Concerning juvenile delinquency.* New York: Cambridge University Press, 1942.

U. S. Department of Health, Education, and Welfare. *Child abuse and neglect: An overview of the problem.* Washington, D.C.: U. S. Government Printing Office, 1975.

U. S. Department of Health, Education, and Welfare. *Child abuse and neglect: The problem of its management.* Vol. 1. Washington, D.C.: U. S. Government Printing Office, 1975.

Weaver, D. J. & Wilson, C. D. *Description of the treatment given child abuse cases in South Carolina with implications for more adequate delivery of services.* Unpublished MSW thesis, University of South Carolina, Columbia, 1973.

Zax, M. & Stricker, G. *The study of abnormal behavior.* New York: The Macmillan Co., 1968.

Zietz, D. *Child welfare: Principles and methods.* New York: John Wiley & Son, Inc., 1959.

14

Social Learning Theory and Child Abuse Interventions

STUART VEXLER

Research Coordinator
Texas Youth Council
Austin, Texas

This paper is not on social learning theory and how it explains the relationship between child abuse and delinquency. Rather, it is on what the assumptions of a relationship between the two mean with regard to the types of interventions we want to develop to deal with both problems. Fairly consistently in the papers presented in this conference, people have in various ways related child abuse to delinquency. While I reinforce and support the existence of that relationship, I don't really think that's at issue. The question we need to be addressing now is: given this understanding of child abuse and delinquency, what sorts of programs are required?

EXPLANATION OF SOCIAL LEARNING THEORY

By social learning theory, I refer to assumptions that behavior is controlled by environmental shaping and indirect environmental and developmental influences which include parental influences, our social service interventions, our public school systems and the ways all of these reinforce different kinds of behavior and different sorts of relationships. The two major factors in social learning theory which appear to relate to child abuse are modeling and reinforcement. With regard to modeling, it has been fairly well demonstrated that children tend to imitate and follow the behavior of adults with whom they identify most strongly, particularly their parents. The real problem, or pitfall, that we see if we adopt the modeling approach is that if a child has been raised in an environment where he or she is abused, where physical punishment is the dominant method the parent uses to control the child's behavior, then the child is going to grow up feeling that this is an appropriate way of life, at least to raise children, and, perhaps, to deal with all sorts of conflicts and problems. We then have a self-perpetuating phenomenon. A child who was raised in a home where he is beaten is going to raise children by beating them.

A second social learning force is social reinforcement. Even when you have behavior demonstrated, the controlled experimentation with modeling shows that if there is no social reinforcement, the behavior will usually be extinguished. When there is reinforcement for aggressive behavior, when there are sub-cultures or neighborhoods which tend to condone, tolerate or reinforce physical abuse or extreme physical punishment for children's behavior, then child abuse is going to go on. The child will grow up in an environment where this sort of behavior is acceptable.

RELATED INFLUENCES

We can then analyze a few lesser psychological influences which are related to the above. One is that there is a fairly well established relationship between the severity of physical punishment in the home and aggressive behavior in the children (Eron, Walder, and Lefcowitz, 1971). The research shows that where children have been exposed to varying severity of punishment, the more severe the physical punishment, the more often spanking and other forms of physical punishment are used to control children, the more likely they are to demonstrate hostile behavior among their peers and in schools.

Another factor is that mental health research (Becker, 1964) shows that most 'messed up' youth, children who are referred for services and are placed in mental health, child welfare and delinquent services, came out of homes where there is a lack of consistency in the disciplining of children.

In terms of child abuse, as little as is known about the behavior of parental abuse, it seems evident that also it is not a consistent behavior. What we have is a situation where periodically, for one reason or another, this physical abuse will take place and the child will grow up not understanding what is expected of it. Children need fairly consistent boundaries in terms of behavior in order to understand the limitations and in order to develop their own self control. Try to take the child's point of view. There may be some stress, high anxiety in the home. The child commits an act, perhaps an innocuous act. The parent responds with an outburst of temper, followed closely by the child being grabbed, squeezed and hit. The child, in this confusion, may well see this beating as a random response. So we now have two problems. The child has learned nothing about what is to be considered appropriate behavior for himself. At the same time, he has witnessed that an appropriate response to confusion or personal displeasure or high anxiety is physically lashing out.

The last factor to be mentioned is that verbal skills are very important in our society. Some of the best short-term studies on child development show that in middle class homes the mother consistently uses verbal skills in order to control the child's behavior (Hess, Brophy and Shipman, 1968). She talks to the child in giving instructions to him or her, verbal controls are used for adjustment. Verbal reinforcement is used when the child is committing the desired behavior. Verbal skills are most likely not being used in homes where abuse is taking place. Parents in these homes often react and respond physically rather than verbally. We could just say that this is a case of modeling and that children who learn how to resolve problems with their verbal skills, how to talk problems out or how to reason with teachers in the classroom, will be much better adjusted than those who know no other way to react than with physical response. The extent and quality of verbal controls in homes in which child abuse has occurred are topics upon which relatively simple research designs could shed some light.

INTERVENTION ASSUMPTIONS

In a previous paper on the subject, I've made two strong assumptions about interventions. I want to pass these on because they are the basis for the sorts of interventions presented. The first of these is that I believe in a behavioral orientation. In order to define what the problem is with which we're trying to deal, we need to define the objectives that we want to reach through our intervention. From my frame of reference, this means that we need a behavioral orientation. We must be able to define a problem in terms of observable phenomena. We define the behavior as the parent beating the child. (I avoid the subject of emotional abuse and I will discuss why I think it's wise for us, both in terms of program administration and academic orientations to the subject, to stick to physical abuse.) We have the problem: the child is being beaten by the parent, a problem we can treat.

Then we look at an objective. The objective that I think is useful in this frame of reference is normalized development. What we want as an end product is not necessarily a parent who doesn't beat his or her child any more or a parent who necessarily raises that child in a traditional middle class way. The goal should be a child growing up in a normal fashion. We can use whatever frame of reference we might want to for what that means. Norms of acceptable behavior and cultural values vary greatly even within homogeneous groups but we can generally make statements about what is acceptable and what is not.

The second frame of reference is that I see child abuse as a community problem. As discussed in a previous paper, for the last 60 or 70 years, when community problems have been identified, the community has chosen to use the government as its instrument for intervening. As far back as revolutionary times we had poor houses which were community responses to the problem of poverty and to the problem of not being able to feed, house and clothe people. Public school education, even in colonial times, was regarded as a community responsibility passed over to the government. Community leaders decide that they do not want to have a hodgepodge of community schools, so they set up an independent school district that taxes everyone. Schooling then becomes a government responsibility.

In the field of child abuse, I think we've made a mistake by treating child abuse as a government responsibility. Analysis of the current rise of child abuse as a critical problem may shed light on that judgment on my part. One of the factors that people have talked about here and in the media, consistently, is the decline of the support system that .we used to have in this country which may have served to prevent child abuse. The extended family served as a very valuable resource. If the parents were under real stress, they could send the child to his grandparents or his uncle who lived around the corner and know that the child would be taken care of. If a parent was not particularly skilled at parenting, the grandparents, aunts and uncles, or the godparents were going to be monitoring this child's rearing and were going to be able to tell them, "You know, you really shouldn't beat the child. You need to, the next time this happens, come talk to me and we'll talk to the kid about it." We don't have these extended families anymore.

The neighborhood — the old neighborhood, the old neighbor down the street who would tell my mother whenever I did anything wrong—is much less prevalent than it was 20 years ago when I was growing up and I think that perhaps all of us can relate to this. I live in a neighborhood now where neighbors are mere acquaintances at best and I don't really expect them to intervene in helping me raise my pets, or my children.

This social decline is a real problem but it gives us a partial key to a solution. This solution is that if those support systems in the past helped prevent delinquency or child abuse, then maybe we need to look at interventions which will reinforce and support the development of artificial support systems that can serve in similar capacities.

I believe we need to look at the family orientation. Everybody is getting very family oriented. President Carter is family oriented, and the Texas Department of Public Welfare is family oriented, but I think that we miss a point when we talk in terms of general family orientation, and that is that we're dealing with a child with a specific problem. The child's problem is that he is not growing up in a normalized way and we're going to intervene. Do you as taxpayers and program decision makers want to have blanket policies for child abuse?

When I've heard people say that federal policies on child abuse are needed, it concerns me. I wonder how the federal government can come up with some sweeping program to work with a problem that is really multifaceted. There is no central, national source of child abuse, though I'm sure we can make classifications of abuse and identify situations where abuse occurs. I would imagine that in every abuse situation there are special elements, special problems that lead to the abuse in that situation. What we need to have are different problems and interventions tailored to local needs. In terms of children, if we're dealing with a younger child, then I believe we need to look at support for the parents, trying to reinforce the family, trying to help the parents look at other ways of raising their children without abusing them. As the child gets older, if the child has been consistently abused, it may really be too late for that kind of educational intervention and we may need to consider the standard response of removing the child from the home. I think that we can set up systems for handling this that are not arbitrary. We can look at the situation of the child abuse, look at the age of the children and then decide what should be done.

In terms of the problems of the adult involved, I'd identify two situations where child abuse occurs. One of these is an acute situation when there is a great deal of stress. The parent has just become unemployed, just lost a parent or just run out of gas. The child acts out and the parent responds with some kind of abuse. I think that is a different problem from what I would call a more chronic child abuse which may be attributed simply to a lack of education about other ways of raising children. In a previous paper, I told an anecdote about a young girl who slapped her child around as a light exercise and a way for her to get the child to perform. She was not conscious of other ways of controlling the child and was completely unaware that her current actions were destructive.

Focus on the Child and His/Her Needs

Age	Deficits	Intervention
0 - 4	Consistent parent/ child interaction Inappropriate model of frustration - aggression	Remove child to more "loving" -- work with parent - self-control - parenting skills Provide appropriate model to work with child and parent(s)
4 - 10	Poor verbal skills, poor impulse control These characteristics will often be developing but require parent models or other significant adult	Remove child to more supportive environment, work with parent (same as above), offer enrichment through the schools, recreation programs
11 -	Inappropriate peer models, poor verbal skills, poor impulse control	Groups with "pre-delinquent" focus on communication skills, impulse control, structure after school programs, work with parents - same as above - remove from the home to a more structured environment

(from Vexler and Raffaniello, 1977)

We know that psychologists and social workers know some ways of dealing with stress. Minicourses in stress management are now very popular at universities and community colleges. I think that for some people we need to look at ways of delivering to them some skills in adapting to stress so that they won't respond with physical acting out.

In the other situations, where the problem is simply a lack of education, I think we need to look at a better educational model and better methods of communicating child rearing, nutrition and other information to parents, and to look at ways of delivering parenting skills to people. We might want to consider requiring parenting skills be taught in the public schools. Perhaps this could be done in the same way that health education or sex education are now being offered. I think we need to look at effective ways of delivering this information. I don't think we need to rely on a teacher getting up in front of a class and talking about parenting. When I think of parenting, I believe people can relate to it in real ways. They may have younger siblings, and have watched their parents raise them. We can inject some reality into this situation. Perhaps we can even work older people into the same classrooms as younger people, which might make the education much less threatening or demeaning to both groups. This would have to be done as part of a general strategy of government intervention, some elements of which are presented in the section which follows.

GOVERNMENT POLICY

I would like to see interventions which reemphasize community responsibility. I think any interventions that we come up with that allow people to believe that the government is going to take care of their problem are a real mistake. I believe that 1) they probably won't work, since governmental services are not well-suited to private, personal, subculturally reinforced behaviors; 2) government intervention into child rearing practices raises strong concerns about personal privacy and 1984; 3) communities can more effectively intervene separate from the government; and 4) that use of government interventions will undermine the community's interventions and its abilities to intervene. If we allow people to look at the government as responsible for taking care of all of our needs, we will lose the ability to provide for ourselves.

It is important here to differentiate between government taking some responsibility for acting on a problem and the government establishing programs of direct service delivery aimed at the problem. I support childcare agencies being vigilant in identifying dangers to youth. It does not follow that I support governmental employees establishing caseloads of problem families with attendant supervisory bureaucracies. Units of government at various levels can spend funds to stimulate the development of services (i.e., education) by agencies at the local level and should set up monitoring and evaluation systems to gauge the impact of funds spent in this manner. To the extent that we can create artificial extended families, to the extent that we can get retired people or people in nursing homes to 'adopt' children and get them involved in child rearing and in family life, we've not only gotten an experienced, concerned person in to monitor child rearing but we've also relieved the boredom in the old age home. This is one of the things that's been done in some areas of the country as a way of creating what I would call an artificial extended family.

We need to use more public campaigns to arouse community interest in this subject. I know that in Texas there were 30-second spots on television which said: "If you see a neighbor abusing a child call this number and report it to the caseworker." That arouses public interest a little bit. But it is looking at the problem as a government responsibility. Don't do anything yourself. Call the government and they send a caseworker out. This is a step in the direction of making people aware of the extent of child abuse and perhaps making them aware of the damage that child abuse does. If people don't care about child abuse, they certainly care about crime right now. If we can get people to understand the linkage between crime and delinquency and child abuse, maybe they'll start caring about child abuse in their community.

What I would like to see is direct government action reserved as a last resort. If people see a neighbor abusing a child they could go over and talk to the neighbor. If the neighbor responds extremely defensively and says: "Get the hell out of here, you're not going to tell me how to raise my kid," then they can always call the caseworker after that. But I think if we can keep the problem at a person-to-person level, get neighborhood involvement and the individual will have gotten some real benefit above that of sending in a professional caseworker.

The second policy would be a commitment to normalized development. When government intervention is necessary, we should minimize the extent of intervention into the family. I don't think we need to put people on childcare caseloads for the rest of their lives. We need to develop short-term interventions where we can try to deal with the problem of child abuse, then get back out of the home. To the extent that we need to do follow-ups, monitoring to see how effective we were, I think we should maintain contact. But we need to minimize the interventions. We do not want to foster dependence on governmental interventions.

In line with minimizing the intervention, we need to present parenting skills in a non-threatening unobtrusive, unintrusive. If a parent is ordered to go to a caseworker at the local child welfare clinic or the local child guidance center, they are going to feel that they have been identified, they may feel defensive about it and they're going to feel labeled. I think we're all very sensitive to labeling theory in delinquency. I think it applies equally well to parents who are having trouble raising their kids. One vehicle for doing this is to offer parenting education through our educational systems as I was mentioning earlier. Offer it through the junior college, offer it through the community college or the high school continuing education program. I think that this may be a useful way of presenting needed skills most effectively.

A third set of policies would try to develop community support systems. It is well-acknowledged in the field of mental health that interventions occurring at times of crises have the best opportunities for success. We can identify crisis situations where people are most open to suggestions and where they are most ready to change. When individuals are in a crisis, if you come to them with a solution at that particular moment, you're most likely to be able to effect change. I think most professionals would agree on that. But there's a little problem. That is, if you come out of the blue and offer them solutions in their crisis, they're liable not to respond to it terribly well. You need to have built some credibility or some history with these people. Now we obviously can't have caseworkers going around and introducing themselves to everyone in the neighborhood so that if a crisis ever comes up, they won't have to come in as a stranger, if only because there isn't enough money.

What we can use are natural bridges, the priest in the community, the lady that runs the laundromat, the grocer, people that come in contact with large numbers of people in the community every day. They have established credibility. They can serve as bridges between the professional and the person in need of childcare services. I think that we need to begin looking at more and more ways of involving those people.

I think what we need to do as social service administrators and as people involved in social services is to encourage the observers of the world to go ahead and get involved. The worst thing that can happen is they can be told to butt out, to leave the situation alone. But that doesn't hurt anyone and they will have at least made an effort to tell parents that child abuse is really not the best thing to do. This alternative is easily preferable to directly going to the last resort. The last resort should be: if you've been abusing your child, that's against the law, you will go to jail and/or have your child taken away from you.

I think that we really need to look at these lesser measures before we resort to governmental and legal interventions. Restricting direct governmental intervention to the last resort may make it more effective. It will almost certainly be more efficient.

In closing, I'll refer back to Peter Forsythe's presentation where he talked about the question of values in this problem. What he was saying in particular was that many of the policies that we have enacted have tended to erode our old support systems. In some ways we have opted for lifestyles which reinforce the erosion. Examples are conscious policies and decisions that were directed at higher values, individual freedom, equal rights for women and greater mobility. I think that we need to be very conscious of these values. Every intervention that we propose is value-loaded. I think that we make a real mistake in ignoring the values and trying to pretend that we are being objective. I think that being against child abuse is very much an expression of middle class values, middle class child rearing and behavioral norms in this country, and I think we have to say this and not feel defensive about it. It has turned out that raising children with verbal skills, not beating them, turns out adaptive, well-adjusted members of our society who can contribute and raise families of their own without problems. And I think that we can't be ashamed to say, "Oh gee, I hate to come out of my middle class bag." This is really the best way to raise children in terms of our society. These are the values we want to project. There is room for a great deal of diversity within 'good child rearing practices.' The message here is don't ignore the values, try to figure out what values are expressed in the programs you're considering using and try to work in terms of even higher sets of values. Certainly we don't want to erode personal freedom.

I've limited myself to physical abuse primarily because of personal values. When we speak of physical abuse, we have a clear line we can draw. We can speak of direct blows, bruises, internal damage. Emotional abuse raises narrow questions. Isolating a child can be emotional abuse. Is it abusive to send a child to his room when he won't behave? Screaming at children can be emotional abuse. Is it abuse to scream at your child when he has the radio on so loud that he can't hear you otherwise? The only way to monitor emotional abuse is to place monitors in the home. How many of us want a government monitor observing all of our behavior in our homes?

Government agents at all levels are making decisions about the kind of society we will have. We should not make such decisions in a knee-jerk manner and we should be aware that the manner in which we deliver social services shapes our society for large numbers of families.

REFERENCES

Becker, W. C. Consequences of different kinds of parental discipline. In M. L. Hoffman & L. W. Hoffman (Eds.), *Review of child development research*. New York: Russell Sage Foundation, 1964.

Eron, L., Walder, L. & Lefkowitz, M. *Learning of aggression in children*. Boston: Little, Brown & Co., 1971.

Hess, R., Shipmen, V., Brophy, J. & Bear, R. Mother-child interaction. In I. Gordon (Ed.), *Readings in research in developmental psychology*. Glenview, Illinois: Scott-Foresman 1971.

Vexler, S. & Raffaniello, E. Interventions into child abuse and delinquency. Paper presented at 2nd Annual Conference on Child Abuse, Houston, 1977.

15

Report on the Relationship between Child Abuse and Neglect and Later Socially Deviant Behavior

JOSE D. ALFARO

Project Director
Select Committee on Child Abusc
New York, New York 10007

INTRODUCTION

The New York State Assembly Select Committee on Child Abuse was established in 1969 by then Assembly Speaker Perry B. Duryea. It was the first, and remains perhaps the only, legislative committee devoted solely to the issues of child abuse and neglect. The Select Committee was formed in response to widespread concern about the effectiveness and adequacy of the child protective system in New York State, a concern aroused by the death of an abused child who had been in the care of a number of agencies and courts. There was an immediate investigation into the handling of this particular case, but there were also questions about the functioning of the system as a whole. The mission of the Select Committee was to determine whether the child protective system was suffering from administrative problems, new legislation was necessary, or both.

In 1969, Article 10 was added to the Family Court Act, and it was substantially revised the following year. Article 10 created a special child abuse part in the Court, formulated a more practice-oriented definition of abuse and neglect, and established special rules of evidence and procedure in child protective cases. In 1973, the Child

Protective Services Act created a unified and uniform system to report, investigate, and treat cases of suspected child abuse and neglect in every community throughout the state. It specified in clear detail the functions of the local child protective service, as well as the responsibilities of the state department of social services, and it provided protection for the rights of parents and children named in reports of suspected child abuse and neglect.

In preparing these legislative changes, the Select Committee held several series of hearings throughout the state over a three year period. This testimony emphasized that many professionals had observed that abused and neglected children often grow up to become problem children who returned to the care and attention of societal institutions as delinquent and ungovernable juveniles. Several Family Court judges of long experience were especially emphatic about this.

After the passage of the new child abuse laws, the Select Committee was responsible for monitoring their implementation. This task kept the Select Committee involved with the problems facing social agencies and the Family Court. The more the committee confronted the problems, the more it became apparent that the line drawn between child abuse or neglect and other social problems was thin, confusing, or fictitious. The children and their families were often the same or faced the same underlying personal, familial, or social difficulties. This experience only confirmed the testimony that had been given about the connection between child maltreatment and juvenile delinquency or ungovernability.

Thus, the Select Committee became convinced that the nature of the apparent relationship between child abuse and these other social problems had to be examined. In fact, it seemed reasonable, at first, to believe that this possible link had been studied already. The generally accepted knowledge about the decisive importance of early childhood experiences, moreover, would indicate that child maltreatment must have a profound forming influence on children. Yet, as the Committee's search of the literature indicated, nearly all of the research on the consequences, or sequelae of child maltreatment has been limited to physical and short-term emotional effects. Most of these studies use small samples of children who are usually followed for a year or two. There has been little published research about the long-term effects of child maltreatment on the subsequent behavior of adolescents and adults.

The paucity of such studies is an important gap in our knowledge, not just about child abuse or neglect, but also about whatever other social problems with which it is associated. Understanding the possible relationship between child abuse or neglect and juvenile delinquency or ungovernability could have enormous significance for the way our society approaches the problems of child maltreatment and juvenile misbehavior. The Select Committee undertook this study with a grant from the New York State Division of Criminal Justice Services because its policy implications were of genuine legislative concern, and also because the Select Committee had access to the records of agencies and courts which would be needed for such a study. The biggest obstacle to this type of longitudinal study is finding and obtaining access to relevant records. Though most courts and agencies were very helpful and cooperative, the legislative authority of the Select Committee guaranteed that the committee could perform the study.

This report presents the basic findings of the study. Given the amount of information collected and the number of variables in it, the range of possible analyses is great. This report does not attempt to prove that child maltreatment causes juvenile delinquency, or that every abused or neglected child will become a delinquent. It does show that maltreated children have a significantly greater likelihood of becoming delinquent or ungovernable, and though the data is conservative, the rate of juvenile delinquency among families in which abuse or neglect have occurred is considerably higher than among the general population of children living in the same communities.

The absence of documented evidence on the long-term social consequences of child maltreatment has limited severely the ability of planners to design effective treatment programs for children and juveniles. Social policy is not usually based on unverified observations and beliefs, no matter how accurate they may be. Knowledge must be demonstrated convincingly before it can be acted upon. This report offers evidence that there is a definite relationship between child maltreatment and juvenile misbehavior and criminality. To be useful, this report must be the beginning, not the end, of a process of finding the most effective arrangement of our social institutions meant to help children and families in trouble.

METHODOLOGY

This study is based on official records of child protective agencies and courts—officially recorded reports of suspected child abuse or neglect and alleged juvenile delinquency and ungovernability. Children and families were not sought out or interviewed. The study examines, from the perspective of official records, children and families who were known to the child protective system or the court end of the juvenile justice system.

Basing a study on official records—the only concrete data available—has its own unique problems, but it also has its advantages. A positive aspect is the certainty that something actually happened, and there was intervention in the life of a child and family. None of the interpretive and subjective problems associated with interviewing someone after the fact exist in this study. Whether a report was made, and whether it was found accurate, are known, not guessed. The specific, verifiable concreteness of the data collected is a firm base for analysis.

This is not an experimental research study made under the controlled conditions possible in a laboratory. It is an empirical study based on the official records. These records are used as the basis for a longitudinal examination of children who were in families reported for child abuse or neglect and children who were reported as delinquent or ungovernable. It was not possible to devise a pure 'control group' against which to make comparisons. It was not possible to construct a sample of 'normal' or 'average' children from the general population because every group of children or families that might be studied has been identified for a particular problem or reason. The fact that they are available to be put into a control group means that they do not share the anonymity—the unlabeled status—of children and families who have not gotten into trouble, who have not been referred to an agency or court for one reason or another. Constructing a birth cohort, the only true control group possible, was beyond the scope and funding of this study.

The difficulty, if not impossibility, of constructing an adequate and usable control group was described by Lynch (1977):

> As the factors associated with child abuse are so complex it is a matter of great debate how one can obtain meaningfully matched controls. For example,

it could be argued that in Elmer's study (1976) the controls matched so exactly her index group that no differences emerged. Could they have even been abused and not identified? In direct contrast to this, others advocate seeking controls from among those with perfect child rearing techniques. It could be questioned whether anyone is in the position to identify such "super parents." In the absence of controls many studies rely on using tests with well established norms, which at least provide a background of data against which results can be interpreted (p. 5).

When possible, discussions of the findings of this study include comparing the children or families in the study with children and families from the general population, or other groups identified for specific reasons. For example, some of the characteristics of children who were reported as abused and neglected and who later were involved in a juvenile contact with the Family Court are compared to the general population of children similarly reported to the Family Court for juvenile misconduct. The demographic characteristics of the families in the study are compared to the general characteristics recorded in the 1950's, 1960's, and 1970's Census reports. (See, for example, Findings Nos. 2,3,6 and 11. Any considerations to be taken into account in these analyses are discussed as part of the individual findings.)

The study was conducted in eight counties of New York State: Broome, Erie, Kings, Monroe, New York, St. Lawrence, Suffolk, and Westchester. Most of the contacts included in the study were between 1950 and 1972, though some go as far back as 1930.

1950's Sample

Two different groups of children were studied. The first group consisted of 5,136 children from 1,423 families which were reported for suspected child abuse or neglect in 1952 or 1953. Not all of the children in this group were involved in a child protective contact during the sample year; some were never involved in a contact, but were included as siblings of the children who were; 4,465 of these children did have contact with at least one agency or court for child abuse, neglect, juvenile delinquency or ungovernability.

These children and their families were identified from the records of public or private child protective agencies and the Children's Court. Court docket books, agency intake registers, master index files, petitions, legal files, and case records were used to identify the children and families to be included in the study. All data obtained on individual contacts came from legal files and case records. In three of the counties, all the reported child protective cases in the sample year were included in the study; in three other counties, the case load for two years was used to generate a sufficiently large sample. In the two New York City counties, the sample included all the cases reported in three months (February, July and October) distributed through the sample year, because of the large volume of cases.

The history of each child in a family reported for suspected abuse or neglect during the sample year was recorded in the study, including siblings who were not named in the report but who were part of the family either before or after the sample year contact. All of these children were then traced through the records of the Family Court, or its predecessor Children's Court, for later juvenile delinquency or ungovernability cases; court contacts for abuse or neglect were also recorded. All the juvenile contacts involved situations that were considered serious enough to take the child to court.

Two aspects of this study of the 1950's sample were never undertaken as originally planned. The initial intention was to check the names of the children in this sample through the centralized state criminal records for possible later, adult contacts with the criminal justice system; the state-wide centralized records include every arrest for a 'fingerprintable' offense, which would include all the serious crimes. Because the officials then responsible for maintaining these records did not agree to conduct this research in a way meaningful to the study, this part was not done.

It also was planned to check the names of the children in the 1950's sample through the records of the New York State Department of Mental Hygiene, which has a rather extensive data file on children and adults receiving mental hygiene services in New York state. Although the department was willing to cooperate in the study, a change in the mental hygiene law removed the department's discretion to do so, and the impass was not resolved. It was thought that a number of the children in this sample, especially among the girls, might have had contact with the state's mental hygiene system. (One hypothesis was that girls would have greater contact because of their greater tendency to internalize aggression than boys; if so, this might balance the boys' greater tendency to commit delinquent acts.)

The number of children and families in the 1950's sample may surprise some people; they represent a substantial child protective caseload from twenty-five years ago, when child abuse and neglect were not noticed to the extent they are today. In the last ten years, child maltreatment has received more attention than ever before. Public and professional willingness to admit its existence began to develop only near the end of the period under study. Yet, child abuse and neglect are not new problems, and child protective efforts have existed for many years in most communities in New York State. In the past, there was no central register to keep track of cases, and no one counted them, but they were there. Table 1 summarizes the number of children and families reported for suspected child abuse or neglect included in the 1950's sample.

Almost all of the contacts recorded in the 1950's sample were with public or private child protective agencies. Contacts with the Children's or Family Courts were either for child maltreatment, juvenile delinquency or ungovernability. Out of

TABLE 1 OFFICIAL REPORTS OF SUSPECTED CHILD ABUSE OR NEGLECT, 1950's SAMPLE

County	No. of Families	No. of Children in Families	No. of Children with Contacts
Broome	107	309	281
Erie	325	1,459	1,290
Kings	184	756	625
Monroe	128	593	545
New York	291	915	840
St. Lawrence	24	131	101
Suffolk	132	375	308
Westchester	222	597	453
	1,423	5,136	4,465

TABLE 2 CONTACTS - 1950's SAMPLE

County	Private Agency	Public Agency	Court	Probation Intake
Broome	0	83	403	21
Erie	3,054	72	1,009	0
Kings	916	141	559	46
Monroe	1,167	0	317	7
New York	1,305	222	568	48
St. Lawrence	0	63	140	4
Suffolk	1	371	47	17
Westchester	1	5	662	65
	6,450	957	3,705	208

the 11,445 contacts, only 131 were with other agencies and are not used in the study. 76% of the child protective contacts were with a public or private protective agency, while 24% of the contacts were with a court. (In two counties, Broome and Westchester, most of the contacts are court contacts because of the destruction of agency records. In Suffolk county, most of the contacts were with the public child protection agency because a fire destroyed the Court building.) There were 1,648 court contacts for juvenile delinquency or ungovernability. Table 2 lists the number of contacts with each type of agency or court in each county in the study.

The high percentage of contacts with private child protective agencies in Erie, Kings, Monroe and New York counties reflects the fact that these private agencies were the prime protective service agencies in their communities in the early 1950's. In many communities, public agencies did not become the prime child protective agencies until the mid or late 1960's. Then, amendments to the Social Security Act, requiring the provision of child protective services for children in families on welfare, changed the funding patterns for child protective services. As a result, a number of private agencies went out of business or at least ceased to serve as the prime child protective agency in their communities. The Monroe and Westchester county Societies for the Prevention of Cruelty to Children, for example, merged with the local Department of Social Services, which then became the prime protective agency; their records, and at least some personnel, were incorporated into the public agency. This study found no evidence that these changes altered the philosophy of child protective services; usually the services were still provided by the same individuals but under the aegis of a different agency. This does not mean that all the child protective cases involved families on welfare, but the shifting of funds and their availability from the federal government under the revised laws undermined the financial base of the private agencies.

The extremely low number of contacts with the Probation Intake Services in the 1950's sample is not a sign of the actual number of cases adjusted or diverted by the Intake Service. In most counties, no record is kept of such contacts for more than six months or a year. Keeping permanent records on such cases is considered to contravene the philosophy of diversion—the desire to avoid scarring a child with a 'record.' This policy makes it impossible to use such contacts in the study, and it precludes ever studying the effectiveness of such contacts.

A system of codes was devised to record the referral reason(s) for each contact.

TABLE 3 PRIME CHILD ABUSE REFERRAL REASONS, 1950's SAMPLE

	1950's Sample	
	%	
Battered Child	9.2	(65)
Other Physical Attacks	61.9	(437)
Risk of Physical Injury	17.4	(123)
Sexual Abuse	11.5	(81)
Total		706

These codes denote the experiences of children that led to their being reported as abused or neglected or the behavior that led to their being reported as delinquent or ungovernable. For each contact, these referral reasons are specifically and uniformly coded. These codes were constructed to allow us to describe the referral reasons in a way that was not affected by the changes in legal definitions that occurred during the period being studied. Until 1962, for example, when the Family Court was created, ungovernability, or status offenses, were considered a form of juvenile delinquency. The Family Court Act separated them into two distinct categories, and delinquency was then reserved for criminal acts committed by juveniles. The status offenses, or juvenile ungovernability, were put into their own category and called PINS offenses, meaning a person in need of supervision. Similarly, until Article 10 of the Family Court Act was enacted in 1969, child abuse was considered an aggravated form of child neglect. Article 10 distinguished between the two. The analysis in this study is not based on the legal label applied to a child, but to the type of child maltreatment or juvenile misconduct. The child abuse contacts recorded before 1969 are not treated as child neglect, but as child abuse. The status offenses recorded before 1962 are not treated as delinquent offenses, but as juvenile ungovernability. These distinctions were possible because the referral reasons for each contact were individually recorded in accordance with the system of codes devised for this purpose. Thus, the study uses actual or alleged treatment of children and behavior of juveniles. The coded types of behavior are discussed throughout this report.

The system of recording referral reasons allowed up to six reasons for each contact. Almost half of the contacts in the study involved two or more referral reasons. This study is based on an examination of the prime referral reasons only. Since the distribution of all referral reasons closely corresponds to the distribution of the prime reasons, this procedure does not seem to create any distortions in the data. The prime reason, moreover, is the first reason mentioned in a case record or a court petition, and it can be assumed reasonably that the first one was considered the most important. For example, homicide was never listed as a second or lesser referral reason.

Child abuse was the prime referral reason in only 8% of the child protective contacts in the study, while child neglect was the prime reason in 92%. By comparison, in 1976, neglect accounted for 81% of all child protective reports. Only 3% of the child protective contacts were for reasons not specified in the coding system, an indication of how inclusive and usable it is. Table 3 summarizes the prime child abuse referral reasons.

TABLE 4 PRIME CHILD NEGLECT REFERRAL REASONS, 1950's SAMPLE

1950's Sample		
Referral Reason	%	Number
Inadequate Supervision	35.0	2746
Inadequate food, shelter and clothing	23.9	1876
Parental Alcoholism	12.9	1013
Abandonment	7.1	561
Parental Sexual Misconduct	4.9	385
Parental Mental Illness	3.1	242
Involuntary Parental Absence	3.0	242
Parental Fighting	2.9	225
Educational Neglect	2.7	210
Impairment of Mental or Emotional Health	2.3	183
Medical Neglect	1.3	100
Parental Drug Use	0.4	31
Malnutrition	0.2	12
Parents Previously Abused Another Child	0.1	4
Total		7,830 contacts

There were 7,830 protective contacts in which child neglect was the prime referral reason. Three reasons accounted for 72% of these contacts: 1) inadequate food, shelter and clothing; 2) inadequate supervision; and, 3) parental alcoholism. Parental alcoholism was the prime referral reason in 13% of all the child protective contacts, and usually it was in association with other referral reasons. Parental drug addiction was the prime referral reason in only 0.4% of these contacts; this reflects the fact that drug addiction was not widespread in the early 1950's. Table 4 lists the prime referral reasons for child neglect.

Until the definition of child maltreatment was revised with the passage of Article 10 of the Family Court Act in 1969, moral neglect or the sexual behavior of parents was a reason for child protective intervention, although it was usually associated with other forms of neglect, such as leaving children alone unattended. It was the prime referral reason in almost 5% of the child protective contacts in the study, and it was present more often as a secondary referral reason. With the revised definition, however, such conduct, in itself, was no longer considered sufficient reason for suspecting child abuse or neglect. In 1969 the focus was shifted from the behavior of the parent to the harm or potential harm to a child. Since parental sexual misconduct accounted for only 5% of the referral reasons, it is apparent that it was not considered a major form of child neglect even under the old definition. This implies that the change in 1969 might have been a ratification of general policy and belief.

1970's Sample

The second group of children studied consists of 1,963 children who were reported to the Family Court or Probation Intake Service as delinquent or ungovernable

TABLE 5 CHILDREN REPORTED AS DELIQUENT OR UNGOVERNABLE, 1970's SAMPLE

	1970's Sample	
County	No. of Children	No. of Families
Broome	278	259
Erie	177	162
Kings	504	480
Monroe	293	273
New York	311	303
St. Lawrence	41	38
Suffolk	204	187
Westchester	155	149
	1,963	1,851

(PINS) in 1971 or 1972. They were identified from the records of the court and intake in the same way as the children in the first group were identified. The histories of the children in this group, however, were traced backward for prior involvement in child abuse or neglect cases. Thus, the first group was examined to see in which direction they went after their contact with the child protective services system, while the second group was examined to see from which direction they had come before their contact with the juvenile justice system. In the second group, information was not collected on siblings, in part because the records of juvenile cases, unlike protective records, do not always include information on brothers and sisters. The data in this group were kept separate from the data on the first group of children and families, although a few comparisons were made to examine possible differences and changes in the handling of cases.

The children in the second group came from 1,851 families. The number of children and families are not identical because siblings were sometimes charged together for being delinquent or ungovernable; they got into trouble with each other. Table 5 lists the number of children and families in the second group, by county.

The children in the 1970's sample had 2,688 contacts with the Family Court and 2,379 contacts with the Court's Probation Intake Service. They also had 688 contacts with public or private child protective agencies. Table 6 lists the number of contacts with each type of agency or court in each county studied. The court or probation contacts include some for child abuse or neglect.

Unlike the first sample, there are many Probation Intake contacts in the second sample. The second group is more recent—the data on it were collected only a year or two after the sample year contact—and the Probation Intake data had not been destroyed yet, except in Broome County, where it is kept for only two months. The lack of any contacts with private child protective agencies in Broome, St. Lawrence, Suffolk, and Westchester counties reflects the fact that there are no such agencies in these counties. In the other counties private agencies were still active as the prime child protective agency in the community, and most of the child protective contacts in the second group occurred before public agencies became the prime protective agencies.

The referral reasons for delinquency or ungovernability in the second sample are

TABLE 6 CONTACTS - 1970's SAMPLE

Contacts - 1970's Sample				
County	Court	Probation Intake	Private CPS Agency	Public CPS Agency
Broome	468	1	0	124
Erie	211	229	46	46
Kings	700	988	57	42
Monroe	405	413	106	1
New York	626	230	88	131
St. Lawrence	55	18	0	10
Suffolk	159	233	0	12
Westchester	64	267	0	25
Totals	2,688	2,379	297	391

consistent with the distribution of referral reasons for all juvenile cases in the judicial year 1971-72. (Until 1976, the Office of Court Administration statistics were based on a year beginning on July 1 and ending on June 13.) Table 7 lists the prime referral reasons for delinquency and ungovernability in the second sample and compares their distribution with the official statistics for all the juvenile cases in the state (1). The official state figures include filed petitions; the referral reasons from the study also include Probation Intake cases that may have been adjusted, and this may alter the percentage distribution somewhat. The differences between the sample and the entire juvenile caseload are small enough to indicate that the sample is representative of the state as a whole.

The prime PINS or ungovernability referral reasons for the contacts included in the study of the second sample also correspond closely to the percentage distribution of PINS referral reasons throughout the state. Table 8 summarizes these referral reasons and compares their distribution in the sample with the state-wide count of petitions filed.

The difference in the distribution of truancy in the sample and the state-wide figures is probably related to the sampling technique—the second sample was primarily drawn from three months, February, July and October. These months, especially February and October, may be heavy ones for truancy cases; in many school districts, they are the second months of a new semester. There were also 261 miscellaneous referral reasons in the second sample, which mostly relate to previous contacts; 118 were for placement, and 71 were for violation of probation.

The Counties Studied

Broome County is located in the central area of the state in the Catskills. Bordering on Pennsylvania, it is considered part of a standard metropolitan area along with Susquehenna county in Pennsylvania. Its largest city is Binghamton, whose population declined from 80,000 to 64,000 people during the period under study. Between the 1950 and 1970 Census, Broome County lost 6.6% of its population, excluding births and deaths. In the previous decade, its population had been steady, with a slight 0.2% decrease. From 1950 to 1970, the non-white population almost tripled, but it comprises only 1.4% of the total population of the county. Many of the child

TABLE 7 DELINQUENCY CONTACTS - 1970's SAMPLE

Delinquency Referral Reasons	No. of Prime Reasons	% of Sample	% Distribution in State Caseload (2)
Burglary	661	20	20
Robbery	515	15.5	11
Larceny	471	14.2	13
Assault	391	11.8	10
Malicious Mischief	247	7.4	4
Narcotics Violation	198	5.9	3
Auto Theft	139	4.2	2
Disorderly Conduct	126	3.8	1
Unauthorized Use of Auto	105	3.1	8
Receiving Stolen Property	74	2.2	3
Possession of Dangerous Weapon	72	2.1	4
Arson	46	1.3	1
Other Sex Crimes	43	1.3	1
Possession of Burglar's Tools	19	0.57	1
Rape	14	0.42	1
Homicide	7	0.21	0.37
Gambling	2	0.06	0.03
Unlawful Assembly	2	0.06	0.08
	3,312 contacts		

TABLE 9 AVERAGE NUMBER OF CONTACTS, BY COUNTY

	1950's Sample	1970's Sample
Low Contact Counties		
Broome	1.80	2.15
St. Lawrence	2.07	2.02
Suffolk	1.53	2.00
Westchester	1.57	2.86
High Contact Counties		
Erie	3.20	3.01
Kings	2.67	3.60
Monroe	2.73	3.19
New York	2.62	3.64
Total Sample - All Counties	2.56	3.03

TABLE 8 UNGOVERNABILITY CONTACTS - 1970's SAMPLE

Ungovernability (PINS) Referral Reasons	No. of Prime Reasons	% of Sample	% Distribution in State Caseload
Habitual Truancy	582	39.4	24
Running from Home	392	26.5	24
Refusal to Obey	258	17.4	21
Staying Out Late	146	9.8	9
Sexual Misconduct	44	2.9	2
Associating with Bad Companions	18	1.2	6
Glue Sniffing	17	1.1	0
Intoxication	10	.68	1
Using Vile Language	9	.61	2
	1,476 contacts (3)		

protective records in Broome County were destroyed for the years before 1963 after a merger of the Broome County Department of Social Services with two other more local departments that served the cities of Binghamton and Union—Johnson. This was the only county in the state that had such a tripartite division of its public social service agency.

Erie County contains the second largest city in the state, Buffalo, with a population of 462,000. Between 1950 and 1970, the population of Buffalo decreased by 80,000 people while the population of the county increased by 215,000 people. Many of the people who left Buffalo moved into suburban communities that are within the county. Erie County has a total population of over 1,100,000 people. A special feature of the county is its rural communities, which are not isolated, but within a half hour's drive of Buffalo or one of the smaller cities in the county. During the period under study, the non-white population of the county doubled to almost 10% of the total population. In recent years, the movement of industry away from this part of the state has had a severe impact on Buffalo and Erie County, although most of it occurred after the period of the study. The records in this county were relatively complete.

Kings County, also known as Brooklyn, is part of New York City, and today it includes some of the worst slum areas of the city. Kings County has experienced a dramatic change in its population during the period under study. Between 1950 and 1960, it lost a total of 13.6% of its population, and another 10.7% from 1960 to 1970. Besides this significant decrease in total population, there was an enormous change in the racial and ethnic composition of the county—an influx of blacks from the South and Puerto Ricans from the Island, accompanied by a large exodus of whites to Queens County and the suburban communities outside the city. The non-white population almost quadrupled from 1950 to 1970, now accounting for 27% of the total population of the county. The records in this county were well preserved.

Monroe County contains the third largest city in the state, Rochester, with a population of 295,000 people. As in Buffalo, the population of Rochester declined, while the population of the county increased from 487,000 people in 1950 to 711,000 people in 1970. From 1950 to 1970, the non-white population of the county increased from 1.7% to 7.9% of the total population. Although experiencing a change, Rochester has not suffered the severe economic difficulties of Buffalo; two large, international corporations, with close ties to the Rochester community, have maintained their headquarters in Rochester. This county had the most complete set of records of all the counties in the study.

New York County is also called Manhattan, and in most people's minds it is synonymous with New York City, the largest city in the state, the largest city in the United States, and one of the largest cities in the world. When people think of urban problems, they think of New York County. Like Kings County, a substantial change in population occurred between 1950 and 1970. From 1950 to 1960, the total population decreased 18.1%, and from 1960 to 1970, it decreased by an additional 12.9%. But the change in racial composition was not as drastic as in Kings County. The non-white population was 20.6% in 1950 and 29.2% in 1970. The records in New York County were relatively complete.

St. Lawrence County remained a rural county throughout the period under study. It is not a rural community of larqe agribusiness farms, but of smaller, family farms. It is not a wealthy community. There are no large cities in this county, and the largest community, Potsdam, has only 16,000 people. The total population of

St. Lawrence County increased from 98,000 to 112,000 during the period 1950 to 1970. There was a net migration of 4% of the population out of the county. Of all the counties in the study, St. Lawrence County changed the least during the period studied. Less than one percent of the population is non-white, increasing from 0.2% to 0.6% of the total population between 1950 and 1970. The records were relatively complete.

Suffolk County experienced a tremendous increase in population and change in status during the period studied. In 1950, Suffolk was primarily a rural county with large farms; potatoes were a large staple crop. By 1970, Suffolk County had become a suburban 'bedroom' community for people who had moved out of New York City and often remained employed in the city. Toward the end of the period under study, Suffolk County had begun to grow further—to become less dependent on New York City for jobs and to create its own self-contained economy, capable of locally employing an increasing percentage of its residents. At the same time, poor people and families on welfare began to make the same judgments about New York City as the middle class that had already fled, and they, too, began to migrate into Suffolk County in search of a 'better life.' From 1950 to 1960, the population of Suffolk County increased 116.5%, and from 1960 to 1970 it increased another 49.3%. The percentage, though not number, of non-white remained almost constant, from 4.9% in 1950 to 5.2% in 1970. Many of the records in this county were missing—the wooden Family Court Building was struck by lightning in 1956 and burnt to the ground.

Westchester County was already a suburban community for New York City in 1950 and became more so by 1970. The population increases, however, were negligible compared to the increases in the other suburban communities around New York City. From 1950 to 1960, the population of Westchester County increased 17.6%, and from 1960 to 1970 it increased by another 2%. Westchester is a diverse county, with some of the wealthiest communities in the state, bordering alongside the even wealthier communities of Connecticut, and with a growing number of poor sections, especially in the southern part of the county bordering the northern most county of New York City, the Bronx. The population increased from 6.2% to 13.2%. Many of the social service records in this county were destroyed after the Westchester Society for the Prevention of Cruelty to Children went out of business and merged with the Westchester County Department of Social Services. The court records were intact.

In both the 1950's and the 1970's samples, there is a similar pattern to the average number of contacts for the children living in different counties. The eight counties in the study can be classified into two broad groups—low contact and high contact counties. Table 9 gives a breakdown of the average number of contacts for each sample in each county.

In three of the low contact counties—Broome, Suffolk, and Westchester—a significant number of records had been destroyed. St. Lawrence County is the most rural and sparsely populated county in the study. The four high contact counties all have major urban centers; the four high contact counties include the first, second, and third largest cities in the state.

The considerably higher average number of contacts in the 1950's Erie County sample may reflect the aggressive outreach policies of the private child protective agency in the county during the period studied. The higher average number of contacts in the 1970's sample may be explained in two ways. The difference may be a function of the sample; in the 1950's group, the sample is child protective cases, while the 1970's group is juvenile delinquency and ungovernability cases that were referred to court and includes the contacts preserved in the records of the Probation Intake Service. The higher average may also be a function of the more recent time of the sample—there has been less time for records to be destroyed or lost.

FINDINGS

The findings of this study confirm that there is an empirical relationship between child abuse or neglect and juvenile delinquency or ungovernability. It must be emphasized, and understood, that the findings presented in this report are conservative and underestimate the relationship between child maltreatment and juvenile misconduct for a number of reasons. These are related to the fact that the study is based on official records. One significant conservative factor is the destruction or preservation of official records. If information is not preserved, it cannot show up in a study such as this one.

Another consequence of having to rely on official records is that the findings are made conservative by the under-reporting of child abuse and neglect. Until the development of reporting laws and specialized child protective services, many situations of child abuse or neglect were not reported, or if they were, they were not called child maltreatment or protective cases, but were hidden in referrals based on a generalized need for services. Saying that parents 'cannot cope,' for example, is a way of saying that children are not being properly cared for without invoking the spectre of child abuse or neglect. Both labels refer to the same problem, but they result in a different approach to the family, and the generalized approach probably leads to a less assured protection of endangered children because the actual or potential harm to a child is more easily ignored.

Child protective professionals universally acknowledge that even today, despite publicity, reporting laws, and elaborate child protective systems, child maltreatment is not being reported nearly to the extent that it occurs. Many professionals estimate that only about one-tenth of the actual abuse or neglect situations are ever reported. All of the protective contacts in this study, in both samples, occurred before the recent wave of professional and public concern about maltreated children. During the time of the study, under-reporting was even greater than it is now. Based on the 1950 Census Reports, it is possible to make a good estimate of the reporting rate of child abuse and neglect during the sample year. As Table 10 shows, it was about half the rate of reporting today; data are drawn from the 1950 Census (pp. 142-152); and the *1976 Annual Report* of the Child Protective Service, Table 16.

TABLE 10 REPORTING RATES FOR SUSPECTED CHILD ABUSE AND NEGLECT, SAMPLE YEAR RATE

County	1952-53	1976
Erie	0.5%	0.8%
Monroe	0.4%	0.8%
St. Lawrence	0.3%	1.5%
Kings and New York (4)	0.5%	0.8%

Being based only on official records of child protective agencies and the courts introduces another conservative factor in the study. To show a relationship between child maltreatment and later juvenile misconduct, a child must be officially reported twice, but a child may have been reported only once. For example, a child may have been reported as abused or neglected and later engage in juvenile misconduct but not have been officially reported to a court as delinquent or ungovernable. Similarly, a delinquent or ungovernable child may have been abused or neglected without being reported to a child protective agency.

That the contacts for juvenile delinquency or ungovernability (PINS) were limited to the Children's or Family Courts and their Probation Intake Services is another important conservative factor in the study. Thus, the bulk of the possible contacts with the juvenile justice system, which do not result in a referral to court, were excluded from the study. A basic tenet of the juvenile justice system is that court action should be used only as a last resort; the system is designed to keep all but the most dangerous or incorrigible juveniles out of court. Morris & Hawkins (1970), for example, found that only 40% of the arrested youths reached the intake service of a juvenile court. Moreover, the Probation Intake Service itself 'diverts' cases away from the court without formal action. During the period of the study, about one-half of the cases referred to juvenile courts in the U. S. were diverted or adjusted without official court intervention (HEW Children's Bureau, 1974.) When a case is adjusted, the Intake Service either arranges an amicable settlement of the issue and the case is dropped or it refers the juvenile to a special program, instead of involving the court officially.

The 1970's sample includes contacts with the Probation Intake Service of the Family Court, but the 1950's sample does not because the records of these 'unofficial' cases were not preserved. Other contacts with the juvenile justice system—including the estimated 60% of the juveniles whom the police arrest but do not refer to court—were not included in the study. Such contacts are real and have meaning—they often lead to a referral to a special youth program—but contacts with the police and pre-court diversion programs are problematic and subject to varying interpretation. No one agrees about the meaning of the arrest of a juvenile who is not referred to court. Including such contacts with the juvenile justice system would have statistically increased the results of the study but would have also increased the subjectivity of its analysis. Thus, the juvenile justice contacts in both samples are only those cases that were considered serious enough to require court action, and the reasons for them are specified in detail on court petitions.

Another noteworthy conservative factor in the study is the migration of families in and out of the counties studied during the period of the study, 1950 to 1972. This migration limits the relationship that can be found between child abuse or neglect and juvenile delinquency or ungovernability. Children who were reported as delinquent or ungovernable may have been living elsewhere when they were abused or neglected, and other abused or neglected children may have moved out of the county before becoming involved in delinquent or ungovernable behavior. In addition to the significant demographic changes that occurred in some of the counties, families involved in abuse or neglect, and perhaps with delinquent or ungovernable children, move more frequently than the average family, according to the literature on child maltreatment.

The population of Kings and New York Counties, besides experiencing a substantial gross decrease in population, also experienced an enormous change in the ethnic and racial composition of their populations. Over one million people moved into Suffolk County during this period, while some upstate communities also lost or gained in population. The Census Reports for 1950, 1960, and 1970 record these changes in gross population excluding changes due to births and deaths; counting the movement of people in and out of the counties, they provide a picture of the net change in the population of each county in the study. The migration changes are as follows:

Population Changes, Percent by County

County	1950 - 1960	1960 - 1970
Broome	+ 0.2	- 6.6
Erie	+ 4.6	- 4.8
Kings	- 13.6	- 10.7
Monroe	+ 6.6	+ 9.4
New York	- 18.1	- 12.9
St. Lawrence	- 3.5	- 9.0
Suffolk	+ 116.5	+ 49.3
Westchester	+ 17.6	+ 2.0

The experience of other research efforts, in which families were being interviewed, reveals how difficult it can be to follow-up children after they have been reported as abused or neglected because they cannot be located. A study in Denver, Colorado, (Martin, et al., 1974) was able to locate only 40% of the children as soon as one year after the report had been made. In a two year follow-up study in Australia, (Birrell & Birrell, 1968), 33% of the children were unlocatable. In a follow-up study in Rochester, New York, 25% of the children could not be found five years later (Friedman & Morse, 1974). Why these children could not be located cannot, of course, be known for sure. It is obvious, however, that their families had moved. In view of the high correlations between child maltreatment and juvenile misconduct found among the Monroe County children in this study, it is interesting to note that the number of children who could not be located in these other studies was significantly lower in the Rochester study, even though the follow-up period was two or three times longer than in the Denver or Australian studies.

The data in this study are county-based , and the cross referencing for later delinquency or ungovernability or earlier abuse and neglect, was limited to the county in which the children and families were identified. There is no way of accounting for children and families who moved in or out of the state.

Children were lost from the study in other ways, too. Some may be so seriously abused that they die or are institutionalized for life; an example would be a child who is brain-damaged to the extent that he has to be placed in a mental retardation facility. Other children are placed in foster homes for long periods of time, and they may become known by the name of the family with which they live. If the child is placed for adoption, his name is changed automatically, and the records are sealed to prevent the tracing of his history. In this way, the relationship between child maltreatment and juvenile misconduct is underestimated by these conservative factors. Estimating the impact of these factors is not really possible, though the data collected indicate that at least 1% of the children in the sample had died by the time the data were collected. Their deaths are known only because they were recorded in the official records studied; other children may have died without their deaths being recorded in the case records of a child protective agency or Family Court. Checking the names of all the children through the vital statistics records of counties or the state was considered, but it proved to be technically impossible.

One additional factor understates the possible relationship between child maltreatment and juvenile misconduct that the study can portray. Children could be charged with delinquent behavior only between their seventh and sixteenth birthdays, and with ungovernable behavior from their seventh to eighteenth birthdays. In practice, the active age range for delinquency is ten to sixteen, and for ungovernability it was, until recently, seven to eighteen; thus, the period of most juvenile misconduct is limited to about six years. This means that some children in the study were never 'eligible' to be charged with delinquency or ungovernability during the period studied, while most of the others were 'eligible' for only part of that period. For example, a sibling who was over sixteen at the time of the sample year contact could not be charged with a juvenile offense. Or, a child who was included because of a maltreatment contact when he was two could not possibly have been charged with delinquency for another five or nine years.

Similarly, the 'eligibility' of the children in the study is limited by the number of officially recorded contacts included in the study. The number of contacts for each child varies greatly, ranging from none to twenty-two contacts. Only considering the first contact, already 11% of the children were not available to the sample to have a later delinquent or ungovernable contact; and only 37% of the children with one contact were old enough to be charged with delinquency or ungovernability. By the second contact, almost half of the children were no longer available for a juvenile contact because they did not have three or more contacts, and almost half of those who were available were too old to be charged with delinquency or ungovernability.

These are the limiting contexts in which the data in this study had to be collected and analyzed. The findings are conservative and underestimate the relationship or association between officially reported child maltreatment and later officially reported juvenile delinquency or ungovernability. The interrelationships described in this report are all minimal, bed-rock figures. Bare and uninflated, they are persuasive because they are conservative.

Finding No. 1: As many as 50% of the families reported for child abuse or neglect had at least one child who was later taken to court as delinquent or ungovernable.

An examination of the relationship between child maltreatment and juvenile delinquency or ungovernability should include the families from which the children came. Most of the families in the 1950's sample had two or more children, some of whom were involved in various contacts, and some of whom were not. In the samples, 42% of the families with at least one founded contact had one or more children who were taken to court as delinquent or ungovernable. In the five counties with relatively complete records, 49% of the families had such a child. In the county with the most complete set of records, Monroe, 64% of the families were in this situation. Table 11 summarizes these data by county.

The correlation between child maltreatment and juvenile misbehavior among the families is twice that among the children. There is a simple explanation for the differences in the relationships by children and families. In some families, only one child was reported as delinquent or ungovernable. For example, 3.4% of the boys had only a founded delinquency or ungovernability contact and were never involved

TABLE 11

	# of Families in 1950's Sample	# of Families with Founded Contact	# of Families with Inter-Relationship	% of Families with Inter-Relationship
Broome	107	92	23	25
Erie	335	325	163	50
Kings	184	170	84	46
Monroe (5)	128	128	82	64
New York	291	199	76	38
St. Lawrence	24	20	10	50
Suffolk	132	97	26	27
Westchester	222	210	57	27
Totals	1,423	1,241	521	42

in a child protective contact for abuse or neglect. Some children in the families were never involved in any type of contact, while not every child who was reported as abused or neglected was later reported to the court delinquent or ungovernable. In a particular family, only one of the children reported as abused or neglected may have been later reported as delinquent or ungovernable.

Findings indicate that children who were reported as abused or neglected accounted for a disproportionate percentage of delinquent and ungovernable children. This implies that families reported for child abuse or neglect account for an even more disproportionate number of delinquent and ungovernable children. There are no data on the number of families with children under 16 in the 1950's, but it is obvious that only a small fraction of the families in the counties under study were reported for child abuse or neglect in the 1950's sample. Yet, in the counties with complete records, about half of these families produced at least one child who was taken to court as delinquent or ungovernable.

Finding No. 2: In Monroe County, the rate of juvenile delinquency and ungovernability among the children in the study was 5 times greater than among the general population.

In Monroe County, it was possible to compare the rate of juvenile delinquency and ungovernability of the children in the 1950's sample with the children living in the county as a whole. The rate of delinquency-ungovernability of all children between the ages of 10 and 16 in Monroe County between the years 1957 and 1967 was 2%. These are the years during which the children in the 1950's sample had most of their delinquency or ungovernability contacts. At the same time, the rate of delinquency or ungovernability for the children in the sample averaged almost 10%—five times greater. It should be remembered that the 1950's Monroe County sample was substantial—almost 600 children. This is the most convincing proof possible that there is a definite relationship between child maltreatment and later juvenile delinquency and ungovernability. Table 12 gives a detailed comparison of the delinquency-ungovernability rates for Monroe County in the years 1957 through 1967.

These figures are conservative because the rate for the general population of

TABLE 12 COMPARISON OF DELINQUENCY-UNGOVERNABILITY RATES IN MONROE COUNTY, 1957-1967*

	Total Population of Children 10-16 Years		1950's Sample Children 10-16 Years	
Year	Children 10-16	# Children Contacted	Children 10-16	# Children Contacted
1967	81,726	2025 (2%)	154	26 (17%)
1966	81,726	1897 (2%)	221	20 (9%)
1965	81,726	1662 (2%)	236	33 (14%)
1964	81,726	1322 (2%)	246	22 (9%)
1963	81,726	1085 (1%)	242	15 (6%)
1962	67,038	709 (1%)	243	24 (10%)
1961	67,038	759 (1%)	229	17 (7%)
1960	67,038	496 (1%)	205	18 (9%)
1959	67,038	588 (1%)	184	25 (14%)
1958	67,038	737 (1%)	169	12 (7%)
1957	67,038	645 (1%)	159	13 (8%)
Average		1.47%		9.6%

* Based on 1950, 1960 and 1970 Census Reports; Annual Report of the Monroe County Children's Court; and the Monroe County Family Court, 1957-1967.

children between 10 and 16, the years during which most delinquency and ungovernability happens, includes the 'unofficial' or adjusted cases, while the rate for the children in the 1950's sample is almost exclusively 'official' cases for which a petition was filed. (There were only 7 Probation Intake contacts in the Monroe 1950's sample.) The sharp increase in juvenile cases between 1962 and 1963 reflects the creation of the new Family Court in 1962 and the establishment of a separate category for juvenile ungovernability or status offenses. The pre-1962 figures do not separate the status offenses from the other delinquency cases, but it is safe to assume that the increased attention created by the establishment of the Family Court heightened awareness about the problems of juvenile misbehavior, thus encouraging more cases to be brought to court. Moreover, the greater promise of solving the problems of juvenile crime and misbehavior, which were made in the process that led to the establishment of the Family Court, also could have prompted more professionals and citizens to use the facilities of the new court.

It is important to note that the socioeconomic backgrounds of the children in the 1950's sample of reported abuse and neglect cases and the general population of children reported to the court as delinquent or ungovernable are comparable. It is generally believed that many, if not most, of the families reported for suspected child abuse or neglect are from the lower socioeconomic strata of our society. It is also generally believed that most children taken to court as delinquent or ungovernable are also from the lower socioeconomic strata of our society. Indeed, a recent survey by the New York State Division for Youth (Ordes, 1977) found that 74% of the children placed with the Division as a result of a delinquency or ungovernability finding in the Family Court are from families that have been supported by public welfare funds. A 1973 study (Juvenile Injustices) found that 59% of the families of children charged with delinquency or ungovernability in the Family Court were receiving public assistance. It seems clear that families reported to child protective agencies and families that produce delinquent or ungovernable juveniles are weighted toward the lower socioeconomic levels of our society. This does not mean that all abused or neglected children, and all delinquent or ungovernable juveniles, come from impoverished or low income families. The socioeconomic factors that are said to affect the reporting of child maltreatment also seem to affect the reporting of juvenile misconduct.

This comparison could be made only in Monroe County, because no other county kept records of the number of delinquency-ungovernability cases for the years involved in this study. It was possible to know how many official and unofficial juvenile cases had occurred each year in this county. The state-wide data collected by the Office of Court Administration only goes back to 1965 or 1966, too late to be of any use in this study, and does not include cases adjusted by the Probation Intake Service.

Knowing the exact number of juvenile cases in Monroe County for each year of the period under study meant that it was possible to make an exact comparison between the rate of delinquency in the general population and the children in the 1950's sample. With the exact number of total cases for each year between 1957 and 1967, the rate of delinquency-ungovernability could be calculated in the same way it was for the children in the 1950's sample, based only on court contacts.

Finding No. 3: In high contact counties of the 1950's sample, 25% of the boys and 17% of the girls with at least one founded maltreatment contact were later reported to court as delinquent or ungovernable.

In addition, 3.4% of the boys and 1.9% of the girls were siblings of children who had been reported as abused or neglected but who had never been part of a child protective report. In Monroe County, 32% of the boys and 24% of the girls were later reported as delinquent or ungovernable.

It should be noted that these figures, like the ones in Finding No. 2, are very conservative. They are gross statistics for the entire sample, without regard to the limiting factors described in the introduction to this section. Among these limiting factors are several that involve the loss of children from the sample or their 'ineligibility' to be available for a later delinquency or ungovernability contact in this study.

Table 13 summarizes the gross interrelationship data available for the whole sample:

TABLE 13 CHILDREN WITH A FOUNDED CHILD PROTECTIVE AND JUVENILE DELINQUENCY OR UNGOVERNABILITY CONTACTS, ENTIRE 1950's SAMPLE

	Broome	Erie	Kings	Monroe	New York	St. Law.	Suff.	West.
Boys	11%	26%	22%	32%	19%	27%	8%	13%
Girls	7%	16%	17%	24%	14%	8%	2%	8%

The low figures in Broome and Suffolk Counties may reflect the destruction of records in those counties. In Westchester County, social service records were also destroyed, but this seems to have had slight effect on the study. Since all the court records were intact, this would indicate that a high percentage of the child protective cases in this county were referred to court, and the generally higher placement rates in the sample from this county would support this indication. The counties with low figures do not adversely affect the total average because the sample in these counties is small.

Though the 1950's sample is almost evenly divided between boys and girls, 51% boys and 49% girls, a much greater percentage of the boys were later reported to the Family Court as delinquent. This difference between boys and girls reflects the fact that considerably more boys than girls are charged with, and probably commit, delinquent acts. During the period of the study, about 90% of the juveniles charged with delinquency were boys. For example, in the judicial year 1967-68, 14,431 delinquency petitions were initiated against boys, while only 1,250 were initiated against girls (6). At the same time, ungovernability cases were almost evenly divided between girls and boys. In the judicial year 1967-68, 54% of the ungovernability petitions were filed against boys, while 46% were filed against girls.(*Administrative Board of the Judicial Conference of the State of New York, 1970, p. 301.*) Because of the greater number of delinquency petitions, and the tremendous weighting of them toward boys, 78% of all juvenile proceedings in the Family Court that year involved boys. Thus, it is no surprise that more boys than girls in the 1950's sample were later taken to court for juvenile misconduct.

There is some indication, however, that there is a higher association between maltreatment and delinquency among girls than boys. Although only 10% of the delinquency cases in the state involved girls, 22% of the children in the 1950's sample with maltreatment and delinquency contacts were girls. The distribution of ungovernability contacts among boys and girls in the 1950's sample is close to the sex composition of the entire sample. Table 14 summarizes this finding.

Finding No. 4: A significant percentage of children reported as delinquent or ungovernable in the early 1970's had been reported as abused or neglected.

As the reporting rates for child abuse and neglect in the 1950's sample showed, about 0.5% of the children between birth and 18 were reported as abused or neglected twenty years ago. Today, the reporting rate is nearing 1%, and in some communities it is closer to 1.5%. Children who are reported as abused or neglected are a small percentage of the population. Yet, the study of juveniles reported as delinquent or ungovernable in the early 1970's shows that 21% of the boys and 29% of the girls had been reported, when younger, as abused or neglected children. In high contact counties, this relationship is even greater. In Erie County, 41% of the boys and 36% of the girls had earlier contact with the child protective system; in Monroe County, 36% of the boys and 53% of the girls had such an earlier contact. In New York County, 31% of the boys and 45% of the girls had an earlier abuse or neglect contact. Thus, the small percentage of children who are reported as abused or neglected account for a significant part of the juvenile delinquency and ungovernability caseloads in the Family Court.

This finding may seem puzzling in view of the findings in the 1950's sample. In the first sample, which began from the perspective of child abuse and neglect and then

TABLE 14 COMPARISON OF CONTACTS BY SEX, 1950's SAMPLE

	Boys %	Girls %
Total 1950's Sample	51	49
Maltreatment & Delinquency in 1959's Sample	78	22
Maltreatment & Ungovernability in 1950's Sample	48	52
Delinquency Court Cases in State, 1967-68	90	10
Ungovernability Court Cases in State, 1967-68	54	46

looked at what became of the children, the relationship between child maltreatment and later delinquency or ungovernability was one-third greater among the boys. In the 1970's sample, which began from the perspective of delinquency or ungovernability and looked backward to where the children came from, the relationship is reversed. Among girls, the relationship is almost one-third greater in the 1970's sample. In only one county, Erie, was the relationship greater among the boys in the 1970's sample; 40% of the boys had been reported earlier as abused or neglected.

The relationship in the 1970's sample varies from county to county much more than it did in the 1950's sample, and this variation does not coincide with the degree to which records had been preserved in the county or the population increased or decreased. Table 15 lists the relationship by boys and girls in each county. As in the 1950's sample, these figures are based on children who had at least one founded contact for child maltreatment, delinquency or ungovernability. Children with no founded contacts were omitted.

One reason for the difference in the relationship between boys and girls may be the size of the sample. Unlike the 1950's sample of children reported as abused and

TABLE 15 CHILDREN REPORTED AS DELINQUENT OR UNGOVERNABLE WHO HAD BEEN REPORTED EARLIER AS MALTREATED

County	Percentage of Boys Reported as Abused or Neglected	Percentage of Girls Reported as Abused or Neglected
Broome	13.5	16.7
Erie	41.4	35.6
Kings	12.3	18.4
Monroe	36.3	53.0
New York	30.9	44.6
St. Lawrence	21.4	40.0
Suffolk	7.9	10.9
Westchester	21.1	28.7

neglected, the 1970's sample is not half boys and half girls; almost 78% of the children are boys. In terms of the children with a founded contact, the 1970's sample consists of 483 girls and 1,272 boys (139 boys and 66 girls had no founded contacts of any type). Perhaps the significantly smaller number of girls in the sample increases the chance that other contacts involving them will be found. The amount or type of screening that occurs before a juvenile is referred to court may also be different for boys and girls. To be referred to court, a girl's behavior or situation may have to be much worse than a boy's. The system's natural tendency to be more lenient toward girls in trouble may mean that in any sample of juvenile delinquents or ungovernable youth, the girls included in it would come from families with more severe, intractable problems, including a history of child maltreatment.

Finding No. 5: Delinquent children who were reported as abused or neglected tend to be more violent than other delinquents.

When the delinquency contacts in the 1970's sample are associated with prior abuse or neglect contacts, there is a greater association between violent delinquent acts and prior child maltreatment than between non-violent delinquent acts and prior child maltreatment. The sample of some of these contacts is small, but taken as a whole, a clear pattern emerges. Table 16 shows these differences.

Except for unauthorized use of autos and possession of burglar's tools, the correlation between delinquent referral reasons in the 1970's sample and earlier reports of child abuse or neglect drops consistently in the non-violent categories. This trend often counters the distribution of delinquency referral reasons in the sample, although the variation in the number of referral reasons for some violent acts, such as homicide and rape, and such non-violent acts as possession of burglar's tools, may, in part, be accounted for by their relatively small number. The violent categories with a large number of referral reasons, assault and disorderly conduct, which includes fighting, show a pattern of relatively high relationship, over 20%. Robbery and burglary, both of which have a potential leading to violence (robbery more so, since it involves a personal confrontation with the victim, such as a mugging for example) fall in between. The bulk of the non-violent acts against property have a relationship of 16% or less.

All of this implies that delinquent children who were involved in child abuse or neglect contacts are somewhat different from delinquent children who were not reported as abused or neglected. They are 'over-represented ' among the group of juveniles who commit, or are charged with committing, violent acts. A larger sample of juveniles charged with the most serious violent acts, homicide, rape and arson, would be useful to see whether the high rate of association would hold. Some studies based on interviews suggest that the correlation would remain high, but they, too, are based on a small sample (7).

Finding No. 6: Child maltreatment cannot be used as an indicator or predictor of a particular type of juvenile misbehavior.

Although the study of the 1950's sample confirms that there is a relationship between child abuse or neglect and juvenile delinquency or ungovernability, it also indicates that almost any type of child maltreatment can lead to any type of later

TABLE 16

Reasons for Delinquency Referral	Total No. in 1970's Sample	Percentage in 1970's Sample	Percentage Related to Prior Abuse/Neglect Contacts
Violent Acts			
Homicide	7	.21	28.6
Arson	46	1.3	23.9
Rape	14	.42	28.6
Other Sex Crimes	43	1.3	11.6
Assault	391	11.8	22.0
Disorderly Conduct	126	3.8	21.4
Possession of Dangerous Weapons	72	2.1	19.4
Acts Against a Person			
Robbery	515	15.5	18.4
Acts Against Property			
Burglary	661	20.0	19.2
Auto Theft	180	5.4	9.9
Unauthorized Use of Auto	105	3.1	26.7
Larceny	471	14.2	16.3
Malicious Mischief	247	7.4	14.6
Unlawful Entry	139	4.2	10.8
Rec'g Stolen Property	74	2.2	13.5
Possession of Burglar's Tools	19	.57	47.4
Victimless Acts			
Narcotics	198	5.9	13.1
Gambling	2	.06	0.0
Unlawful Assembly	2	.06	0.0

behavioral problems, with no clear pattern of predictability. Not every child reported as abused or neglected was later reported as delinquent or ungovernable. Child maltreatment does predispose a child toward later delinquency or ungovernability more than a childhood without abuse or neglect, but other factors apparently help direct this predisposition toward a specific type of delinquency or ungovernability. Examples of such factors may be peer relationships with other juveniles, or the neighborhood environment. In many families reported for child maltreatment, only one or two children were later reported for juvenile misconduct; even children who experienced the environment of the same family, often at the same time, went in different directions as they passed through adolescence into adulthood.

This limitation on constructing a formula of predictability should be remembered by anyone tempted to use child maltreatment as a predictor of specific juvenile criminality. For example, the children in the 1950's sample who were later charged with homicide had been reported earlier, not as physically abused, but as neglected, as inadequately supervised. But most inadequately supervised children did not become murderers. Making predictions about the type of anti-social behavior to be expected of abused and neglected children is extremely risky, as are all behavioral

TABLE 17

Delinquency Referral Reason	Percentage of Referral Reasons in 1950's Sample	Percentage in State, 1967-68 Judicial Year
Homicide	.8	.1
Arson	2.0	2.0
Rape	.9	1.0
Other Sex Crimes	1.6	1.0
Narcotics Violation	1.1	2.0
Robbery	8.6	10.0
Burglary	19.8	10.0
Assault	13.7	14.0
Auto Theft	4.6	6.0
Unauthorized use of auto	2.7	6.0
Larceny, not auto	19.5	16.0
Possession of dangerous weapons	1.9	2.0
Malicious mischief	11.6	5.0
Unlawful entry	5.5	3.0
Possession of Burglar's Tools	.2	1.0
Gambling	0.0	.1
Receiving Stolen Property	1.0	1.0
Unlawful Assembly	.5	.3
Disorderly Conduct	3.9	2.0

(For state-wide statistics, see Administrative Board of the Judicial Conference, State of New York, 1970, p. 309).

predictions. Apparently, the experience of being abused or neglected as a child is more important and consequential than the type of maltreatment suffered.

The distribution of the delinquency referral reasons for children in the 1950's sample demonstrates the general lack of any predictability in the outcome of child maltreatment. This distribution is similar to the distribution of all delinquency referral reasons in the general population; no special clustering is evident. The children in the 1950's sample were not disproportionately involved in one or more types of delinquency. Table 17 compares the distribution of the prime delinquency referral reasons of the children in the 1950's sample with the distribution of all the delinquency referral reasons in the state in a year in which these children were involved themselves. (The year 1967 had the highest involvement in the Monroe County sample.)

The general lack of any significant difference between the delinquency contacts of the children in the 1950's sample and the general population of delinquency contacts is apparent. In most categories, the distribution is almost exact; burglary and malicious mischief are the only categories with any noteworthy difference. This difference may be either a fluke of the sample or a variation in the general pattern without any true significance. A possible psychological explanation is that these types of delinquency, acts against property, are attention-getting activities.

A comparison of the ungovernability contacts of the children in the 1950's sample with the general distribution of all such contacts in the state shows a similar agreement in distribution. Table 18 compares these.

Again, as with the delinquency referral reasons, the distributions among the contacts in the 1950's sample and the general population are similar. The difference in

TABLE 18

Ungovernability or Status Offense Referral Reason	Percentage of Referral Reasons in 1950's Sample	Percentage in State, 1967-68 Judicial Year (8)
Running Away From Home	20.3	21
Habitual Truancy	33.1	21
Refusal to Obey	26.2	22
Sexual Misconduct	11.7	2
Staying Out Late	3.9	9
Associating with Bad Companions	1.8	5
Using Vile Language	1.5	2
Intoxication	1.0	1
Glue Sniffing	.4	1

truancy and sexual misconduct may reflect fluctuations that would occur for reasons unrelated to the behavior of children. The possibility of attention-getting behavior among the children with these contacts may be real. There is not a higher percentage of running away from home among the sample of abused and neglected children. Acting out behavior, such as truancy and sexual misconduct, may be a desperate attempt to provoke love or caring from indifferent parents. Sexual misconduct may be a misguided way of searching for love or affection; adult promiscuity is often similarly motivated, and there is no reason to assume it does not serve the same function for adolescents who feel unloved.

TABLE 19

Child Maltreatment Referral Reasons	% of All Contacts in Sample	% Related to Ungovernability Contacts	% Related Delinquency Contacts
Battered Child	.8	.76	.37
Other Attacks	5.1	8.6	6.8
Risk of Injury	1.4	.76	1.1
Sexual Abuse	.9	1.7	.5
Mental/Emotional Impairment	2.1	2.6	3.0
Inadequate Food, Shelter, Clothing	21.9	20.0	20.6
Malnutrition	.1	0.0	.19
Educational Neglect	2.5	3.0	4.7
Medical Neglect	1.2	.87	1.4
Abandonment	6.6	5.0	5.1
Involuntary Parental Absence	2.6	3.5	5.9
Parental Drug Use	.4	.1	.28
Parental Alcoholism	11.8	9.4	8.3
Parental Sexual Misconduct	4.5	5.4	3.1
Parental Mental Illness	2.8	3.0	2.2
Parental Fighting	2.6	2.0	2.6
Inadequate Supervision	32.1	27.0	27.5
Other	2.9	4.7	6.2

To double check that there is no special pattern in the delinquency or ungovernability contacts of the children in the 1950's sample, a comparison was made between the distribution of the child abuse or neglect referral reasons in the sample with the distribution of those associated with later delinquency or ungovernability. Again, the pattern reflected no special relationships other than the distribution of child maltreatment referral reasons in the sample. The distribution of correlated child maltreatment referral reasons is similar to the distribution of all child abuse and neglect referral reasons in the entire 1950's sample. Table 19 shows this distribution.

This lack of sure predictability may disappoint those who like neat formulas, but it is important to know reality as it is, not as it may be pleasing to comprehend. The lack of a formula, in itself, is an important finding because of its implications for treatment. It means that no type of child maltreatment can be given less priority than another in long-range planning for the treatment of children and parents. Priorities are often set in the investigative stage because of the apparent, immediate danger to a child, but these priorities must end when treatment services are provided. Every abused and neglected child is in equal need of treatment services, and the potential social costs of ignoring any of these needs is equally great.

Finding No. 7: Few services were provided to abused and neglected children or their families.

Professionals who treat abused and neglected children or their families recommend a wide range of rehabilitative services to help families overcome the problems that lead to child maltreatment; in most cases, child abuse or neglect are found to be symptoms of other problems, not isolated in themselves. Current understanding indicates that a complex combination of personal, familial, social or situational problems prompt parents to abuse or neglect their children. Therapeutic services such as counseling are used to help relieve the personal distress of marital discord, and other forms of psychological treatment are often recommended to help parents overcome their personal problems. Other services are directed toward the parents' current situation. Day care, homemaking, employment and even recreational services are used to help parents manage the external problems of daily living which confront many families without provoking child abuse or neglect.

The need and utility of services to treat child abuse and neglect are not entirely the product of recent wisdom. In the early 1950's, the provision of a complex array of services was the treatment ideal, just as it is now. Vincent DeFrancis wrote about the use of services in 1955 (The American Humane Association). "Disregarding the infrequent deliberate or willful neglect, we know for the most part it is unintentional and is the product of the parent's inability to cope with a variety of personal and family problems." DeFrancis was quite specific about the types of services that should be provided to abused and neglected children and their parents.

> Obviously we cannot be expected to probe into the subconscious to reach down to experiences or incidents responsible for... personality disorders. That is a job for psychotherapists. For the most part as caseworkers we can deal only with the immediate problems of inadequacies which are the direct cause of the neglect.
>
> We have called these the "proximate causes of neglect." Unless there are

symptoms of deep neurosis or psychosis, these proximate causes are the focal point of treatment.

It is very difficult sometimes to distinguish between cause and effect. Arbitrarily, perhaps, we have chosen the more basic as causes. For example, inadequate housing may well be the cause for neglect. In this context, however, we have thought of it as an end result of some deeper problem, possibly a lack of sufficient finances. Other problems in this category would be non-support and unemployment; physical illness or disability, abandonment or desertion, separation, divorce, or death of a parent with the concomitant family breakdown.

In the area of emotional problems we encounter the same difficulty in distinguishing cause and effect. As interpreted earlier we are thinking here of the emotional difficulties which are the direct causes for the neglect. We know that these causes themselves may be the products of deeper emotional tensions, stresses or problems. In this concept, we would identify emotional immaturity, emotional maladjustments, marital discord, mental deficiency, neurosis, psychosis, alcoholism, the emotional concomitants to separation, divorce, or death, and psychopathic personality.

The level of knowledge about the prevention and treatment of child abuse or neglect in the 1950's is similar to that today, although one might add to it. Yet, an analysis of the dispositions of the abuse and neglect contacts in the 1950's sample shows an enormous gulf between knowledge and implementation. Perhaps the most outstanding, if not shocking, finding of this study is the absolute paucity of services provided to children and families. Less than 7% of all the child protective contacts in the 1950's sample led to the provision of any services, and the chief service offered was casework supervision. Fewer than 0.1% of the contacts resulted in the provision of any other type of service. Table 20 summarizes this finding for each county.

Most of the child protective contacts of the children in the 1970's sample of delinquent and ungovernable children would, of course, come later than the protective contacts of the children in the 1950's sample. In the 1970's sample, the provision of services in child protective cases was extremely low; 12% of these protective contacts led to supervision of the parents, and 1.2% led to the provision of some other type of additional service. Thus, the difference is almost negligible, and may be due to the sampling method. The 1970's sample was drawn from a population of children reported to the Family Court as delinquent or ungovernable, and, unlike the 1950's sample, does not represent either the complete child protective case load for a given year or a substantial part of it.

More recent data on the provision of child protective services indicate that current cases of suspected child abuse or neglect still are not receiving needed services.

TABLE 20

Type of Service	Broome	Erie	Kings	Monroe	New York	St. Law.	Suff.	West.
Supervision	13%	2%	4%	2%	15%	8%	11%	16%
Supervision & Other Services	.4%	.6%	.9%	0	0	0	0	.7%

TABLE 21 36,629 TOTAL CHILD RECIPIENTS WITH A GOAL OF 3 (PROTECTIVE SERVICES)

	%
Adoption	3
Adult Education	7
Day Care	6
Education	1
Employment	2
Family Planning	3
Foster Care Adult	1
Foster Care Children	22
Health Related	5
Home Management	4
Homemaker	2
Housekeeper	1
Housing	3
Preventive	10
Protective Adult	1
Protective Children	34
Group/Senior Citizen	.8
Social Adjustment	5
Transportation	4
Unmarried Parent	1

Statistics released by the State Department of Social Services (*Child Protective Services in New York State: 1976 Annual Report,* p. 31 -) show that the traditional reliance on casework supervision and placement as the prime protective service response continues. Two forms of casework supervision account for 44% of the services provided, and placement accounts for another 22%. The total adds up to slightly more than 100%, because some children received more than one service. Most of the overlap occurs with the children who received casework supervision, plus one or more other services. Table 21 summarizes the distribution of these services.

Preventive and protective children are, essentially, two different classifications of case work supervision.

These figures do not come from the State Central Register of child abuse and maltreatment cases, and they do not portray the distribution of services to all families reported for suspected child abuse or neglect. Instead, they show the distribution of services given to children through Title XX in which protective services were designated as a treatment goal, which may include children not reported as abused or neglected. These figures are the only ones available, and they confirm the trend that has prevailed for the last thirty or more years. They show that few services, other than placement or supervision, are being provided to children and families who are considered in need of protective services, as defined in Title XX procedures. The gap between defined, recognized need and the actual delivery of services is still immense.

The lack of services should be kept in mind because it has an important bearing on the other findings of this study. It means that little, if anything, was attempted to undo the effects of abuse or neglect on the children, and that little, if anything, was done to alter the home environment in which the children lived. Yet, it should be remembered that 79% of the child protective reports in the 1950's sample were considered to be "founded," or in some way accurate. Thus, for most of the children and families in the 1950's sample, the child protective intervention had little impact on their lives, and the same can be said of the children in the 1970's sample who had been reported as abused or neglected earlier in their lives. It would seem that protective services are generally limited to stopping a recurrence of abuse or neglect, and that even these efforts do not conform to the state-of-the-art knowledge of the time.

Finding No. 8: Most of the founded child protective contacts ended in no action.

Sixty-two percent of the contacts led to no further action. The high rate of 'no further action' is not a sign that the contacts were inaccurate or false reports. Of the protective contacts, 79% were founded, and another 4% involved families or children who were already 'active' with an agency or court. Yet, 69% of the child protective contacts in the 1950's sample resulted in no change in the child's status; the child remained in the same home without any services being provided. Another 6.9% of the contacts resulted in supervision or services for the family whose child remained in the home. Thus, in the 1950's sample, about 75% of the child protective contacts led to no change in the child's status, and little change in his circumstances.

Of the protective contacts, 5.4% led to the change in custody of the child, though the child remained in a home, either a different parent's or another relative's. Interestingly, in Westchester County, 33.2% of all the protective contacts in the 1950's sample led to a change in custody. No other county comes near that level of switching custody.

The removal of endangered children from their homes has long been an integral part of child protective work. When protective agencies were first established a century ago, removal was the main emphasis, and even today it is often the only image evoked by the thought of protecting abused and neglected children. It is generally believed that the less punitive emphasis of keeping children in their own homes is a recent development. The study of children reported as abused or neglected in the early 1950's shows that this philosophy was already in operation at that time.

In the 1970's sample of children reported as delinquent or ungovernable, the disposition of the child protective contacts shows a similar pattern as in the 1950's sample. Of these protective contacts, 61.3% led to the child remaining in his or her own home, and another 9.4% ended up in the home of a different parent or another relative. The slightly different distributions of the protective contacts in the two samples may reflect the different way in which each was identified.

Table 22 shows these data for the 1950's sample, and Table 23 shows it for the 1970's sample, for each county.

The disposition figures do not total 100% because the figures for placements and other dispositions are discussed in other findings. See finding No. 9 for figures on placements.

Finding No. 9: The placement rate in child neglect cases was higher than in child abuse cases.

Abuse and neglect have been considered either as part of a continuum or as entirely different problems. In both views, however, abuse is usually treated as more serious than neglect, which has not received the public and professional attention

TABLE 22 NON-PLACEMENT DISPOSITION OF CHILD PROTECTIVE CONTACTS, 1950's SAMPLE (%)

Disposition	Broome	Erie	Kings	Monroe	New York	St. Law.	Suff.	West.
Child in Same Home	43	83	56	74	75	36	64	34
Child with Different Parent	.4	1	2	1	2	3	8	27
Child with Other Relative	5	.3	3	3	2	0	3	6
Totals	48	84	61	78	79	39	75	67

TABLE 23 NON-PLACEMENT DISPOSITION OF CHILD PROTECTIVE CONTACTS, 1970's SAMPLE (%)

Disposition	Broome	Erie	Kings	Monroe	New York	St. Law.	Suff.	West.
Child in Same Home	56	75	61	59	55	67	93	40
Child With Different Parent	4	4	0	4	9	0	7	10
Child with Other Relative	4	0	7	7	6	0	0	0
Totals Placed Other	64	79	68	70	70	67	100	50

that has been given to neglect (See Polansky, et al.). Given the prevailing opinion that abuse is more severe than neglect, one finding of the study may seem strange; the percentage of neglect contacts leading to placement was higher than the percentage of abuse contacts leading to placement. Among the abuse contacts, 16% resulted in placement, but 20.3% of the neglect contacts ended in placement. Table 24 shows the differences in placement rates in each county in the 1950's sample.

A 5% difference may seem small, but it is a 20% variation among all the child protective placements recorded in the study. This finding indicates that neglect may be more difficult to treat than abuse, that protective agencies find abuse more amenable to treatment. As Polansky, et al. indicate, neglect "is chronic, pervasive, resistant to specific treatment, and transmitted in intergenerational cycles (p. 337)."

Polansky has argued that child neglect has not been studied to the extent that it deserves as a problem in itself. This finding supports his contention that neglect is difficult to treat, and it calls for greater study. It also serves as a reminder that neglect, in most states, accounts for 85% or more of the child protective caseload.

TABLE 24 PLACEMENT RATES IN 1950's SAMPLE

Contacts	Broome	Erie	Kings	Monroe	New York	St. Law.	Suff.	West.
Abuse	14	9	16	20	15	55	5	24
Neglect	47	16	21	14	19	59	16	41

More children are reported as neglected than abused, and they have a greater chance of being placed in foster or institutional care as a result.

Moreover, it has been suggested that neglect may have a higher social cost than abuse. Glasser and Garvin (1977) have compared the family characteristics associated with abuse, neglect, ungovernability and delinquency. They found similar patterns of family dysfunction in both abuse and ungovernability cases, while the dysfunction in neglect and delinquency cases were also similar to each other. The patterns were more similar between abuse and ungovernability, or neglect and delinquency, than between abuse and neglect or ungovernability and delinquency. The data in this study neither confirm nor contradict Glasser and Garvin's findings. It seems clear, however, that the implications of these findings demand further study and ultimate translation into programatic policy making. It is yet another reminder that abuse and neglect are equally serious and require an equal treatment commitment from professionals and communities.

Finding No. 10: The placement rate for ungovernability was higher than for juvenile delinquency.

In the 1970's sample, the placement rate for ungovernability was almost twice the rate for delinquency: 19.4% of the ungovernability contacts led to placement, while only 11.3% of the delinquency contacts led to a similar placement. Similar to the greater seriousness usually attributed to abuse over neglect situations, delinquency is usually considered a more serious offense than ungovernability; it is, after all, criminal activity of juveniles. Yet, a substantially higher percentage of ungovernable children were placed as a result of their contact with the Family Court. The explanation is, probably, that ungovernable children are 'beyond the lawful' control of their parents, who may also not want them, and thus placement becomes the only alternative for them, unless the court insists that the parents care for them. But if the court did so and the parents refused, the court would then have to declare the parents neglectful and place the children under a different label.

The placement rate for ungovernability and delinquency varied from county to county, as shown in Table 25. Interim dispositions 'referred to court,' or 'referred to another agency,' have been excluded.

These data contradict the belief that officials and Family Court judges upstate are 'tougher' on juvenile delinquents. The placement rate for delinquency was greatly lower in Erie, Monroe, St. Lawrence, Suffolk, and Westchester Counties than in New York County. Kings County was about the same as Erie and St. Lawrence Counties, and Broome County had the highest placement rate. Suffolk County had, by far, the lowest placement rate. This implies that a juvenile accused of a delinquent act has a much greater chance of being placed if he lives in Broome or New York County.

TABLE 25 PLACEMENT RATE FOR EACH CONTACT (%)

	Broome	Erie	Kings	Monroe	New York	St. Law.	Suff.	West.
Ungovernability Contacts	35.4	12	17.4	11.2	35.9	14.3	1.2	10.5
Delinquency Contacts	29.9	8.6	8.5	4.9	20.2	8.3	2.1	4.8

The placement rates for ungovernability were also much higher than for delinquency in the 1950's sample, about one-third greater. Table 26 shows these rates for each county.

An interesting difference between the placement rate of juvenile contacts in the 1950's sample and the 1970's sample is the lower placement rate in the more recent sample. Whether this is a feature of how the samples were constructed or a reflection of an actual change in the policy of placing juvenile offenders cannot be determined by the data collected. Some further analysis of the data is possible to determine whether the children involved in a protective contact have a higher rate of placement than other children named in a delinquency or an ungovernability case in the 1970's sample.

Finding No. 11: Children reported as abused or neglected and children reported as delinquent or ungovernable come from similar families, which are significantly different from the general population.

Researchers studying child abuse and juvenile delinquency have argued that various aspects of family composition affect these two problems. Gelles observed that a repeated finding in child abuse research is the positive association between child abuse and family size (See also Gil, 1971). Many have suggested that pregnancies occurring before marriage or early in a marriage may reflect an unwanted pregnancy or a severe stress on an already stressful relationship, and premarital pregnancies, unwanted pregnancies and children born out-of-wedlock have been shown to be associated with child abuse (Zalba, 197l; Bennie and Sclare , 1969; Wasserman, 1967). Finally, abused children have been shown to disproportionately

TABLE 26 PLACEMENT RATE FOR 1950's SAMPLE JUVENILE CONTACTS (%)

	Broome	Erie	Kings	Monroe	New York	St. Law.	Suff.	West.
Ungovernability	50	31	34	27	49	40	22	35
Delinquency	17	19	25	23	30	25	20	28

Average Totals (%)

	1970's Sample	1950's Sample
Ungovernability	19	34
Delinquency	11	23

come from female-headed households (Gil, 1971). A study of New York City delinquency and ungovernability cases (*Juvenile Injustice*) found that 52% of the children came from a one-parent family, and that another 16% came from families in which the mother was living with a boyfriend; 28% of the children were born out-of-wedlock.

The families in both the 1950's and 1970's samples, which were identified for different reasons, share certain basic characteristics in common, which distinguish them markedly from most families living in the same communities. In general, these families were larger, had a greater percentage of illegitimate children, and were one-parent households with either parent missing. Families belonging to minority groups appear to be 'overrepresented,' even though almost 60% of the 1950's sample were white children.

Thus, the demographic data for the children and families in both samples give a picture of dysfunctional, multi-problem families which probably did not fit easily into the normal life of their communities. Regardless of the reported child maltreatment or juvenile misbehavior, many of them could have otherwise been considered families in trouble, children and parents who needed help to overcome a variety of problems.

There is no question that the families in both samples were larger than the average. According to the 1950 Census, only 12% of all American families with children had four or more children, but 42% of the families in the 1950's sample were at least that large, almost three and a half times greater than the national average. According to the 1970 Census, only 16% of the families in New York State had four or more children, but 53% of the families in the 1970's sample were at least that large. In the 1970's sample, 10% of the families had eight or more children, while only 1.5% of the families in the United States were so large.

A positive association between family size and child abuse appears to be a consistent finding in child abuse research (Gelles, 1977). In Table 27 this consistent finding is confirmed by the sample data. When compared to the general population of the eight counties studied, the families in the sample of maltreated children are always twice as large, and often as much as three times as large, as the average family size in the communities in which they live.

The data presented here support the previously found association between family size and child abuse, but Table 28 goes further by suggesting that coming from a large family may increase the chances of being in contact with official agencies over a longer time and for more types of contacts, both maltreatment and juvenile offenses. Perhaps large families are more known and visible and therefore more likely to come to official attention for any given type of behavior. Or, possibly, large families are simply more stressful social settings.

The greatest difference between the families in both samples and the general population is in the large percentage of children born out-of-wedlock. In the 1950's sample, the rate of illigitimate births is 450% higher than the national average, and in the 1970's sample it is 261% greater. Of the children in the 1950's sample, 18% were born out-of-wedlock, while the national average was 4% from 1940 until 1955. Of the children in the 1970's sample, 13% were born out-of-wedlock , while the national average from 1955 to 1960 was 4.9%.

It has been argued that children born out-of-wedlock are more likely to be abused than other children. Table 28 clearly shows a disproportionate number of children in the 1950's sample were born out-of-wedlock, when compared with children in the

TABLE 27 AVERAGE POPULATION PER HOUSEHOLD

	General Population 1950	Total 1950 Sample Children	1950 Sample Children with Maltreatment Contacts & JD Contacts	PIS Contacts
Broome	3.35	5.84 (281)	5.14 (14)	5.11 (9)
St. Lawrence	3.63	9.02 (101)	8.36 (14)	0.0 (1)
Suffolk	3.31	5.29 (308)	4.78 (9)	6.67 (9)
Westchester	3.40	5.08 (475)	5.30 (30)	6.48 (27)
Subtotal	NA	5.66 (1165)	5.84 (67)	6.50 (46)
Erie	3.42	7.52 (1290)	7.81 (167)	8.17 (149)
Kings	3.36	7.39 (625)	7.63 (67)	7.66 (59)
Monroe	3.26	7.64 (545)	8.04 (80)	7.52 (97)
New York	2.80	6.13 (838)	7.02 (54)	6.74 (68)
Subtotal	NA	7.16	7.71	7.66
Total	NA	6.77 (4463)	7.42 (435)	7.53 (419)

general population of these eight counties. And in low contact counties this is even more apparent: more than three times as many children were born out-of-wedlock among those with maltreatment contacts than in the general population.

The literature does not address the question of whether an unwanted pregnancy increases or decreases the association between maltreatment contacts and juvenile misconduct contacts. The small number of children in low contact counties with both maltreatment contacts and juvenile contacts precludes assessing the effect of out-of-wedlock birth on these children. Yet, they are more likely than children in the general population to be born out-of-wedlock.

In high contact counties, the evidence generally suggests that being born out-of-wedlock increases the probability of having official contact for maltreatment. With the exception of children in New York County with maltreatment contacts **and** ungovernability contacts, children with **both** types of contacts are no more likely to have been born out-of-wedlock. Children with both maltreatment and juvenile contacts are, however, about as likely as other maltreated children (or their siblings) to be born out-of-wedlock.

In New York County one can speculate about why it is children with maltreatment and PINS contacts, and not maltreatment and delinquency contacts, that are much more likely to be born out-of-wedlock . Perhaps status offenses are typical of children not just born out-of-wedlock, not just children of unwanted pregnancies,

TABLE 28 PERCENT BORN OUT-OF-WEDLOCK

	In the General Population	In the Total 1950 Sample	Among Children With Maltreatment Contacts with PINS Contacts	JD Contacts
Broome	3	16 (274)	0 (9)	0 (14)
St. Lawrence	4	13 (101)	0 (1)	21 (14)
Suffolk	2	12 (307)	11 (9)	0 (9)
Westchester	5	20 (471)	11 (27)	13 (30)
Subtotal	NA	16 (1153)	9 (46)	10 (67)
Erie	5	12 (1276	9 (149)	14 (167)
Kings	8	19 (624)	14 (58)	10 (67)
Monroe	6	21 (539)	23 (96)	28 (79)
New York	18	27 (836)	43 (68	24 (54)
Subtotal	NA	19 (3275)	20 (371)	18 (367)
Total	NA	18 (4428)	19 (417)	17 (434)

but truly **unwanted** children. Table 28 summarizes the out-of-wedlock status of children in the 1950's sample and the general population of each county.

Large families, of course, in themselves are not harmful, even though the trend, or fashion, recently has been toward small ones; they may even be healthier than one-child families. Moreover, many people believe that the stigma of 'illegitimacy' is more harmful than the simple fact, in itself. But these situations can be a sign of trouble when they occur in conjunction with other events. The data from both samples, though especially the 1950's sample, show that a large percentage of the families were missing one parent. In the 1950's sample, 40% of the children did not have a father living with them, and 15% did not have a mother living with them. The data on the 1970's sample is less conclusive because it was not known for about 40% of the children; the 1970's sample was comprised of delinquent and ungovernable children, and these data apparently were not considered as important as in child protective cases. The information was not recorded in many case records. Where available, the data indicate that 28% of the children came from a home without a father, while 7% had no mother living with them. The combination of large families, illegitimate births (which often means different fathers for each of the children) and one-parent families has important consequences for parents and children, as well as for the community in which they live.

We have become more conscious of racial and ethnic influences and discrimination than ever before in our history, and we are more willing to attribute motivations to these differences. There is a temptation to do so with the data in this study. Although 58% of the 1950's sample, in which ethnicity is known, is white, 21% of the children were black and 6% were Hispanic, at a time when non-whites accounted for only 6.5% of the population of the state. The ethnicity of 14.5% of the children was not indicated in the records of the agencies or courts. In the 1970's sample, 39% of the children were white, 31% were black and 12% were Hispanic, when only 13% of the population was non-white. It should be noted that 85% of the Hispanic children in the 1950's sample lived in New York County (Manhattan), while 34% of the black children lived in Kings County. In the 1970's sample, 91% of the Hispanic children and 57% of the black children lived in New York County. Only in St. Lawrence County is the proportion of whites in the sample about equal to the proportion of whites living in the county.

Thus, one could say that non-whites are 'over-represented' in both the 1950's and the 1970's samples. This would mean that non-whites were 'over-represented' in the reports of suspected child abuse and neglect in the early 1950's and reports of alleged delinquency and ungovernability in the early 1970's. The possible significance of this is difficult to assess, given the high proportion of large, broken, one-parent families in both studies. It is possible that these problems had more to do with the situations that led to the children being reported as abused, neglected, ungovernable or delinquent than any other characteristic of their families, including race. It is also possible that the non-white families in the counties studied had a higher incidence of such family dysfunction; 'over-representation' cannot be claimed unless these other factors are known.

Saying that a group is 'over-represented' sounds like an important discovery, it even sounds like an accusation. But it only means something when the true level of incidence of a problem like child abuse or juvenile delinquency within that group is known, not the level of reporting, but the true level of incidence. A group may be 'over-represented' only because it is being reported out of proportion to the incidence within it. Even if it is being reported frequently, and out of proportion to its size in the general population, it is not being 'over-represented' in reporting if the level of incidence within it is correspondingly high. Of course, knowing the true level of incidence of a social problem within each group in our society is not within the grasp of our knowledge and data-gathering techniques. The true level of incidence of child abuse, for example, is not even known, though it is debated, for the entire society, let alone a segment of that society.

Much has been said in the debate about the role of poverty in reported child abuse and neglect cases. It is generally believed that most official cases of child maltreatment involve impoverished families; similarly, it is generally held that many, if not most, juvenile delinquents or ungovernable children grew up in families at the lower socioeconomic levels of our society. Despite the importance some attach to these arguments, the official records of child maltreatment and juvenile offense cases generally do not include any information about the economic status of the child's family. Sometimes there might be a reference to a family's receiving public assistance, but, in general, most case records were mute on the issue. Apparently, the socioeconomic status of children and families is not considered important enough to be recorded in these records, and, one must assume, to be considered in devising treatment plans. It should be noted, however, that whatever the merits of this debate, most impoverished families do not abuse and neglect their children or produce juvenile delinquents. It is unfair to the many impoverished but devoted parents in our society to assume that they are not successful parents. They are just as loving and successful as any other parents in our society.

CONCLUSION

The findings of this study confirm that there is an empirical relationship between child abuse or neglect and socially deviant behavior. Since the data in the study are 'time-ordered,' which means there is a demonstrable sequence of protective service contacts followed by juvenile justice contacts, the study certainly suggests that child maltreatment leads to later juvenile misbehavior. Yet, it is not clear whether it is possible to prove that child abuse or neglect causes juvenile delinquency or ungovernability. Not all maltreated children become behavior problems as juveniles, and not all delinquent or ungovernable children were abused or neglected when younger. Moreover, one must remember that in most systems of logic, attributing causation to temporal sequence is a fallacy. One fact is resoundingly clear: a considerable percentage of children, in both the 1950's and the 1970's samples, were abused or neglected and reported as delinquent or ungovernable when they were older. An important implication of this study is that the relationship between child abuse or neglect and later socially deviant behavior is more complicated than a simple cause and effect association, and that this complexity raises questions about how we are responding to the problems of child maltreatment and juvenile crime.

An important factor in the relationship between child maltreatment and juvenile misbehavior, highlighted in this study, is the amazing lack of services provided to most children and families. Though human behavior is difficult to change, and undoing the emotional consequences of child maltreatment may be even more difficult and unappealing, little effort was made to try to help children and parents. Except for families involved in special or experimental programs, which can reach only a small fraction of the child protective caseload, there is no reason to suppose that things are any better now than during the time under study. The complaint that we have improved reporting laws, but that few services are available to respond to new cases is almost universal. Even allowing for the recent developments that occurred in child protection, the state-of-the-art system described by Vincent DeFrancis in 1955 exists more on paper than in reality. One must wonder whether reality has made any additional advances since then, despite the changes in the current state-of-the-art knowledge about what works and what is needed.

In both samples in the study, the prime services provided, if they are to be called that, were either placement or casework supervision, and for most cases, nothing else. It is possible, of course, that the families involved needed nothing else, but the outcome in terms of the later problems indicates that more was needed, unless the children and parents were going to be discarded as hopeless. The criticism that child protective services do not do much for the child, that it is oriented toward helping the parents, is not a novel perception, but it is true. Most services, most child protective efforts, are directed toward getting the parents to stop the abuse or neglect. Little is done to help the child overcome the experience of being abused or neglected. C. Kempe summed up the situation in these words:

> It is a fascinating question to consider why it is that during the past seventy years of active protective services work on behalf of troubled families, the focus of treatment, and indeed of diagnosis, has been upon the mother rather than on each member of the family, but it is not surprising. For one thing, the mother was more readily available to a social worker who was beginning to provide

diagnostic and treatment services to a family while the father was at work during the time the social worker was available. Moreover, the philosophy of protective services for the past fifty years has been very much geared to the feelings that if a mother could be helped to be more competent or more loving to her child, or able to stabilize her marriage, even though the father might be the primary abuser, that good things would of necessity happen in regards to the abused child and the other children in the family. It is not surprising, therefore, that while there is an extensive literature on casework with mothers, there is much less on work with fathers and virtually nothing on the abused child.

Numerous studies have chronicled the psychological, as well as the physical, effects of child maltreatment. Elmer and Gregg (1967) found that 40% of the abused children studied were emotionally disturbed. Green, et al. (1974) found that both abused and neglected children were significantly more impaired in ego competency, self-concept, body image, reality testing, defensive functioning, object relations and basic thought processes; they also had greater levels of aggression, low impulse control, anxiety and self-destructiveness. Johnson and Morse (1968), in a study of 101 abused children, found nearly 70% to be below normal in physical and emotional development.

It is natural to assume that abuse will provoke aggression in a child, but there has also been some indication that neglect can lead to serious behavioral consequences. James Prescott (1975) has written that he believes "that the deprivation of body touch, contact and movement are the basic causes of a number of emotional disturbances which include depressive and autistic behavior, hyperactivity, sexual aberration, drug abuse, violence and aggression." He has backed up his belief with intensive neurological research. The findings from the 1950's sample indicate that child neglect can have the same serious consequences as child abuse for the child's later behavior.

All of this implies that abused and neglected children need mental health services to undo the emotional damage of child maltreatment. There does not seem to be any doubt that child abuse and child neglect evoke aggressive feelings in children, which are either directed inward or outward. Like all feelings, this hostility will be expressed, in one way or another, and the chance is that it will take the form of antisocial behavior. Inhibited aggression, or aggression turned against oneself, which has been frequently described in abused children, eventually reaches a point where it breaks through in a violent rage. Yet, if a survey were taken, not many children would be found to be receiving mental health services, despite evidence that they are effective, especially if the children are reached when they are very young (10). As one study concluded:

> Abused children have the capacity to make changes. The younger they are, the more resiliency they have. Children between the ages of two and four in the therapeutic day care setting, will make more changes and at a faster rate, than children between the ages of four and eight seen in play therapy once or twice a week. This pilot study has demonstrated that it takes quite some time to establish a trusting alliance with an abused child. For that reason, short-term therapy has significant limitations. However, other modalities such as intensive, short-term , daily contact might result in quicker progress (Beezley, Martin, and Kempe, 1976, p. 211).

Psychotherapy alone, of course, would not be enough. As the data from both the 1950's and 1970's samples indicate, the families from which both abused or neglected and delinquent or ungovernable children come tend to suffer from a range of other problems. Although the study does not prove that child abuse causes juvenile delinquency, it leads to a more important conclusion: child maltreatment and juvenile misconduct are products of a common family environment. They are shared symptoms of the deeper problems afflicting families and children. Other studies, such as Glasser and Garvin (1977), point to the same conclusion, and we can expect additional studies in the future to add evidence to document and explain the perceptions which social workers, psychologists and family court judges have discussed over the years, that family dysfunction and parental inadequacy are closely related to the problems of child abuse or neglect and juvenile delinquency or ungovernability. A chicken or the egg discourse on which comes first, which could become quite complicated and inconclusive when the multi-generational aspects of these problems were addressed, would probably be less helpful than the development of family oriented services.

The demographic data on the families in both the 1950's and 1970's samples graphically depict the inordinate dimensions of the family breakdown experienced by children reported as abused, neglected, ungovernable or delinquent. Services and treatment approaches must be oriented toward the family as a whole. In the words of Brandt Steele, "Abuse and neglect must be understood as problems of interaction between members of a family." But in the system we have today, the family is not treated as a unit; instead, services are offered piecemeal for a specific individual or a specific problem. Unrealistic distinctions have to be made to fit a family into a categorical program whose area of expertise or jurisdiction often conforms to legislative or administrative mandates instead of the true needs of children and parents.

The legal distinctions made between the different categories assigned to children and families often are misleading and hinder treatment efforts. This is true not only in child protective services, but in the treatment of delinquency and ungovernability. The very words used to describe these children may be at fault. Many juveniles accused of delinquency could have been reported as abused or neglected, and often were. The apparent differences between delinquent and ungovernable acts are often unclear. The label or category assigned to a child appears to be more an accident of time and place than of any condition or behavior inherent in the child or family. Over the years, children are pushed through various systems with changing labels. The terms 'abused child,' 'neglected child,' 'juvenile delinquent' or 'ungovernable youth' frequently describe the same child or juvenile, or his brother or sister, during different stages of his early life.

These categories and distinctions were created by a system of categorical funding, usually initiated at the federal level, and then duplicated at the local and state level to qualify for the federal funds that become available. Over the years, an enormous hodgepodge of programs has been established to deal with various problems, or parts of problems. Every time a new problem is discerned, another program is created and funded without any reference to other programs that already exist; each new program becomes another lump on the pile. Sometimes someone is asked or required to coordinate the new with the old to avoid duplication, but coordination cannot solve the weaknesses built into a system that has developed by accretion over several decades of intense governmental action. The time has come for someone to undertake the monumental task of examining the entire system of categorical programs in order to realign them with reality. This is not a task to be undertaken lightly, and it will upset established or vested interests who will fear the uncertainty of change. But it is necessary if children, parents, and families are going to be served and helped. If our goal is to help, this necessary re-examination cannot be postponed or ignored.

As they stand today, neither the child protective nor the juvenile justice systems are organized to deal with one of the major underlying causes of child maltreatment and juvenile misconduct—family and community disorganization and weakness. Thus, institutionalization becomes one of our prime treatment options, and, in terms of the system as it exists, it is a necessary option that has to be used with some frequency. Many children are institutionalized, not because they 'need' or 'deserve' it, but because there is no alternative when the environment from which the child comes is unsuitable. Non-institutional remedies to the problems of family breakdowns are needed, but as long as the existing system blinds us to the necessity of developing a full range of treatment services, as long as it binds us to the inadequate or unsuccessful formulas of the past, the needed improvements will not happen.

Services cost money, and that is another important obstacle to overcome. There is no indication from this study that short-term miracle cures exist. As another study (Lynch, 1977) noted: "Clinical experience has already shown us that many abused children and their families need help years after the initial identification (p. 2)." Many of the families in the study required intensive, long-term help, perhaps for a generation or more. In one sense, they got it in the form of repeated, but intermittent, involvements with the child protective or juvenile justice systems as individual problems were brought to the attention of agencies and courts. But there was no long-term commitment to supporting families with an organized array of services to help them overcome their problems. We must face the fact that some families will require this kind of help for a long period of time. It would probably be foolish to promise that money would be saved in the long run; legislators do not really believe that argument any more, unless they are inexperienced. Perhaps it could be pointed out that we seem more willing to spend the money on correctional services than on services to rehabilitate families. It all depends on where we are going to place the major thrust of intervention; either it is early in the life of a child from a dysfunctional family or it is later when the child has grown up to be a social problem.

The juvenile or family courts that hear cases of child abuse or neglect and delinquency or ungovernability also need to be family-oriented; they are a part of both the child protective and juvenile justice systems. Though, in theory, they are used only as a last resort when all else fails, they are used; and they are limited by the types of services, if any, available to them. They, too, are affected by the categorical system of thinking. Attempts have been made to make courts more family-oriented, and an interesting approach was developed in Scotland, after much public and professional examination of their judicial system, for children and family problems.

As described by Professor Sanford Fox (1974), this system uses what is called a Children's Hearing to decide all cases in which a child "may be in need of compulsory measures of care." This would include situations that we label child abuse, child neglect, juvenile delinquency and juvenile ungovernability. The focus is on the child's and family's need for help. From the beginning of the court process, including a strong attempt to resolve the situation without a hearing, the entire family of the child is involved. The parents are required to attend and participate in conferences and the hearing itself. The nature of this parental involvement reinforces the idea that the parent has a role and responsibility for his children, and the purpose of the pre-court conferences and the hearing itself is to devise a mutually acceptable plan to improve the situation. Everything that is considered in the hearing, including reports from social workers and agencies, is openly discussed with the child and parents. Professor Fox observed that "the level of involvement in the conversation by the child and his parents is qualitatively different from what, to my knowledge, is achieved when the juvenile and his family stand before a judge." Whether or not such a system could be implemented in our country, it is important to realize that even a court can function in terms of family instead of an individual child or parent.

The effect of the 'children's hearing' in the Scottish juvenile court is to erase the distinctions made by categorical labels, and to look at a child or family as in trouble and needing help. If a court can do this, there is no reason that social agencies cannot, provided the underlying legal framework is modified to allow it. This does not mean that we can make the problems of child abuse, child neglect, juvenile delinquency and youthful ungovernability disappear, or that we can end family dysfunction. But we can deal with them more effectively than we have been; we can create a system that at least has a chance of reaching some of the underlying problems that lead to child maltreatment and juvenile misconduct. For, perhaps, the greatest finding of the study is that these problems all come from a common family environment, and that problems which are family-oriented in nature can be treated only by recognizing the role played by the family and the problems confronting some families in our society.

The family dysfunction and parental inadequacy that blights the families in which child maltreatment or juvenile misconduct occur can no longer be ignored. Twenty years ago, when the children in this study were being processed through the child protective and juvenile justice systems of their communities, a juvenile court judge wrote about the problems and the children she had seen after adjudicating 30,000 cases. Titling her book *Other People's Children,* she wrote:

> In spite of all that has been said and written on the subject of juvenile delinquency, there is little understanding of the problems of the children who are called juvenile delinquents. Lurid headlines and sensational newspaper accounts play up the superficial aspects of the subject, while the real story of what goes on in the hearts and minds of youthful offenders remains untold.
>
> Perhaps these are other people's children, not yours or mine, or even our neighbors'. But the time has passed when we can ignore their troubles. Just as we now know that smallpox in the slums constitutes a danger to the homes in our garden districts, so do we know that human failure, whether it be in high places or hovels, affects us, our families, our communities, and ultimately the nation (Levy, 1956, p. iii).

Twenty years later, few people would quarrel with what the judge wrote or deny that her statement is still true. The time for action has arrived. Enough is known to reshape the systems we have developed to help families and children in trouble. The child protective system in many communities has been recently upgraded and given new stature, while the juvenile justice system has often turned out to be a disappointment to those who worked so hard to establish it. All of the disparate systems that affect children and parents must be reexamined and redirected to deal with the total reality of the problems that afflict families, children and parents.

A study such as this one, of course, raises more questions than it answers, and it cannot give us a blueprint for what must be done. It can clarify our thinking and point out the choices that face us. It can tell us that the consequences of child maltreatment are more serious than we would probably like to imagine. If we do not help children in trouble, they will grow up to make trouble. Child abuse and neglect are not isolated problems unrelated to the life of families and our society; the comforting thought that they afflict only someone else is an illusion that must be discarded. The effort to help maltreated children, in the end, unites the forces of compassion and common sense in our society. Yet, though the study points out the direction that lies ahead, it cannot compel us to begin the journey. That is something that we, as a society, must decide, and this study gives us some verified facts to help us decide. The task ahead is the responsibility of both professionals and the public; without their mutual support, its achievement will not be possible.

NOTES

1. The Office of Court Administration figures for a year include all the petitions that were filed in a given year and were disposed of by the time the statistics were gathered. A data card is filed on each case after it has been completed; the slight variations in the distribution of cases in the sample and all the cases in the state are probably due to the delay in entering these data, as well as fluctuations between counties.

2. *Report of the Board of the Judicial Conference of the State of New York for the Judicial Year July 1, 1971 Through June 30, 1972,* p. 364. These figues are for boys only; girls were the subject of 85 petitions alleging one of the referral reasons on this list—an insignificant number.

3. *Ibid.* p. 357. The state figures for PINS combine boys and girls, unlike the same figures for delinquency.

4. Only the counties from which a full year's or a computable partial year's protective caseload were obtained are included. Kings and New York counties are combined because the available 1976 figure is for New York City as a whole.

5. The high rate in Monroe County—only one child was not found abused or neglected in the sample year—was double-checked to make sure the records on unfounded cases had not been destroyed. The officials now and from the past reported that all records were preserved, which agrees with the condition of the records observed by project staff in the course of the study. Since the high founded rate applied to both court and protective agency contacts, one can only conclude that it was either a bad year for children or that stringent standards were used, which seems more probable. It should be kept in mind that the founded rate for the entire 1950's sample is rather high.

6. *Report of the Administrative Board of the Judicial Conference of the State of New York for the Judicial Year July 1, 1968 through June 30, 1969,* Legislative Document No. 90 (1970), p. 309. The figures for 1968-69 are compared to 1967-68.

7. See, for example, Easson, Williams, and Steinkilber, "Murderous Aggression by Children and Adolescents," *Archives of General Psychiatry, 4,* June, 1961. This study took a representative sample of the entire delinquency caseload, but an 'unrepresentatively' larger sample of juveniles charged with homicide, rape and ar-

son would be worth further study and comparison with the large sample of other delinquent acts included in this study.

8. *Report of the Administrative Board,* p. 301. The judicial year reports are based on cases completed within that year, or before the data collection period for that year is terminated, and this method may introduce fluctuations of its own. Types of cases that last longer might not be recorded until the next year.

9. In this table, contacts which lead to an interim but not final disposition, such as referral to court or another agency, have not been included. The 15% average for placement in abuse cases is based on 611 abuse contacts, while the 20% average for placement in neglect cases is based on 6760 contacts.

10. Given the low level of services being provided to abused and neglected children, more longitudinal research may be needed on the long-term effectiveness of various types of services. In the meantime, there is clinical evidence that mental health services can help children who need them, whether or not they have been maltreated.

REFERENCES

American Humane Association. *The fundamentals of child protection: A statement of basic concepts and principles in child protective services.* Englewood, Colorado: Author.

Beezley, P., Martin, H. P., & Kempe, R. Psychotherapy. In *The abused child: A multidisciplinary approach to developmental issues and treatment.* Boston: Ballinger Publishing Company, 1976.

Birrell, R. G., & Birrell, J.H.W. The maltreatment syndrome in children: A hospital survey. *Medical Journal of Australia,* 1968, *2,* 1023-1029.

Elmer, E. & Gregg, G. Developmental characteristics of abused children. *Pediatrics,* 1967, *40*(4), 596-602.

Fox, S. Juvenile justice reform: Innovations in scotland. *American Criminal Law Review,* Winter, 1974.

Friedman, S. B. & Morse, C. W. Child Abuse: A five year follow-up of early case finding in the emergency department. *Pediatrics,* 1974, *54,* 404-410.

Gelles, R. Etiology of violence: Overcoming fallacious reasoning in understanding family violence and child abuse. Presented at a symposium, Child Abuse: Where Do We Go From Here? Washington, D. C.: Children's Hospital National Medical Center, February, 1977.

Green, A. H., et al. The psychiatric sequellae of child abuse and neglect. Paper read at the American Psychiatric Association Annual Meeting, 1974.

Johnson, B. & Morse, H. Injured children and their parents. *Children,* July-August, 1968, *15*(4), 147-52.

Levy, A. V. *Other people's children.* New York: The Ronald Press Company, 1956.

Lynch, M. The follow-up of abused children—A researcher's nightmare. Paper presented at the Second World Conference of the International Society of Family Law, June 13-17, 1977.

Martin, H. P. (Ed.) *The abused child: A multidisciplinary approach to developmental issues and treatment.* Boston: Ballinger Publishing Co.

New York State Department of Social Services. *Child protective services in New York State: 1976 annual report.*

Office of Children's Services, Judicial Conference of the State of New York. *Juvenile injustices.* October, 1973.

Prescott, J. W. Body pleasure and the origins of violence. *The Futurist*. April, 1975, 64-74.

Report of the Administrative Board of the Judicial Conference of the State of New York for the Judicial Year July 1, 1968 through June 30, 1969. Legislative Document (1970) No. 90.

Report of the Administrative Board of the Judicial Conference of the State of New York for the Judicial Year July 1, 1971 through June 30 1972.

16

An Inquiry into the Problem of Child Abuse and Juvenile Delinquency

CHRIS M. MOUZAKITIS

Graduate School of Social Work
University of Arkansas
Little Rock, Arkansas

Child abuse/neglect has received considerable attention in recent years from the fields of medicine, social work, psychology, psychiatry, sociology and other related human services professions. Statistics have been compiled in reference to the extent of the problem; several etiological theories have been developed; and new, innovative programs on a local and nationwide basis are underway (Justice & Justice, 1976). Juvenile delinquency, on the other hand, has received the attention of the various professions for a long time, and more intently during the past two decades (Cavan, 1975). Although there is an abundance of literature related to both areas, no studies were found relating to the possible association of child abuse and juvenile delinquency.

Writers and the sparse number of researchers in the child abuse field have focused primarily on the etiological variables of child abuse. As a result, several theories have emerged. The psycho-pathological theories, which emphasize the parents' emotional instability and individual pathologies, have such proponents as Birell & Birell (1968), Steel (1968), D'Ambrosio (1970), Spinetta & Rigler (1972) and Fontana (1971). Fontana conclusively states that children who are mistreated are likely to grow up having an unusual degree of hostility toward the world in general and they are likely to become child abusers and violent people themselves.

Gil (1973), a primary proponent of sociocultural theories, emphasizes environmental factors. For Gil, poverty and its correlates, inadequately served neighborhoods, a large number of children especially in one parent, mainly female-headed, households, can facilitate the abusive attacks toward children. He considers poverty not the direct cause of child abuse but the source which triggers abusive behavior. Toby (1967) expressed a similar view in "Affluence and Adolescent Crime," stating that poverty cannot cause crime, but resentment of poverty is more likely to develop among the relatively deprived of a rich society than among the objectively deprived in a poor society. Others, such as Holter and Friedman (1968), have attributed the etiology of child abuse to such factors as mental retardation; and Mouzakitis and Spieker (1977) to excessive use of alcohol.

Many writers and researchers whose primary interest is juvenile delinquency have pointed to such etiological factors as emotional disturbance, delinquent companions, social class norms, delinquent subcultures, immaturity , aggressiveness as a common reaction to frustration or conflict, antisocial personalities, organic impairment and morbid parent-child passions (Cohen, 1955; Lambo, 1971; Schwarz, Berthold and Ruggieri, 1959). Lambo states:

> If we accept the theory of a slow development of the aggressive motive, we might expect a correlation with later parental encouragement of, or punishment of, aggression. Excessive punishment tends to harden the child and increases his wish to punish in return, possibly through reinforcement of imitating his parents' behavior.

Findings by Sears, Maccoby and Levin (1957) on child rearing practices in the United States support Lambo's views. In their study, it was found that mothers who were most severely punitive had the most aggressive children.

Several studies make reference to violence in the home as the primary source of family breakdown, subsequent abusive behavior and delinquency (Levinger, 1966; Toby, 1975). Flynn (1977), in a study conducted in Kalamazoo, Michigan, reported, among other findings, that: 1) over one-half of the assaulters had parents involved in assaultive behavior; 2) two-fifths had been abused as children; 3) one-third of the cases indicated that the assaulter was said to also abuse his children; and 4) that there is a direct relationship between being a victim or an assaulter and having been a witness to parental violence in one's own childhood.

Preliminary results of the Family Services of Detroit and Wayne County indicate that both abused and abusing clients had experienced violence in early childhood directed toward themselves, violent behavior between the parents and/or between parents and children. Parents were strict and authoritarian as well as punitive, rather than over-permissive. In most cases, loss of one or both parents had occurred in childhood, especially to the abusive and violent person. As young adolescents, they had demonstrated violent behavior. Ackley (1977) similarly points to the role of violence in the adolescent and adult life of abused children. She states that:

> ...not only do they abuse their own children, but they also frequently engage in other forms of violent behavior such as murder and assault. Such violence is not surprising: thinking of parents as models, children see violence as acceptable behavior.

The literature on female juvenile delinquency is sparse. This is understandable, since four or five times as many boys appear before juvenile courts as girls (Fine, 1968; Offord, 1969). A study of Elkind (1967) points to the fact that parents' pathology is obviated in the child's behavioral symptoms. Similarly, girls from unstable home environments usually have fathers who are either abusive or absent (Fine, 1968). Gold's (1970) study of 2,490 delinquents on the character of delinquent behaviors also found that the girls' running away was due primarily to problems in the home. Trese (1962) also reports that 73% of the delinquent girls were the products of multiproblem environments and broken homes. There is a general agreement by most experts in the field of juvenile delinquency that a girl's delinquency is closely related to personal pressures at home and the desire to excape them.

METHOD

Data for this study were obtained from the Arkansas Diagnostic Reception Center and Girls School (Girls Training School) at Alexander, Arkansas, a state-operated facility for delinquent girls and/or girls in need of supervision. The Graduate School of Social Work, University of Arkansas at Little Rock uses this facility for field placement of first and second year graduate social work students. Commitments to this Center of all those girls under the age of 18 who have been adjudicated delinquents or in need of supervision (status offenders) are made by the juvenile courts of the State of Arkansas and/or circuit courts.

This study explored the possible associations between abuse by the parents and the delinquent behaviors committed by the 60 young girls, and between marital and economic status of the parents and the girls' delinquent behavior. The population of this study included the 60 girls who were committed in this facility the first two weeks of February, 1977.

Data were collected by a questionnaire which sought demographic information about the population, reason for commitment to the School, information related to delinquent behaviors committed prior to their admission, overall conditions at home, the ways they were disciplined by their parents, reactions to such discipline, effects of such discipline, whether or not they were sexually abused and their feelings toward the parents. The questionnaire was administered by six graduate social work students at the four cottages of the setting. The data were analyzed in terms of percentage distributions. To assess significance of association between variables, Chi Square was used.

DEFINITION OF TERMS

Child Abuse and Neglect "The physical or mental injury, sexual abuse, negligent treatment of a child under the age of 18 by a person who is responsible for the child's welfare which is harmed or threatened thereby." Specifically, child neglect refers to: inadequate physical care; absence of or inadequate medical care; cruel and abusive treatment; improper supervision; exploitation of the child's earnings; unlawfully keeping the child out of school; exposing the child to criminal or immoral influence that endangers his morals (Meier, 1964).

Emotional Abuse: A home environment where the child feels unwanted, unloved and insecure and where his/her achievements were neither respected nor recognized (Zaphiris, 1975).

Physical Abuse: For the purpose of this study this term refers to the application of force through the use of hands, belts, other objects (e.g., cords, hangers, brushes, pots, sticks).

Verbal Abuse: Refers to the use of verbal expressions (screaming, etc.) as means of discipline.

Sexual Abuse: For the purpose of this study the term refers to sexual intercourse the girls had with members of their immediate family, i.e., fathers, siblings, uncles and family friends.

Juvenile: Any person, whether married or single, who has not yet reached his/her 18th birthday.

Delinquent Juvenile: Refers to any juvenile who: 1) has committed an act other than a traffic offense which, if such an act had been committed by an adult would subject such adult to prosecution for a felony or misdemeanor under the applicable criminal law of this state; or 2) has committed an offense applicable only to a juvenile (Pasvogel, 1976).

Juvenile in Need of Supervision: Refers to any juvenile who: 1) while subject to compulsory school attendance is habitually and without justification absent from school; or 2) is habitually disobedient to the reasonable and lawful commands of his parents, guardian or custodian; or 3) has absented himself from his home without sufficient cause, permission or justification.

Runaway, Truant, Incorrigible: Refers to a juvenile in need of supervision as it has been defined above.

Status Offense: Refers to such delinquent behaviors as runaway, truancy or incorrigibility.

Non-status Offense: Refers to such acts as sexual promiscuity, stealing, use and possession of drugs, violation of probation, use and possession of alcohol, forgery, robbery, breaking and entering and armed robbery.

FINDINGS

The findings are presented in the following order: 1) selected demographic characteristics of the respondents; 2) analysis of the respondents' delinquent behavior in relation to age, race, their parents' marital condition, economic status and delinquent behaviors prior to their commitment at the Girls Training School; 3) analysis of the means through which the respondents were disciplined, the effects of such discipline on the respondents, the possible neglect at home, the sexual abuse they had experienced and their possible association to the delinquent behaviors.

Of the 60 girls who responded to the questionnaire, 40 (67%) were white and 20 (33%) were black. The median age for the entire population was 14.8 years. The youngest girl was 12 years of age and the oldest girls (7) were 17 years of age. The rest of the 52 girls were almost equally distributed between the ages of 13 and 16 years old.

The majority of the girls, 44 (73%), came from single-parent, female-headed households. Specifically, the parents' marital statuses were: 15 (25%) lived together; 4 (7%) were separated; 27 (45%) were divorced; 1 (1.6%) the mother was deceased; 10 (16.6%) the father was deceased; and the remaining 3% were equally distributed under the categories 'Never knew their parents,' 'Parents never were married' and 'Both parents were deceased.'

One-half of the delinquent girls' parents were receiving public assistance,

TABLE 1 AGE DISTRIBUTION OF 60 DELINQUENT GIRLS COMMITTED AT THE GIRLS' TRAINING SCHOOL WHO PARTICIPATED IN THIS STUDY IN FEBRUARY, 1977

Age	Number	Percentages
Twelve	1	1.6
Thirteen	10	16.6
Fourteen	14	23.6
Fifteen	15	25.0
Sixteen	13	21.6
Seventeen	7	11.6
TOTAL	60	100.0

TABLE 2 DISTRIBUTION BY PARENT'S MARITAL STATUS

Marital Status	Number	Percentages
Living Together	15	25.0
Separated	4	7.0
Divorced	27	45.0
Deceased Mother	1	1.6
Deceased Father	10	16.6
Deceased Both	1	1.6
Never Knew Them	1	1.6
Never Married	1	1.6
TOTAL	60	100.0

TABLE 3 DISTRIBUTION OF TYPE DELINQUENT BEHAVIORS

Delinquency	Numbers	Percentages
Runaway	10	17.0
Truancy	12	20.0
Incorrigibility	11	18.3
Sexual Promiscuity	2	3.3
Stealing	8	13.4
Use & Possession of Drugs	7	11.6
Violation of Probation	2	3.3
Use & Possession of Alcohol	2	3.3
Forgery	2	3.3
Robbery	2	3.3
Breaking & Entering	1	1.6
Armed Robbery	1	1.6
TOTAL	60	100.0

although the data did not suggest an association between the parents' economic status and the delinquent behaviors committed by the girls.

The offenses for which the girls were committed were almost equally distributed between status and non-status offenses, 33 (55%) and 27 (45%), respectively. It should be noted that the heaviest concentration among the non-status offenders was in stealing and use and possession of drugs, i.e., 60% of all non-status offenses.

In order to test the association between age and delinquent behavior, the age distribution was divided into two categories: 14 years of age and below, and 15 years of age and above. The percentages were distributed as follows: offenses committed at age 14 or below, 25 (41%) of the respondents. compared to those 15 years of age or older, which were 35 (59%). No statistically significant association was found between race and delinquent behavior when the Chi Square test was applied.

The data related to the parents' marital status and the girls' delinquent behavior revealed that 45 (75%) of the delinquent acts were committed by those whose parents were either divorced, separated or deceased. Of these 45 who came from broken homes, 27 (60%) had committed status offenses or were in need of supervision, and 18 (40%) of them had committed non-status offenses. This concurs with the findings of many researchers who have indicated that there is a strong association between broken homes, female-headed households and juvenile delinquency.

TABLE 4 DISTRIBUTION OF AGE OF THE RESPONDENTS ACCORDING TO THE TYPE OF DELINQUENT BEHAVIOR

Delinquency	12 Yrs.	Percent	13 Yrs.	Percent	14 Yrs.	Percent	15 Yrs.	Percent	16 Yrs.	Percent	17 Yrs.	Percent
Runaway			1	1.6	1	1.6	2	3.5	4	6.1	2	3.5
Truancy			3	5.0	5	8.0	2	3.5	2	3.5		
Incorrigibility	1	1.6	2	3.5	4	6.5	3	5.0	1	1.6		
Sexual Promiscuity			1	1.6			1	1.6				
Stealing					2	3.5	2	3.5	2	3.5	2	3.5
Use & Possession Of Drugs			1	1.6			4	6.6	2	3.5		
Violation of Probation			1	1.6							1	1.6
Use & Possession of Alcohol							1	1.6	1	1.6		
Forgery											2	3.5
Robbery			1	1.6								
Breaking & Entering									1	1.6		
Armed Robbery					2	3.5						
TOTAL	1	1.6	10	16.5	14	23.1	15	25.3	13	21.4	7	12.1

An analysis of the girls' self-reported delinquent behavior, for which they were not apprehended by the authorities, showed that in the three years preceding their commitment to the Training School, during the first year 48 (80%) had committed delinquent acts. Of these acts, 23 (38%) were non-status offenses, with 11 (22.5%) of these being for use and possession of drugs. The second year prior to their commitment, 31 (52%) had no problems. Of the remaining 29 (48%) who had problems, 19 (65%) had committed status offenses. The third year prior to their commitment, 38 (63%) had no problems. The 22 (37%) who had problems were primarily status offenses by 18 (47%) of them. These findings indicate the progression of delinquent behavior as the age of the girls advanced. Whereas only 11 (36%) of the girls had problems three years prior to their commitment, 48 (80%) had problems one year prior to their commitment.

The respondents' siblings, with the exception of 20 (33%), had all committed various delinquent acts. The majority of their siblings' offenses were non-status offenses, i.e., 24 (40%), and the remaining 16 (27%) were status offenses. This indicates that most of the respondents came from homes where delinquent behaviors were exhibited by their siblings, who could have become models for their own behaviors.

The questions attempting to determine the means through which the 60 girls were disciplined were answered as follows: 13 (23%) were disciplined through the use of hands and belts; 30 (52%) through the use of hands and objects; and 8 (13%) through the use of hands. A total of 51 (86%) of the 60 girls had received physical punishment and only 9 (14%) were verbally disciplined. As a result of the physical punishment, 31 (51%) recalled bruises, 15 (25%) recalled scars, 23 (38%) recalled bleedings, and 12 (20%) recalled no apparent physical effects. These findings plainly indicate that the major means of disciplining the respondents was the use of force. Such force was exercised not only through the use of hands or belts, but also through such objects, in a great number of cases, as pots, pens, sticks, cords, chairs, knives and a number of other items. Furthermore, the effects of such discipline indicated that the respondents were physically abused. Although 12 (20%) reported no apparent physical effects, they felt that they had been abused. The 9 (14%) of the population studied who had been disciplined through verbal means, i.e., screaming and "hollering," could also have been abused verbally, but since no specific information was gathered concerning the content of the verbal communication, the 9 girls were considered to have not been abused.

Furthermore, the data indicated that 13 (25%) of the 51 girls who had been physically punished had been so since infancy, and only 3 (6%) had been punished since the age of 14 years old. The rest of the respondents were distributed as follows: 6 (12%) between the ages of 2 and 4 years; 12 (23%) between the ages of 5 and 7; 8 (16%) between the ages of 8 and 10; and 9 (18%) between the ages of 11 and 13 years. It should be noted that the majority, 37 (73%), of these girls received physical punishment when they were young, i.e., below the age of 10 years old.

The assertion that the parents in this study were forced to use physical discipline in order to restrain the acting out behavior of their teenage daughters is not supported by these findings, since the girls were relatively young. Thus, it becomes apparent that physical force was exercised as a means of discipline throughout the formative years of these youngsters.

The findings related to the frequency of such punishment were also revealing, since 15 (29%) were punished once a day; 2 (4%) more than once a day; and 20

(39%) once a week. The abusive behavior of the parents became clear when the effects on the girls were considered, e.g. scars, bruises and bleedings.

In reference to the girls' reactions to the parents' abusive behavior, it was found that 8 (15.5 %) had run away and 15 (29.5%) went out in the streets, i.e., a total of 23 (44.8%) of the girls. These findings suggest that, as a result of such punishment, the girls left their homes and sought, either through companions or possible delinquent behaviors, to relieve their frustrations and anger. The remainder of the girls retreated to their rooms, swore, cried and one attempted suicide. Only four girls thought that their parents' violent behavior toward them was justified. Of the nine girls who were verbally disciplined, one ran away and the rest either cried or retreated to their rooms.

Further analysis revealed that although they had come from broken homes, the discipline was administered by the parents, i.e., either mother or father and/or stepparents in 42 (70%) of the cases. Since the majority of the girls came from single-parent, female-headed households, the mother had administered the physical punishment in 19 (37%) of the cases. In only 9 (19%) of the cases was discipline administered by siblings, grandparents and foster parents.

The findings related to the feelings of the 51 physically punished girls seem incongruent to the treatment they had received from their parents. Thirty-nine (76.5%) felt that their parents loved them, as compared to 12 (23.5%) who felt that they did not. A possible explanation for this may be the fact that these youngsters' extended kin relationships were rather limited, since they came from broken families, and the only person to whom they could claim any attachment was the parent. On the other hand, findings by many researchers indicate that abused children are protective of their parents; this is supported by the findings in this study.

Examining more analytically the delinquent offenses these girls had committed, 29 (57%) were status offenses and 22 (43%) were non-status offenses. The heaviest concentration, in the physically disciplined girls, was in the non-status offenses of stealing, 8 (16%), and use and possession of drugs, 7 (14%).

Furthermore, it was found that 32 (53%) of these girls felt that they had been sexually abused, meaning that they were forced to have sexual intercourse. The percentages for those 19 girls who had been sexually abused by their father, siblings, uncles and family friends were equally distributed. These girls indicated that the involuntary sexual contact was for over a six month period, as contrasted to the 13 (21%) who were sexually abused by strangers and whose sexual experience was, in most of the cases, a one-time involvement. Further analysis related to the delinquent behaviors committed by these girls indicated that they tended to become runaways, truants, incorrigible, sexually promiscuous and drug users.

Analysis of their delinquent behavior during the three successive years prior to their commitment in the Training School revealed a progressive trend in delinquent behavior. The first year prior to their commitment, all but 4, i.e., 47 (92%), had demonstrated various delinquent behaviors; the second year, 24 (47%); and the third year, 14 (21%). Although many other factors could explain the girls' progressive delinquent behavior, the physical punishment and constant abuse they were experiencing could explain this delinquent acting out. In many instances, this acting out behavior, especially with the runaways, truants and incorrigibles, could be construed as a call for help, since the majority of them expressed no desire to return home.

No association was found between the various forms of delinquent behaviors committed by the girls and specific aspects of neglect by the parents related to food, clothing, heat and medical care. The only exception was the provision of supervision, with 29 (48%) indicating that they did not have any. There also seemed to be an association between supervision and school attendance. Forty-one (68%) had missed school regularly. Further analysis, related to the 51 girls who had been physically punished, revealed that 31 (60%) had no supervision, and 36 (71%) had missed school regularly. As a result of these findings, one may wonder about the real intent of physical punishment and its effectiveness, since almost two-thirds of the girls thought that they did not have any supervision and about two-thirds were regularly truant from school. One could speculate that the intent of the parents was not to discipline and correct undesirable behaviors but rather, through physical punishment, to use the girls as scapegoats for their own personal problems.

DISCUSSION AND CONCLUSIONS

Findings in this study have suggested several conclusions. *First,* girls committed to the Girls Training School had been physically abused by their parents, and only a fraction of the girls had not been abused. If the general definition of abuse, which includes emotional abuse, had been applied to this small fraction, they also could have been considered abused. Similarly, the physically abused girls could be considered emotionally abused. There is no universally accepted definition of emotional abuse. Authors such as Ackerman (1958), Zaphiris (1975), and Pollak (1958) make references to the emotional climate within the family and to the intra-family relationships as necessary conditions for healthy, emotional growth of the child. Josselyn (1953), describing the importance of the total emotional atmosphere, states that "just as inadequate oxygen results in only partial combustion, so psychological metabolism is incomplete without healthy emotional elements in the family atmosphere."

Second, the parents' use of physical 'disciplinary' methods were not sporadic occurences, but were consistent and persistent from an early age of the subjects. What else could traumatize a young child during the formative years of life but the confrontation of violence and possible rejection? The immaturity, emotional instability, inability to trust and relate to people and the unrealistic expectations which were characteristic of these girls' personalities could be thought of as an associated symptomatology of the effect of abuse they had experienced. It is not surprising that these abused girls demonstrated violent and delinquent behavior. The models of violence to imitate were always around them, as the study has suggested. Other authors who have studied the effects of parental role also found that there exists an interrelationship between 'delinquent' criminal behavior and types of discipline, parental rejection, absence of maternal warmth, etc.

Third, although this study did not attempt to find out the specific elements of the girls' home atmospheres, it would seem fairly accurate to state that there was a lot to be desired. It is not only the presence of force and violence and the absence of complete family structure, but also the absence of parental warmth, the feeling of security, acceptance and love so necessary for a child's normal growth which were absent in the girls' home environments. Of course, the study found that the majority of the girls felt that their parents loved them. It seems incongruent to think that the parent, not the one who disciplines a child, but the one who constantly beats the child severely, also loves the child. But child abuse theory tells us that the majority of parents who abuse their children do so not because of lack of love for their children but because of emotional and, mainly, personal, problems. The parents of the abused girls undoubtedly had their own problems, since the majority of them were without a spouse, had many children and a rather limited income.

Fourth, the finding that the majority of the physically abused girls also had been sexually abused leads us to certain conclusions: a) the sexual abuse by their fathers, siblings and uncles, with the accompanying emotional strain and possible alienation, could have served as an additional precipitating factor in their acting out delinquent behavior; b) sexual 'abuse' by strangers was in itself an acting out behavior resulting from the physical maltreatment they were experiencing at home. This researcher is hesitant to accept the girls' statements that they had been abused sexually by strangers. It is most likely that the sexual contact was provoked by them, or at least was a mutual consent affair.

Fifth, a partial explanation for some of the girls' delinquent behavior can also be found in their reaction to their parents' abusive behavior, since they either ran away or tried to find consolation in the streets for a period of time following each incident of abuse. It is not difficult to determine the whereabouts of a child who has been beaten physically and is frustrated and angry. When the child is young, she probably stays in the immediate vicinity of her home, with her friends; but when she is older, she would seek companions elsewhere and, perhaps, use other means to relieve her frustration and anger. Not all of the girls in this study were demonstrating acting out delinquent behavior when they were younger, but one year prior to their commitment in the Training School practically all of them had demonstrated delinquent behavior.

One would expect that as a result of the abuse these girls were experiencing at home and their acting out delinquent behavior, a number of professionals could have been involved with them or their families. The findings have shown the complete absence of professionals, except in three cases, where two social workers and one physician were involved. It is ironic, to say the least, that with all of the programs under way on behalf of abused children and their families, as well as other programs for acting out juveniles, such troubled families and troubled children never received any kind of professional help. It seems that early detection systems, if there are any, are ineffective. Furthermore, it seems that our child abuse and juvenile delinquency programs are geared neither toward prevention nor toward treatment.

Primary prevention, by social workers, public health nurses, school teachers and all of those who come in contact with the child and his/her family ought to be prepared to break the vicious cycle of child abuse and juvenile delinquency. It is the contention of this author, suggested by the findings of this study, that juvenile delinquency and physical and emotional abuse are interrelated. Abuse, physical, sexual or emotional, is one of the many factors which can contribute to a child's delinquent behavior. There is a need for relevant treatment services for these children and their families and a need for more systematic research in this area.

REFERENCES

Ackerman, N. W. *The psychodynamics of family life.* New York: Basic Books, 1958.

Ackley, D. C. A brief overview of child abuse. *Social Casework,* 1977, *58*(1).

Birrell, R. G. & Birrell, J. H. W. The maltreatment syndrome in children: A hospital survey. *Medical Journal of Australia,* 1968, *55,* 1023-29.

Cavan, R. S. (Ed.) *Readings in juvenile delinquency.* (3rd ed.) Philadelphia: J. B. Lippincott Co., 1975.

Cohen, K. A. *Delinquent boys: The culture of the gang.* New York: The Free Press, 1955.

D'Ambrosio, R. Treatment of a battered child. In *No Language but a cry.* Garden City, New York: Doubleday, 1970.

Elkind, D. Middle class delinquency. *Mental Hygiene,* 1967, *51,* 80-84.

Fine, R. H. & Fishman, J. J. Institutionalized girl delinquents. *Diseases of the Nervous System,* 1968, *29,* 17-27.

Flynn, J. Recent findings related to wife abuse. *Social Casework,* 1977, *58*(1).

Fontana, V. J. We must stop the vicious cycle of child abuse. *Parents,* December, 1975, 8.

Gil, D. *Violence against children.* Cambridge: Harvard University Press, 1973.

Gold, M. *The character of delinquent behaviors.* Wadsworth Publishing Co., 1970.

Holter, J.C. & Friedman, S.B. Principles of management in child abuse cases. *American Journal of Orthopsychiatry,* 1968, *38,* 127-136.

Jensen, G. F. Parents, peers, and delinquent action: A test of the differential association perspective. *American Journal of Sociology,* 1972, *78*(3), 562-575.

Josselyn, I. M. The family as a psychological unit. *Social Casework,* 1953, *20,* 338-339.

Justioe, B. & Justice, R. *The abusing family.* New York: Human Sciences Press, 1976.

Keller, O. J. Hypothesis for violent crime. *American Journal of Corrections,* 1975, *37*(2), 7.

Lambo, T. A. Aggressiveness in the human life cycle within different sociocultural settings. *International Social Science Journal,* 1971, *23,* 79-88.

Levinuer, G. Sources of marital dissatisfaction among applicants for divorce, *American Journal of Orthopsychiatry,* 1966, *36*(5), 803-807.

Offord, D. R. Youth and rebellion. *Corrective Psychiatry and Journal of Social Therapy,* 1969, *15*(2), 6-17.

Pasvogel, G. *Arkansas juvenile law and procedures.* School of Law, University of Arkansas at Little Rock, 1976.

Pollak, R. Commentary. *Social Casework,* February-March, 1958, 84.

Richette, L. *The throwaway children.* Philadelphia: J.B. Lippincott, 1969.

Schwarz, E. B. & Ruggieri, A. B. Morbid parent-child passions in delinquency. In S. Glueck (Ed.), *The problem of delinquency.* Boston: Houghton-Mifflin Co., 1959.

Sears, R. R., et al. Some child rearing antecedents of aggression and dependency in young children. *Psychological Monograph,* 1953, Vol. 47, 135-234.

Spieker, G. & Mouzakitis, C. Alcohol abuse and child abuse and neglect: An inquiry into alcohol abusers' behavior toward children. Paper presented at the 27th Annual Meeting of the Alcohol and Drug Problems Association of North America, New Orleans, Louisiana, September, 1976.

Spinetta, J. J. & Rigler, D. The child abusing parent: A psychological review . *Psychological Bulletin,* 1972, *77,* 296-304.

Toby, J. Affluence and adolescent crime. In R. Cavan (Ed.), *Readings in juvenile delinquency.* Philadelphia: J. B. Lippincott Co., 1975.

Trese, L. *101 delinquent girls.* Notre Dame: Fides Publications, 1962.

U. S. Department of Health, Education, and Welfare Office of Human Development, Office of Child Development, Children's Bureau, National Center on Child Abuse and Neglect. *The problem and its management.* Publication No (OHD)75-300073.

Walters, D. R. *Physical and sexual abuse of children.* Bloomington & London: Indiana University Press, 1975.

Zalba, S. R. The abused child: I. A survey of the problem. *Social Work,* 1966, *11* (4).

Zaphiris, A. Paper presented at the Institute of Training the Trainer in Child Abuse and Neglect, Hot Springs, Arkansas, June, 1975.

17

Child Abuse as Causation of Juvenile Delinquency in Central Texas

STEVEN C. WICK

Central Texas Youth Services Bureau, Inc.
Belton, Texas 76713

This paper presents a research study of 50 cases of the Central Texas Youth Services Bureau, Inc., to determine causes for delinquent behavior or, for the purposes of this research, the 'troubled child syndrome.' Although an hypothesis of parental causation of such behavior was postulated, the high correlation of the troubled child syndrome with the abused child was an unanticipated finding. The results of this research are presented, with a discussion of child abuse as a cause of juvenile delinquency in Central Texas.

The old adage that 'crime does not pay' is probably as questionable a statement today as it ever has been in the past. Leonard Hancock, Chief of the Temple, Texas, Police Department, recently stated that approximately 70% of the actual offenses committed are never made known to law enforcement agencies (personal communication, August, 1975). In addition, there is increasing concern that a large percentage of offenders who are caught are given too lenient sentences by courts. In any event, it is generally agreed that the incidence of crime has steadily risen in recent years, with little or no evidence of this trend decreasing or altering. In 1972, major crimes committed in the U.S. numbered 309,349, compared to 115,693 cases ten years earlier, in 1962. This represents a 37% increase during this ten-year period *(1974 Criminal Justice Plan for Texas, p. 13).*

What effect this trend has on young people is a wide open area for research. It does appear that crime committed by youth is increasing, and that an analysis of juvenile crime in any one geographic area of the country would show similar results to any other area. For instance, during 1974, some 417 juveniles were handled by the Temple Police Department, representing a 72% increase over the 301 juveniles processed in 1973. From January to September, 1975, 335 juveniles were processed, indicating a projected increase of 7% over the previous year. The Juvenile Division of the Killeen (Texas) Police Department reported that during 1974, 851 juveniles were processed, demonstrating a statistically significant increase over the 360 arrests for 1973. Through September, 1975, a total of 887 youths were processed, indicating a projected increase of 28% (Texas Youth Council, Community Assistance Program Proposal, 1975, p. 5).

That young people are committing offenses of every degree of severity can be indicated by any statistical compilation of any police department. Such statistics are useful for determining overall trends of activity, but do not reflect the humanistic pressures, values and attitudes that influence such activity, nor do they portray the extent of human suffering and pathos involved.

A considerable amount of literature related to juvenile delinquency and its causation was reviewed by the author. The extent of research devoted to causation in proportion to the extent devoted to examining other elements of delinquency was found to be inadequate. Most of the literature examined either does not treat causation, or relegates a chapter or section of the manuscript to causation. As a matter of explanation, it appears that most research in the area of delinquency has centered on 'cures' or rehabilitation of the delinquent. In other words, the focus has been somewhat after-the-fact. As this observation was confirmed, it seems plausible that delinquency continues to be a major problem in our society.

The intent of this research was to establish (in a limited context) the cause, or causes, directly influencing the incidence of crime among young people in the Bell County, Texas, area. The research focused particularly on parental causation of juvenile crime or delinquency. However, the term 'delinquency' carries a wide range of meanings, in addition to eliciting a wide variety of emotional responses. Technically speaking, the term delinquency is a legal word used to describe the state of a minor who has been declared a delinquent by a juvenile court judge in court. Consequently, in the strict definition of the word, any child who has experienced difficulties with the law or who actually has been taken into custody is not necessarily a delinquent. In addition, many children have violated the law at one time or another and to various degrees of severity, but cannot be considered delinquent (such as minors smoking cigarettes, being truant from school, and so forth.) Such actions can, and often do, indicate a troubled child, however. Consequently, the triad "troubled child syndrome" was used in this research to describe problematic behavior exhibited by a child and considered unacceptable by the society or community of which he is a member. Such behavior includes delinquent activity in the legal sense, as well as nondelinquent, but problematic, activity.

It is hoped that the results of this research will directly affect current rehabilitation endeavors in the Bell County area by confirming the importance of the immediate family, parents in particular, on the children. The results should encourage efforts toward delinquency prevention, prevention of child abuse and neglect, mental illness prevention and significantly demonstrate to the community the importance of parent training. Mr. Walter Minica, Chief Probation Officer of the Bell

County Juvenile Probation Department stated, "If delinquency is to be truly curbed in our community, more research is needed to determine causes of delinquency, not just in St. Louis or Los Angeles, but right here at home (personal communication, Belton, Texas, October, 1975).

STATEMENT OF THE PROBLEM

This research analyzed the factor of parental causation of the troubled child syndrome in relation to other pre-selected causative factors. Parental causation was analyzed by the following questions:

1) Was the major parental influence due to the lack of positive values, attitudes and discipline (either too much or too little)

2) Was the major parental influence due to any known incidence of abuse or neglect?

3) Is there evidence of failure by the parents to provide proper communication?

Two basic assumptions have been accepted within the context of this paper: There is more than one cause of the troubled child syndome, since there is an almost infinite variety of individual characteristics and individual environmental situations; and the methods used in data collection (case files, worksheets, and narrative forms) were accepted as basically accurate.

DEFINITION OF TERMS

The following terms have special meanings in the context of this research paper:

1) *Troubled Child Syndrome.* Any problematic behavior exhibited by the child and considered unacceptable by the society or community of which he is a member.

2) *Delinquent (or) Delinquency.* In contrast to the strict legal definition of the term, which applies to a minor who has been designated a delinquent by a juvenile judge in a juvenile court, delinquent or delinquency will be used synonymously with 'troubled child syndrome.'

3) *Child Abuse.* This term applies to: a) any deliberate and excessive violence administered to a child 17 years old or younger which causes physical or mental pain; and b) the deliberate denial of necessities for physical/mental health.

4) *School.* This term, when referring to causation of the troubled child syndrome, is used in a broad sense to include all aspects of the school-related environment, including administration, teachers, classmates, school codes or policies, physical plant, etc.

5) *Family Conflict.* This term applies to any form of abnormal activity deriving its source from within the family unit.

6) *Parent.* This term covers natural parent, parent substitute or guardian.

METHODS AND PROCEDURES

The collected data were scored on a simple percentage basis and were interpreted both qualitatively and quantitatively.

The purpose of this research was to demonstrate the following four hypotheses:

l) The primary cause of the troubled child syndrome stems, or originates, from the parent (or guardian).

2) Parental causation of the troubled child syndrome is due both to lack of

teaching the child positive values and attitudes, and to discipline, which may be excessively administered or insufficiently administered.

3) The parental causation of the troubled child syndrome is caused by failure of the parents to impart effective communication skills on any level other than the most superficial communication necessary for communal living.

4) Parental causation of the troubled child syndrome is due to known incidents of physical or mental abuse or neglect (mental or emotional abuse or neglect is included).

The research was conducted in Bell County, which represents a population of 160,900 people, with approximately 75% of the population residing in a series of five cities, beginning with Killeen in the west to Temple in the east (Chamber of Commerce, August, 1975). The western portion of the county includes Fort Hood, comprising 216,915 acres, with a population of 71,688 military personnel. This Army reservation is the largest in the free world.

To accomplish this task, 50 case records were compiled from the files of the Central Texas Youth Services Bureau, Inc. Because of the Youth Services Bureau's policy, and because the agency works with any youngster and her/his family concerning any problem, the Bureau readily lends itself to study of the troubled child syndrome on all levels.

A case file is kept on each client. It contains a 'work sheet,' or vita, on which is recorded statistical data regarding the client and his family. A parental approval form is attached, along with any other documents necessary for working with the families. Finally, narrative forms contain a running account of the problem(s), cause(s), relations with the counselor and any other significant development. From this case file, cause and effect relationships can be analyzed to determine the source(s) of problems, their severity, etc. Case files were randomly selected. However, if a selected case file did not contain sufficient information to determine causal factors, that case file was rejected and the next random sample selected in its place.

Eight categories of potential causes were pre-selected and included the following: a) parent or family conflict; b) peer group pressure or gangs; c) drug abuse; d) sexual promiscuity; e) mental retardation; f) mental illness; g) school; and h) other. Under the category of parent or family conflict, three sub-categories were included: 1) values, attitude and discipline; 2) abuse or neglect; and 3) communication.

Other data were collected under the headings of broken home, comments and client problems. An additional form was used to collect data under the headings of race, sex, age, religion, military dependent, and contact with the law (police or probation).

As was anticipated, some of the data contained in the narrative portions of the case files had to be interpreted by the author. However, case files were selected on the basis of sufficient material to determine causal factors. For instance, statements such as "client severely spanked for breaking dish," or "mother admitted to maintaining extra-marital affair," could be interpreted, in the first example, as an abuse of discipline, and in the second example, as deviation of moral values. Such statements, and each case history, were interpreted in the context of the entire case file.

In some instances, it was difficult to categorize individual problems, as some overlap occurred. In the example, "client severely spanked for breaking dish," the parent could be classified as using excessive discipline or as possibly physically abusing the child. In such an instance the predominant or primary problem was classified in the context of the case file.

FINDINGS

The results of this study indicate that of the 50 cases, none was caused by peer group pressure, sexual promiscuity, or mental retardation. The results did indicate that one case was due to mental illness, one to school problems, 3 to drug abuse, and 45 to parental causes.

Of these troubled child syndrome cases involving parental causes, 60% (27 cases) were due to lack of values, attitude and discipline; 29% (13 cases) were due primarily to abuse or neglect; and 11% (5 cases) were due to communication problems.

Twenty-five subjects (50%) came from broken homes in which either divorce, separation, dealth or abandonment took place. Six additional cases experienced one parent incapacitated by serious illness. Thus, the total number of cases in which at least one parent no longer resided in the home or was severely limited from participation in normal family life was 31 (62% of the total cases).

The ages of the subjects ranged from 5 to 18 years old, with a mean of 13.8 years old.

One-half of the subjects had had contact with legal authorities (police or probation) at least once.

Twenty-seven cases (54%) were dependents of active or inactive military personnel.

Thirty-six subjects (72%) were Caucasian, 9 (18%) were Black, 3 (6%) were of Spanish descent, and 2 were unknown.

In the category of religion, 8 denominations were represented; but the significant factor was in the subcategory of 'unknown,' which indicated either that the child's denomination was unknown or that the child did not claim any denomination. Since the actual unknown factor in the other categories ranged from 2 to 4, we can safely estimate that the unknown factor within the religion category is also between 2 and 4. This implies that approximately 21 cases (42%) probably do not claim a religious affiliation.

CONCLUSIONS

The findings of this research overwhelmingly confirm Hypothesis 1, that the primary cause of the troubled child syndrome in Bell County is parental, since 45 out of 50 cases indicate parental causation.

Hypothesis 2, that the lack of appropriate values, attitudes and discipline were among the causal factors, proved to be the primary subfactor in parental causation, in that 60% were found in this category.

Hypotheses 3 and 4, that known incidents of child abuse and neglect (including physical and mental) are a significant causal factor, is supported, in that 29% were found in this sub-category. Communication breakdown between parent and child was also confirmed to be a causal factor, although only 11% were found in this sub-category. The research also confirmed that there are other causes of the troubled child syndrome, but these 5 cases amounted to only 1% of the entire study.

Some additional data was found that had not been anticipated, but did lend support to the hypothesis of parental causation. Over one-half (62%) of the cases studied came from broken homes or homes in which at least one parent was not consistently involved.

COMMENTARY

Of particular import here is that 29% of the 45 juvenile delinquency cases found to be caused by parents indicated child abuse and/or neglect as the primary causative factor of the juvenile delinquency. Also, as a point of discussion, the 60% of the cases involving lack of appropriate values, attitudes and discipline could be interpreted, in many instances, as child neglect which in turn propagated at least one delinquent act. If healthy values and attitudes are not taught by parents through communication and by example, the values and attitudes of other powerful influences (such as peer group) will be accepted by the child. Furthermore, a lack of discipline administered through concern and used as a teaching tool usually results in a child with an abnormally poor self-image or, at best, a definitively negative self-image. Such a child is in essence saying, "If my parents don't teach me how to control myself, I must not be worth controlling. Therefore, I will prove to them, myself and others just how bad I am."

Although no definitive or easy answers exist to the problems of child abuse and juvenile delinquency, there do exist three levels of approach, some of which have already demonstrated great potential.

Both child abuse and juvenile delinquency, having essentially the same root causes, are, in one sense, symptoms of a vicious spiral of social and cultural factors with historical origins, rejuvenated contemporary impetus and a promise of continuation, unless the spiral is broken.

Social ills, such as inflation, poverty and discrimination (racial, sexual, social prestige, economics) are the fuels that feed intrafamilial problems which may result in child abuse, delinquency, mental illness and family break-ups. Society must continue to work toward alleviating and eliminating these social inequities in an effort to improve living conditions for everyone. If we as a society can be reawakened to respect for the life of the individual, many of these inequities will begin to disappear.

Large corporations, for example, need to consider the effects on spouses and dependents of moving their employees from one location to another. The military branches of service need to concern themselves with the results of an indoctrination philosophy that teaches the most efficient means of eliminating an enemy and how that affects the soldier's family.

The second level of potential solution to juvenile delinquency and child abuse lies in parent education. The often used expression that 'parenting is the most important, but least prepared career' is a truism in our society. Parent education seminars and clinics providing such programs as Parent Effectiveness Training and Systematic Training for Effective Parenting need to be available in all communities through community centers, agencies, churches, school systems, and so forth. Marriage preparation, sex education, and child raising should be an essential part of the school curriculum for students of both sexes, extending from elementary through high school.

Third, local community agencies stressing voluntary participation of clients should be available in all communities. Dumping the problem of child abuse on the State Department of Public Welfare or juvenile delinquency on police and probation departments has been, in most cases, a traditional 'cop-out.' Rarely does placing a delinquent in detention or sentencing an abusive parent to jail solve the problem with the child, the family or the community. This is not to be interpreted to mean that the arm of the law should not be used in such cases. What is meant is that coercion should be used only as a last resort, and not the only resort, to such problems.

The most effective solution to juvenile delinquency and child abuse is to elicit the voluntary cooperation of child and parent, even if 'voluntary consent' is persuasively provided through court order. Only if unexcused non-participation results should the full arm of the law be imposed by the court system.

The Central Texas Youth Services Bureau, Inc., established in 1971, is a case in point. This program attempts to prevent juveniles who are indicating behavior problems from entering the juvenile justice system and attempts to divert those juveniles in the system from returning. The Bureau works closely with the child and the family and seeks to diagnose causes of the child's behavior and then seeks solutions with each family member participating. When specialized services, such as testing and therapy, are needed, referral is made to the appropriate agency. Supportive services and temporary residential care also are available and all services are free. One of the keys to the Bureau's success is the voluntary participation by the child and the parents.

As of April, 1977, the Youth Services Bureau has worked with 3,027 documented cases, at an approximate cost of $108 per family, or $27.16 per person. The statistical success rate, based on known cases referred to law enforcement agencies or reopened, is a 94% diversion rate which, in turn, is based on 547 cases worked with from January, 1975, to April, 1977. Of these 547 cases, over 234 were runaways, many of whom were running from an abusing home environment.

From January, 1976, through May, 1977, the Bureau has worked jointly with CANDO, a child abuse and neglect prevention and treatment organization in Bell County. Of 20 child abuse and/or neglect cases referred to the Bureau, 19 cases were considered successfully treated.

Such programs providing voluntary local services should be available in every community and be subsidized by local, state and federal funds. These programs provide more efficient services at less cost than their often bureaucratic and megalithic public counterparts. Such state agencies are necessary, but could be far more effective by moving away from direct service provision and, instead, serve as funding sources and provide evaluation and technical assistance services to private service providers.

Through cooperation by the community, city, state and federal governments, the problems of juvenile delinquency, child abuse and neglect can be alleviated by providing social action, education and direct services. The question is: Do we, as individual citizens, value our youth enough to cooperate and are we willing to pay the price?

18

The Influence of Child Abuse on Psychosexual and Psychosocial Development and Implications for Delinquency

FRANK B. RAYMOND

Professor, College of Social Work
University of South Carolina
Columbia, South Carolina 29208

Major theories of human development have emphasized that the individual normally passes through certain stages of development, and that at each stage certain developmental tasks must be accomplished and particular developmental crises must be resolved. If early stages are not passed through normally, difficulties will result in later stages which may manifest themselves in several ways, including deviant behavior such as juvenile delinquency. It is the contention of the writer that child abuse can inhibit the child from successfully completing various stages of development.

This paper briefly reviews the research which has been done regarding the characteristics of abusive parents, the characteristics of abused children and the subsequent effects of abuse on the children. While the research in each of these areas tends to stand alone, the components can be interrelated and better understood through the application of the concepts of psychosocial and psychosexual development. The psychosocial and psychosexual development during five stages of childhood are therefore presented in this paper, and it is shown how normal development during each of these periods may be impeded by child abuse, with delinquent behavior being a theoretically likely result. Research which supports the relationship between frustration of normal developmental stages and subsequent delinquency is cited. Finally, in order that the theoretical perspective developed in this paper may be examined more fully, several questions for further research are presented and related proposals for research are suggested.

PREVIOUS RESEARCH

A substantial amount of research has been done regarding the characteristics of abusive parents, the characteristics of abused children and the after effects of abuse. The theoretical concept of the child's passage through stages of development and the parent's role in this passage provides a means of integrating the findings of these three areas of research. The findings in each of these areas will be presented first, and these will be discussed later in relation to the child's developmental stages.

Research Concerning Abusing Parents

Child-abusing parents cannot be characterized by race, social class, religion, education, or occupation (See Raffali, 1970; Rubin, 1966; Terr, 1970). "Parents may be college graduates and professional persons, as well as high school dropouts. They come from high-, middle-, and low-income groups and from various cultural, religious, and racial groups (Rubin, p. 231)." The commonalities which abusing parents share are more psychological than sociological. It has been found that they tend to be immature, dependent, socially isolated and impulse-ridden (Holter and Freedman, 1968). Often they are rigid, self-centered and feel rejected and angry (Holter and Freedman, 1968). They tend to share certain serious social problems including marital difficulty, financial mismanagement and faulty relations to the community (Zalba, 1966). Very often the extended family lives far away and their involvement with the immediate family is minimal. When the parents also have little involvement or poor relations with the neighbors they are left in a lonely situation (Montgomery County Public Schools, 1974, pp. 5-6). Often abusing parents are unable to develop genuine relationships with other persons, have a feeling of being loved insufficiently as children and have difficulty in delaying gratification (Wasserman, 1967). Several studies have revealed that a high percentage of abusing parents have been abused as children (U.S. DHEW, *Working with Abusive Parents*, 1975, p. 9) . Their dependency seems to be an expression of their own emptiness; they yearn for the caring and warmth which they never experienced. As a result of the immaturity of the abusing parents they tend to see the child as more mature than he is and expect him to act as an older child. Because of their generally poor knowledge of child development and consequent excessive expectations of the child, abuse often results. For example, they may require the child not to cry, or expect the child to assume an inappropriate parental role in order to satisfy their immature needs. On the other hand, abusive parents often feel they cannot allow the child to become too dependent, so they will not comfort him when he cries. They feel that it is necessary to show the child "who is boss" to teach him respect for authority and to prevent him from becoming sassy or stubborn (*Working with Abusive Parents*, p. 9).

Research Concerning Abused Children and the Effects of Abuse

Although abused children cannot be characterized in terms of race, age or social class, they do tend to share certain behavioral characteristics. Behavioral extremes seem common among abused children. They either cry much or little; they are either fearless or very fearful of adult authority; and they are either aggressive and destructive or passive and withdrawn. Furthermore, although they are often hungry for affection, they are generally unable to relate to other children or adults (U.S. DHEW, *Child Abuse and Neglect* 1975, pp. 4-5). Abused children generally appear to be alert to danger and wary of physical contact with adults (Montgomery County Schools, p. 37). The abused child often has learning difficulties in school and is truant. The truancy may reflect the parent's neglect of educational needs or may be due to the fact that the parent kept him at home to hide the physical evidence of the abuse.

Although there have been many theories about the long-range effects of abuse upon the child, there has been little empirical research in this area. Evidence does seem to indicate that abused children are likely to become adults in whose behavior violence plays an important role. As noted above, most abusing parents were themselves objects of violence as children. In rearing their children they recreate the pattern by which they were raised as children (Kempe and Helfer, 1972, pp. 104-111). Hence, for the abused child violent behavior probably occurs because of role modeling, with the small child accepting his parents' behavior and imitating the parents. In addition to learning that abusive behavior is a way of rearing children, the abused child learns that violence is an effective and appropriate means of resolving conflicts (Hetherington, 1975, p. 191). Furthermore, this learned violent behavior becomes exaggerated by the fact that the child who has been brutally treated feels an unusual degree of hostility toward his parents, and this hostility is transferred toward the world in general. This hostility may be expressed in delinquency in the juvenile or through crime in the adult—in either case a striking out in bitterness (Simmons, 1970, p. 52).

The research findings in this section regarding the abusing parent, the abused child and the effects of abuse will be drawn upon to explain the impact of abuse on the child's passage through the normal stages of childhood development.

PSYCHOSOCIAL AND PSYCHOSEXUAL DEVELOPMENT

The effects of abuse on the later behavior of a child can best be understood by an examination of developmental theory. Developmental theory assumes that the individual passes through distinct stages of development as the personality unfolds. These stages are sequential, although the point in time at which individuals enter or leave each stage varies from person to person. At each stage certain psychological events must occur, and the psychological development that takes place at each stage will have a significant impact upon all subsequent stages and affect a person's behavior throughout life.

Psychoanalytic theory focuses on the development of the emotional and social life of the individual. While much of Freud's theory has been revised, many of his original assumptions persist among contemporary psychoanalytic theorists. Freud suggested that all behavior is motivated; hence, all behavior has meaning and no behavior occurs randomly or without purpose. While Freud hypothesized two basic psychological motives—sexuality and aggression—other personality theorists suggest other motives such as the will to power (Adler). According to Freud, every behavior has, as part of its meaning, a sexual or aggressive message. However, many behaviors are unconsciously motivated.

Freud also described three components of the personality— the id, the ego, and the superego. The *id* is the source of instincts and impulses, the primary source of psychic energy throughout life. It operates without concern for reality and presses for expression and gratification. The *ego* includes all mental functions which are involved with reality, and its primary purpose is to gratify id impulses within the constraints of reality. The *superego* develops later in childhood and includes prohibitions about moral behavior and ideals about one's potential as a moral person. The ego often functions to allow expression of id impulses without offending the superego. The stages of development described by Freud reflect his interest in the role of sexuality as a driving force. Each stage involves a period of life during which a particular body zone is of heightened sexual importance. During these stages—the oral, anal, phallic, latent, and genital—there is conflict between individual impulses and social regulations, and the components of the personality are involved in trying to reduce this conflict (Blum, 1953).

Psychosocial theory also suggests stages of development. As articulated by Erikson (1950) the theory describes eight stages, the first five of which correspond in part to the stages of development proposed by Freud. However, psychosocial theory emphasizes that at each stage the person is confronted with a unique problem which requires him to integrate his own needs and skills with the demands of the culture. Erikson therefore refers to the psychosocial crises of each stage, which describe the person's psychological efforts to adjust to the psychic demands of the environment at that stage. Psychosocial theory also emphasizes that at each stage the individual must master certain developmental tasks, which consist of sets of skills and competencies that are acquired by the individual as he attempts to adjust to the environment. Mastery of tasks of later stages of development often depends on the acquisition of earlier, simpler skills. Finally, psychosocial theory deals with the process of coping, which refers to the active efforts on the individual's part to resolve stress and to create new solutions to the problems that face him at each developmental stage. Through coping, the individual is able to grow and develop and move successfully through the stages of life.

Based on the foregoing concepts, the following integration of psychoanalytical and psychosocial perspectives on development will explain how child abuse may interfere with normal development and result in deviant behavior, including delinquency.

Infancy

This period, which lasts until approximately 1½ to 2 years of age, covers the period that Freud described as the oral stage of development. During this time the individual obtains primary satisfaction from reducing the drives of hunger and thirst. Although oral behavior may later be influenced by experience, in the beginning it is a drive, an instinctual pleasure. The infant is governed by id impulses, with little ego development. He is very dependent, and any significant events occurring during this stage, particularly those associated with oral satisfaction, will influence later behavior in the area of dependency. Affection becomes associated with the oral stage as the parents display positive emotions in meeting the child's oral needs.

During this period the infant is engaged in resolution of the psychosocial crisis of trust versus mistrust. Trust is "an emotional feeling of well-being and confidence that one's needs will be met (Newman and Newman, 1975, p. 41)." The process through which this trust evolves is the repeated interaction with responsive caregivers, as through receiving satisfaction of oral needs from the parents. A negative resolution of this crisis leads to the development of a sense of mistrust which is characterized by lethargic, withdrawn, grief-stricken behaviors. Through repeated successful interaction with the caregiver, the infant accomplishes the social tasks of learning object permanence and developing social attachment. That is, he learns that the caregivers are separate beings from himself but that he can trust them to remain a part of his environment and he therefore develops a social relationship with them that enables him to feel secure enough to explore further his environment.

Child abuse and neglect can have a profound influence upon the child's satisfaction of basic needs, accomplishment of developmental tasks and acquiring a sense of trust. For example, if an infant who is hungry or uncomfortable is fed, diapered and cuddled, his sense of trust will develop. However, if his needs are not responded to consistently or if he is punished for expression of his needs through crying, his trust is not developed and the ability to relate appropriately to other people is not acquired. Both neglecting and abusing parents tend to demand a great deal from their infants and become distressed by the child's inadequate response. However, the neglecting parent responds to his distress by giving up and abandoning efforts to care for the child, whereas the abusing parent seems to have more investment in the active life of the child and punishes him for his failure to perform adequately (Helfer and Kempe, 1974, p. 105) . In either case, the result will likely be deleterious to the child's development of a sense of trust and consequent ability to establish satisfactory relationships with others. As mentioned earlier, child-abusing parents (who, themselves, have often been abused) generally lack this ability to relate appropriately to others. Furthermore, although the full effects of infantile deprivation are not known, research has indicated that such children continue to suffer other serious deficiencies, such as impairments in the capacity to delay when frustrated, which interfere with their abilities to solve problems; a failure adequately to generalize what they learn; an undue concreteness in thinking; and failure to expect and seek help from other adults (Ainsworth, 1962). Such difficulties may be manifested later in delinquent behavior.

Toddlerhood

During the toddler years (two through four) the child is in the anal stage of development (and may enter the oedipal stage towards the end of this period). While in the anal stage, which corresponds closely to the toilet training period, the anal areas become more pleasurable to the child. As opposed to the oral stage, the child during this period has behavioral expectations placed on him which sometimes result in hostile conflict between parent and child. Not only is he expected to choose the appropriate time, place and method for urination and defecation, but his parents seek to shape his other social behavior. The child's ego, which began to develop during the infancy period, becomes more highly differentiated, and the foundations of the superego begin to be formed.

According to psychosocial theory the child must deal with the crisis of autonomy versus shame and doubt during the toddler period. A primary developmental task at this stage is that of learning self-control, which involves the child's ability to control his own impulses and his feeling that he can control the events around him. If the parents' responses to the child are such that he experiences feelings of failure or inadequacy, self-doubt will result. On the other hand, if the parents provide appropriate interaction, acceptance and discipline, the emergence of autonomy and individuation will occur.

Abuse on the part of the parent can preclude the child's successful accomplishment of the tasks of the toddler period. Not understanding normal childhood behavior, abusing parents may be unable to tolerate the toddler's infraction of rules and consider his expressiveness an indication of his being 'bad.' They may therefore either seriously constrict the child or foster undue hostility in him by grabs, slaps and whippings. Aggression develops within the child, but since the child cannot win in overt conflict he will find covert means of combat. However, since he is still closely identified with his mother, hostility and aggression toward a parent is also aggression toward the self. Because he needs his parents and seeks to love them, he may find it better to feel guilty and direct his hostility against himself, rather than toward the abusing parent.

Research tends to support the idea that repression of normal behavior during toddlerhood through unreasonable disciplinary practices such as abuse can contribute to delinquency. For example, the Gluecks concluded that unreasonable disciplinary practices ". . . during the early years when they are developing a sense of power may be baneful sources of emotional distortion and ultimately result in ambivalence toward, or defiance of the authority of the parents and later of school and law (Glueck and Glueck, 1968, p. 15)." It has also been found that harsh discipline such as abuse during this period tends to heighten aggression in children, which may later be expressed through delinquency (Haskell and Yablonsky, 1974, p. 455). Not only does the child have heightened aggressiveness as a result of the abuse, but he has learned through his parents' models that violence is a way of self-expression (Deykin, 1972).

Early School Age

During the early school age years (5-7) the child is in the phallic stage of development, which represents a period of heightened genital sensitivity in the absence of the hormonal changes which accompany puberty. According to psychosexual theory, children at this stage direct sexualized activity toward both sexes and also engage in self-stimulation. The Oedipal or Electra conflicts occur during this period, with the child's feeling strong attraction to the opposite-sex parent and hostility and competition with the same-sex parent. The normal outcome of the conflict is the development of a positive identification with the same-sex parent, and the emergence of a well-differentiated ego. This results in the repression of the sexualized and aggressive impulses which the child had directed towards the parents.

Similarly, psychosocial theory points out that two developmental tasks during early school age are the development of sex role identification and early moral development. In sex role identification the child must learn the gender label, acquire sex-role standards, establish a sex preference and identify with the same-sex parent. The child's development of moral behavior involves an integration of his moral judgments, his understanding of the reward structure, his parental identifications and his empathy for others (Newman and Newman, p. 116). Obviously, the response of the parent is crucial in the child's accomplishment of the tasks of sex-role identification and moral development. The psychosocial crisis of this period is that of initiative versus guilt. Initiative is the active inquiry and investigation of the environment, and positive resolution of the crisis involves the development of a sense that the active cognitive investigation of the environment is an informative and pleasurable experience. The negative resolution of this crisis results in a feeling of overwhelming guilt, a feeling that curiosity itself is taboo. The child who resolves the crisis in this negative way must rely almost totally on external authority to direct his life. He is unable to distinguish between legitimate and inappropriate areas of investigation, and must develop a strict moral code which restricts many areas of living. Again, the role of the parents in helping the child resolve this crisis positively is crucial.

The child's behavior during this period of life may not be understood by the abusive parent who has a poor understanding of normal childhood development. For example, the child's attachment to the opposite-sex parent and rivalry with same-sex parent may be misperceived by the latter. The parent's inability to cope with the child's behavior could lead to aggressive and abusive acts toward the child. The trauma of such abuse could result in the child's inability to achieve adequate superego development or moral development. Furthermore, research has demonstrated that harsh discipline in child-rearing results in conformity to rigid parental rules for a short period of time, but the child shows a lack of internalization of moral values or behavioral control useful in other situations over long periods of time (Shore, 1971, p. 462). The lack of adequate internal controls and ability to make appropriate moral judgments for himself therefore leaves the abused child in a vulnerable position when faced with a choice between delinquent and non-delinquent behaviors.

Middle School Age

Psychoanalytic theory has relatively little to say about the child's development during this time and considers this to be a period of latency, a time of transition and consolidation between the closing of the Oedipal period and the onset of puberty. The child has come to terms with his position in the family, repressed sensuous desires for the opposite-sex parent and internalized controls. He is now investing his energies and interests outside the family, in his peers and in learning. Later psychoanalysts emphasize that this is a crucial time for personality development, especially in terms of the child's forming relationships with peers.

Psychosocial theory gives even more emphasis to the child's development of social skills during the juvenile period. The crisis of this period is that of industry versus inferiority. During his day-to-day experiences with success and failure the child learns that work, effort and perseverance bring him rewards of competence, mastery and approval. This success enables him to internalize these behaviors and to develop a sense of industry and a willingness to confront future problems without fear. On the other hand, if he experiences many failures during this time he may internalize a sense of inferiority, so that when he confronts future problems he will feel inadequate and unable to succeed. Developmental tasks during this period include learning social cooperation, engaging in self-evaluation, developing various skills and learning team play. While engaging in these tasks the child becomes acutely sensitive to the evaluations that others make of his performance. Thus, the social dynamics of the family, the peer group and the school environment play a part in supporting feelings of mastery or failure. If the child's resultant self-concept is positive, he becomes better able to guide his own behavior as he begins to emerge from the family during adolescence. However, if his self-concept is poor he may tend to withdraw, become unable to accept challenges and be unable to utilize his own judgment appropriately when faced with moral decisions. Whereas the younger child exhibits what Piaget calls a "morality of constraint," during the middle school age years he should develop a "morality of cooperation" (Lidz, 1968, p. 282). That is, the young child accepts a rigid code of standards of behavior from his parents because of their superior positions as adults and because of the fear of punishment. However, as he enters the juvenile years he begins to judge the morality of behavior in terms of the motivation behind it and the social implications of the act.

If the child is abused during the middle school years it is likely that a poor self-concept will result. During this time when he is most vulnerable to the evaluations of others as he tries to experiment with autonomous behavior, the effects of abuse can be devastating. In fact, the literature on delinquency has indicated an association between a poor self-concept and delinquent behavior. It has also been found that delinquents with such self-concepts generally come from families which prohibit initiative and ego development through rejection, deprivation or abandonment (Rubenfeld, 1965, pp. 117-118).

Furthermore, abuse during the juvenile period will likely inhibit the child's progression from a morality of constraint to a morality of cooperation. Such progression depends on the social environment in which the child lives. Rigid and arbitrary parents foster fixation at the earlier level, and parents who enforce rigid standards with abusive behavior make it even more difficult for the child to learn to use judgment, to formulate his own rules or to govern himself (Lidz, p. 283). Lacking these abilities, the child may not be able to decide appropriately whether or not to engage in delinquent behaviors when faced with new situations offering this potential.

Adolescence

According to Freud, the final phase of development, the genital stage, begins with the onset of puberty. During this period the individual directs his sexual impulses toward an opposite-sex object. This period brings a resurgence of the Oedipal or Electra impulses and a reworking of earlier infantile identifications. Tension exists during this stage because of the sexual threat which the adolescent poses to the family unit. In order to diminish this threat the adolescent withdraws from his family and temporarily discounts his parents' adequacies. At the end of adolescence the relationship with the parents becomes restored, as the teenager has selected a sexual partner outside the family and the internal family threat is dissipated.

According to Erikson, the psychosocial crisis is that of ego identity versus ego diffusion. That is, one must develop an "accrued confidence that one's ability to maintain an inner sameness and continuity is matched by the sameness and continuity of one's meaning for others (Erikson, 1959, p. 89)." This identity carries with it the mastery of the problem of childhood and the readiness to face the challenge of adulthood. Just as a sense of trust was earlier required for the infant to enter into new childhood experiences, a sense of identity is necessary for the person to be able to make adult decisions such as the choice of vocation, a marriage partner or whether or not to have children.

Tasks of this period include achieving autonomy from parents and development of memberships in peer groups. The emerging autonomy from parents requires considerable energy at this stage. Although the person is constantly involved in the process of self-differentiation, it is during adolescence that a true departure from parental dominance should take place. This developing sense of autonomy has implications outside the home. As the young person becomes more confident about his own independence, he begins to evaluate the judgment of other authority figures rather than automatically accepting their legitimacy and adequacy as he did earlier. The pressure for peer group membership and social acceptance becomes intense during this period. In fact, Newman and Newman (p. 197) posit an additional psychosocial conflict which confronts an adolescent—group identity versus alienation. Psychological growth is facilitated by group acceptance, whereas if the adolescent is unable to identify with or be accepted by peer groups he will experience a strong sense of alienation and some degree of self-depreciation.

Child abuse during adolescence will likely reinforce the young person's withdrawal from his parents and may result in the relationship's not being restored as is normally the case. Also, abuse may make it difficult for the child to achieve adequate ego identity. Evidence indicates, in fact, that abusing parents (many of whom were abused as children) generally lack adequate ego identity (Helfer and Kempe, 1974, p. 109). Furthermore, if the young person does not develop an adequate sense of autonomy during this period because of restrictive, abusive parents he will likely be unable to make appropriate judgments of the legitimacy and adequacy of other persons in positions of authority, and his inadequate judgments may result in behavior of a delinquent nature. Finally, in seeking to establish peer relationships during adolescence the child may select delinquent-oriented groups if his parents are abusive. It has been demonstrated that the type of peer group the adolescent selects is a function of the relationship within the home environment. When he experiences positive and intense relationships within the family, there is an increased probability that the values held by the family will be matched by the peer group he selects. On the other hand, weak or unpleasant relationships within the family increase the likelihood that the adolescent will accept outside and different cultural influences such as those of a delinquent group (Stanfield, 1966, p. 413).

QUESTIONS FOR RESEARCH

Infancy

It is theorized that children who are abused during infancy are less likely than other children to develop a sense of trust in others and that this lack of trust will be manifested in later life in delinquency, as well as other forms of deviant behavior. To test this proposition, four purposive samples of young people could be selected and compared in terms of their responses to an attitude scale measuring "trust of others." The four groups would include: 1) non-abused, non-delinquent; 2) non-abused, delinquent; 3) abused (during infancy), non-delinquent; and 4) abused (during infancy), delinquent. It is predicted that the level of trust in others will be found to range from highest to lowest among the four groups in the order they are listed above. Also, the same attitude scale could be given to a group of young people who have been abused at different ages. It is predicted that those who were abused during infancy will have a lower sense of trust than those who were abused at later points in life.

Toddlerhood

It is theorized that abuse occurring during toddlerhood will make the child more disposed towards aggressive behavior than non-abused children, and more disposed towards aggression than children abused at other ages. To test the first proposition, two matched samples of children abused (during toddlerhood) and children not abused could be compared in terms of defined indices of aggression. In order to test the second proposition, children who have been abused at different ages could be compared in terms of defined indices of aggression, which would reveal whether or not child abuse during toddlerhood is more conducive to later aggressive behavior than abuse which occurs at other periods. The relationship between abuse during this period and later delinquency could be measured by studying a group of delinquent youth who have committed aggressive acts and who have also been abused. It is predicted that a significantly larger proportion of those young people will be found to have been abused during toddlerhood than during other periods.

Early School Age

During this period the ego becomes well-differentiated and the child develops adequate behavioral control mechanisms under normal circumstances. However, it is theorized that this development will be hampered by abuse occurring during this period, predisposing the child to later delinquency. This proposition could be tested through administering psychological tests aimed at measuring ego functioning to four purposive samples of children 1) non-abused, non-delinquent; 2) non-abused, delinquent; 3) abused (during early school age), non-delinquent; and 4) abused (during early school age), delinquent. It is predicted that the ego development will range from strongest to weakest among the four groups in the order they are listed above. Also, the same psychological test could be given to a group of young people who have been abused at different ages. It is predicted that those who were abused during the early school years would display weaker ego strength than those who were abused at other times during their development.

Middle School Age

Since this is a crucial period for self-evaluation and development of a self-concept, the effect of child abuse on the development of the self-concept might be measured. Abused and non-abused children passing through this stage of life could be assessed in terms of their self-concept through appropriate psychological tests. It is predicted that the abused children would show poorer self-concepts than the non-abused children. Furthermore, if children having been abused at different points in life were tested in terms of their self-concepts, it is predicted that those abused during middle school age years would have the weakest self-concepts. As discussed earlier, the relationship between self-concept and delinquency has been demonstrated through previous research. Since the middle school age years are crucial for self-concept development, the relationship of abuse during this time and delinquency could be demonstrated through giving self-concept tests to four groups: 1) non-abused, non-delinquent; 2) non-abused, delinquent, 3) abused (during middle school age), non-delinquent; and 4) abused (during middle school age), delinquent. It is predicted that the self-concept would range from strongest to weakest among the four groups as ordered above.

Adolescence

In view of the fact that the breaking away from the parents and establishing individual identity and autonomy is crucial during this period, research relating this issue to delinquency would be appropriate. First, it is theorized that young people abused during this time are less able to develop an adequate ego identity which will enable them to make later adult decisions properly. As mentioned earlier, research has demonstrated that abusing parents generally lack adequate ego-identity. Similar research could compare the ego-identity development of a sample of young people abused during this period with a sample of young people not abused. The relationship to delinquency could also be assessed by measuring the ego-identity of four purposive samples of adolescents: 1) non-abused, non-delinquent; 2) non-abused, delinquent; 3) abused (during adolescence), non-delinquent; and 4) abused (during adolescence), delinquent. It is predicted that ego identity will range from strongest to weakest among the four groups in the order listed. Furthermore, research could be directed at assessing the attitudes toward authority of the abused, as opposed to the non-abused, adolescent. It is predicted that the abused adolescent will have poorer attitudes toward authority than the non-abused adolescent. Again, the variable of delinquency could be assessed by measuring the attitudes toward authority among four groups differentiated by both variables, as discussed above. Finally, the choice of peer groups could be assessed through research. It is predicted that the peer groups selected by non-abused adolescents will represent cultural patterns similar to those of the adolescents' families, whereas the peer groups selected by abused adolescents will represent cultural patterns significantly different from their parents.

CONCLUSION

This paper has examined the phenomena of child abuse and delinquency through an analysis of the psychosexual and psychosocial stages of development. It has been theorized that insofar as relationships exist between child abuse and delinquency, they are best explained in terms of the impact of abuse on the child's normal development. It has been demonstrated how the occurrence of abuse during each of the five stages of childhood development can result ultimately in delinquent behavior. Selected research findings concerning the characteristics of child abusers, characteristics of abused children and the effects of abuse are drawn upon to illustrate the heuristic value of the proposed theoretical perspective. Research questions and related proposals for research which would examine the relationships discussed in this paper have been presented.

REFERENCES

Ainsworth, M. S. *Deprivations of maternal care: A reassessment of its effects.* Public Health Papers, No. 14. Geneva: World Health Organization, 1962.

Blum, G. S. *Psychoanalytic theories of personality.* New York: McGraw-Hill Book Co., Inc., 1953. Deykin, E. Y. Life functioning in families of delinquent boys: An assessment model. *Social Service Review,* 1972, *46,* 90-91. Erikson, E. H. *Childhood and society.* New York: Norton Press, 1950.

Erikson, E. H. Growth and crises of the 'healthy personality.' *Psychological Issues,* Vol. 1, No. 1, Monograph No. 1. New York: International Universities Press, 1959.

Glueck, S. & Glueck, E. *Delinquents and non-delinquents in perspective.* Cambridge, Mass.: Harvard University Press, 1968.

Haskell, M. R. & Yablonsky, L. *Crime and delinquency.* (2nd ed.) Chicago: Rand-McNally College Publishing Co., 1974.

Helfer, R. E. & Kempe, C. H. (Eds.) *The battered child.* Chicago: University of Chicago Press, 1974.

Hetherington, E. M. (Ed.) *Review of child development research.* Vol. 5. Chicago: University of Chicago Press, 1975.

Holter, J. C. & Freedman, S. B. Principles of management in child abuse cases. *American Journal of Orthopsychiatry,* January, 1968, *28,* 130-132.

Kempe, C. H. & Helfer, R. *Helping the battered child and his family.* Philadelphia: J. B. Lippincott Co., 1972.

Lidz, T. *The person.* New York: Basic Books, Inc., 1968.

Montgomery County Public Schools. *Proceedings from Project Protection.* Child Abuse and Neglect Conference and Workshops. Rockville, Md.: Montgomery County Public Schools, 1974.

Newman, B. & Newman, P. *Development through life.* Homewood, Ill.: Dorsey Press, 1975.

Raffali, H. The battered child—An overview of a medical, legal, and social problem. *Crime and Delinquency,* April, 1970, *16,* 139-150.

Rubin, J. The need for intervention. *Public Welfare,* July, 1966, *24,* 230-235.

Shore, M. F. Psychological theories of the causes of antisocial behavior. *Crime and Delinquency,* 1971, *17.*

Simmons, H. E. *Protective services for children.* (2nd ed.) Sacramento: The Citadel Press, 1970.

Stanfield, R. E. The interaction of family variables and group variables in the etiology of delinquency. *Social Problems,* Spring, 1966, *13.*

Terr, L. C. A family study of child abuse. *American Journal of Psychiatry,* November, 1970, *127,* 665-671.

U. S. Department of Health, Education, and Welfare. *Child abuse and neglect: An overview of the problem.* Washington, D.C.: U.S. Government Printing Office, 1975.

U. S. Department of Health, Education, and Welfare. *Working with abusive parents.* Washington, D.C.: U. S. Government Printing Office, 1975.

Wasserman, S. The abused parent of the abused child. *Children,* September, 1967, *14.*

Zalba, S. The abused child: A survey of the problem. *Social Work,* October, 1966, *2,* 6-7.

19

Adolescent Perceptions of Parental Discipline and Juvenile Delinquency

JEANETTE R. ABRAMS

Doctoral Candidate, Department of Sociology
University of Washington
Seattle, Washington 98195

Pfohl (1977) observes that early concern with the relationship between child neglect and juvenile delinquency stimulated the development of institutions for juveniles whose parents were not providing adequate care as early as 1825. Then, as now, child abuse, neglect and delinquency were viewed as especially prevalent among the lower SES groups. Yet, the presumed relationship between the three variables—child abuse, neglect and delinquency—remained, until recently, an untested hypothesis. This paper examines data bearing on perceived parental discipline and juvenile delinquency, testing that hypothesis on a sample of rural adolescents.

BACKGROUND

What we know about abusive and neglectful families indicates they are on opposite ends of a continuum of controlling behaviors. Parents who are abusive have patterns of responding to their children quite different from those of neglectful parents (Conger, 1975). Young (1964) described abusive parents as those who go far beyond the usual techniques of discipline in controlling their children. Indeed, the response of those who consistently abuse their children by beating, punching, kicking, burning and throwing is punishment in the old sense of the word. It does not seem to have much to do with the control of children's inappropriate and undesirable behavior. Neglectful parents, on the other hand, are characterized by a profound indifference to their children, typically expressed by failure to provide adequate hygiene, nutrition and general care. Discipline and control are lacking, since they require more effort than these passive parents can generate.

Another characteristic of abusive parents is their determination to restrict the lives of their children as much as possible. Demands for immediate compliance and punctuality, for example, are rigidly enforced and punished. All of this indicates an extreme preference for control. Neglectful parents, on the other hand, are happy to have others assume responsibility toward their children and to establish sound relations with them. This unwillingness to exert control over their own lives and those of their children stands in stark contrast to abusive parents (Young, 1964).

Young's data indicate differences in SES between neglectful and abusive families, as do Conger's. Neglectful families were much more likely to come from low SES groups, while abusive parents appear to come from all SES groupings. However, the findings are somewhat contradictory in Elmer's (1967) small (N, 31) study, the median family income was lower for both abusive and neglectful families when compared with the median family income for the population from which the sample was drawn. A disproportionately higher percentage of Elmer's families were on welfare compared with the total population. Curiously, the mean number of years of education in her sample was the same for abusive and neglectful families as for the total population.

Elmer's data are particularly informative about abusive parents. Her sample was selected by radiologists from X-ray files of a children's hospital in a large city. The criteria for selection were injured or broken bones, an absence of bone disease (an alternative hypothesis) and a history of gross neglect and assault, or an absence of a history showing convincingly that the injuries were accidental. The striking factor about these abused children is their extremely young age. Most of them were under one year old, many injured soon after birth. This extremely young age at which children are likely to be abused has both methodological and theoretical implications. The methodological issues have to do with the determination of causal links between early child abuse and neglect and later delinquency. So many events intervene between infancy or early childhood, when most abuse occurs, and the preteen and teen years, when delinquency usually begins, that even longitudinal studies cannot accurately identify and measure the multitudinous variables operating within this time period.

Young's data on the type and amount of delinquency among abused and neglected children in her study are inconclusive, in large part due to the limited information available for delinquent items. For between 50% and 75% of her cases she could secure no information. She attempted to measure truancy, fighting and stealing, but only the data on truancy were reliable enough to report. She found that children of neglectful parents were more than twice as likely to be truant from school as were children of abusive parents. That is, these children appear to model themselves after their parents. Neglectful parents tend to avoid their problems; their children's truancy suggests avoidance of school, perhaps even encouraged to do so by their parents.

THEORETICAL ISSUES

Before turning to the data, it is necessary to review findings from those theoretical perspectives which bear on the hypothesized relationship. The Skinnerian perspective, based on a vast accumulation of empirical evidence, posits that behavior is a function of its consequences. With respect to the effects of punishment it is especially informative. The greater the frequency and magnitude of punishment, the greater the suppression of behavior. The more immediately and the more variably punishment follows behavior, the greater the suppression of behavior. Two issues are especially pertinent. One is that the most devastating characteristic of punishment is that it is likely to lead to generalized suppression of all behavior. Seligman's (1975) work on learned helplessness illustrates this. But further, the younger the organism when uncontrolled punishment is administered, the greater the suppression of behavior and the greater the duration of such suppression.

If we extrapolate from these well substantiated findings, what do they show about the relationship between early child abuse and later delinquency? It suggests that there may very well be no relationship. Elmer's data suggest that abused children mature into good and compliant people, rather than delinquent. However, there is one irreducible fact which may alter this proffered hypothesis. Children grow up. As they do, they develop resources of their own. They can run away, hit back, choose devious means of behaving as they grow larger. In short, their very growth over time alters the pattern of behavioral responses between child and parent, even when the parents, attitudes toward their children remain the same or similar to earlier attitudes.

The difficulty, however, of measuring the relationships between early child abuse and later delinquency remains problematic. What can be done to resolve it? In this study, lacking both longitudinal and observational data, cross-sectional data from a survey on adolescents was utilized, focusing on variables which measure behavior attitudes at one point in time, drawing inferences from that. This technique has one limitation: Measures are verbal reports or perceptions rather than actual measures of observed behavior. If, however, we can agree with the observation of W. I. Thomas (1918), there may be a resolution. Thomas observed that "if a thing is perceived as real, then it is real in its consequences." If we assume that it is how a child or adolescent perceives his parents' response to him which affects his own behavior independently of actual parental behavior, we can utilize the survey data.

METHODOLOGY

The data presented in this paper constitutes only a fragment of the data gathered for another research project, which is concerned with a test and extension of social control theory as articulated by Hirschi. The primary aim of this larger research is on the psycho-social etiology of adolescent drug use. An advantage of this study is that it includes non-delinquents as well as delinquents, thus increasing the range of variation in the dependent variable, and allowing more careful evaluation of the relative contribution of many variables, including that of parental disciplinary techniques, which are as related to delinquency and drug use.

In this study there are two measures of parental discipline: 1) perceived parental strictness; and 2) perceived unfair parental punishment. Each of these variables, particularly at their extremes, touch on characteristics of abusive and neglectful parents. Parents who are perceived as never being unfair, and as never being strict, touch on the non-interactive parent categorized as neglectful. These two measures are reflective, rather than perfectly valid measures, of abusive and neglectful parental disciplinary techniques.

TABLE 1 CORRELATIONS AMONG SEVEN DELINQUENCY ITEMS FOR TOWN AND COUNTRY BOYS BOYS ONLY (N = 515)

	Ran Away	Cheated on test	Truant	Fight	Suspended	Steal less than $10
Cheated on test	.16					
Truant	.22	.44				
Serious Fighting	.32	.36	.34			
Suspended	.17	.16	.19	.25		
Steal less than $10	.10	.42	.32	.31	.22	
Steal more than $10	.15	.29	.26	.29	.21	.49

The seven measures of self-reported delinquency include cheating on a test at school, running away from home, truancy, fighting, suspension from school and stealing items worth less than and worth more than $10. These measures are also imperfect measures of delinquency, which can be seen in the correlations among these seven delinquency items in Table 1. Correlations range from a low of .10 between stealing less than $10 and running away from home, to a high of .49 between stealing less than $10 and stealing more than $10. Further, not all of these measures can properly be considered delinquent acts, since some are without legal penalty in many of the newer juvenile codes. This includes cheating on a test at school, running away from home and serious fighting. These last two behaviors, however, have frequently been among those for which adolescents could be committed to a juvenile detention center. However imperfect these measures are, they are all positively correlated with each other, and constitute a usable delinquency measure.

The data were generated from a sample of 6th to 12th grade adolescents in a small rural county in a northwestern state. A proportionate stratified cluster sampling technique with a constant sampling fraction was used. Classes at each grade constituted the clusters. They were numbered serially and then randomly selected. All students in each of the selected classes were then included in the sample. Only those students in each of the classes whose parents signed affirmatively an informed consent form were included in the survey. The overall response rate was 65%. A comparison of respondents and non-respondents indicated that females were slightly overrepresented in the sample, when compared with the population for these grades. It is the younger students with higher self-reported English grades who were more likely to participate in the survey. The number of usable questionnaires was 1371, of which boys constitute 48%.

The hypothesis to be tested is that derived from a Skinnerian perspective, and ignores the effects of growth. This hypothesis posits no relationship between parental punishment items and delinquency on grounds that punishment tends to suppress all behavior, and that severely punished children will have learned to comply with demands made by others; hence, they are likely to be non-delinquent. While this hypothesis refers to measures of actual parental behavior, which are unmeasured in

TABLE 2 GAMMA COEFFICIENTS BETWEEN SEX, FATHER'S EDUCATIONAL LEVEL AND EACH OF SEVEN DELINQUENCY ITEMS (N = 1371)

Since school began last fall how often have you done the following?	Sex	Father's Education
Ran away from home	.09	.06
Cheated on a test at school	.04	.03
Stayed away from school because you felt like it	.00	.07
Gotten into a serious fight at home or school	.00	.01
Been suspended from school	-.33	.02
Taken something which did not belong to you worth less than $10.	-.16	.05
Taken something which did not belong to you worth more than $10.	-.39	-.16

this study, the hypothesis is extended to a child's perceptions of his parents as well. The hypothesis can then be stated as one in which there is no relationship between the perceptions which a child holds concerning parental disciplinary techniques and delinquent behavior by the child. For those who argue that internal cognitive states, or attitudes and perceptions, have but limited effect on behavior, this hypothesis is quite tenable.

Before the data bearing on this hypothesis are examined, the relationships between sex and delinquent behavior, and father's educational level, as a measure of parental socioeconomic status, and delinquency are shown. Only the gamma coefficients are presented in Table 2. The gamma coefficients indicate that it is only for the two most serious items of delinquency—stealing—that sex differences exist. Boys are more likely to engage in these activities than are girls. But there are no differences in predicting between boys and girls with respect to running away, cheating, being truant or fighting, as indicated by the gamma coefficient.

Again, with the exception of the most serious delinquency item, there is no relationship between father's education, as a measure of familial socioeconomic class; and delinquency. And, for this item—stealing something worth more than $10—there is only a weak negative relationship, suggesting that the lower the family SES, the more likely a child is to steal.

Before examining the relationship between perceived parental discipline and delinquency, the relationship between SES, as measured by father's and mother's education and parental disciplinary techniques was examined. Neither measure of parental strictness or unfair punishment was found related to either father's education or

TABLE 3 GAMMA COEFFICIENTS FOR EACH ITEM OF PARENTAL DISCIPLINE AND ADOLESCENT DELINQUENCY FOR ALL CASES (N = 1371)

Since school began last fall how often have you done these things?	Are your parents strict with you?	Do your parents punish you unfairly?
Ran away from home	.09	.33
Cheated on a test at school	.02	.05
Stayed away from school because you felt like it	.00	.11
Gotten into a serious fight at home or school	.06	.25
Been suspended from school	.06	.31
Taken something which did not belong to you worth less than $10	.01	.23
Taken something which did not belong to you worth more than $10	.02	.36

mother's education. All statistics, including chi-square, lambda, tau-b, gamma and eta-squared indicated no relationship between these two variables, thus graphically illustrating the contention that child rearing practices are unrelated to SES.

Table 3 informs specifically on the relationship of each item of parental discipline to each of the delinquency items. Gamma coefficients are presented to indicate the strength of the relationship between the items. The data show that parental strictness is unrelated to delinquency. However, the relationship between unfair punishment and delinquency is moderately positive. The more the parent is perceived to punish children unfairly, the more likely will the child engage in delinquent acts. There is a further implication to the data. The strength of the gamma coefficient varies with the seriousness of the delinquency item. In general, the less serious items report lower gamma coefficients, while the more serious items report highest gamma coefficients. The highest gamma coefficient is for the most serious act of delinquency, stealing something worth more than $10. Thus, unfair parental punishment is positively related to delinquent acts, and the more serious the delinquent act the stronger the relationship.

If we take a look at each of those items for which the gamma coefficient is among the strongest, the patterns become more obvious. The following series of table informs clearly on the relationships. Table 4 suggests that there is a slight curvelinear relationship existing between parental strictness and running away from home. Parents perceived as either always strict or never strict have children who report higher proportions of running away from home. This pattern holds for serious fighting also, as can be seen in Table 5. Thus parents who are at extreme ends of the continuum of strickness have the strongest effect on the delinquent acts of their children.

The relationship of unfair parental punishment is much clearer. It is a linear relationship. The more unfairly parents punish, the more likely is an adolescent to run away; the less unfair the parental punishment, the less likely is the adolescent to run away. This linear relationship can be seen in the following tables.

TABLE 4 RELATIONSHIP BETWEEN UNFAIR PARENTAL PUNISHMENT AND RUNNING AWAY FROM HOME

	Unfair Parental Punishment				
Ran away from home	Always	Usually	Sometimes	Rarely	Never
Five plus times	24%	12%	9%	5%	4%
One to five times	5	2	2	1	1
Never	71	86	89	94	94
	100%	100%	100%	100%	99%
Number of cases = 1335	63	66	270	503	433

Missing observations = 36

Gamma = .33

TABLE 5 RELATIONSHIP BETWEEN UNFAIR PARENTAL PUNISHMENT AND SERIOUS FIGHTING

	Parental Strictness				
Gotten into a serious fight at home or school	Always	Usually	Sometimes	Rarely	Never
Five plus times	30%	25%	26%	28%	30%
One to five times	21	12	13	13	20
Never	49	63	61	60	50
	100%	100%	100%	101%	100%
Number of cases = 1335	141	324	518	296	56

Missing observations = 36

Gamma = .06

TABLE 6 RELATIONSHIP BETWEEN PARENTAL STRICTNESS AND SERIOUS FIGHTING

	Unfair Parental Punishment				
Gotten into a serious fight at home or school	Always	Usually	Sometimes	Rarely	Never
Five plus times	37%	35%	35%	25%	21%
One to five times	29	30	17	12	9
Never	35	35	48	63	70
	100%	100%	100%	100%	100%
Number of cases = 1337	63	66	271	504	433

Missing observations = 34

Gamma = .25

TABLE 7 RELATIONSHIP BETWEEN UNFAIR PARENTAL PUNISHMENT AND SCHOOL SUSPENSION

	Parental Strictness				
Been suspended from school	Always	Usually	Sometimes	Rarely	Never
Five plus times	6%	8%	6%	6%	9%
One to five times	5	0	2	0	4
Never	89	92	92	94	88
	100%	100%	100%	100%	100%
Number of cases = 1334	141	324	518	295	56

Missing observations = 37

Gamma = .06

TABLE 8 RELATIONSHIP BETWEEN PARENTAL STRICTNESS AND SCHOOL SUSPENSION

	Unfair Parental Punishment				
Been suspended from school	Always	Usually	Sometimes	Rarely	Never
Five plus times	18%	9%	10%	6%	4%
One to five times	3	5	2	1	1
Never	79	86	88	93	95
	100%	100%	100%	100%	100%
Number of cases = 1336	63	66	271	503	433

Missing observations = 35

Gamma = .31

TABLE 9 RELATIONSHIP BETWEEN UNFAIR PARENTAL PUNISHMENT AND STEALING LESS THAN $10.00

	Parental Strictness				
Taken something which did not belong to you worth less than $10	Always	Usually	Sometimes	Rarely	Never
Five plus times	25%	23%	24%	27%	25%
One to five times	19	10	12	9	6
Never	56	67	64	64	70
	101%	100%	100%	100%	101%
Number of cases = 1333	141	324	517	295	56

Missing observations = 38

Gamma = .01

The same tendency toward a curvilinear relationship between parental strictness and serious fighting exists (Table 5), although it is much less pronounced. A look at the total number of cases in each column of this table indicates that parents are more likely to be viewed as strict than not strict. A comparison with column totals in Table 6 indicates most parents are not perceived as punishing unfairly. However, in this table, the positive linear relationship between unfair parental punishment and serious fighting prevails. Parents perceived as being unfairly punitive are more likely to have a child who gets into serious fights than parents not so perceived.

In Tables 7 and 8, the relationship between the two different measures of parental discipline and being suspended from school indicates that whatever tendency toward a curvilinear relationship existed for parental strictness, it no longer obtains, but that the relationship between unfair parental punishment is moderately positive. In fact, the relationship between parental strictness and being suspended from school is null. The increasing strength of the relationship between unfair parental punishment and seriousness of delinquency is becoming more evident. Tables 9 and 10, concerning stealing items worth less than $10, and Tables 11 and 12 on stealing items worth more than $10, reinforce this finding.

The data presented support the null hypothesis of no relationship between parental strictness and any delinquent activities. Parents perceived as strict are as likely as those perceived as not strict to have children who engage in delinquent behavior. It appears that strict parents do not suppress delinquent behavior any more than parents who are never strict fail to suppress delinquency. Walters and Parke (1971), examining the behavioral contingencies for delinquent models, conclude that when there is no negative outcome for deviant behavior, the incidence of deviant behavior is likely to increase. In their words, "no outcome" or "non-reward" (for deviant behavior of models) appears to operate similarly to a positive reinforcer and may be conceptualized as withdrawal of punishment rather than as a simple "non-reward."

The data do not support the hypothesized null relationship between perceived unfair parental punishment and delinquent behavior. The relationship between unfair parental punishment is moderately positive for all but one item of delinquency. This relationship is more difficult to explain, especially given the lack of measures of various parental disciplinary practices reported by either parents or their children.

TABLE 10 RELATIONSHIP BETWEEN PARENTAL STRICTNESS AND STEALING ITEMS LESS THAN $10.00

Taken something which did not belong to you worth less than $10	Unfair Parental Punishment				
	Always	Usually	Sometimes	Rarely	Never
Five plus times	27%	21%	30%	27%	18%
One to five times	24	24	16	11	5
Never	49	55	54	62	77
	100%	100%	100%	100%	100%
Number of cases = 1335	63	66	271	503	432

Missing observations = 36

Gamma = .23

Children often see their parents as unfair when their own expectations for rewards are unmet, regardless of whether the parents are being punitive or unfair. Unfair punishment may refer, perceptually, to a discrepancy between what a parent says (s)he will do and what is actually done in a given situation. Or it may refer to a discrepancy in how parents respond to different children in the family who emit the same behavior. It may be that the magnitude, frequency, duration and unpredictability of parental punishment coalesce into a holistic perception of parents as unfairly punitive. What is not to be discounted is that parents who are perceived as unfairly punitive are more likely than those who are not so perceived to have children who commit delinquency acts. Even without measures of actual parental punishment, perceptions themselves affect behavior. The question remains, however, concerning how such perceptions operate on behavior. It may be that children who are unable to control or avoid their parent's unfair punishment may choose to vent accumulated anger and frustration on others, as suggested by Freud's displaced aggression hypothesis.

TABLE 11 RELATIONSHIP BETWEEN PARENTAL STRICTNESS AND STEALING MORE THAN $10.00

Taken something which did not belong to you worth more than $10	Parental Strictness				
	Always	Usually	Sometimes	Rarely	Never
Five plus times	7%	7%	8%	8%	2%
One to five times	6	1	2	3	3
Never	87	92	90	90	95
	100%	100%	100%	101%	100%
Number of cases = 1334	141	324	518	296	55

Missing observations = 37

Gamma = .02

TABLE 12 RELATIONSHIP BETWEEN PARENTAL STRICTNESS AND STEALING MORE THAN $10.00

Taken something which did not belong to you worth more than $10	Unfair Parental Punishment				
	Always	Usually	Sometimes	Rarely	Never
Five plus times	18%	17%	8%	7%	4%
One to five times	5	9	3	2	2
Never	76	74	89	91	95
	99%	100%	100%	100%	101%
Number of cases = 1336	63	66	271	504	432

Missing observations = 35

Gamma = .36

TABLE 13 PARENTAL DISCIPLINE AND DELINQUENCY INDEX (PERCENT DELINQUENT)

	Parental Strictness				
Delinquency Index	Always	Usually	Sometimes	Rarely	Never
Number of Acts					
Two or more	22%	13%	17%	15%	20%
Once	41	38	40	42	34
None	37	49	44	43	47
	100%	100%	101%	100%	101%
N = 1329	139	323	515	296	56

Gamma = -.0005

In an effort to specify the relationship between perceptions or parental disciplinary techniques and delinquent activity, other variables were examined. It was suggested earlier that the effects of age on the relationship between child abuse and delinquent activity were such that child abuse would decrease with age. This was hypothesized as so, since with age the child's ability to manipulate his environment would increase, and since the very nature of growth would enable the child to have access to additional resources.

First, the relationship between age and delinquent activities was examined, and found, predictably, to be positively related to age (gamma equals .26). The older the child, the more likely (s)he is to commit delinquent acts, and the more serious those acts are. When the relationship between age and delinquent activity was examined separately for boys and girls, the relationship was stronger for girls (gamma, .36) than for boys (.18). However boys are more likely to be delinquent at any age than are girls.

The relationship between age and each of the two items of parental discipline also was examined. One would guess that parents would be more likely to be strict with younger children, at an age when they are more impressionable and parents are attempting to inculcate them with good habits. There is, however, no relationship between parental strictness and age (gamma equals .01). Nor is there any relationship between unfair parental punishment and age either (gamma equals .02). A curvilinear PRE measure, eta squared, also indicates no relationship between each of the two measures and age.

A delinquency index was then constructed, adding all of the delinquency items, thus maximizing the variation in delinquent activity. Each item of parental discipline was cross-tabulated against this delinquency index. Table 13 indicates the lack of relationship between parental strictness and delinquency. This finding supports the data presented earlier for each delinquent behavior. However, the relationship between perceived parental unfair punishment and the delinquency index is still moderately positive, with a gamma of .27. In fact, all the PRE measures indicate that the relationship between perceived unfair parental punishment and each delin-

TABLE 14 PARENTAL UNFAIR PUNISHMENT AND DELINQUENCY INDEX (PERCENT DELINQUENT)

Delinquency Index	Unfair Parental Punishment				
	Always	Usually	Sometimes	Rarely	Never
Number of Acts					
Two or more	37%	20%	23%	14%	9%
Once	38	38	41	43	36
None	25	32	36	43	55
	100%	100%	100%	100%	100%
N = 1331	63	66	268	502	432

Gamma = .27

quent item is statistically significant beyond the .001 level. The data in Table 14 illustrate the relationship. If parents have the view that punishment is effective, the data indicate that unfairly applying the rod spoils the child, since the child is more likely to engage in (bad) behavior. This finding is theoretically significant, even without actual measures of parental disciplinary techniques, since merely the perception of unfair parental punishment is related to delinquency.

Since the relationship between the two items of parental discipline was moderately positive (gamma, .36), an indcx of parental discipline was constructed, additively combining the two items. At the extreme end, where parents are always strict and always unfair, such a combination touches on the qualities typical of parents who abuse their children. The relationship between the parental discipline index and the delinquency index was weaker (gamma, .19) When these two indices were examined separtely for boys and girls, the gamma coefficient was stronger for boys (gamma, .21) than for girls (gamma, .16). But for both boys and girls, the more likely a parent is to be both strict and unfair, the more likely the child is to engage in delinquent activities.

Since a number of other variables measuring facets of the parent-child relationship were available, a multiple regression technique was utilized to examine the relative effects of disciplinary practices when other variables were included in the equation. These other items include measures of communication between parent and child, supervision by the parent, identification of the child with the parent, as well as the two measures of parental discipline. The multiple regression coefficient for all these variables, using the delinquency index as the dependent variable, was .35 (for all boys). Thus it is only moderately positive. Parental unfairness contributed .12 of that multiple R. Of all the items, unfair parental punishment is the most strongly related to delinquency. Given Hirschi's hypothesis that the communication patterns obtaining between parent and child and the child's identification with the parent are indicative of the bonds which inhibit a child from engaging in delinquent acts, this is surprising. Even the zero-order correlation between unfair punishment and delinquency was .25, while parental strictness was much less, .08. Hence, the more precise measure of association, Pearsonian correlation, parallels that obtained by gamma, an ordinal PRE measure.

In addition, epistemic coefficients, which measure the relationship between concepts utilizing sets of indicator items; were calculated between parental discipline and supervision. These coefficients indicate there is no relationship between disciplinary techniques and supervision of the child by parents, even though each is related to delinquency. This suggests that both supervision and disciplinary practices are two independent factors in parental response to children. It does not appear that discipline should be confused with supervision, although often it is, at least subjectively by the parent.

SUMMARY

What can be said in conclusion about these findings? First, there is additional support for the finding that there is no relationship between parental SES and discipline or delinquency. There is a slight tendency for boys to commit acts of more serious delinquency, as compared to girls. There is, also; no relationship between delinquency and parental strictness, for any one item of the seven delinquency behaviors, or for the delinquency index.

The clearest finding has to do with perceived unfair punishment. Regardless of what it is that a parent does, merely being perceived as unfair is related to all but one delinquent item, and to the delinquency index. The more serious the delinquent act, the stronger does the relationship become. It must be acknowledged that these data do not provide any futher information of just what it is that a parent does that results in a child's perceiving his or her parent as unfairly punitive. Nor do we know, given this relationship between delinquency and unfair punishment, what is the link between the two variables. The cautionary note that correlation or association is not causation must be kept in mind. Just what triggers a child who perceives his parent as unfairly punitive to commit delinquent acts remains a puzzle. While a possible theoretical link is provided by Freud's theory of displaced aggression, other variables, unmeasured in this study, are likely to be important in facilitating or inhibiting this nexus.

One final point is necessary. In discussing the relationship between a child's perceptions of a parent's disciplinary practices and delinquent behavior, it has been assumed that the perceptions are antecedent to delinquency. It is quite possible that the child begins to view the parent as unfairly punitive only after he has been disciplined by the parent for delinquent behavior. Longitudinal studies can resolve the temporal and causal ordering which resides in this issue. Hopefully this kind of data will be more available in the future.

The limitations of these findings are obvious. What they do is point the direction for further research. One would like more specific measures of parental responses to a variety of situations and their children's behavior, as well as children's perceptions of their own, as well as of their parents', behavior. Undue concentration on parental discipline and punishment, however, without concern with other factors, such as parental norms and expectations about children, would be unwise. Only by including other variables can we assess the relative direct and indirect effects which parents have on their children's behavior. If we focus exclusively on discipline and punishment, we fail to understand when, where and how such undesirable consequences as delinquency are mitigated by other unmeasured factors, which may prove, in the end, to be of greater importance.

REFERENCES

Conger, R. D. *A comparative study of interaction patterns between deviant and non-deviant parents. (Doctoral Dissertation, University of Washington, Seattle) 1976.*

Elmer, E. Ch.ildren in jeopardy: A study of abused minors and their families. Pittsburgh: University of Pittsburgh Press; 1967. Hirschi, T. *Causes of delinquency.* Berkeley: University of California Press, 1969.

Linden, E. *Interpersonal ties and delinquent behavior.* (Doctoral Dissertation, University of Waahington, Seattle). 1974.

Littman, R. A., Moore, R. C. A., & Pierce; J. Social class differences in child rearing: A third community comparison with Chicago and Newton. In E. Zigler & I. L. Child (Eds.) *Socialization and personality.* Reading, Mass.: Wesley Publishing; 1973

Pfohl, S. The. 'discovery' of child abuse. *Social Problems,* 1977, *24*(3), 310-323.

Seligman, M. E. P. *Helplessness: On depression; development and death.* San Francisco: W. H. Freeman & Company, 1975.

Thomas, W. I. & Znaniecki., F. *The Polish peasant Europe and America.* Chicago: University of Chicago, 1918, 5 vols.

Walters, R. H. & Parke, R. D. Influence of response consequences to a social model on resistance and deviation. In A. Bandura (Ed.)m *Psychological modeling: Conflicting theories.* Chicago; Aldine, Altherton, 1971.

Young, L. *Wednesday's children: A study of child neglect and abuse.* New York: McGraw-Hill, 1964.